QUIET NEIGHBORS

QUIET NEIGHBORS

PROSECUTING NAZI WAR CRIMINALS IN AMERICA

Allan A. Ryan, Jr.

HARCOURT BRACE JOVANOVICH, PUBLISHERS

San Diego   New York   London

Requests for permission to make copies of any
part of the work should be mailed to:
Permissions, Harcourt Brace Jovanovich, Publishers,
Orlando, Florida 32887.
With grateful appreciation to Random House, Inc.,
for permission to reprint the quotation from
A Man for All Seasons by Robert Bolt.

Library of Congress Cataloging in Publication Data
Ryan, Allan A.
Quiet neighbors: Prosecuting Nazi War Criminals in America.
Includes bibliographical references and index.
1. War crime trials—United States. 2. War crimes.
3. War criminals. 4. World War, 1939–1945—Atrocities.
I. Title.
KF221.P6R9 1984 345.73′0238 84-6540
ISBN 0-15-175823-9 347.305238

Designed by Ellen Lo Giudice

Printed in the United States of America

First edition

A B C D E

To Nancy, my wife

"The wrongs which we seek to condemn and punish have been so calculated, so malignant and so devastating that civilization cannot tolerate their being ignored because it cannot survive their being repeated."

—Justice Robert H. Jackson, Chief
American Prosecutor, Trial of the Major
Nazi War Criminals before the International
Military Tribunal, Nuremberg, 1946

ALICE: "While you talk, he's gone!"

MORE: "And go he should, if he was the Devil himself, until he broke the law!"

ROPER: "So now you'd give the Devil benefit of law!"

MORE: "Yes. What would you do? Cut a great road through the law to get after the Devil?"

ROPER: "I'd cut down every law in England to do that!"

MORE (roused and excited): "Oh? And when the last law was down, and the Devil turned round on you—where would you hide, Roper, the laws all being flat? This country's planted thick with laws from coast to coast—man's laws, not God's—and if you cut them down—and you're just the man to do it—d'you really think you could stand upright in the winds that would blow then? (Quietly) Yes, I'd give the Devil benefit of law, for my own safety's sake."

—Robert Bolt, *A Man for All Seasons*

September 1939 frontiers

Line of departure, German invasion of the Soviet Union, June 22, 1941

✿ Capitals

CONTENTS

Photographs appear between pages 178 and 179.

ACKNOWLEDGMENTS

When I joined the Office of Special Investigations in the Department of Justice soon after its formation in 1979, I knew very little about Nazi war criminals in the United States. When I left in the fall of 1983, I knew a good deal more, and many of the themes and conclusions of this book first emerged, in my own mind, as I worked day to day with a truly dedicated group of professionals.

OSI was an eclectic group. We were veteran trial lawyers and lawyers just graduated, historians who were doctors of philosophy and historians who had fought the Nazis, retired intelligence analysts, student volunteers, and criminal investigators. The secretaries, paralegals, and other assistants were full members of the team and made our work possible.

We came from diverse backgrounds and distinct disciplines, yet we worked with unusual harmony and with respect for each others' skills, and each of us learned much from our colleagues. There is no way that I could have written this book had I not been informed, challenged, and stimulated by their contributions, day after day for nearly four years. As Director of that Office, I tried to bring out the best in each of them, and if I succeeded it is largely because each of them had a great deal to offer. I hope they will recognize their contributions throughout this book. I will remember them always with respect and affection.

Deputy Assistant Attorney General Mark Richard, Criminal Division, U.S. Department of Justice, played a greater role in the success of OSI than anyone will ever know. A wise counselor, a good friend, and the very best kind of public servant.

I am grateful also to Elie Wiesel for reading portions of the manuscript and providing his comments, to Jeffrey Mausner and

Jovi Tenev, who graciously allowed me to use their photographs, and to Jim Schweitzer for his assistance.

Joseph and Muriel Nellis believed this book should be written long before I was ready to do it and Marie Arana-Ward, my editor at Harcourt Brace Jovanovich, gave it unity. My parents, and my brothers and sisters, share in this as well.

I owe special thanks to Ray and Julia Foote, who lived through the writing of this book and helped in very many ways. It is for my children, Elisabeth and Andrew, and above all for their mother.

QUIET NEIGHBORS

NAZIS AND AMERICA:
The Indictment

In the barrens of Poland in 1942, an outpost of hell was created on earth. The Nazis built it of bricks and wood and barbed wire and connected it to the world by one railroad track. They called it Treblinka. Treblinka's commandant called it Dante's Inferno come to life.

No one knows how many people were murdered there. The most conservative estimate is 700,000; the most accurate may be 1,200,000. In thirteen months, from July 1942 to August 1943, thousands of hump-roofed little boxcars rumbled to the end of the line and disgorged their cargo at a movie-set railroad station. The cargo had names. They were whole families—whole communities—of Jews from Poland and other countries: infants carried by their mothers; fathers and sons, hand in hand; husbands searching frantically for wives they had not seen since the trains had pulled out of Warsaw a day or two before.

They were set upon by uniformed guards cracking leather whips with little lead balls in the tips. The guards drove the dazed and fearful Jews like livestock from the trains to be processed—clothing removed, hair shorn—some snatched out of the streams of people and told to stand aside. Families who had managed to stay together during the suffocating train ride slowly fell apart, their screams, their outstretched arms no match for the disciplined and experienced guards.

After their hair was removed, the naked cargo was herded onto a dirt path packed hard by the feet of thousands of people before them. At its end lay gas chambers and, beyond them, deep smoldering pits that sent up thick black smoke to darken the sky.

For gas at Treblinka, the Nazis used the engines of captured Russian tanks: huge, noisy machines that pumped exhaust fumes into the tightly sealed chambers containing the fathers, mothers, and children packed in by the hundreds. This took time—too much time, the Nazis decided when they designed the more efficient gas chambers at Auschwitz—but it was always fatal, eventually.

There was a man responsible for pumping the carbon monoxide into the chambers and turning it off when the screams fell silent. He repaired the motor and maintained it in peak operating condition. The Germans needed a mechanic but they got a sadist—a muscular young Ukrainian named Ivan. When he was not tending to his engine, he sometimes walked the camp with an iron pipe, smashing skulls. The Jews who had been plucked from the train cargo and put to work carrying bodies from the gas chamber to the burning pits did not know this man's last name, but they did not need to. In a bitter reference to a czar of Russia who had killed thousands of Jews himself, they called the engine man Ivan Grozny—Ivan the Terrible.

Several thousand miles from Warsaw is Seven Hills, Ohio, a suburb of Cleveland, full of tree-lined streets and neat homes, many with gardens and barbecue grills in the back yard. Families live here. Some of the men bring home paychecks from the Ford plant near the airport, and through the fifties and the sixties and the seventies this was a steady livelihood—not exciting, but reliable.

In Seven Hills, John Demjanjuk and his wife and kids were no different from their neighbors. Mr. and Mrs. Demjanjuk came here in 1952, among the last in a wave of Eastern European immigrants uprooted by the war and the descent of what was then called the Iron Curtain. Six years later, they became citizens of the United States of America. She was a housewife, raising three children. He worked for the Ford Motor Company as a mechanic at the plant. He was a member of the union, and served on the board at St. Vladimir's Ukrainian Orthodox Church. He did not talk much about himself, but he was a good worker, a responsible citizen, a quiet neighbor.

On February 10, 1981, the United States Department of Justice went to federal court in Cleveland to prove that Ivan the Terrible from Treblinka was living in Seven Hills, Ohio, and that his name was John Demjanjuk.

The nation that is now called Yugoslavia has always been a place of suspicion and intrigue. Its inhabitants have been peoples of dissimilar culture, religion, and politics. Amidst great natural beauty, Serbs,

Croatians, Montenegrins, Bosnians, Slovenes, and others have lived for centuries, sometimes in uneasy peace, more often in conflict.

During World War II, Hitler and Mussolini plunged knives into the back of this Balkan land, creating and sustaining a vicious government called "The Independent State of Croatia." Its führer was Ante Pavelic, a thoroughly repugnant Croatian separatist who carried out a campaign of genocide with all the force he could summon against Serbs, Jews, and the hapless gypsies. The terror was as suffocating as any in Europe during the war. It was not an efficient slaughter. The Pavelic government unleashed a force of roving paramilitary fanatics who gouged, stabbed, tortured, and dismembered several hundred thousand people, in the fields or in primitive concentration camps.

The minister of the interior, the director of "public security," the enforcer of Croatian racial purity, was a lawyer and Croatian nationalist named Andrija Artukovic. Short and stocky, a bachelor until the age of forty-two, an accomplished orator, he oversaw the concentration camps and carried out Pavelic's order to save Croatia for the Croatians, which required that it be rid of Serbs and Jews.

As Hitler lay dead in his bunker in May 1945, Andrija Artukovic began his escape across Europe—first to Austria, then Switzerland, then Ireland—always one step ahead of the Allies seeking to bring him to trial for his crimes. By July 1948, Artukovic had run as far as he could go in Europe. Agents of his archenemy Josip Tito were on his trail, and the British government had submitted his name to the House of Commons as one of nineteen Yugoslav traitors to be arrested if located. Artukovic walked into the American legation in Dublin and produced some Swiss identity papers in the name of "Alois Anich." He said he was a professor who wished to visit his sister-in-law in California for a few weeks. He was issued a tourist visa good for sixty days and he bought a ticket for New York. At Idlewild Airport, he showed his papers to immigration officers and immediately got on another plane to Los Angeles.

Two years later, he was discovered, still in California, and was ordered deported from the United States.

He is still living in California.

This book is the story of John Demjanjuk and Andrija Artukovic and other Nazi war criminals who came to the United States. It is the story of how they came here, and how, some forty years after their crimes, a small office of the U.S. Department of Justice was created to bring them to trial. The story stretches from the Kremlin to the Supreme Court, from the walls of Auschwitz to the walls of Jerusalem, from the streets of Berlin and Budapest and Warsaw to the streets of New York, Chicago, Philadelphia, and a dozen other cities in this country.

This is not a story of Nazi Germany. It is a story of America.

"We have but one aim and one single, irrevocable purpose," Winston Churchill told the House of Commons in June 1941. "We are resolved to destroy Hitler and every vestige of the Nazi regime."[1] Six months later, in December, President Roosevelt issued a similar summons to his nation in a radio address: "Modern warfare as conducted in the Nazi manner is a dirty business. We don't like it—we didn't want to get in it—but we are in it and we're going to fight it with everything we've got."[2] Two hundred thousand American soldiers, twice as many British, and fifty times as many Russians died on the battlefield to fulfill these vows. America and the Allies destroyed the Nazi regime, as Churchill had promised, but at enormous cost in human lives.

Nazism was far more than a military threat. Eleven million innocent people were put to death by the Nazi machine; six million of them were Jews whose only crime was to be Jewish, whose only weapon was their faith. Forty years have passed since the defeat of Nazism, yet the horror of these crimes has not dimmed. The healthy and necessary reanalysis of history by new generations has offered no explanation, no perspective, that would even slightly rehabilitate Nazi rule. Nazism remains the embodiment of man's most profound capacity for evil. "This trial's mad and melancholy record," said Justice Robert H. Jackson in his closing argument at Nuremberg, "will live as the historical text of the twentieth century's shame and depravity."[3] Forty years later, Jackson's contemporaneous indictment has only grown more solid.

Yet from time to time in the past few years, books or other accounts have appeared claiming to expose some newly-discovered conspiracy by the CIA, or the military, or a cabal of lawless bureaucrats, to bring Nazi collaborators to the United States after the war. Of course it is shocking to think that the government that sent men to die for freedom should then bring back their killers to live in America, but these accounts have offered dubious evidence and have been unable to survive any objective analysis. To be sure, there were instances where American officials, after the war, employed or drew assistance from ex-Nazis. The Klaus Barbie episode, which is set forth here, is one example. Otto von Bolschwing is another, and Bolschwing immigrated to the United States. Surely if it were to be proven tomorrow, let us suppose, that the CIA or the Army or any other agency had knowingly assisted a Nazi war criminal to enter this country after the war, we would be angry and indignant; we should become angry when a government official breaks the law, and we should always be indignant that a Nazi persecutor should find sanctuary in the United States.

But my indictment is, or ought to be, far more disturbing: Nazi war criminals came here by the thousands, through the openly deliberated public policy of this country, formulated by Congress and administered by accountable officials. And it is the more disturbing because the proof is abundant.

The overwhelming majority of Nazi criminals came through the front door, with all their papers in order. They came here not by conniving with lawless government officials but by the infinitely easier method of simply deceiving the honest ones. They were the beneficiaries of a law that virtually excluded Jews while welcoming their oppressors. And these immigrants were not merely "ex-Nazis," or Nazi sympathizers, or Nazi collaborators. They were the war criminals, the handmaidens of Nazism who had personally, and quite willingly, taken part in the persecution of millions of innocent men, women and children. They had no assistance from anyone in particular; they did not need it. All they needed was the ability that any twelve-year-old might possess to tell a lie; we did the rest. And we did it with all democratic processes intact and functioning.

The law that made it so easy for Nazis to come to America—the Displaced Persons Act—was hardly a secret at the time. Indeed, it was one of the most thoroughly deliberated and openly administered laws of the postwar years. Those few critics who predicted that the DP Act would make America a haven for Nazi criminals were ignored by a Congress whose concern for the future of Europe's refugees was laced with very definite prejudices as to which of those refugees ought to be allowed entry to America.

The consequences of the DP Act proved the critics right—but by then America was far more concerned with the new enemy of Communism than with the old enemy of Nazism, and it paid little attention to the consequences.

And so these criminals, once in this country, found both shelter and anonymity in a citizenry that did not seem to care whether they were here or not. For nearly thirty years, we ignored the evidence that Nazi war criminals were in America, and we allowed the government's law enforcers to look the other way as well. We simply were not interested in the possibility that those who had killed innocent people might have found sanctuary among us.

This indifference persisted well into the 1970s, when at last a few determined men and women in Congress insisted that the Justice Department investigate these criminals and take legal action against them. This book is, to some extent, an account of the activities of the office created to do that—the Office of Special Investigations, which I directed for most of the first four years of its life.

But this book is, more importantly, an attempt to answer some troubling questions. Who were these Nazi war criminals who came here? How were they able to get in? What was done about them in the thirty years after their arrival, and why was it so little? After paying so dear a price to defeat Hitler, why did we show so little concern when his henchmen became our neighbors?

1

DISPLACED PERSONS:
"You've Got Everything in This Camp Except Hitler"

Wolodymir Osidach was born in the western Ukraine, that flat and fertile grain belt above the Black Sea. The flag of the Ukraine was a blue band over gold: vast sky over vast wheat. Like many of his countrymen, Osidach was solid, sturdy, muscular, a man of the fields. He was from a town called Rava Ruska, population about 12,000, some thirty miles north of the ancient city of Lvov, the spiritual capital of the Galicia region, both Polish and Ukrainian.

But Wolodymir Osidach was not in the Ukraine on the sixth of July, 1949. For nearly four years, since October 1945, he and his family had been displaced persons living in a camp in Neu Ulm, Germany. He was in the American consulate in Munich, in the United States zone of occupied Germany, applying for a visa to emigrate to America.

To get a visa, Osidach had to account for every year of his adult life—where he had lived, how he had earned a living, what he had done during the war. This was not difficult to answer. Osidach wrote that he had lived in Rava Ruska and, in broken English, stated that his occupation from 1936 to 1944 had been that of a "dairy technic," employed by the "Dairy Association of Rawa Ruska."[1]

It was a plausible story. The Ukraine was full of farmers.

He handed his application to a vice-consul of the United States who looked it over and asked Osidach a few routine questions. Osidach was polite, even deferential.

Behind the desk, the vice-consul scanned the forms, took up a stamp, and pressed it to the paper. Osidach was going to America.

In the displaced persons camps of occupied Germany, Wolodymir Osidach and his family were no more distinctive than grains of sand tossed onto a beach and left behind in the turbulence of war. There were Ukrainians, Lithuanians, Latvians, Poles, Romanians, Czechs, Jews, with nothing in common beyond a desire never to return to their homelands. Each, for his own reason, had to begin a new life somewhere else.

In the spring of 1945 when the Red Army met the American troops at the Elbe to end the war in Europe, Germany and its neighbors were teeming with human debris of the war. Nobody knows how many these homeless were; the best estimate was eight or nine million in Germany and Austria alone.[2] By the end of the summer of 1945 seven million or so of these had returned home, but they were mainly Western Europeans who returned by choice to France, Italy, Scandinavia; or those in Soviet-controlled areas railroaded home, forcibly if need be, by the Russians. That left a million or more who could not, or would not, go back to their former countries.

They were a mass of diverse faces: Eastern Europeans who had gone to Germany in wartime as laborers, some voluntarily, some by force; other Eastern Europeans who had stayed in their homelands to help the Germans and who had retreated with them, a step ahead of the Red Army; Jews who had survived the Nazis by hiding in woods and fields; Jews who had been put to work in concentration camps and who had been liberated by Allied troops; people whose homes or farms had simply been destroyed. They were Catholics and Protestants as well as Jews; some well-fed, others, including the Jews, little more than skeletons. Some were the wreckage of war; some were the makers of war. And many had been the handmaidens of Nazism in their homelands. In the DP camps, the makers of war, their victims, and the bystanders all gathered together.

To understand how such a volatile mix was thrown together in the DP camps at war's end, one must look to Hitler's invasion of the Soviet Union in 1941. Two years earlier, Hitler had invaded Poland; once Poland was subdued, he turned to the West. Nineteen forty was a year of blitzkrieg: Holland, Belgium, France, the Battle of Britain. But by the summer of 1941, Hitler was ready to move eastward again, toward Moscow.

On June 22, 1941, he launched Operation Barbarossa—the invasion of the Soviet Union. Panzer and infantry divisions roared into

Soviet territory, aiming first at the Baltic countries of Latvia and Lithuania, and the Ukraine to the south. The Germans advanced with astonishing speed against the unprepared Soviets. Within ten days the Baltic capitals of Riga and Kaunas fell; in the south, the Wehrmacht troops surged across the Ukraine, reaching the outskirts of Kiev just twenty days after the invasion began. By the end of the summer Leningrad was cut off by the Germans and the advance to Moscow itself was launched.

But military conquest of the Soviet Union was not Hitler's only objective. The "East"—*Ostland*—was to become an annex of the German Reich, sheltering and nurturing the master race as it grew over a thousand years. To make room for the Aryans, the Slavs would have to be subjugated, but that could wait. The elimination of the Jews came first.

And so, traveling with the army across the plains of Russia, the dreaded Einsatzgruppen—mobile killing units of SS troops—attended to the Jews. The Einsatzgruppen men looked like soldiers, but there was a difference. They had no military objective; no bridges, factories or high ground interested them. Their victims did not shoot back. There were no Purple Hearts in the Einsatzgruppen. In the villages and cities of the Baltics and the Ukraine, the SS men marched the Jews out to nearby forests, forced them to dig their own graves, stripped them naked, lined them up, and shot them. Within five months, five hundred thousand Jews were massacred.[3]

Unlike the Poles, however, many Ukrainians welcomed the Germans. Some were "Volksdeutsche"—the descendants of German settlers of the seventeenth century. They had names like Deutscher and Lehmann; they had clung to German culture; and they welcomed their modern-day kinsmen.

Some other Ukrainians saw in the Germans their liberators from Soviet rule. These Ukrainians were a nationalistic people, restless for change and unhappy to be the "Ukrainian Soviet Socialist Republic," ruled from Moscow through local Ukrainian communists.

Whatever their background, well-organized groups of Ukrainians not only cheered the advancing Germans but helped them in the slaughter.* And the Germans desperately needed help killing all the

---

*Not every Ukrainian was a fascist, of course. Some detested the Nazis as much as they did the Bolsheviks, and many joined the partisans. But for the Jews, this made little difference. There were enough Ukrainian Nazis for the task.

Jews. There were only four battalions of Einsatzgruppen troops, about 3,000 men. By the end of the summer, they were responsible for over 500,000 square miles—from the Black Sea to the Baltic—where four million Jews lived.[4] Three thousand men were nothing against those numbers. So they relied on indigenous forces of sympathizers willing to take up arms against Jews.

Formed as "auxiliary police" or "militia," Ukrainian collaborators guided the Einsatzgruppen to the Jewish quarters of a thousand cities and towns, drove the trucks of human cargo to the forests, guarded the frightened men, women, and children. One German officer reported back to Berlin on the slaughter: "It was done entirely in public with the use of the Ukrainian militia. . . . The way these actions which included men and old men, women and children of all ages was carried out was horrible. The great masses executed make this action more gigantic than any similar measure taken so far in the Soviet Union."[5]

One Einsatzkommando in Radomyl agreed to deal only with adults; it let the Ukrainian militia kill the Jewish children.[6] Said one German leader: "We were actually frightened at the bloodthirstiness of these people."[7]

To the Jews of Rava Ruska, like Jews throughout the Ukraine, death was delivered by neighbors. The Germans organized a Ukrainian militia there, armed them, outfitted them in blue uniforms, chose a commandant, and set them upon the Jews.

Philip Langer was a Jew in Rava Ruska: "Any militia had a free hand. If a militia[man] decided to take, say, my kid or my brother's kid and just take him and beat him to death or take him and throw him anywheres he felt like it, he could have done it and the same as the Germans could have done that, too.

"In 1942 there was like an action. We used to call it a razia, but that was an action. I seen the trucks and the militia people and Germans driving by to the [train] station."

Q. "And there were people in the trucks?"
"Yes."
Q. "Who were these people?"
"The Jewish people."
Q. "Now did you go home that night?"
"Yes."

Q. "And what did you find when you went home?"
"My house was empty."
Q. "There was no one there?"
"No one there."
Q. "Before the action, who was living in your house?"
"My mother. My sister and her baby. My sister's sisters [sic] and
two kids."
Q. "Did you ever see these people again?"
"No."

Anna Weinfeld was a Jew in Rava Ruska: "I went to the phar-
macy. I had a small girl with me, leaving. And I told her, 'Remem-
ber, if you are in need, come to the pharmacy and ring three times;
maybe they will let you in and tell them you want to go to me.'

"And I didn't want to go to hide. I was standing in the window,
a small window. Every pharmacy in Europe had a small window. When
somebody wants to pick up a medicine during the night, they gave
them through this small window.

"All of a sudden I heard some shooting and crying. I went to the
window. I saw, like, after a big storm, the block was running. And
then I saw some people picking up Jewish children by the feet and
banging their heads to the wall."

Q: "These people you have just described—doing these things?"
"They were German and Ukrainian police. And then I went in-
side and I heard three times the bell ring and the girl came but they
didn't let her in. After this I heard three shots and the next day . . .
she was lying there next to the pharmacy."

In the Baltic countries of Latvia, Lithuania, and Estonia, the horror
was repeated. In Latvia, Einsatzgruppe A recruited the Arajs Kommando, under the leadership of Victor Arajs. The commando had one
purpose: to kill all the Jews of Latvia. In June 1942 Einsatzgruppe A
reported back to Berlin: "The number of Jews in Latvia in 1935 was
93,479—4.79 percent of the entire population. . . . At the present
time there are only a few Jews in the ghettos who are doing specialized work. . . . Aside from these Jews, Latvia has become free of
Jews in the meantime."[8]

In Lithuania, a force of 150 locals set to work, seizing and shooting 500 Jews a day, every day, all day and night.[9] By January 1942,
the Einsatzgruppe reported: "Executions by shooting are carried out

everywhere . . . In Lithuania, the country and the smaller towns have been completely purged of Jews.''[10]

So zealous were the Lithuanians that the Germans sent a battalion of them to neighboring Byelorussia to continue the carnage. In Slutsk, the German civil administrator asked that the Jewish craftsmen of that city be spared. He was ignored. Furious, he sent a cable to regional headquarters: ''The whole picture was worse than disgusting. With indescribable brutality, both German Police officials and, even more, the Lithuanian partisans (Auxiliary Police) herded the Jews out of their houses. Shots were to be heard all over the town and in some streets the bodies were piled high.''

In Estonia, the local auxiliary joined the Einsatzgruppe there; Jews were rounded up, driven off, and shot. June 1942: ''The Jews were seized by and by, avoiding all unnecessary trouble in the economic life of Estonia. Today there are no more Jews in Estonia.''[11]

Within one year of the invasion of the Soviet Union, the Einsatzgruppen, with meticulous attention to detail, counted 481,887 Jews killed in German-occupied territory.[12] These were men and women, boys and girls, killed one after the other by men firing rifles. Reported one Einsatzgruppe leader: ''The nervous strain was far heavier in the case of our men who carried out the executions than in that of their victims. From the psychological point of view they [the executioners] had a terrible time.''[13]

By 1944 one million Jews in the Ukraine and the Baltic countries had been killed by the Germans and their Baltic and Ukrainian helpers.[14]

In that year, the Red Army began pushing the Germans back toward Berlin; thousands of Balts and Ukrainians fled with the Germans. When Germany collapsed a year later, so did they. Literally and figuratively, they threw off their Nazi uniforms. When the war ended, they were ''refugees,'' lying on the German beach like so much driftwood left by a vanishing tide. The Allies were in control now, and the first task after survival for those who had fled was to ingratiate themselves with the victors.

Faced with the staggering task of dealing with millions of people who had no place to live, the Allied forces, particularly the Americans and the British, hastily organized some 900 ''assembly centers'' throughout Germany, Austria, and Italy.[15] ''Assembly center'' was a euphemism for any place people could be stored short of an open field: former German barracks, military training centers, bombed-out buildings, warehouses, even, near Rome, the Cinecittà movie lot.[16]

Some of the "assembly centers" were in fact the concentration camps themselves: Dachau was an assembly center; so was Bergen-Belsen, near Hannover. In April 1945, in the final weeks of the war, the Germans pulled out of Bergen-Belsen and left 28,000 Jewish inmates to fend for themselves. "Typhus and diarrhea raged unchecked, corpses rotted in barracks and on dung heaps. Rats attacked living inmates, and the dead ones were eaten by starving prisoners."[17] Three months after the war had ended, some 7,000 Jews were still there.[18]

Living conditions, especially for Jews who had survived the camps, were atrocious: DPs were treated as prisoners, or worse. Many camps had barbed-wire fences; sanitary facilities, clothing, and shoes were almost nonexistent; diet was primarily black bread and coffee. One U.S. investigator concluded in August 1945: "As matters now stand, we appear to be treating the Jews as the Nazis treated them except that we do not exterminate them. . . . Beyond knowing that they are no longer in danger of the gas chambers, torture, and other forms of violent death, they see—and there is—little change."[19]

Other dwellings of the displaced, however, were far more livable; in fact, they were not camps at all but villages with pleasant grounds, neat, well-tended homes and gardens, well-fed residents. Here one found not Jews but Latvians, Lithuanians, Ukranians who had fled to Germany with the retreating Wehrmacht. They took up residence in Germany, and stayed there.

The Balts and Ukrainians made a wholesome impression on the Americans. One congressman touring the camps reported that most of the Balts were "unmistakably intelligent, conscientious, industrious, energetic, and showed every sign of having come from good stock and good breeding."[20]

Another American official was similarly impressed. "There is no doubt that if those who favored Germans could be eliminated," he noted, "the remainder would make most desirable immigrants."[21]

Yet the fact was that the camps were rife with "those who [had] favored the Germans." Whatever the proportion of collaborators, persecutors, and killers among Eastern Europeans and Balts during the war, the proportion among DPs was almost certainly far higher,

because the collaborators had greater reason to flee. This was no secret at the time to Americans—military personnel, touring congressmen, relief workers, journalists. One American official became
convinced that "most of these men and women were pro-German and
had voluntarily come to aid the Nazis; they had responded to the lure
of lucrative salaries and during the war had enjoyed a relatively luxurious life on the lootings from other countries. Now they posed as
war victims . . ."[22]

Another American camp official wrote in frustration to his chief:
"[I]t is time we begin to review a little more carefully a policy which
lumps together a few thousand dazed and bewildered Jewish survivors of Nazi terror with . . . the collaborationists of every hue who
populate DP camps throughout Germany, Austria and Italy . . ."[23]

In October 1945 Drew Middleton of *The New York Times*, reporting from Baltic-populated camps, concluded that "many thousands of former allies of Germany are being well fed and housed" by
the American military in "camps for collaborators." He reported reliable estimates that "one-third and probably more of the Balts" had
fought for the Germans or had been "members of the Gestapo and
SS." In fact the Balts were not only inhabiting the camps but running
them, maintaining a "tight control" over the issuance of passes,
clothes, cigarettes, and information inside the camps. "Most of the
Balts speak English," Middleton reported, and "have made a good
impression on the American Military Government's officers."[24]

A few months later, an official Army investigation confirmed
Middleton's allegations. "In two camps containing Baltic nationals at
Mainfranken," the Army found, "a majority of those investigated were
found to consist of voluntary pro-Nazi exiles."[25]

One U.S. Army major summed it up bluntly when he welcomed
United Nations social workers to the DP camp at Wildflecken. "You've
probably got everything in this camp except Hitler," he said, "and I
wouldn't be surprised if you turned up that bastard when you get started
on the registration."[26]

The Army, which was administering camps in the U.S. zone together with the International Refugee Organization (IRO) of the United
Nations, was caught in an unhappy squeeze. Whoever these refugees
were, turning them out to fend for themselves was unthinkable; they
had nowhere to go. Sending them back to their homes in Eastern Europe was also out of the question; anyone who was in a DP camp in

1946 was voting with his feet—he did not want to go back home. Whatever their true motivation, they quickly learned to announce that they preferred death to life in a Communist regime. Forcible repatriation was also ruled out; the United States would not send anyone to a Communist regime against his will.[27]

In 1946 the camps continued to swell with the homeless. Some Western European countries accepted some immigrants in 1946 and 1947, but not enough to put any appreciable dent in the numbers. And those taken were usually the young, strong, and unmarried. A few refugees were trickling into America through the normal immigration channels, helped somewhat by President Truman's directive in December 1945 that DPs would have first call on the annual quotas for immigration. But the quota for all citizens of Eastern European countries in 1946 was a mere 13,000 people—fewer than two percent of those living in the camps.[28] It was like dislodging the bathtub plug a crack while water came gushing through the faucets above.

In the summer of 1946 a new and ominous development added to the misery. In Poland, the persecution of Jews, briefly interrupted by the liberation, resumed. Jews who had returned to Poland after war's end came streaming back to Germany with gruesome tales of an officially sanctioned pogrom. Jews were being shot, kidnapped, beaten, mutilated. Hundreds were murdered. In the summer of 1946 more than 100,000 Jews fled Poland for the West, and most of those flocked to the gates of the DP camps that could barely shoehorn them in, but somehow did.[29]

The United States could not continue indefinitely to be the reluctant landlord for hundreds of thousands of displaced Europeans. However humble the food and shelter of the camps, the task of keeping the refugees alive was putting a major strain on the military occupation government. Reconstruction of the German economy—a major American goal—could not proceed with so many homeless people in the way. Clearly, something had to be done.

On August 16, 1946, President Truman recommended that Congress amend the immigration laws to enable 200,000 refugees to come to America, regardless of immigration quotas. This was the moment of conception for the Displaced Persons program—the first attempt by the United States to open its doors to people who had no other place to go.[30]

Truman's announcement may have been historic, but in 1946 it was not an idea whose time had yet come. Fully three-quarters of the American people, according to one poll, opposed the very idea of allowing refugees to come to America.[31] This may have been based on the widespread belief that "DP" meant "Jew" and probably "Communist."[32] Although in fact only about one DP in five was a Jew, anti-Semitism as well as anti-Communism was flourishing in postwar America. Yet within two years, by the summer of 1948, the United States Congress had passed, and President Truman had signed, the Displaced Persons Act of 1948, allowing 200,000 Europeans to come to the United States.[33]

Many of those 200,000 would sail past the Statue of Liberty and her noble plea to give America the tired, the poor, the huddled masses yearning to breathe free. But it was perfectly obvious that "the lady who lifted the lamp beside the golden door did not write the DP Act."[34]

The Displaced Persons Act of 1948 was a brazenly discriminatory piece of legislation, written to exclude as many concentration camp survivors as possible and to include as many Baltic and Ukrainian and ethnic German Volksdeutsche as it could get away with. The DP Act was not a fishnet spread wide across the DP camps; Congress had very definite preferences in mind, and the waters it was fishing had more than a random share of Nazi collaborators. Had Congress tried to design a law that would extend the Statue of Liberty's hand to the followers and practitioners of Nazism, it could not have done much better than this without coming right out and saying so.

The words of the DP Act of 1948 authorized the entry of 200,000 displaced persons over a two-year period. But they were not to be chosen at random. Instead, Congress inserted four crucial provisions that gave a decided cast to who those lucky people would be.

First, only refugees who had arrived at the camps by December 22, 1945, would be eligible. This drastically early cutoff date automatically excluded those 100,000 Jews who had fled from Poland in 1946. And it did not greatly benefit the Jews who had traded a Nazi concentration camp for an Allied one, since at least half of them had gone to Palestine in 1946 and 1947. Only about 10,000 Jews, roughly one percent of the DP population, had been in the camps since December 1945. Thus, "carefully but without ostensible prejudice," Congress hung out a sign saying, in effect, 85 percent of the Jews in DP camps need not apply to come to America.[35]

Having excluded nearly all the Jews, Congress then extended America's hand to the Balts. It required that 40 percent of the immigrants be from countries that had been "de facto annexed by a foreign power"—a diplomatic euphemism for Latvia, Lithuania, and Estonia, whose incorporation into the Soviet Union in 1944 the United States had never officially recognized.

The third discriminatory provision was an outright preference given to farmers, who were entitled to 30 percent of the available slots. This provision favored Ukrainians (and Poles, to a certain extent) at the expense of Jews, fewer than four percent of whom were farmers.[36]

Finally, Congress wrote into the DP Act a special preference for Volksdeutsche, the German ethnics of the East—"the notorious Nazi Fifth Column," in the words of one critic[37]—if they had managed to get to Germany during or after the war. Volksdeutsche could not even qualify as DPs under the rules laid down by the IRO, since they had not left their homelands involuntarily or under the threat of persecution. So Congress simply ignored the IRO and wrote a legislative ticket for 50,000 of the Volksdeutsche in Europe.[38]

It was no accident that the DP Act excluded the vast majority of Jews in the camps and gave preference to the very groups that had been found to be infested with Nazi collaborators by reporters and official government studies. The House and Senate committees that produced the bill were dominated by isolationists who had no desire to throw open America's gate to any European huddled masses, and particularly not Jews. There was nothing subtle about the December 1945 cutoff date; it was understood by its proponents and critics alike to be a closing of the door to as many Jews as possible. Its congressional sponsors reflected the beliefs of the chief counsel of a Senate committee, who had reported that, unlike the industrious Balts, the Jews "do not desire to work, but expect to be cared for . . . It is very doubtful that any country would desire these people as immigrants."[39]

In the congressional debate, anti-Semitism sometimes wore the thinnest of veils. Senator Alexander Wiley of Wisconsin, the chairman of the Senate Judiciary Committee, was quoted as warning the Senate to be "careful about letting displaced persons into this country." That meant America should seek "good blood" and keep out the "rats." Said Senator Wiley of the "rats": "We've got enough of them already."[40]

His colleague, Senator William Chapman Revercomb of West Virginia, was more direct. "We could solve this DP problem all right," he was quoted as saying, "if we could work out some bill that would keep out the Jews."[41]

The preference given to farmers and Volksdeutsche was sponsored by a senator who believed that not every immigrant flocking to American shores should be "related to residents of New York City."[42] Everybody knew what *that* meant.

This lurking anti-Semitism was aggravated, with tragic irony, by what appears to have been a profoundly misguided attempt by Jewish leaders in America to ensure the widest possible coverage of the DP Act. Although only about 20 percent of the DPs were Jews, the persistent image in the public's eye was that all, or nearly all, the DPs were Jews. To generate widespread support for DP legislation, American Jewish leaders put together an ecumenical group of American church leaders and public figures, named it the Citizens Committee for Displaced Persons (CCDP), and undertook a massive public relations campaign to publicize the fact that half the DPs were Catholic, most were refugees from Communism, and nearly all were honest families who worked hard, feared God, and loved freedom. To support this new image, CCDP brochures and lobbying efforts featured Latvians (who were largely Catholic), Lithuanians (who were largely Protestant), and other non-Jewish Eastern Europeans. CCDP gave little publicity to Jewish DPs, except to note that they comprised only 20 percent of the camps' population.

CCDP also concluded that, in order to make room under the DP Act for 100,000 Jews, the act should authorize 400,000 visas.[43] What would be the makeup of the other 300,000? Correspondence of the American Jewish Committee, one of the components of the CCDP, was startlingly frank. "A calculated risk . . . should be taken" that Nazi collaborators would receive some of those 300,000 visas. This is "unavoidable if a haven were to be found in this country for any really significant number of displaced Jews."[44]

Thus, the leadership of the organized American Jewish community not only supported but encouraged the greatest possible generosity for European refugees, believing that the Jewish survivors of the Holocaust would find space on the boats for themselves only if there was plenty of room for the others. The goal of the CCDP, therefore, was to convince the public, and through them the Congress, that there was room enough for all. And the more appealing a face it could put on the DPs as a whole, the better the chances that Congress would be generous.

The publicity campaign of the CCDP was successful—too successful. It created a favorable public climate for the admission of DPs, a climate that Congress could not ignore. But as the act was hammered out in committee, the CCDP was trapped in a roaring backfire. The newly created sympathy for Eastern European, anti-Communist Christians generated what came to be officially known as "the Baltic preference" with its reservation of 40 percent of DP Act visas for the Balts, yet the early cutoff date left most Jewish DPs ineligible.[45]

The CCDP's approach infuriated some American Jews who were not at all pleased at CCDP's "calculated risk" of casting the net wide enough to include three non-Jewish DPs for every Jew. This tactic, wrote one Jewish critic, "utilized the feelings of mercy built up by the sufferings of Nazism's victims to make propaganda for all DP's, including the murderers, by its undiscriminating plea for all."[46]

This argument, however, had little effect on the Congress. Abraham Duker, a former member of the prosecution staff at Nuremberg and a specialist in the Nazi atrocities of the Ukraine, culled out official wartime German reports of the slaughters there, detailing the assistance rendered by the Ukrainian militia.[47] Duker forwarded his report to every member of Congress. One congressman inserted it in the back of the *Congressional Record* with a pro forma observation that "all such suspects should be rigorously examined."[48]

When the bill passed, Duker provided the epitaph: "These Balts and other self-proclaimed 'farmers' and 'political persecutees' will [now] receive priority in admission to the U.S.A. . . . . As Americans, [we have] no business flooding our shores with criminals of this kind. The handling of the DP problem . . . has obviously proved a failure, and one which will have tragic consequences."[49]

Shortly after the act was passed, a *New York Post* reporter, touring the DP camps, wrote, "The DP camps today are shot through with collaborators, with those who actively collaborated in the nazi [sic] design, with former members of the SS and Wehrmacht, and with men who played a role in the extermination of the Jews."[50]

A *New York Times* report was equally blunt: "As matters stand, it is easier for a former Nazi to enter the United States than for one of the Nazis' innocent victims."[51]

If the act made the entry of Nazi war criminals easy, it stopped short of actually making it legal. Congress could hardly have failed to recognize that it was stacking the deck in favor of groups that had more than their share of Nazi collaborators, but of course no congressman was eager to appear to be a sponsor for ex-Nazis. The proponents of the act's lopsided priorities regularly expressed their faith that individual applicants would be "screened" to keep out Nazi collaborators.

"Screening" was actually a two-step process, although neither step was to prove terribly effective. The first step was a requirement imposed by the International Refugee Organization, which was screening and certifying refugees for any nation that wanted to take them in. The IRO Constitution specifically provided that certification as a "displaced person" was not available for any "war criminal" or any person who "can be shown to have assisted the enemy in persecuting" civilians or to have "voluntarily assisted the enemy forces" in military operations.[52] Thus, if the IRO determined that a refugee had been a Nazi collaborator who had taken part in persecution, it would, in theory, refuse to certify him as a "displaced person" and thus doom any chance he had for emigration to the West.

But the IRO's investigations were superficial and, in the eyes of some, corrupt. One employee of the DP Commission who worked closely with IRO staff resigned in disgust, calling the IRO certification process "a complete racket."[53] Many of the IRO clerks, he charged, were former collaborators themselves who coached the applicants in the techniques of successful deception or who simply filled out the papers on behalf of applicants, submitting them for rubber-stamp approval by unsuspecting IRO officials.

Beyond this, Congress had created a gigantic loophole in whatever protection the IRO offered when the DP Act authorized some 50,000 visas for Volksdeutsche. Because the Volksdeutsche, in IRO's view, had left their homelands voluntarily to assist the war effort in Germany, they were not considered "displaced persons" at all, and IRO refused to have anything to do with them, even to the point of screening them for possible evidence of past collaboration. When the Congress extended America's hand to the Volksdeutsche, therefore, it was reaching into a pool that had not been strained for impurities even by the IRO. The act that Congress passed should have been called "The Displaced Persons and Volksdeutsche Act of 1948."

The second step in the displaced persons' screening process (and, for Volksdeutsche, the only step) was imposed not by the IRO but by Congress. The act created the Displaced Persons Commission and provided that the commission would investigate each applicant to ensure that he had not "been a member of, or participated in, any movement which is or has been hostile to the United States or the form of government of the United States"—a provision broad enough to cover Communism and Nazism both.[54] If an applicant flunked this investigation, he would not get a visa.

As matters turned out, the DP Commission delegated the actual investigation to the Counter Intelligence Corps (CIC) of the U.S. Army. CIC's problem was that it had no access to the records that would indicate that a Ukrainian, Baltic, or other Eastern European applicant had been a Nazi collaborator. The CIC's investigation consisted of a personal interview of the applicant, a "neighborhood check," a check of the CIC security files for "classified security information," checks of U.S. military government records, German police records and U.N. "local camp records," and the records of the Berlin Document Center (BDC).[55]

Although officials of the Displaced Persons Commission were fond of describing how many such steps CIC took in investigating applicants, the CIC's investigation, except for the BDC check, was limited to the applicant's behavior since he had entered the camp, or at least since he had entered Germany. The neighborhood, the military government, the German police, and the United Nations would know of nothing else.

It was through the Berlin Document Center—the repository of Nazi party and SS personnel records, captured by the Army in the final days of the war—that the Army thought, or at least claimed, it was getting information on an applicant's Nazi background. The DPC later claimed that "the availability of the Berlin Document Center with its 20 million names on record in one spot meant an incalculable saving in time and money for the whole DP program, and an unimpeachable source of security data."[56] But the BDC contained only records that had been generated in Berlin. For German or Austrian applicants, this was fine; if they were Nazi party or SS members, their records would be in the BDC.

But Hitler's record keepers had shown no interest in sympathizers in the Ukraine, the Baltic countries, or most other areas of Eastern Europe. Indeed, members of the Ukrainian militia, or the Latvian political police, or the Estonian Selbstschutz, or the Croatian Ustashi, or the Hungarian Arrow Cross were usually not members of the Nazi party of Germany, but of their own local fascist organizations. Their records were simply not in Berlin, and never had been, so the "BDC check" was utterly useless for these people. The records the Army needed—personnel rosters, paybooks, membership cards, and so forth from German-occupied areas—were either destroyed or behind the Iron Curtain, far from the reach of the United States Army.

So, after giving an overt preference to groups that were laced with Nazi collaborators, the act could not very effectively keep out the Nazis of the Baltics, the Ukraine, and Eastern Europe simply by declaring that Nazis were ineligible. The task of identifying Nazis was almost impossible. Very few would admit it. IRO investigators, Army investigators, and DP Commission investigators were swamped with a million DPs and could not mount exhaustive background checks of each one. The applicant filled out his own application form; if he said he had been a farmer in Poland (as many of them did to obtain the farmer's preference), who was to prove him a liar? The guards at Treblinka and Maidanek and Auschwitz had left few eyewitnesses behind.

Occasionally it happened that a Jewish DP might recognize a Ukrainian militia man by chance, or fellow DPs might inform on one, or a hapless applicant might admit that he had been a member of the auxiliary police or one of the other "inimical organizations" in his homeland, but these cases were rare. The DP Act had cast U.S. nets into waters known to be rife with sharks, and it was inevitable that sharks would be brought in.

To compound the difficulties inherent in identifying non-German Nazis, the individual screening of applicants quickly degenerated into a haphazard and unreliable business. As one scholar put it later:

> Most frequently, Army youths between the ages of 18 and 23 were given twelve hours of training before being sent out to determine eligibility [of DP applicants]. In this short period, they were taught about European minorities and dialects, national enmities, German occupation policies, Russian government methods, ploys, guises and tricks, and the differences between

false and genuine documents. In one and a half days they were expected to learn what it had taken more experienced individuals years to master.[57]

Predictably, screening techniques were slipshod. Whether an applicant was approved or rejected often depended on his examiner. Yet in 1947 88 percent of non-Jewish DPs were approved.[58]

"In one group of 20 Latvians," according to one account, "there were 12 former SS officers who bore the SS mark on their arms. All were approved for DP status. Each of the men claimed that he had received the identical mark from a burn, a wound, or an accident, and the American interrogator accepted the explanation."[59]

One DPC employee wrote his superiors in disgust in 1949. "Through false documentation," he said, "individuals who served the Nazis as traitors of their own countries, and persons who committed atrocities against the Jews . . . are being processed with little possibility for detection. These types of individuals are poor material for United States citizenship."[60]

As late as 1949 an Army intelligence report echoed the conclusions of a similar report over three years earlier. It confirmed that "hundreds, if not thousands, of Nazi collaborators have been and still are residing in DP camps."[61]

As if all of this were not enough, camp officials soon discovered that Congress had grossly overestimated the number of Balts who were eligible for visas. Forty percent of the visas were reserved for this select group, but only 19 percent of the DPs could qualify for them. The DP Commission literally could not give out these visas fast enough. In the first year of operation, Balts received 30 percent of the visas— "far in excess of their proportion among the DP population," the DP Commission reported, "but still below the statutory 40 percent."[62]

Such shortages posed a critical problem to the operation of the act. Because Balts were entitled to 40 percent of the visas, every two visas given to Balts meant that three visas became available to non-Balts. Finding a Latvian and his wife who could go to America meant that three Poles or Czechs or Jews or Hungarians could go too. Particularly in the first year of the DP Act, therefore, there were strong pressures to pass through as many Latvians, Lithuanians, and Estonians as possible

The same rationale applied to farmers with their 30 percent preference—every three visas given to farmers would free seven visas for others. But the DP Commission could not always find enough farmers. By June 1949 only 26 percent of the visas, instead of the statutorily required 30 percent, had gone to farmers. At one point, DP officials stopped handing out visas to anyone else and scoured the camps looking for farmers who wanted to go to America.[63]

Because Balts and farmers, in effect, went to the head of the line, and because there was a lot of room there, falsification of documents became a growth industry, and many DPs who hardly knew a hoe from a pitchfork passed themselves off as farm workers, foresters, and dairy technicians—all entitled to the agricultural preference.[64] As one DP Commission employee observed, "[P]eople who have falsified documents and who have much to hide in their personal history records have their cases pushed along without an investigation to ascertain the validity of their documents. Thus many persons are finding their way with completely false information about themselves."[65]

It was particularly easy for anyone with calloused hands or a strong back to concoct a history as a "farmer"; no tests were given, no experience need be shown. And counterfeit farmers came through in droves. For the farmers in America who had volunteered to sponsor a DP family or two by providing jobs, the results could be disconcerting. Said one farmer in Virginia: "[W]e apply for farmers, and get such things as civil engineers and electricians and aviators." Said another, who had agreed to sponsor a lumberjack: "When this man arrived I was appalled when I found he not only was inexperienced and did not even know how to properly handle an axe but that he was an office worker as a bookkeeper and an accountant."[66] By 1950 over 40 percent of the DPs were already living in such farming communities as New York City, Chicago, Philadelphia, Detroit, Cleveland, Los Angeles, Baltimore, and Pittsburgh. By 1951 90 percent of the "farmers" were no longer with their American farm sponsors.[67]

The institutional pressures on the various organizations involved in the process were formidable. The IRO was charged with resettling DPs, not with keeping them in camps. The Army, which was charged with investigating DPs, wanted them out of Europe. State Department officials, charged with granting visas, were indoctrinated with the "humanitarian purposes" of the DP Act. The whole purpose of the DP program was to move people out of the camps.

DP employees who were responsible for ascertaining the background of applicants had, according to one, "very little" opportunity to interview applicants face to face. "I was told that it would take too much time," he said, "and that we must pass the cases along to meet our quota."[68]

The final report of the Displaced Persons Commission made no bones about it. "From the beginning to the end, there was public pressure on the Commission. . . . American Government authorities, including first and foremost the occupation authorities in Germany and the allied authorities in Austria, were insistent in their desire to press for physical departure of eligible applicants to alleviate the difficulties in those countries."[69] Like General Motors turning out Chevys, the Displaced Persons Commission saw its goal as maintaining "expected levels of production."[70]

By 1949 the discriminatory and unworkable provisions of the DP Act had become too great to ignore. Aided by the Democratic victories of 1948, sentiment in Congress ran high to amend the act. Led by the new chairman of the House Judiciary Committee, Emanuel Celler of Brooklyn, proponents of a more liberal act eventually outlasted the restrictionists in the Senate, led by Pat McCarran of Nevada. In 1950 Congress extended the DP Act for another two years and lifted the ceiling to 350,000 DPs and 54,000 Volksdeutsche. More significantly, Congress eliminated the 1945 cutoff date, thus opening the doors to thousands of previously ineligible Jews; it removed the preferences for Balts and farmers, which DP officials had admitted they could not fill no matter how hard they tried; and it added a provision that no one who had taken part in persecution would be eligible for admission to the United States.[71]

But the final figures are instructive. By the time the DP Act finally expired on June 30, 1952, nearly 400,000 immigrants had come to the United States under it. Some 337,000 (85 percent) of those were DPs, the rest were Volksdeutsche. One-third of them (including many Ukrainians) listed their country of birth as Poland (the DP Commission did not keep separate figures for Ukrainians); some 18 percent were born in the Baltics, 15 percent in Germany, nearly all the rest from Yugoslavia, Hungary, Czechoslovakia, or other Eastern European countries. Fully three-quarters of them settled in New York, Illinois, Pennsylvania, New Jersey, Michigan, Ohio, California, and Massachusetts, in that order.[72]

In its final report in 1952, the DP Commission concluded an exhaustive study of its production:

> In the vast preponderance of cases, they have made fine neighbors and good workers. Their children have adjusted well to the schools, and the adults have begun to take their part in the normal community life. . . . [I]n a relatively short time, the displaced persons are almost indistinguishable from the rest of the people in the communities which welcomed them.[73]

Wolodymir Osidach and his family sailed slowly past the Statue of Liberty on July 29, 1949. They walked down the gangplank and transferred to a train that took them the few miles to Philadelphia. He quickly obtained work—as a butcher. The family moved into a small home in a Philadelphia neighborhood. Most of their neighbors were Ukrainians, and the Osidachs drew no attention to themselves. They were four of the 116,000 DPs who settled in Philadelphia.

It would be wrong to leave the impression that the DP Act, even in its first two years, was entirely misbegotten, or that a majority of Ukrainian, Baltic, or Volksdeutsche immigrants had taken part in Nazi atrocities. The number who had actually taken part in persecution, as opposed to those who had merely been sympathizers, was almost certainly a small part—although no one will ever know how small. Yet a small part of 400,000 immigrants is still a large number.

How many Nazi persecutors came to the United States? No one knows and no one ever will. All one can do is conjecture. There were 393,000 immigrants under the DP Act. If one estimates that only two and a half percent of that number took part in persecution, then nearly 10,000 Nazi war criminals came to America.

Look at the groups with demonstrable patterns of collaboration. Some 53,000 immigrants were Volksdeutsche, most from Yugoslavia, Germany, Poland, and Romania. Of the 340,000 others, 68,000 listed themselves as Balts. The DP Commission did not keep figures on Ukrainians; they were included in the Polish numbers, of which there were 125,000.[74] The United Ukrainian American Relief Committee estimated that 138,000—about fourteen percent—of the DPs in Germany and Austria were Ukrainian.[75] If 14 percent of the DPs coming to the United States were Ukrainians, it would mean 48,000.

That means 116,000 Baltic and Ukrainian DPs, and 53,000 Volksdeutsche. If even five percent of those people had taken part in persecution, then over 8,000 Nazi criminals came here. This figure does not include non-Volksdeutsche immigrants from Germany, Austria, and Eastern European countries where persecution took place, nor is it meant to cast exclusive blame on Ukrainians, Balts, or Volksdeutsche. Collaboration was found in all countries and areas occupied by the Germans.

Such estimates are hardly scientific. Indeed, they are speculation dressed in very light clothing. But they give a certain perspective to the question of how many Nazi persecutors came to this country. It is a number not to be measured in scores, or even hundreds, but very likely thousands.

The numbers also give perspective to how people who had taken part in such unimaginable crimes managed to come to this country. It was not all that hard. It even had a certain inevitability to it, given the undeniable facts.

And the facts are undeniable: in many areas of Europe occupied by the Nazis, there was widespread collaboration. As the war ended, many of the collaborators fled rather than remain to endure the retribution of the victors. They ended up in DP camps with the victims of war. The United States took in hundreds of thousands of the camps' inhabitants, and the preferences went to groups with known patterns of collaboration. The pressure to move bodies, to stimulate production, was intense, and individual investigations were cursory and unreliable. As a result, the applicants were sifted through a screen of very coarse mesh.

The decision to open America's doors to 400,000 European refugees was a peculiar mix of generosity and racism. In the first two years of the DP Act, racism prevailed. The act sorted out applicants not according to need but according to race, religion, and nationality: Jews were disfavored; Latvians, Lithuanians, Estonians, and those of German ethnic background were preferred. The 1950 amendments, removing the sanctions against Jews and the preferences for Balts and farmers, went far toward righting the balance in favor of generosity, but the special provisions for Volksdeutsche remained, the screening process was still infirm, and nearly 150,000 immigrants had already arrived.

Had Congress been motivated by a genuine desire in 1948 to extend the lamp of the Statue of Liberty to the most deserving of the homeless, it could have done so easily by giving preference to the real victims of Nazism—the survivors of the concentration camps— and those who could demonstrate that they had been at least neutral during the war. The cockeyed preferences based on country of birth, occupational background, and date of entry to the camps had no rational relationship to need or trustworthiness. They were political, not humanitarian, choices.

Keeping out Nazi collaborators was not a high priority. In 1948 Congress sought out groups that had much to conceal and encouraged them to apply. It erected barriers against those who had nothing to conceal. The disqualification of Jews by means of the early cutoff date was strong and effective; its disqualification of Nazis by means of legal fiat and cursory background checks was weak.

Probably no program that handed out 400,000 visas to America could have totally excluded Nazi collaborators. Deceit and wile and corruption would have prevailed, in some cases, over the noblest and most conscientious laws and the most scrupulous administration of those laws. But the DP Act, particularly in its first two years, was not the noblest law and the administration of it was porous, from the superficial background checks to the hydraulic pressure to maintain production. And all of it was in the open—documented by official congressional and military reports and eyewitness accounts of American journalists.

How did Nazi war criminals come to the United States? We invited them in.

2

INS AND THE NAZIS:
"Just Like Any Other Case"

Surely no enemy in American history was forgotten so soon after defeat as the Nazis. In 1939, Nazism was an ominous and powerful force astride a mightily armed nation threatening all of Europe; four years later, American land, sea and air power was fully engaged from the North Atlantic to Egypt; four years after that, America was trying to return Germany to the Germans as soon as possible. American policy, by and large, was to treat Nazism as a virus from which the German people had suffered but of which they were now thankfully cured; the American job was first to keep the patient alive by administering its government and then to get it back on its feet through a massive program of aid and rehabilitation and thus to establish a strong bulwark against Soviet influence in Europe.

In March 1947, less than two years after the defeat of the Nazis, President Truman announced the policy of the United States to "support free peoples who are resisting attempted subjugation by armed minorities or by outside pressures" and to help them resist "totalitarian regimes forced upon them against their will."[1] The Truman Doctrine was the declaration of a cold war against the expansionism of our wartime ally. By early 1948, reported one opinion poll, nearly three of every four Americans viewed the Russians "unfavorably."[2]

The profound swing in foreign policy permeated nearly every aspect of life at home. But while the widening of the Soviet sphere in Europe, and Soviet espionage at home, was a serious challenge to American security interests, the threat of "internal subversion" of American institutions by Kremlin agents produced debilitating and at times hysterical overreaction. The national commander of the American Legion warned that the United States was being infiltrated by a "secret battalion" of 75,000 "trained Communists" and an "auxiliary corps" of up to "one million dupes, camp followers, secret sympathizers, and casual supporters." Some Americans speculated darkly that the Commies were the source of the comic books that were being so avidly read by American youth. On California's Big Sur coast, the "Russian Inn" changed its name to the "Ocean Inn."[3]

Not every aspect of our reaction was so amusing. In 1947, President Truman, professing a certain reluctance, instituted loyalty review boards, where persons accused of subversive activities could defend themselves—but could not see the evidence against them or know the identity of their accusers. By 1952, the FBI had conducted 10,000 full field investigations, and nearly 3,000 employees were "arraigned," but the loyalty board's national chairman told Congress that "Not one single case of espionage . . . has been disclosed."[4]

The House Un-American Activities Committee, among its many other escapades, tried to root out "Communist influence" in Hollywood in the late forties; ten writers went to jail for refusing to testify, and they and hundreds more were blacklisted long afterward. "Hollywood capitulated to HUAC," said Joseph Goulden.[5]

And, he might have added, America had capitulated to the anti-Communist phobia that HUAC so zealously exploited. In February 1950, Senator Joseph McCarthy stood before a women's club in West Virginia and said "I have here in my hand a list of two hundred and five [men] that were known to the Secretary of State as being members of the Communist Party, and who, nevertheless, are still working and shaping the policy in the State Department."[6] There was no such list, but for nearly four years, McCarthy held America very nearly captive with his undocumented charges that the government was full of Communists. "No bolder seditionist ever moved among us," wrote Richard Rovere, "nor any politician with a surer, swifter access to the dark place of the American mind."[7]

What on earth had happened to Nazis? Who knew? Who cared? In Germany, the Nazis were cured. Nazism was dead; Communism grasped at our State Department, our movie theaters, our comic books. If we wanted criminals, we had only to look around us for members of the "secret battalion." One Legion member had a proposal to do just that: "a system whereby in each block in the city and in each neighborhood in the country someone can be made responsible" for exposing the Communists on his block.[8] The irony is inescapable: in such a vigilante network, who would have been better suited to stand the watch than the displaced persons, the refugees from Communism, those whose homelands had been "incorporated" by the Soviets?

And so, once in this country, the Nazi war criminals who had been laundered through the Displaced Persons Act found that they were, literally, home free. They arrived in an America whose enemies had been their enemies, an America that no longer feared—or even much thought about—Nazis. And not surprisingly, the agenda of the Immigration and Naturalization Service (INS), the enforcer of the deportation laws, reflected the mood of the country. In the quarter century from the end of World War II until the early 1970's, INS sought to remove thousands of "internal security" suspects, but filed no more than ten cases against persons suspected of Nazi collaboration or of persecuting the innocent.* Had INS filed four hundred cases—forty times as many as it did—only one-tenth of one percent of the DPs would have been charged.

The Immigration and Naturalization Service was no shining star in Washington's bureaucratic firmament. Until 1940 it had been part of the Department of Labor, and its transition to a law-enforcement agency was a slow one. Its agents were often culled from applicants who could not qualify for the FBI, Internal Revenue Service, Treasury, or other prestigious operations. It was decentralized; its dozens of district offices throughout the country maintained the files on individual aliens and were subject to only tenuous control by the commissioner and the "central office" in Washington. Within the Justice Department, INS's ostensible parent, there was little interest in immigration issues, and so INS functioned as a quasi-autonomous stepchild that often found itself at the far end of the table when money and resources were being handed out. It took what it could get and made do.

---

*Because INS did not treat Nazi cases as a separate category until 1973, there is no ready means of identifying, in the thousands of deportation cases filed from 1945 to 1973, just which ones involved Nazi collaborators. The cases discussed in this chapter were identified from a variety of sources: an internal INS survey of March 1977; an investigation by the General Accounting Office in 1978; and four years of research by the Office of Special Investigations, and particularly Eli Rosenbaum of that Office, beginning in 1980. I believe the cases discussed here represent INS's complete record in this respect. Two of the cases—Krasnauskas and Spokevicius—were overlooked by both the INS survey and the GAO investigation and are discussed here for the first time. Even if a stray case or two has eluded us all, however, it would not materially affect the conclusions.

INS was also burdened with the task of administering a law that was festooned with obscure and often contradictory preferences, quotas, conditions, and exclusions. Congress did not devise the original immigration act of 1924, nor its successor in 1952 (which is still in effect), with easy administration in mind. No one understood every provision of the immigration law, including those who were expected to enforce and administer it.

Beyond all this, INS was one of the most ingrown agencies in Washington. Where deportation was involved, INS was investigator, prosecutor, judge, and appeals court: a case was investigated by an INS agent, prosecuted by an INS attorney before another INS attorney who acted as judge (or "hearing officer" as they were known then), and appealed to the Board of Immigration Appeals (BIA), a panel of INS employees. In theory, a BIA decision could be appealed to the federal courts, but this happened rarely, and so the fresh winds of judicial inquiry seldom ruffled the stale air of the Immigration and Naturalization Service.

Unlike the FBI, therefore, INS was not a single vessel holding a steady course under the firm hand of the commissioner. It was a fleet of lesser ships, each with its own captain, loosely subject to the commands of an admiral who was never quite sure where all his ships were heading. The influx of 400,000 immigrants in four years affected the various district offices more immediately than the central office in Washington, and Washington let the districts deal with the problems as they saw fit. Even at that, the districts seldom gave any real guidance to their investigators. As one investigator later put it, "When [an] allegation [of Nazi persecution] came in, it was handed to an investigator just like a prostitution case or a fraud case or any other case. It was not given any special consideration. The investigator who handled it had to make his own determination as to the extent of the investigation and how much effort was going into it."[9]

This lackadaisical attitude could produce bizarre results. Among the first cases brought by INS against Nazi collaborators, the defendants were not Nazis at all. They were three Polish Jews, Heinrich Friedmann, Jakob Tencer, and Jonas Lewy. Their cases were not connected—indeed, the defendants probably never even met—but each was called to defend his conduct under Nazi occupation.

In 1942 the Jews of Poland were being slaughtered in appalling numbers. Three million died—two million of them in death camps.[10] But such "dislocations" caused grave problems for the Germans, who needed Poland's factories to turn out planes and tanks for the German war machine. If Poland's factories had no workers, who would build the planes? To supplement the non-Jewish workers, the SS plucked 15,000 to 25,000 of Poland's strongest Jews from the death camp trains and set them to work in the armament factories, where they lived in labor camps, guarded by Ukrainians.[11]

"There was no hope for anyone who could not work," concluded Professor Raul Hilberg in his monumental work *The Destruction of the European Jews.* "Only the best and strongest workers . . . had a chance to live; all others had to die." From the evidence at Nuremberg, he recounted one incident: "When, in 1943, an SS officer (Sturmbannführer Reinecke) seized a three-year-old Jewish girl in order to deport her to a killing center, she pleaded for her life by showing him her hands and explaining that she could work. In vain."[12]

The lucky and the strong, their families dead, worked for their lives, and sometimes worked themselves to death, making planes for the Luftwaffe or bullets for the German army. To keep the inmates in order, and to see that they made the daily trek from camp to adjoining factory, the Germans established a hierarchy of Jews, selecting a Jewish commandant—a "kapo"—to maintain order. These kapos were, of course, themselves prisoners and victims who worked for their masters keeping other prisoners and victims in line. They beat their fellow Jews, which sometimes, not always, protected their victims from worse beatings, or death, at the hands of the Ukrainians or Germans.

Heinrich Friedmann, a thirty-six-year-old Polish Jew from Lvov, was picked by the Germans to be the "commandant" of the 2,150 Jews at the Luftwaffe plant near Mielec.[13] Friedmann beat his fellow victims, sometimes with his hands, sometimes with a rubber hose. He took boots from those lucky enough to have them. But Friedmann also concealed sick or injured Jews, saving them from death, until they were fit to return to work. He surreptitiously destroyed a list of Jews scheduled to be shot. Against SS orders, he allowed prayers to be said. When the Germans liquidated the camp in 1944, killing the remaining Jews, Heinrich Friedmann escaped. He made his way to a DP camp and came to New York on January 13, 1950.

But he was seen in New York, probably by another survivor from Mielec, who notified the INS, which filed for deportation. After trial, Friedmann was ordered deported by an INS judge who found that he had entered illegally under the DP Act because he had taken part in the persecution of innocent people.

Friedmann appealed, and the decision was reversed. An assistant commissioner of the INS, looking at the same evidence of good and bad, ruled that Friedmann's conduct, under the circumstances, did not amount to persecution or inhuman conduct. Friedmann was allowed to remain in the United States.[14]

For Jakob Tencer, a Polish Jew who was in charge of forced laborers at an ammunition factory in Pionki, the story was much the same. He landed in New York in December 1949 as a displaced person; INS was told of his presence and it brought him to trial in 1952. Several survivors of Pionki testified that he had beaten and abused prisoners; twenty-three affidavits were introduced on his behalf, each speaking favorably of him. The judge heard it all and concluded: "Doubtlessly it is true that most of [Tencer's] actions at the camp did in some small way assist the Axis in prosecuting the war against the United States, but so it was too with the actions of every other inmate in that labor camp and all similar camps." Tencer "can [not] be found to have purposefully or by design acted contrary to human decency or civilization on behalf of the Axis." The judge dismissed the charges.[15]

For Jonas Lewy, the third of three Jews to be charged by INS with persecution and collaboration, the results were not as unequivocal. His story was in many ways like that of Friedmann and Tencer. Lewy, a thirty-three-year-old furrier and hat maker, had been a kapo in the Polish ghetto of Piotrkow, near Lodz. The Germans forced 25,000 Jews into the Piotrkow ghetto; ninety percent of them were slaughtered or sent to concentration camps in October 1942. Three witnesses testified that Lewy had done good: hiding them from the Germans, allowing them to keep forbidden food. Four others testified that he had beaten or betrayed them. The judge concluded that Lewy, "having committed the evils, is not excused from [deportation] by the fact that he had done noble actions while a policeman . . ." The order was upheld on appeal. There was no discussion either by the judge or the appeals board of why Lewy's situation was any different from that of Friedmann or Tencer, who had been exonerated. It is quite likely that the judges in Lewy's case were not even aware of the previous cases.

With a rough sort of justice, however, Lewy's case ground to a halt. The appeal was decided in December 1955. Not until January 1958 was Lewy actually ordered deported, to Poland. Nearly five years later, in October 1962, Poland declined to accept him. In 1964 the case was reopened and a new trial ordered because, prior to the 1955 trial, Lewy had not been given the statements of the witnesses against him, and thus his lawyer could not have adequately prepared for cross-examination. In 1965 INS found that, of the four witnesses against him, one had died and one could not be located. Lewy was not put back on trial. In 1980, he died in New York, at age sixty-nine.*[16]

If INS could find Jews who were Nazis, it could also find Baltic police auxiliaries who were not. The first such was Antanas Spokevicius, a forty-nine-year-old Lithuanian who came to Chicago as a displaced person and found a job at fifty dollars a week as a car cleaner in a railroad yard. Spokevicius had obtained his visa by claiming that he had been a "primary school teacher" in Kaunas from 1936 to 1944—a representation that he later admitted was totally false. He had joined the Lithuanian police auxiliary as soon as the Nazis invaded in 1941 and he fled to Germany in 1944 when they retreated. Although the record is bare of any evidence of what he actually did for the Nazis, he almost certainly would have been involved in the liquidation of Kaunas' 27,000 Jews.

Shortly after Spokevicius entered the United States, INS received an anonymous letter claiming that he had been a battalion leader who had worked closely with the Germans. An investigator interviewed Spokevicius, who admitted that he had immigrated under false pretenses, and a deportation case was filed. The judge declared that he was "not impressed" with Spokevicius' claim that he had lied to avoid repatriation to the Soviet Union. Spokevicius' misrepresentation "cut

---

*In the mid-fifties INS busied itself with the case of Andrija Artukovic (see chapter 5)—a case that resulted in Artukovic remaining in the United States.

At about the same time, INS got involved in a long, complex legal battle against Nicolae Malaxa, a Romanian industrialist, who originally came to the United States in 1946. Malaxa left the U.S. in 1954, and when he tried to return a year later INS attempted to bar him on grounds that he had supported both the Iron Guard (the Romanian fascist movement) and the Romanian Communist Party. The Immigration Service's primary concern seems to have been that Malaxa was a Communist sympathizer and may have been involved in financial irregularities in establishing a tubing mill in California. Although the hearings consumed nearly three years and 5,000 pages of testimony, neither of these charges was proven, nor was the charge that Malaxa had rendered overt support either to the Third Reich or the Iron Guard. His admission to the United States was finally upheld in 1958. He died in New Jersey in 1965.[17]

off an avenue of inquiry'' that might have resulted in a finding of actual persecution, and the judge ordered him deported.

Spokevicius took his case to the Board of Immigration Appeals, which reversed the deportation order and allowed Spokevicius to stay. It ruled that the Immigration Act did ''not preclude the issuance of a visa to a bona fide refugee who has made even a willful misrepresentation of a material fact where the misrepresentation was made because of fear of being repatriated to his former homeland.'' [18]

It was an outrageous decision, for any number of reasons. First, forcible repatriation to the Soviet Union from the American zone of Germany had ended by late 1945, long before the DP Act was passed in 1948. In fact, one of the Truman administration's major arguments in support of DP legislation was that the Baltic refugees would not be returned against their will and thus America must find room for them. Second, despite what the BIA said, nothing in any law at any time excused a misrepresentation based on fear of repatriation or any other fear. The whole point of the law was to require absolute truthfulness so the applicant's eligibility could be determined. While this requirement was often evaded in practice, there was no legal defense to it.

Finally, the implications of the ruling were enormous: BIA was holding that an immigrant who had consistently misrepresented his past, and who had admitted the truth only when caught and confronted with it many years later, could nonetheless be protected from deportation if he claimed he once had a ''fear of repatriation''—no matter how specious the claim actually was. BIA was saying, in effect, if you tell the truth and are denied a visa, it's your own fault; if you lie and manage to come here, we will protect you. The Queen of Hearts in Alice's Wonderland could not have improved on that.

A few years later, in 1956, the BIA again turned common sense inside out for the benefit of a Lithuanian collaborator. Felix Krasnauskas had told DP officials that he had been a farmer in Lithuania during the entire wartime period; he got a visa (as a Baltic ''farmer'' he could be counted under both preferences) in 1950 and settled in Worcester, Massachusetts, where he worked as a hotel porter. His ex-wife, who was in a German jail serving a nine-year sentence for trying to murder him, wrote to INS disclosing that Krasnauskas had helped the Germans destroy a Lithuanian village, burning alive dozens of men, women, and children.

Krasnauskas denied to an INS investigator that he had taken part in any such atrocities, but he did admit that his claim to being a farmer had been a total fabrication and that he had been "chief of the political police" in his district, trained by the Gestapo, and had worked closely with the Gestapo in arresting what he called "saboteurs and communists." It was virtually a full confession to Nazi collaboration. The INS judge ordered him deported for having been part of a "movement hostile to the United States"—a class to whom DP visas were forbidden.

Once again BIA upheld the collaborator on appeal. "We think it is obvious from [Krasnauskas'] testimony that, particularly during the German occupation of Lithuania, he was actively engaged in combating sabotage by communist agents and that he had a valid reason to fear enforced repatriation to Lithuania and death or other punishment if his prior activities had become known. . . . [T]here is no evidence that the respondent participated in a movement hostile to the United States."[19]

Just what BIA considered the Gestapo to be, if not a movement hostile to the United States, is difficult to fathom. And its discussion of the fear of repatriation was nonsense. Moreover, if Krasnauskas had indeed been engaged in anti-Communist activity, would he not have proclaimed it loudly in the DP camps of 1948 to the keepers of democracy's gates?

Although the case could not have been prosecuted very vigorously at trial—no evidence was presented of the critical role the Lithuanian police had played in the murder of that country's Jews—Krasnauskas' own admissions were plainly sufficient to prove the government's case. The only explanation is that by 1956 the BIA, deliberately or otherwise, had clamped such blinders on itself that it was willing to consider only *Communist* movements as being "hostile to the United States." That reading, of course, was at odds with the entire history of World War II, but no other explanation makes any sense. Whatever the reason, Felix Krasnauskas, admittedly a Lithuanian auxiliary and a confessed perjurer besides, stayed in Worcester, Massachusetts—a Gestapo-trained bellboy.

There was one case quite different from all the rest. Ferenc Vajta, a Hungarian, became the only Nazi criminal the INS actually deported. And Vajta had been, after the war, in the service of American intelligence in Italy.

In October 1944, Ferenc Szalasi, the leader of Hungary's viciously pro-Nazi Arrow Cross party, came to power—the last Nazi in
Europe to do so—and he appointed Vajta, the thirty-year-old editor
of a fascist newspaper, to the important post of Hungary's general
consul in Vienna, one of the few major cities still firmly in German
control. For Vajta, described by one acquaintance as "one hundred
percent pro-Nazi," and by another as "an extremely handsome, polished and suave sort of person, proficient in several languages and
absolutely without any trace of decency or moral fiber," it was the
chance to ingratiate himself with top German Nazis. He entertained
them at his sumptuous villa in Vienna, the last foreign outpost of a
demented regime in a war that was already lost.

But in Hungary, there were still Jews. Vajta wired Szalasi in Budapest that, if Jews could be sent to Vienna in batches of fifteen to
twenty thousand, the Germans would be "willing and able to accept
and distribute them to the proper places." Szalasi, a rabid anti-Sem-
ite who had suffered for years under more moderate Hungarian prime
ministers, desperately wanted to comply, but time was rapidly running out for the Arrow Cross. In the spring of 1945, when the Red
Army was at Hungary's door, the Szalasi government collapsed and
dispersed. Despite Vajta's efforts, Szalasi was unable to dispatch any
Hungarian Jews to Vienna.

But Vajta's odyssey was just beginning. In May 1945, the war
scarcely over, the Office of Strategic Services (OSS), the U.S. wartime intelligence group, put Vajta's name on a list of Hungarian
war criminals "for having done intellectual work in the service of the
most intensive prosecution of the war and in support of the Arrow
Cross (Fascist) movement." Vajta was captured by American troops
in June and interned at Dachau, where he was interrogated by OSS
agents.

The OSS quickly concluded that Vajta was a thoroughgoing Nazi
and, like many others, he was scheduled to be turned over to the
Hungarian government for trial in Budapest. But early in July 1945,
he escaped from American custody at Dachau. He claimed later that
he had obtained a German uniform and passed himself off as a German POW to be repatriated; American intelligence reports stated that
he had been released by a British officer.

Whatever the fact, Vajta made his way to Innsbruck in the French
zone of Austria where, according to later intelligence reports, he gave
the French information that enabled them to recover a stunning 6,000

kilograms—over six and a half tons—of gold and diamonds from a "gold train" that had left Budapest in the closing days of the war. Even at thirty-five dollars an ounce, six and a half tons of gold were worth over $7,000,000 (at today's prices they would be worth nearly $100,000,000) and the French were profoundly grateful. In what would prove to be a bizarre mirror image of the Barbie episode a few years later, the French repeatedly refused American requests for Vajta's extradition; instead, they procured his escape into Italy in August, 1946, a year after he had come to them.

Vajta's greatest skill was self-promotion, his greatest asset was a silver tongue, and his only objective was to keep out of the hands of the Hungarians. He found an unlikely sponsor in the Americans. In the spring of 1947, agents of the Counter Intelligence Corps of the United States Army in Italy recruited Vajta and put him to work. With the inclusion of Hungary into the Soviet satellite system and the disbanding of the OSS, there was little enthusiasm for turning Hungarian Nazis over to Hungarian Communists, and Vajta quickly took advantage. His handler, an American army sergeant who had earlier described Vajta as a "Hungarian war criminal . . . [and] a conceited adventurer true only to money" later apparently changed his mind when Vajta volunteered his services to the Army. The sergeant gave Vajta a letter commending his "great assistance to Counter Intelligence Corps in Rome giving information on immigrants from Russian satellite states"—a common euphemism for spying on Soviet activities in the Allied zones of occupied Europe.

But word had leaked to the Hungarian government that Vajta was in Italy, and Hungary requested his extradition from the Italian police. Vajta's American handler put Vajta into hiding and quickly made arrangements for him to go to Spain in the summer of 1947. After a few months in Madrid, Vajta approached the American Embassy there and displayed the letter from the CIC. An inveterate name-dropper, Vajta convinced Embassy officials that, under the sponsorship of European Catholic figures and anti-Communist exiles, he was assembling a network of patriotic Hungarians to fight Russian influence in Europe. He wanted to go to America, he said, to explore the possibility of getting official American support for his activities and to enlist Eastern European recruits from the emigré community here. Embassy officials, apparently taken by his suave and sincere manner and his past service to the CIC, gave him a six-month tourist visa and wished him luck.

Vajta arrived in New York in December 1947, and his luck quickly went sour. He had little aptitude for organizing anything; his real priority was to aggrandize his own credentials by seeking a prestigious American publisher for his anti-Communist tracts. But the first Hungarians he approached here recognized him immediately as the same Vajta who had been a pro-Nazi newspaper editor during the war. They tipped off Walter Winchell, who blew the whistle on Ferenc Vajta in his Sunday evening radio broadcast on January 4, 1948— although it is not clear whether Winchell was angrier at Vajta ("slippery as a greased skunk") or the "disgraceful, shameful, disloyal, disgusting conduct of some American diplomatic officers in Madrid" for letting him in.

In 1948, Walter Winchell had clout. Four days after the broadcast, INS arrested Vajta and clapped him into custody at Ellis Island. He was ordered deported in August 1948, although the appeals process dragged on until February 1950, when he was put on a plane for Colombia.

CIC's dalliance with Vajta in 1947 seems singularly ill-considered. It is highly unlikely that this fast-talking opportunist had anything of value to offer American authorities. But there is little reason to conclude that his entry into the United States was covertly sponsored by CIC or any other branch of the government. During his two years of confinement on Ellis Island, Vajta was by his own account "frantic" over the possibility that he might be deported to Hungary, and he inundated American officials in the State Department, the Defense Department, the CIA and elsewhere with letters appealing for help. But his constant refrain was that he was a devoted anti-Communist who could help America fight the cold war. In none of his many letters did he ever claim that he had come here under the sponsorship of the very government that was trying to deport him. And no American official lifted a finger to intervene with INS.

Why was he deported to Colombia, of all places? INS asked the Italians to take him back, but they wanted no part of him, and INS did not want to deal with the new government of Hungary. Vajta's friends, who at one time included the head of the Vatican press office, arranged to have him appointed to the faculty of a small Catholic university in Bogota, and Colombia issued him a visa. INS decided that Colombia was better than no country at all, and they sent him

there in 1951. Vajta spent the rest of his life as an economics professor and newspaper editor, and he died in Bogota sometime in the late
sixties—the only Nazi in his lifetime to be deported from the United
States.

For INS, one of the last cases was brought in 1959 against Laszlo
Agh, a fifty-one-year-old Hungarian army officer from Newark accused of having beaten and mistreated Jews in a forced-labor detachment at a Hungarian barracks far removed from war. Over ten days
of trial the judge heard twenty-five witnesses, many of them Hungarian Jews who had been in the labor unit. They identified Agh as the
man who had beaten them, buried some of them up to their necks,
and forced them to eat their own excrement.

Agh produced nine witnesses, none of whom knew anything about
the barracks but who testified that Agh had a good reputation and did
not appear to them to be anti-Semitic (none of them was Jewish). Agh
himself took the stand, haughtily denied everything, and claimed the
whole case was a frame-up because he was in an anti-Communist
Hungarian organization in this country (overlooking the fact that all
the former victims who testified against him were American residents). The judge found the victims to be honest and credible, concluded that Agh's witnesses were irrelevant and that Agh himself was
a liar, and ordered him deported.

The Board of Immigration Appeals reviewed the transcript of
the trial (as customary, they did not see Agh or the witnesses against
him), pointed out various minor inconsistencies in the victims' testimony, and concluded that the government had fallen "far short" of
proving its case by "reasonable, substantial and probative evidence."
It dismissed the charges and allowed Agh to remain in the United
States.[20]

INS's next case, in 1968, ten years after the Agh case, hardly
seemed worth the effort. It also concerned a Hungarian Nazi, named
Kornel Lang, who apparently was a Volksdeutsche. He came to this
country under the name Janos Tokaji, and the INS, claiming that he
had been a member of a small but fanatic anti-Semitic hit squad in
Hungary, charged him with obtaining his visa by fraud—using a false
name.

The Immigration Act, however, protects an immigrant who ob-
tains a visa by fraud if he is the spouse or parent of an American
citizen and is "otherwise admissible." Since Lang had married a nat-

uralized citizen in 1957 and had fathered two children in the United States, he was immune from deportation unless the government could prove that, for reasons other than using a false name, he was inadmissible to the United States under the DP Act.

The government never charged that he was. It introduced some confusing and inconclusive evidence about his allegedly anti-Semitic actions in Hungary but called no witnesses. The judge ruled, not unreasonably, that INS "should urge some specific ground [of law] on which it believes [Lang] was not . . . admissible to the United States." It did not; the judge could not divine any from the slipshod evidence before him and dismissed the charges.[21] Just why INS decided to bring the case at all is a mystery.

To summarize: of the nine deportation cases filed against alleged Nazi collaborators prior to 1973, three were lost at trial (including two kapo cases); the government did not appeal any of them. Of the six cases that resulted in deportation orders after trial, BIA upheld three (Vajta, Artukovic, and the kapo Lewy) and reversed three (Spokevicius, Krasnauskas, and Agh).

Only one truth is clear from all of this: INS never mounted a centralized, organized effort to investigate and prosecute Nazi persecutors in the United States. But beyond this obvious fact, there is no pattern to these events, no all-encompassing explanation that would make sense of what INS was doing. Its actions were random and unpredictable. Sometimes its prosecutors were prepared, sometimes they were not. Its judges ruled in favor of some defendants, against others. The Board of Immigration Appeals could be remarkably forthright, as in the Artukovic case, or grossly ignorant of both history and the law, as in Spokevicius, which was decided only eight months later.

That only a handful of cases were brought, and that they were brought against such disparate individuals with such disparate results, is evidence enough that the only INS policy on Nazis was that there was no policy at all. One might as well ask what was the policy against brown-eyed aliens, or those whose names began with the letter C. INS did not go out of its way to protect Nazis; it simply never went out of its way to look for them. As one INS official said later, "I don't think there [was] any organized effort" to discourage investigations of Nazis. "At the same time, I don't believe there was the proper inspiration either."[22]

Wolodymir Osidach, of Rava Ruska in the Ukraine, became a natu-
ralized citizen of the United States on August 7, 1963. The following
summer a Soviet newspaper accused Osidach of having been the
commandant of the Ukrainian police in Rava Ruska from 1942 to 1944,
responsible for seeing that the Jews of that town were systematically
and efficiently slaughtered.

The FBI, which monitors Soviet newspapers, reported the story
to INS, which sent it to the Philadelphia office, which sent an inves-
tigator to Osidach's neighborhood to check it out. One neighbor told
the INS investigator that the Osidachs were "very quiet people." An-
other said the Osidachs "seem all right." A third told the investiga-
tor the Osidachs had been "very quiet and not very sociable" in the
past fifteen years. A fourth neighbor, a Ukrainian, said Osidach was
a regular churchgoer who was "definitely against Communism." The
Philadelphia police department had no arrest record for Osidach.

A week later, on August 10, 1964, the investigator interviewed
Osidach. Osidach said "everything put out by the Russian newspa-
pers is a lie" and that he had been a dairy worker during the war.
He admitted for the first time that he had also worked as an inter-
preter for the Ukrainian police in dealing with the Germans, but he
claimed that he never served as an interpreter in any case where the
Jews of Rava Ruska were being sent to concentration camps. He ab-
solutely denied that he could have been considered a policeman him-
self.

Osidach also told the investigator that a former Philadelphia
neighbor named Makar had recently decided to return to the Soviet
Union, for reasons unknown to Osidach.

The investigator submitted his report on September 30, 1964: "[I]t
seem[s] likely, in view of propaganda methods resorted to by officials
of the USSR, that Makar may well have been responsible or instru-
mental in supplying [Osidach's] name and address to the Soviet press,
especially in view of the close proximity of Makar's former residence
[in Philadelphia] to that of [Osidach]." The neighborhood check, he
reported, "disclosed no information supporting allegations made
against subject."

The file on Wolodymir Osidach was closed.

In 1978 the General Accounting Office, the investigative arm of Congress, inspected the records of the INS dealing with the investigation

of alleged Nazi war criminals, or at least what records it could find.*
It concluded that from 1946 to 1973 INS had received allegations of
possible Nazi activity concerning fifty-seven people in the United States
(nine of which, as noted above, it pursued to the point of filing charges
against the defendant).

GAO selected forty of those cases for detailed review. It found
that INS had not even investigated twenty of them, and that its investigation in fifteen of the remaining twenty had been "deficient or
perfunctory." For the twenty cases not investigated, there was justification in only six of the cases (the individuals had died or left the
United States); for the remaining fourteen, GAO could find no reason
for INS's failure to investigate. For the fifteen cases where investigation was "deficient or perfunctory," only three cases could be
identified as flimsy and thus unworthy of investigation. For the remaining twelve (including Osidach), INS had simply not bothered to
follow up on the allegations.[23]

Thus in twenty-six of forty files surveyed by GAO—two cases out
of every three—INS had not done an adequate job.

Why? GAO listed several possible reasons: INS had higher priorities for Communists, smugglers, and gangsters than it did for Nazi
war criminals; little attention was paid to the allegations because, even
at fifty-seven, the number was small; some of the allegations, like
those against Osidach, had originated in the Soviet Union and were
presumed to be propaganda; the "political atmosphere of the cold war"
discouraged U.S.–U.S.S.R. cooperation; the prosecutions in the mid-
fifties had not produced "overall successful results"; other cases
promised greater chances of success. GAO also found that INS was
not guilty of any "deliberate effort to obstruct" the investigation of
Nazi cases.

All of GAO's explanations were variations on a theme, and the
theme was simple: investigating Nazis was too much work for too
little return. Few investigators were willing to put in the time.

---

*The GAO investigation, ordered by Representatives Joshua Eilberg of Philadelphia and Eliz-
abeth Holtzman of Brooklyn, was prompted in part by their apprehensions that INS officials
may have been engaged in a conspiracy to obstruct Nazi investigations or to block them altogether. This theory obsessed one INS investigator and was avidly promoted in a book published
in 1977. An FBI investigation had yielded no evidence of such a conspiracy, and the GAO
study likewise concluded that there was none. Based on my own experience as the Director of
the Office of Special Investigations, I can state that INS's failure to pursue Nazi investigations
vigorously was a matter of neglect, not corruption or conspiracy.

For further thoughts on the reasons for INS's inaction, see the last chapter of this book.

This was not a case of mere laziness. The investigators and su-pervisors of the INS in the fifties and sixties were no different from the rest of middle-class America; in fact they were an integral part of it. They were veterans of the war, many of them, and after the war they raised families and worked forty hours a week in a secure job and brought home a paycheck. If they came across a promising in-vestigation, they pursued it, and did what they had always done, and what their bosses expected them to do. Promotions, assignments, and raises were given out on the basis of what was produced, not on the moral rightness of the cases. And even at that, who was to say that a Communist or a racketeer or a smuggler was any the less righteous a cause than an ex-Nazi? There were plenty of those cases, and they were more promising than Ukrainians or Romanians or Hungarians who had come from places with unpronounceable names, who found themselves accused by the Soviet press. An investigator who had spent months investigating a cell of treacherous Comintern subversives in Philadelphia could not very well be expected to take the pronounce-ments of Moscow at face value just because the subject was Nazis.

The universal assumption was that evidence behind the Iron Cur-tain, particularly in the Soviet Union, was not available. This was partially a reflection of the "too-much-work" mentality. But part of it reflected a very real reluctance on the part of the State Depart-ment—to whom INS was subservient in matters involving foreign governments—to go looking for evidence in Communist countries that could be used to prosecute American citizens, particularly anti-Com-munist American citizens.

INS investigators, and their supervisors, and the district directors, were not interested in protecting Nazis; they were interested in pro-tecting their jobs, and that meant producing results in cases assigned to them. Nazi cases were unpromising, unfamiliar, and uncertain. Given a crewman who had jumped ship last week or a quiet Ukrainian who had done God knows what ten or twenty years ago in the Soviet Union, the choice was not a difficult one. No one, from the commissioner on down to local supervisor, made Nazis a high priority, and so they were not.

In 1964, about the time that INS was closing the file on Wolodymir Osidach in Philadelphia, an inquiry of a very different sort was taking shape in Israel. The investigator was not an INS employee but Simon Wiesenthal, a fifty-six-year-old Jew born near Lvov, Poland (now the

Ukrainian S.S.R.), not far from Osidach. Wiesenthal's budding career as an architect was snuffed out in July 1941, a few weeks after the German invasion, when he was arrested by the Ukrainian militia; four years later, he was liberated by the Americans from the concentration camp at Mauthausen, a skeleton weighing ninety-six pounds.

Within weeks, he was working for the Counter Intelligence Corps of the U.S. Army, locating his former SS captors. In 1947 he established a small office in Austria to track down Nazi killers still free. He had been instrumental in leading the Israeli government to Adolf Eichmann, the engineer of the Final Solution. With Eichmann's conviction and execution in 1962, Wiesenthal became known around the world.

On an April afternoon in 1964, Wiesenthal and a friend sat in a café in the modern and rather colorless city of Tel Aviv. Nearby, three women talked over coffee.

One of the women recognized Wiesenthal and approached him. She had been in Maidanek during the Holocaust, she explained, and Wiesenthal needed no further description. Maidanek had been a killing center created in 1942 near the ancient Polish city and Jewish community of Lublin. Together with Sobibor and Belzec, it was the final stop for the Jews of Lublin, Krakow, Galicia, and even parts of Germany and Holland. It was smaller than Auschwitz but no less ghastly for its tens of thousands of victims.

There had been a woman at Maidanek named Braunsteiner, the woman went on: blond, tough, cruel. She brandished a whip whose straps were filled with lead bullets. "When mothers with small children were brought to the camp, Braunsteiner would tear the children away. She hated children." The woman stopped, torn by the memories. She regained her composure and went on. "I've seen women prisoners scream and faint while she flogged them with her horrible whip. She enjoyed it; she was a sadist."

"Mr. Wiesenthal," the woman said, "I've seen cruel men and cruel women in Maidanek. Women were worse. And Hermine Braunsteiner was one of the most vicious I ever met. Please try to find her."

The trail was not hard to pick up. Wiesenthal found that Hermine Braunsteiner had been convicted in 1949 by a low-level court in Austria for her role, not at Maidanek, but as an overseer at Ravensbrück, a small concentration camp near Berlin. She had been sentenced to three years' imprisonment. Because she had been in confinement awaiting trial, she was released shortly after her conviction.

And Wiesenthal made another discovery.

In July 1964 Joseph Lelyveld, a reporter for *The New York Times,* made his way across the city to Maspeth, Queens, the home of Russell Ryan, a construction worker, who with his wife had just bought a small home at 52-11 72nd Street. There, the reporter found a "large-boned woman with a stern mouth and blond hair turning gray." On this summer day, she wore pink and white shorts and a sleeveless blouse, and was painting the walls of the small living room. She was three days shy of her forty-fifth birthday.

Speaking with a heavy German accent, she readily admitted to Lelyveld that she had been a guard, but, she said, she had served her time in jail for it. "All I did is what guards do in camps now. I was punished enough. I was in prison three years. Three years, can you imagine?"

Lelyveld persisted. Her three years had been for her role at Ravensbrück. New evidence had now come to light, and it had to do with a different and more deadly place—Maidanek. Had she ever been at Maidanek?

The housewife with the stern mouth paled, then burst into tears. But they were not tears of remorse. "This is the end," she cried. "This is the end of everything for me."

The next day the *Times* had the story: "Former Nazi Camp Guard is now a Housewife in Queens."[24]

Hermine Braunsteiner was born in Vienna in 1919. She had a succession of jobs there as a "domestic" and an unskilled worker; then at nineteen she drifted to Berlin, where she held a few more odd jobs until she joined the SS in August 1939, just before the invasion of Poland. She was detailed to the concentration camp at Ravensbrück, where she was soon promoted to head of the "clothing detail." In October 1942 she had been transferred to the death camp at Maidanek, where she stayed until she returned to Ravensbrück as director of one of its outlying camps in January 1944.

After her conviction and release for "mistreatment" at Ravensbrück, Braunsteiner had been given an amnesty. In 1959 she traveled to Canada to marry Russell Ryan, a thirty-five-year-old Brooklyn-born Air Force enlisted man she had met a few years earlier when he

had been stationed in Germany. In April 1959 Ryan and his wife came
to the United States to live. She found a job as a machine operator in
a clothing factory, and on January 15, 1963, she became a naturalized American citizen in ceremonies at the federal courthouse in
Brooklyn. In March 1964 she and her husband bought the house in
Queens—the house she was painting in July 1964 when the *New York
Times* came knocking at the door.

INS officials read the newspaper, and they pulled the file of Hermine Braunsteiner Ryan and opened an investigation. They discovered that when she had applied in Canada for her visa to enter the
United States, she had not disclosed any prior convictions. INS set
about getting records of her 1949 Austrian conviction.

It was an unusual case for INS. Braunsteiner was a citizen, which
meant that she could not be deported unless the Justice Department
proved in federal court, under a little-used provision of American law,
that her citizenship had been obtained illegally or by fraud. If a federal judge was persuaded, he could revoke her citizenship, clearing
the way for deportation proceedings. But INS dealt only with aliens,
and denaturalization suits were beyond its jurisdiction. The Department of Justice would have to decide what to do.

But it took nearly a year to get a certified copy of the 1949 conviction from Vienna, and not until June 1965 did INS send the file to
the Department of Justice with a recommendation that suit be filed to
revoke her citizenship.

The Justice Department looked at the file for nearly six months,
then sent it back to INS. It was uncertain whether the 1957 Austrian
amnesty relieved Braunsteiner from any obligation to disclose her
conviction when she had come to the United States, and it wanted
more information on her activities for the SS.

INS reopened the investigation, contacted Simon Wiesenthal for
the first time, and through him found two survivors of Maidanek who
identified Braunsteiner as a guard there.

In October 1966 INS sent the file to Justice for the second time,
with the new information. Two months later, Justice sent it back again,
asking INS whether there were any charges pending against Braunsteiner in Austria. Seven months later—three years to the week after
the *New York Times* article had appeared—INS sent the file to Justice
for the third time. There were no charges pending against Braunsteiner anywhere.

Justice took another year to make up its mind. It was July 1968 before it sent the file to the United States Attorney in Brooklyn. The file contained little more than it had when Justice saw it the first time, and had no documentary evidence of Braunsteiner's SS membership. On August 23, 1968, more than four years after the public accusation, the United States Attorney filed charges with the federal court on Long Island, alleging that Braunsteiner had entered the U.S. illegally because she had concealed her 1949 Austrian conviction. He asked that her citizenship be revoked.[25]

Throughout this time, Braunsteiner remained free. "My wife wouldn't hurt a fly," Russell Ryan had said at the outset. "There's no more decent person on this earth."[26]

For nearly three years, the case languished in federal court. Finally, on July 28, 1971—seven years and two weeks after the *Times* article—Hermine Braunsteiner Ryan signed a consent decree, relinquishing her citizenship without a trial.[27]

Despite the initial splash of publicity in 1964, the Braunsteiner case had been largely shrouded from public view as it made its weary way through INS, the Justice Department, and the federal court leading to the revocation of citizenship in 1971. There had not been one public hearing. No witness had been called to describe the horrors of Maidanek. The consent decree had been a bloodless document; she had not admitted anything of her past in it. Russell and Hermine continued to live a normal life in their house at 52-11 72nd Street, Maspeth, Queens.

But now that Braunsteiner was an alien and the responsibility of INS once again, Anthony DeVito, an INS investigator, and Vincent Schiano, a trial attorney, were assigned the file to determine if Braunsteiner could be brought up on deportation charges. They began to look for witnesses—witnesses who could tell, in public, the story of Maidanek, witnesses who could persuade an INS judge that Hermine Braunsteiner Ryan ought to be deported from the United States.

Braunsteiner had consented to denaturalization, but there was no way she would consent to deportation. INS would have to prove its case. In February of 1972 Schiano and DeVito had assembled their cast. When hearings opened, the public saw, for the first time, what Braunsteiner was guilty of.

Eva Konikowski, a Polish Catholic who was also living in Queens, recalled her hell at Maidanek. She had been arrested by the Nazis in

1941 for helping Jewish families to escape the Nazis in Lvov and was sent to Maidanek. There she saw Braunsteiner and another guard loading children onto trucks to be carted to the gas chamber. "They gave the children some candy," Mrs. Konikowski recalled. But the children were not deceived. They were screaming, she testified. "They were crying, 'mama!' "

Aaron Kaufman, a frail seventy-one-year-old Jew, had been sent to the woman's camp at Maidanek to serve as a "horse"—a beast of burden, hauling coal and lumber. One day he and some other "horses" were hauling a wagon past a group of three hundred inmates. Braunsteiner was there with her leather whip. "Mrs. Braunsteiner was telling the ladies they have to give their children away because the children were going to a summer camp where they would get milk two times a day," Kaufman recounted.

"The mothers didn't want to give up their children because they knew what would happen. Mrs. Braunsteiner started hitting one old woman with a child so long the woman fell down. The lady was dead and the child was dead. We have to move them aside and get our wagon in."

Mary Finkelstein, a survivor of Maidanek living in Brooklyn, identified Braunsteiner from an old photograph, and provided more incriminating testimony. Finkelstein said she had seen Braunsteiner "clobber" a woman inmate to the ground, shouting, "You pig! You goddamn Jew! Stand up straight!" Said Mrs. Finkelstein, "She dropped, and didn't get up, ever."

A dentist from Poland came to New York to testify. One day at Maidanek she was hauling bricks and sand, but not fast enough. Braunsteiner came over with a dog, the dentist testified, and beat the prisoners with her leather whip. On other days Braunsteiner put the dog away and used her feet, stomping inmates with heavy leather boots. The Jews had a name for her: "the mare."

Asked to identify "the mare," the dentist pointed a finger at Braunsteiner. "The moment I walked in, I recognized her," she said.[28]

At her table, Braunsteiner cracked to her husband, "Easy to say." [29]

The dentist, her eyes on "the mare" for the first time in thirty years, grew noticeably pale, then collapsed on the stand. She could not go on that day.

Despite this stark evidence, the case against Braunsteiner became mired. Unlike federal or state courts, deportation trials in INS do not go straight through from day to day until they are done. They appear and fade away like astronomical phenomena, convening for a day or two to hear testimony of a witness, then recessing for a few weeks, or a month, or longer, until another witness is ready.

The first day of Braunsteiner's trial was February 7, 1972. There were two days of hearings in March, none in April, four days in May, one day all summer, then three in September, one in October. Then it came to a stop. From October 1972 until March 1973 not a witness was heard, not a day of trial held. The case against the mare of Maidanek sat on a table in an empty courtroom.

On March 22, 1973, like an electric charge, the case came alive again. The jolt came not from INS but from the government of the Federal Republic of Germany. The West Germans, preparing a major trial against guards at Maidanek, filed a request with the United States government for Braunsteiner's extradition.[30]

Braunsteiner was immediately arrested, and was jailed at Rikers Island, where, she complained at her arraignment the next day, she had been forced to sleep with prostitutes. She was soon transferred to the more hospitable Nassau County jail, but her days as a free woman were over. When the German government filed affidavits from Maidanek survivors in support of the extradition request, more horrors came out.

A Jewish girl at Maidanek had claimed to be Christian, the better to escape the gas chambers. Braunsteiner was not fooled. This girl was brought to the gallows as an example to the other prisoners. Braunsteiner put the girl on a three-legged stool. As the noose was slipped around her neck, the girl turned to the throng that had been made to witness the event. She took her last breath and shouted, "Remember me!"

An SS man kicked the stool away.

Such testimony—and the Germans had provided 300 pages of similar accounts of Braunsteiner's complicity in the deaths of thousands of Jews at Maidanek—convinced Judge Jacob Mishler. He ruled on May 1, 1973, that Braunsteiner should be returned to Germany to stand trial.

On August 6, federal marshals took Braunsteiner from the Nassau County jail to JFK Airport and handed her over to German police. She smoothed her makeup and brushed her cropped hair. Her handcuffs were removed, and she had a Coke, chatting in German with her new custodians. As she boarded the Lufthansa flight for Cologne, she took out her knitting. The mare of Maidanek looked like any other middle-aged tourist bound for a holiday in Germany.* [31]

As Braunsteiner took her knitting across the Atlantic, however, the complacency that for twenty-five years had attended the question of Nazi war criminals in America was already coming apart.

For years, Dr. Otto Karbach of the World Jewish Congress had been keeping a list. As he read the Yiddish-language press of New York and Canada, he had snipped out stories of survivors recounting their experiences in the Holocaust. Whenever the name of a death camp guard or auxiliary policeman or propagandist or collaborator was mentioned, with an indication that the person was in the United States, Karbach added the name to his list. And, as he saw the legal process close in on Hermine Braunsteiner, he sent the list—fifty-nine names— to Tony DeVito of the INS.

In the past, INS would have yawned and parceled the names out one by one to the field offices near the suspects and gone about its business. But the modest publicity of the Braunsteiner case had made INS increasingly sensitive to its lack of action in the past. To handle Dr. Karbach's fifty-nine names, INS set up a "project control office" in New York to review the accusations and coordinate whatever evidence-gathering could be done. The "office" was INS investigator Sam Zutty. Zutty was, in his own words, "way on the bottom of the totem pole," a career INS investigator given a task of worldwide scope. [33]

The project control office was probably better than nothing. It was, at least, the first time that INS had handled Nazi files as a discrete group. But the agency was too hidebound a bureaucracy to invent any new procedures to fit the unusual and difficult investigations rquired by the allegations. Many of the people on Karbach's list were from the Baltic countries, or the Ukraine, or Eastern bloc nations. Many survivors, all of whom might be potential witnesses, lived in Israel.

---

*Braunsteiner was indicted with fourteen other Germans in Düsseldorf in February 1975 for the deaths of hundreds of thousands of Jews at Maidanek. Seated in the dock, she and her co-defendants, *The New York Times* reported, "looked like any row of elderly, modestly-dressed passengers on a streetcar in a big German city." [32]

    The trial lasted nearly six years; on June 30, 1981, Braunsteiner was convicted of multiple murder. She is now serving a life sentence in Germany.

The documents compiled by the West Germans in their extensive postwar Nazi investigations were sitting in a government office in Ludwigsburg, near Stuttgart.

Zutty had no staff to speak of. He could not communicate, even indirectly through the State Department, with foreign governments. In fact, Zutty could not even suggest that INS headquarters approach the State Department in a given case until he had received the approval of a committee of fourteen INS officials, each of whom had to agree that there was enough of a case to bother State. The committee usually did approve Zutty's recommendation to send the dossier in this or that case to Foggy Bottom. It accomplished nothing.

What INS needed was someone to knock on the doors of the foreign ministries in Bonn, Tel Aviv, Moscow, and elsewhere to enlist the assistance of these governments in locating witnesses, arranging interviews for INS investigators, locating documents from the Nazi era that would prove persecution by those on Karbach's list. Yet not even documents held by the Berlin Document Center—the repository of all known Nazi party and SS personnel files—were available. And the BDC was owned by the U.S. State Department.

State Department officials could not care less about Sam Zutty, the INS, and Nazi war criminals. Foreign policy was their game, and INS was not allowed to play. State Department officers had always treated INS, in those areas where they were forced to work with it, as a distant and somewhat disreputable cousin. State ignored every dossier that Zutty sent over.

But for the first time in twenty years or more, INS's efforts, however halting, to deal with Nazi war criminals in America had some very interested observers on Capitol Hill. One was Congresswoman Elizabeth Holtzman of Brooklyn, a smart, tough, no-nonsense lawyer who had dethroned Emanuel Celler in a stunning upset in 1972, ending Celler's fifty years in Congress. In her first term in Congress, in April 1974, Holtzman blasted INS for what she called "an appalling laxness and superficiality" in their search. "Haphazard, uncoordinated and unprofessional," she said of INS's latest efforts.[34]

INS promptly confirmed every one of Holtzman's adjectives by releasing to the press a list of all the persons it was investigating for Nazi activities, noting that it had "no derogatory information" on many of them, and that many witnesses had not been interviewed.[35]

The other interested observer was Congressman Joshua Eilberg of

Philadelphia, the soft-spoken but persistent chairman of the House Judiciary Committee's subcommittee on immigration—a subcommittee that included Holtzman. In June 1974, with Zutty's task force making little real progress, Eilberg stepped in. He fired off a letter to Secretary of State Henry Kissinger, expressing his "deep concern over the Department of State's failure to cooperate" with INS. The investigations, Eilberg charged, had been "seriously impeded" by State's neglect.[36]

An assistant secretary of state tried to brush Eilberg off. "[T]here is no agreement between the U.S. and the USSR permitting investigations or the taking of testimony or statements of Soviet citizens by U.S. officials in the USSR," he wrote. "Our only practical recourse would be to request the Soviet Ministry of Foreign Affairs to locate alleged eye witnesses and make them available to our officers. While this might be possible, we would have no way to verify the credibility or, indeed, the identity of the witnesses provided us by the Soviet authorities. This caveat would seem particularly applicable to the sensitive issue of alleged war crimes . . ."[37]

Eilberg was not about to be put off by pronouncements about "alleged eye witnesses" to "alleged war crimes." He wrote again to Kissinger, criticizing State's demonstrated "inaction and indifference" and its unwillingness even to raise the matter with the Soviet government.[38] And State's letter had not even mentioned the possibility of contacting West Germany and Israel, two of the United States' most trusted allies in world affairs.

The State Department relented a little. It agreed to meet with INS officials to see what the flap over Nazi war criminals was all about.[39] But Eilberg escalated the matter, writing to President Ford in August 1974, just two weeks after Richard Nixon's resignation. Eilberg urged the president to "use the power of your office" to end the State Department's reluctance to seek the assistance of foreign governments in the search for information.[40]

The Ford White House was happy to oblige a congressman, particularly a congressman from the Judiciary Committee. It put in a word at the State Department, which finally recognized that it had to do something to keep everybody happy, or at least placated. State took Karbach's list from the INS and told the White House that it would think about "planning approaches" to the Germans, the Israelis, and even the Soviets.[41]

Over the next six months American diplomats in Bonn, Tel Aviv, and Moscow raised the matter, in general terms, with their host governments, and found them ready and willing to cooperate in the search for Nazis in America if the United States could suggest some specific way that they could do so. In July 1975, a year after Eilberg's first salvo to Henry Kissinger, State told Eilberg that it would go through Karbach's list of Nazis residing in the United States, one by one, and ask the West Germans to provide whatever information they had. When that was done, State would think about whether it would approach the Soviets with a similar request.[42]

By Halloween of 1975 the Germans had combed their files and had given whatever information they could find to the State Department. The results were disappointing. Of the fifty-nine names, the Germans had information on only six and "additional but unsubstantiated allegations" against ten others. The State Department still refused to commit itself to any approach to the Soviet Union.[43]

But over the next few months the Germans spewed forth more information, a little at a time as they came across it, and by early 1976 they had provided something on nearly half the names that INS had passed on.[44] Holtzman was flogging the State Department regularly in the press for what she termed its "utterly incomprehensible" reluctance to discuss the matter with the Soviets.[45] Finally, Kissinger had had enough. He authorized an advance on Moscow.[46] The American embassy handed the Kremlin fourteen names from Karbach's list and asked for whatever information might be available. The Soviets took the names and told the Americans they would be in touch.

While the State Department tiptoed forward in Bonn and Moscow, INS got in touch with the head of the Israeli police unit on Nazi war criminals and found him ready to locate whatever witnesses he could in Israel. At long last, the ice floes were breaking up overseas. Foreign capitals were getting the message that the Immigration Service was trying to do something—it may not have been clear exactly what—about Nazis.

Still, by June 1976 Zutty's task force had been in business for nearly three years and had only one case to show for it—a suit filed in Detroit by the U.S. Attorney to revoke the citizenship of a Romanian bishop, Valerian Trifa. And that case, which had been brought only after an exposé on Trifa in *The New York Times*, was going nowhere.

Unknown to Sam Zutty, and certainly unknown to the gaggle of assistant secretaries of state, there was an eight-page document in the Soviet State Archives in Lvov, in the Ukraine. It was the report of the District Commission for the Ascertainment and Investigation of the Crimes of the German Fascist Invaders in the Rava Ruska District. The commission had five members, who had interviewed forty-two witnesses in the city of Rava Ruska. Its report was filed on September 30, 1944, three months after the Red Army had driven the Germans from the area, and it was signed by the commission's chairman, Maxim Sidorovich Gavrilenko:

Excerpts:

Upon investigation by the District Commission in the vicinity of the city of Rava-Ruska, large mass graves were discovered in the following locations:

1. In the Jewish cemetery, located 480 meters from the center of the city, four large pits are filled with the bodies of over 5,000 tortured and executed men, women, and children.

2. In the Borove Forest, 3 kilometers from the center of the city and 250 meters from the village of Borove, in a pit measuring 13×8 meters, the bodies of over 1,500 men, women, and children are buried.

3. One thousand meters south of the center of the city of Rava-Ruska, next to the old Jewish cemetery, over 4,000 corpses are buried in pits.

. . .

7. In the Sedliskiy Forest near the village of Selysko, 4 kilometers from the city of Rava-Ruska:

   a) five corpses are buried in a bomb crater;

   b) 50 human corpses are buried in block 53 in a mine shaft measuring 1.5×1.5 meters and 17 meters deep;

   c) 350 human corpses are buried in block 52 in a pit measuring 5×7 meters and 3.5 meters deep;

   d) the bodies of approximately 7,000 executed men, women and children are buried in block 51 in a pit measuring 15×10 meters and 7 meters deep;

   e) the bodies of 60 men and women are buried 450 meters from the road to Yalynka in a pit measuring 4×6 meters and 2.5 meters deep;

   f) 80 human corpses are buried 450 meters from road to

Yalynka in a pit measuring 6 × 8 meters and 3 meters deep;
g) the bodies of 3,500 executed men, women and children are
buried 100 meters from the same road in a pit measuring
8 × 7 meters and 4.5 meters deep.

A total of over 11,000 human corpses are buried in this forest.

The District Commission's investigation, involving questioning of eyewitnesses and witnesses and a review of documents, established the following facts concerning German fascist crimes and atrocities committed in Rava-Ruska District:

. . .

In early September 1941, by order of Kreishauptmann [district leader] Hager, all Jews from the neighboring villages were herded into the city of Rava-Ruska. After registering the Jewish population, the German fascist barbarians proceeded to exterminate the innocent civilian population.

On March 19, 1942, the gendarmerie and Ukrainian fascist police, led by the gendarmerie chief and the city commandant, Senior Sergeant Major Klein, conducted a roundup (police action) in the city. During the roundup more than 2,000 men, women and children were arrested. The German barbarians sent them to be exterminated at a death factory in the little town of Belzec (20 kilometers from Rava-Ruska on Polish territory).

The Gestapo, together with the "Schupo" police and Ukrainian police, carried out a second roundup (police action) on July 30, 1942, under the command of the Gestapo chief, Oberscharführer [technical sergeant] Spät. During the roundup more than 2,000 men, women and children were arrested and sent to the death factory in Belzec. . . .

In the summer of 1942 the German authorities in the city of Rava-Ruska organized a Jewish camp, a so-called ghetto. . . . [A] total of over 18,000 people were settled there.

The ghetto blocks were enclosed with barbed wire, and from December 1942 the ghetto was guarded by police. It was forbidden to enter or leave. Violators were liable to be shot on the spot.

. . .

The third police action, which lasted from December 7, 1942 to January 10, 1943, was the cruelest and bloodiest reprisal. In the course of a month over 14,000 men, women and children were exterminated, nearly 2,000 of whom were sent to the death factory in the small town of Belzec, while the rest were shot. . . . [A]n entire month [was spent] carrying out the execution of the Jewish population, as a result of which the ghetto was completely liquidated. About 800 members of the police and gendarmerie took part in this operation.

During this massacre the streets were filled with corpses and a river of blood. Most of the people to be shot were transported in trucks to the Sidletskiy Forest, near the village of Selysko, where about 10,000 of them were shot; and to the Jewish cemetery, where about 2,000 were shot.

. . .

In this manner, the District Commission established that the German fascist invaders in the Rava-Ruska District, during the period of occupation, exterminated:

a) Innocent civilians   17,500 people
b) In the prisoner of war camp   18,000 people
c) Transported from Rava-Ruska District
   to the death factory at Belzec   6,000 people
   Total exterminated   41,500 people

The District Commission established that the perpetrators of all the crimes described, who should bear the responsibility, are:

There followed a list of twenty-two names—Kreishauptmann Hager, Gestapo Chief Spät, Commissar for Jewish Affairs Holtz, and so forth. But one of the names was not German.

15. Ukrainian police commandant—OSIDACH[47]

In Washington, in June 1976, Congressman Eilberg was taking up the attack again, shifting his sights now from State to the Justice Department. He accused Attorney General Edward Levi of treating Nazi war criminals as a "non-priority issue." As attorney general, Levi was ultimately responsible for what INS did, and Eilberg charged Levi with a "reluctance" to file cases in court, while "the investigation of alleged Nazi war criminals continues to drag on and on." Eilberg urged Levi to "expedite the preparation of cases."[48]

It was becoming increasingly apparent to Justice and INS that the one way to appease Eilberg and Holtzman, and to demonstrate that three years' work had accomplished something, was to bring cases in court formally charging American residents with Nazi persecution. After Eilberg's blast at Levi, INS dispatched a team of attorneys to Israel to talk to the witnesses the Israeli police had located. As soon as they came back, INS issued a press release announcing its intention "to initiate proceedings against seven persons in the United States who are alleged to have committed war crimes during and prior to World War II.''[49]

A few weeks later, on October 13, 1976, INS filed formal deportation charges against two Latvians and a Lithuanian. And in the next ten months it brought seven more cases—one against a Latvian alien, six against U.S. citizens: four Ukrainians, a Lithuanian, and a Polish Volksdeutsche.

It was about the worst possible thing INS could have done. The cases were not ready for trial. They were not even close to being ready. INS had gathered virtually no documents tying the defendants to incriminating events (Israel has many survivors but few documents); witnesses had been hastily interviewed and not adequately prepared for the ordeal of testifying; Soviet witnesses were nowhere to be seen. No attempt had been made to locate survivors in the United States.[50] Legal theories had not been carefully thought out. INS attorneys were unfamiliar with the rigorous standards the Supreme Court had imposed for showing photospreads to witnesses in criminal cases to avoid undue suggestiveness; the INS attorneys had shown Israeli witnesses a sheaf of loose photos in various configurations that could never be reassembled in court to demonstrate their fairness, if indeed they were fair. And even after the cases were filed, INS made no attempt to take the testimony of aging survivors. INS was, in effect, betting that they would survive until trial.

But INS had learned a few facts of life: Eilberg and Holtzman were dead serious, they were not going to go away, and they were convinced that INS was thoroughly inept, if not actually corrupt, on the Nazi issue. In the summer of 1977, a few days before INS Commissioner Leonel Castillo was to face Eilberg's subcommittee to report on the progress of the Nazi cases, INS dissolved Sam Zutty's task force and transferred all responsibility for the Nazi cases to a "special litigation unit" under the supervision of the General Counsel of INS.

On paper, it was not a bad idea: the unit was to consist of five attorneys who would evaluate all pending and future investigations, decide what work needed to be done, and do it. It would not have to rely on INS investigators who had prostitution and fraud cases to worry about along with Nazi cases. It could deal directly with the State Department to coordinate overseas inquiries. The special unit would de-

cide when a case was ready for filing in court and would plan the
trial. All of INS's expertise on Nazi war criminals would be centralized under one roof.[51]

From its beginning in August of 1977, the "special litigation unit"
was a disaster. It quickly bogged down into what Holtzman termed
"a morass of funding, staffing and bureaucratic problems."[52] It had
no vigorous leadership and no clear idea of how it should proceed to
investigate or prosecute Nazis. Two years after it was formed, it had
not filed a single case.

That was the good news. The bad news was that the special litigation unit attempted to try some of the cases that had been filed in
the last few months of Sam Zutty's tenure. From 1977 to 1979 five
cases were tried. Three were lost; one was discontinued; the fifth was
won, but with highly embarrassing consequences.

In the case of Boleslavs Maikovskis, a Latvian police chief working as a carpenter in Mineola, Long Island, allegedly responsible for
the deaths of hundreds of Jews and gypsies in Latvia, INS got off to
a halting start with confusing and conflicting testimony. The case was
temporarily discontinued while INS tried to figure out how to rescue it.[53]

Vilis Hazners, of Whitehall, New York, also charged with being
a Latvian executioner, went to trial over a two-year period from 1977
to 1979. INS attorneys could not find the photographs that had been
shown to the witnesses prior to trial and were forced to substitute what
they contended were "reproductions" to a skeptical judge. A document crucial to INS's case was never put in the record. The judge
found the evidence that was introduced to be insufficient, and Hazners went free.[54]

Karlis Detlavs, a retired factory worker for General Electric who
had entered the U.S. under the DP Act as a "forester," charged with
having been a collaborator in the Latvian political police, went to trial
in Baltimore. The judge in that case dismissed the charges for insufficient evidence, finding that significant aspects of the INS case were
either not supported by any evidence or by documents inserted haphazardly in the record with no testimony as to what they were, or
what they meant. It was later discovered—too late—that INS had ne-
glected to introduce documents showing that Detlavs had been a
member of the notorious Arajs Kommando in Latvia.[55]

Feodor Fedorenko, a naturalized Ukrainian who had been a guard at Treblinka, went to trial in Florida. In the summer of 1978 the judge handed down judgment against the government.[56]

Finally, INS and the U.S. Attorney in Chicago charged Frank Walus with having been a member of the Gestapo in Poland. The case was tried before Judge Julius Hoffman, of "Chicago 7" fame, who ruled in favor of the government and revoked Walus' citizenship. It was a temporary victory. On appeal, Walus produced new evidence that tended to exonerate him, and the court of appeals set aside Judge Hoffman's verdict and ordered a new trial. It turned out that Walus was the wrong man. He had spent the war years on a farm in Germany. (See Chapter 6.)[57]

That left six cases that the special unit, fortunately, did not go to trial on. The oldest—Trifa in Detroit—was by 1979 over four years without a trial; the youngest was two years without a trial. And no trial was in sight for any of them. As bad as the situation had been in 1977, by 1979 it had grown far worse.

Liz Holtzman was fed up. As the new chairman of the immigration subcommittee (Eilberg had been defeated for reelection in 1978), Holtzman wanted INS to have nothing further to do with Nazis, ever. She brought intense pressure on the Justice Department to take on the job with a larger staff and budget. Justice was distinctly cool to the idea. The Nazi cases had become legal lepers—unwanted, incurable, and probably contagious. It did not want them in its house.

But Holtzman was no longer just another congresswoman and she could not be ignored. The immigration subcommittee—which also had jurisdiction over refugee matters and international legal affairs—could make life difficult for the Justice Department in any number of areas, and no one doubted Holtzman's determination to do just that if she was thwarted on the Nazi issue.

Attorney General Griffin Bell yielded to the power. On March 28, 1979, a triumphant Holtzman announced the decision: Justice would take over the effort and Congress would earmark $2.3 million to upgrade the staff dramatically.

"There should be absolutely no question," Holtzman emphasized, "that the Department of Justice and the U.S. government will act unequivocally and vigorously to deny sanctuary in the United States to persons who committed the worst crimes in the history of humanity." But Holtzman was not breaking out any champagne: "Certainly this subcommittee," she warned, "will vigorously exercise its oversight responsibility to assure that all commitments made by the Department today are honored.''[58]

At Holtzman's insistence, the newly named Office of Special Investigations was put into the Criminal Division of the Justice Department, which was headed by Assistant Attorney General Philip B. Heymann, a Harvard Law School professor on leave to the government. Although the Office of Special Investigations would be pursuing civil, not criminal, cases, the Criminal Division had a reputation as Justice's most effective and vigorous branch.

For Heymann, who had not shared Justice's reluctance to get involved with the Nazi cases, the new office represented a mix of both moral imperative and political necessity. He wanted OSI to succeed because it was not right that Nazi criminals live legally in the United States and also because failure would plunge the Justice Department into considerable difficulty with the formidable Holtzman.

Heymann's first move to strengthen the Office of Special Investigations, and to demonstrate to Holtzman that he was indeed setting off in a new direction, was to go outside the Justice Department for leadership. As OSI's first director Heymann drafted Walter J. Rockler, a former member of the U.S. prosecution staff at Nuremberg and a tax attorney with the Washington law firm of Arnold and Porter. Rockler agreed to come to OSI for six months to set up the office, hire staff, and begin to make headway on the disorganized backlog of accusations, files, investigations, and pending cases that INS had been accumulating since the days of Dr. Karbach and his list of fifty-nine names.

On November 20, 1979, the Office of Special Investigations filed a formal complaint in federal court in Philadelphia charging that Wolodymir Osidach, 75, who had come to the United States as a dairyman, had in fact been commandant of the Ukrainian militia in Rava Ruska. OSI charged that Osidach had been the top-ranking Ukrainian collaborator in that city, and had organized, supervised, and carried out the final solution of the Jewish question there.

On September 16, 1980, the trial—OSI's first—began before Judge Louis Bechtle in a packed courtroom. Carefully, the government built its case, calling Anna Weinfeld, Philip Langer, Kurt Lewin, and other Jews who had escaped alive from Rava Ruska. Then, OSI attorney Neal Sher called Osidach to the stand. Slowly he led Osidach through the events of his life, up to the point where Osidach, who had gone to Poland in 1939, returned to his home town of Rava Ruska on the heels of the Einsatzgruppe in the early days of summer 1941. Then Sher's cross-examination turned deadly:

Sher: "And as soon as you got back to Rava Ruska you went back to work at the same dairy cooperative; is that right?"

Osidach: "Admittedly I returned. I presented myself to the dairy farm and started to work."

"And this is the same dairy farm where you worked during the Polish period; is that right?"

"Yes, same, and same director."

"What was that director's name?"

"Czich."

"And you began working again at that dairy farm in June or July of 1941."

"Yes."

"But you only worked at that dairy farm for several weeks; is that right?"

"Yes."

"And after working there for several weeks you left the dairy cooperative to become the Commandant of the Ukrainian Militia; is that correct?"

"Because Mr. Czich has been very busy in the dairy farm and on advice of the people or requirement of the people he made me, or he proposed me, to take his place as the Commandant of the Militia because I knew German language. They knew that I have been Ukrainian nationalist and they knew I will take in protection Ukrainian people [*sic*]."

"And so Mr. Czich asked you to become the Commandant of the Militia?"

"Yes."

"And you accepted?"

"Yes. I accept."

On March 17, 1981, Judge Bechtle handed down his decision, a sixty-page analysis of the facts and the law. He retraced the occupation, the creation of the ghetto, the three actions undertaken by the Germans and by the Ukrainian militia to make Rava Ruska Judenfrei—*free of Jews. "The acts of brutality during this final action, which lasted for weeks, were unspeakable," Judge Bechtle wrote:*

The Ukrainian militia's function was to keep "order" in the streets of Rava Ruska. There were approximately 15 to 25 men in the militia, all of them volunteers, and all under Osidach's command when he became the new commandant of the militia. At that time, there were no other police within the town of Rava Ruska except the militia.''

. . . Overall, the Court finds that [the evidence in the trial] points to four separate categories of activities in which the Ukrainian police were in fact engaged: a) enforcement of ghettoization of Jews and enforcement of other degrading laws enacted for the Jewish population by the occupying Germans; b) guarding and abuse of Jewish forced laborers; c) the deportation of Jews from the ghetto; d) the final action involving the liquidation of the Rava Ruska ghetto.

. . . Osidach's role as an armed, uniformed interpreter for either the Ukrainian police's or the German gendarmes' interrogation of suspects could be classified as both physical and mental persecution. Osidach's personal assignment as an armed, uniformed Ukrainian street policeman constitutes on the present record the form of mental persecution that quite naturally follows from the conspicuous public display of armed force and uniformed authority, regularly, over a long period of time in a repressive ghetto-type atmosphere. The mere presence of the watchful eye of the conqueror or his deputies, coupled with the often demonstrated presence of both the means and the inclination to persistently inflict various indignities, physical abuse, injuries or even death, without notice or reason, is the personification of mental persecution, to anyone, let alone innocent civilian men, women and children reduced to various degrees of substandard mental and physical well-being.

. . . In summary, the Court finds that, under §13 of the [Displaced Persons Act], Osidach was ineligible to enter this country in 1949 as a displaced person because of, first, his willing membership in the Ukrainian police . . . and second, because he was a participant affiliated with the Ukrainian police who personally committed acts of persecution . . . in the town of Rava Ruska from 1942 to 1944.

Judge Bechtle ordered that Wolodymir Osidach be stripped of his naturalized citizenship on grounds that he obtained it illegally and through fraud.[59]

Two months later, on May 26, 1981, Osidach died of a heart attack in Philadelphia.

3

THE MOSCOW
AGREEMENT:
Old Allies, New Realities

It was a bitterly cold day in Moscow the 27th of January, 1980. That night the temperature would drop to twenty degrees below zero, and I squeezed my eyes shut against the stinging wind of a darkening afternoon as I pressed across the desolate tarmac at Sheremetyevo International Airport. Behind me, the British Airways jet from London hovered on the ground, its engine running, its crew eager to refuel and get on their way. For them, Moscow was only a frigid stop on a flight to Tokyo.

As I made my way toward the terminal, it was easy to imagine the killing power of a Russian winter. Thirty-eight years before, this weather had paralyzed Hitler's advancing army only a few miles from this airport and had sustained the massive Soviet counteroffensive that had pushed the Germans out of Russia, defining forever the farthest reach of the Third Reich. In the fields beyond the terminal lay the entrails of Nazi tanks and the rusted trucks of the Red Army, artifacts of that awesome battle of a generation ago, a battle that had begun three years before I was born.

Pushing my way across the windswept Moscow airport in the middle of winter had not been a part of my plans just a few weeks before. I had been an assistant to the solicitor general of the United States, representing the U.S. government in the Supreme Court, arguing matters of federal and constitutional law in striped pants and tails before nine justices in a well-heated building.

It had been challenging and stimulating work, involving a wide variety of cases, from veterans' rights to the law of the sea. Once a case was briefed and argued, I usually forgot about it in the press of new cases coming in. But one case had been different; I could not forget about it.

That case was the INS prosecution of Feodor Fedorenko, a former guard at the Treblinka death camp, then a retired factory worker living in Florida. INS had lost at trial in Florida when the judge ruled that there was insufficient evidence that Fedorenko had committed atrocities at Treblinka. The solicitor general must approve any government appeal from an adverse verdict at trial, and the Fedorenko case had been assigned to me, purely by chance. By the time I had read the transcript, and the judge's decision, I was convinced that the case could be won on appeal, and the solicitor general agreed.

INS had been sufficiently impressed with my reasoning to ask me to write the appeal brief and to argue the case in New Orleans, which I had done, successfully. The court of appeals had reversed the trial judge, ruling that Fedorenko's role as a guard at a death camp was enough to disqualify him from immigration—and citizenship—under the Displaced Persons Act, whether he had committed atrocities against individual victims or not.*

The Fedorenko case had fascinated me. The idea that Nazi criminals had come safely to America and were still living here was a new and troubling one for me, and I had followed with great interest the formation of the Office of Special Investigations in the summer of 1979. When Walter Rockler was appointed Director of OSI, I went to see him, and then Phil Heymann, the head of the Criminal Division. My main purpose was to discuss how the recent court of appeals' decision in *Fedorenko* might be applied to similar cases. I also wanted to work on more of these cases.

Rockler's appointment was temporary, Heymann told me; after the office was staffed and in full operation, he would go back to his law firm. Would I be interested in coming on as Rockler's deputy for a few months, and then taking over when he left? After all, Heymann

---

*There is little doubt in my mind now that Fedorenko was a brutal man who had taken part in the beatings of Jews who arrived at Treblinka. The routine of Treblinka was such that he could not have avoided it, though at his trial he claimed to have done so. But INS had relied on the in-court identifications of Treblinka survivors, and had provided the judge little evidence of what the role of the guards at Treblinka was, which made Fedorenko's story more believable than it should have been. For more discussion of Treblinka—and how OSI successfully prosecuted the case of another man who was there—see Chapter 4.

told me, I had argued one Nazi case; that made me as much an expert as anyone, and I had won it, which made me unique.

It was a question of leaving a secure post in a prestigious office doing something I enjoyed for a highly uncertain future in a new office born in political controversy and saddled with the undistinguished record of INS's defeats. OSI would be the first serious effort to do something the government had never done before. Its future was uncertain, difficult, controversial—and bound to be exciting. My wife Nancy and I talked it over. She knew what my answer would be before I did. "Forget security," she said. "What do you really want to do?"

I told Heymann I wanted the job.

Whatever risk I was taking was minor compared to Heymann's risk in appointing me. Over the years, INS's bumbling efforts against Nazis had angered more than Elizabeth Holtzman and Joshua Eilberg. Several major Jewish organizations, including the Anti-Defamation League of B'nai B'rith and the Jewish War Veterans, had strongly criticized INS and had given full support to Holtzman's plan to upgrade the operation and move it to the Justice Department. Their leaders had come calling on Heymann soon afterward to underscore their concern and to urge him to give OSI top priority within the Criminal Division. Heymann was well aware that the Jewish community would be watching him closely.

And I was not a Jew. Heymann believed, as I did, that this was essentially irrelevant, and that while American Jews were understandably sensitive to the government's poor record in the past, the prosecution of Nazi criminals in America was not exclusively a Jewish issue. What was needed was tough, fair, vigorous prosecution. Still, the complaint of American Jewish representatives was that INS had not been committed to the prosecution of Nazis, and that it was insensitive to the jarring injustice that the murderers of eleven million people—six million of them Jews—should find haven in the United States. Heymann could certainly have found a good lawyer who was Jewish, whose family had been scarred by the Holocaust, whose commitment to vigorous prosecution would be taken for granted. Could a good lawyer who was not Jewish have the same commitment?

Heymann thought so; I thought so. I told him that I believed that Jewish leaders would be fair enough to give me—and Heymann— enough time to judge whether that commitment was there, and whether

I could produce results. If I could, my religion would not matter; if I could not, I deserved to get the sack. Heymann could have played it safe; instead, he gave me the job.

Walter Rockler and I, the director and the heir apparent, were at the Moscow airport soon afterward.

Winning the cooperation of the Soviet Union was a critical step in our plans for OSI. The priorities embedded in the DP Act, particularly from 1948 to 1950, invited large numbers of Latvians, Lithuanians, and Ukrainians to America after the war and many of the active investigations OSI had inherited from the Immigration Service had implicated these emigrés in atrocities. But we needed the documents that recorded the names of those enrolled in auxiliary police units, or official correspondence, pay records, unit diaries, or anything else that would establish their affiliations and their individual actions. These records, created by German officials in occupied areas, had been captured by the Red Army in 1944 and had been held in Soviet archives ever since.

We also needed witnesses to atrocities: bystanders, colleagues, victims, neighbors. Some of these, particularly victims, we might find in America, or Israel or Canada or elsewhere in the world. But most of the neighbors and bystanders had never left home, and some of the criminals themselves had been captured, tried, and imprisoned by Soviet authorities. They had since been released from prison but they were still in the Soviet Union, and if we were to have their testimony, we needed the permission of their government.*

In mid-January 1980—three months after Attorney General Benjamin Civiletti had forcefully raised the matter with Soviet officials—we were notified that Moscow had approved our request for visas.

---

*Latvia, Lithuania, and Estonia, the Baltic countries, have been ruled since the end of the war by the Soviet Union, which considers them Soviet Socialist Republics, like the Ukraine or Russia itself. The United States has never diplomatically recognized this fact, and the State Department clings officially to the fiction that the Baltic countries are independent republics under "occupation" by a hostile power. This policy provides some sustenance to the Baltic emigrés in this country, most of whom are resigned to the fact that their homelands will never be free of the Soviet Union, but it has little practical effect. Whenever necessary, the United States government deals with Moscow on matters affecting the Baltic countries, and then solemnly pronounces that whatever it has done is not inconsistent with the non-recognition policy. Because many of these dealings benefit the Baltic communities in this country—an emigration is facilitated from Lithuania or a Christmas package is passed on to a cousin in Latvia—the emigrés, too, accept the reality while proclaiming the fiction.

We were told nothing else. We had requested an appointment with the Procurator General of the Soviet Union, the highest-ranking legal officer, but there was no word on whether that request had been granted. The Soviet embassy staff had been stiffly formal in its dealings with us—neither friendly nor unfriendly, and certainly not inclined to chat about what sort of reception we might expect in Moscow.

Their silence was more than a little ominous. The Soviet Union had invaded Afghanistan only four weeks earlier. President Carter had reacted with a strong and public denunciation, and relations between the two countries were speedily deteriorating. Then, two days before the visas were granted, the Soviet government had banished the eloquent dissident Andrei Sakharov to the closed city of Gorky, a move that immediately brought harsh criticism from many quarters in the United States.

We would be the first official U.S. visitors to the Soviet Union since the banishment of Sakharov, and there was a distinct possibility that we were being admitted so that we could be dressed down and sent packing back to Washington with the message that the United States ought to mind its own business on "internal" Soviet matters such as the treatment of dissidents. The coolness of the Soviet embassy staff was unsettling. Perhaps they knew something that Rockler and I did not.

Our reception at the airport did nothing to encourage us. The vast, empty terminal was being remodeled for the thousands of visitors expected to arrive for the summer Olympics. Its floors were earth, the light was dim, and there was almost no one in sight. Except for the absence of the stinging wind, it was as chilly inside as it had been on the walk from the plane.

A sullen Soviet Youth, a KGB corporal on border guard duty, glared at my diplomatic passport, my visa, and me and then repeated the sequence, and repeated it again. He said nothing. When at last he seemed convinced that my papers were in order and that there was nothing he could do to prevent my entry into his country, he tossed the passport back to me and jerked his head toward the wooden gate leading to the reception area. As I walked through, I was approached by a lone figure, clad in a great cloth coat and a Russian fur hat, who had been watching me.

He was American, from the embassy. He took us to a waiting Chevrolet outside, where a Russian driver sat rubbing his hands under the heater, smoking American cigarettes.

As we pulled out of the airport, the embassy man gave us the first bit of good news. The Soviets had scheduled a meeting in the morning, at the office of the Procurator General. But he knew no more than that; what the Soviets had in store for us was still a mystery.

The long drive into Moscow took us down a dark, undivided highway, punctuated every mile or so by small shuttered houses, their single lightpoles in the yards giving the only light. It was like driving through North Dakota in the middle of a moonless night.

After three quarters of an hour, we came over a slight rise in the highway and suddenly the entire vista changed. As we crossed the Moscow River, there was a glowing, shadowless light everywhere; broad boulevards replaced the narrow highway, and apartment buildings and small food shops crowded the deserted sidewalks. A few cars and trucks passed us on their way out of the city. The driver swung down one street after another and emerged in the vast empty plaza at the center of the city, directly in front of Red Square. Through the buildings I caught a glimpse of the colorful onion-dome spires of St. Basil's Cathedral, floodlit in the cold, clear night, as distinctive a symbol of Moscow as the Capitol dome is of Washington. Beside the cathedral a red star burned brightly atop the brick steeple marking the entrance to the Kremlin.

The driver pulled to a stop in front of the Hotel Metropol, an imposing pre-revolutionary hotel whose czarist design was evident despite sixty years of proletarian renovations. As I got out of the car, a shudder of disorientation swept over me. What was I doing here, in this strange city in a strange land? In the shadow of the red star, we were turning back the clock four decades. It seemed like forever.

That night, in my room at the Metropol, I reviewed the proposals we would make—we hoped—in the morning, to representatives of the Procuracy, perhaps to the Procurator General himself.

We were asking the Soviets to do two things that had never been done before: to allow Soviet citizens to come to the United States to testify, or where that was not feasible, to allow trial testimony to be taken from them on Soviet soil. They were the witnesses whose testimony would be crucial to our cases: not Jews, most of them, since the Einsatzgruppe executioners and their local collaborators had left no Jews alive in many of the villages, but Ukrainians and Latvians and Lithuanians who remembered what had happened in those villages forty years before. Some of these people had themselves collaborated with the Nazis and had served jail sentences for it after the war.

We knew of course that the simplest way to bring back evidence was the most direct way: to find the witnesses, interview them, and bring them to the United States to testify in court. But we recognized that the chances that the Soviets would let significant numbers of their citizens travel to the United States—or indeed that the witnesses themselves would want to undertake such a journey—were far from certain. So our back-up plan was to ask the Soviets whether, in such cases, we could take depositions of the witnesses in the Soviet Union.

A deposition is simply a means of obtaining the testimony of a witness who cannot attend the trial itself, for whatever reason. Several weeks or months before the trial is to take place, the witness appears at a place convenient for him and there he is questioned by the attorney who wants the testimony for trial. A deposition does not require the presence of the judge, but it does require that the attorney for the other side be given the chance to attend and cross-examine the witness to the same extent he would if the witness were actually testifying at trial, because, in effect, that is exactly what he is doing.

Normally, a verbatim record of the questions and answers is made by a stenographer and, when the trial is held, the transcript is submitted to the judge and becomes part of the record in the case. But this procedure—laying a typewritten transcript on the judge's bench—deprives the judge of the opportunity to see the witness and observe his demeanor: whether his answers are spoken firmly or with hesitation, whether he can look his questioner squarely in the eye, whether he squirms in his chair, whether, indeed, he speaks with any feeling at all—and judges have traditionally relied on this opportunity to help them decide whether a witness is telling the truth. In the United States, therefore, lawyers and judges in recent years have made increasing use of videotape, substituting the living color of a twenty-five-inch screen for the flat gray transcription of a witness's words. The judge can see the witness, if not in person, at least on television.

So the third point we intended to raise with the Soviets, after seeking to have the witnesses testify at trial or, if not, then at depositions, was to ask that any depositions be videotaped for playback at trial. This was a gamble on our part, for we had no idea of how the witnesses would come across on camera. For all we knew, the bright lights could reveal them to be hesitant, evasive, and uncomfortable men and women, whether they were telling the truth or not. The very act of testifying, we assumed, would be a novel experience for most of them, and the prospect of doing so with all the trappings of a television studio—and in front of Americans yet—would not ease their situation.

But we had little choice. In one sense, we felt an obligation to lay before the judge as accurate a picture of their testimony as we could, whatever it might show, and from a prosecutor's point of view we had to assume that the videotape would bring out the vividness of their testimony in a way that a stenographic record never could. We did not think that a judge would revoke citizenship of a flesh-and-blood American based on witnesses he had never seen. So we had to fly blind: put the witnesses on tape first, worry about how effective they were later.

We knew that the witnesses existed, at least in some of our cases. Since 1976, when the American embassy in Moscow had requested Soviet cooperation in Nazi cases, Soviet investigators had taken statements from some witnesses and had passed them to our embassy, which had forwarded them to INS, which had done nothing with them. These statements gave us an idea of what the witnesses knew, and which of our cases might be strongest, but they were useless as evidence because the witnesses had not been subject to cross-examination by the defense. Indeed, in most instances there was no defense because the lawsuits had not even been filed. Yet we knew also that the Soviets were puzzled, and somewhat annoyed, that all the statements they had been sending had apparently been ending up in a file cabinet. One of our tasks in the morning would be to explain why the Soviet statements were helpful in pointing us in the right direction and alerting us to the prospect of hard evidence, but fell short of what we needed to try the cases in court.

Before we had left Washington, an officer on the Soviet desk at the State Department had urged us to take every opportunity to make known to the Soviet side the United States' stern disapproval of the invasion of Afghanistan. I had no intention of following his advice. We had come to Moscow for one purpose only—to seek Soviet cooperation in our search for Nazi war criminals. If the Soviets were prepared to cooperate, we were not going to jeopardize the chances of an agreement by bringing up Afghanistan. If they were not going to help, we would pack our bags and come home. Either way, we would leave foreign relations to the State Department.

As I settled into my narrow bed in the small Moscow hotel room, I thought of Nancy, eight months pregnant with our first child, and wondered how she was spending the afternoon in our white frame home behind a stand of boxwoods at the edge of our town in the Blue Ridge Mountains of Virginia. From the edge of Red Square, that pleasant place seemed like a different planet.

The next morning was, to no one's great surprise, numbingly cold. Walter and I stood in the lobby of the Hotel Metropol waiting for an embassy car to pick us up for the trip to the Procuracy. Around us, the hotel was in the process of cleaning itself up for the Olympics, six months away. The prognosis was uncertain. The lobby was packed with rolled-up carpets, scaffolding, paint buckets, and unopened boxes. Before us, a dozen wide marble steps led to two rows of glass doors and the street outside. We noticed that no one held the heavy doors for those who might be behind; people pushed their way out and let the doors swing back without a glance. Little things can occasionally be clues to larger. Breakfast in the hotel's coffee shop, for example, was a curious experience. The coffee was strong and not at all bad when laced with hot milk and plenty of sugar. But there had been no eggs and no meat. I finally ordered what the menu called (in English and Russian) "breakfast pastries." The waitress brought me a little dish of elegant frosted petits fours garnished with delicate yellow sugar flowers. They were, I believe, four days old.

When the embassy's black Chevrolet station wagon pulled up to the hotel, it looked like the *Queen Elizabeth* in a harbor of little Russian tugboats. Inside were Tom Hutson, the American consul in Moscow, and Dennis Reece, on his first tour in the Foreign Service. Both spoke Russian fluently, and we were glad to have them along for our negotiations. The driver, a Russian employee of the embassy and, we assumed, a KGB informant as well, took us through the streets crowded with men and women on their way to work and to shop. Every man in Moscow, including our fellow Americans in the car, wore the distinctive Russian fur hat. I was wearing an Irish tweed cap I had picked up hurriedly in London. As I sat in the big black car, returning the stares of curious pedestrians as they scurried by, I was sure I could not have been more conspicuous on the streets of Moscow had I been wearing Mickey Mouse ears.

The Procuracy was on a narrow street near the center of the city. It was set back from the street by a circular driveway attended by a single Soviet guard who did not bother to come out of his warm little hut as we drove in. If he did not come out to examine Americans advancing on the Procuracy, I wondered, what is the purpose of having him there at all?

We were met at the door of the building by a man who introduced himself as Zhukov, a stocky middle-aged fellow whom I first took to be the doorkeeper. In fact, as we would later learn, he was a lawyer on the Procurator General's staff. The Procuracy appeared to have been at one time a small hotel, with a reception desk attended by a clerk who was busily engaged in discussion with a Soviet citizen and who paid us no attention at all as we walked by in Zhukov's trail. Zhukov led us up a grand wooden staircase covered with a worn Oriental rug, exchanging pleasantries with Hutson and Reece, and smiling and nodding in our direction. He spoke no English but apparently did not want Rockler and me to think he was ignoring us. Desperate for omens of what was to come, I latched onto his nodding head as a good sign.

On the second floor, Zhukov led us to an office whose sign proclaimed, as best I could make out with my imperfect knowledge of the Cyrillic alphabet, that it belonged to one Rogoff. Zhukov opened the door and motioned for us to precede him in. Rogoff, whoever he might be, obviously outranked Zhukov. We entered the room and there, standing stiffly straight, was a tall and broad-shouldered man, perhaps in his early fifties, with thick black hair. He wore a deep-blue uniform with inconspicuous gold bars, the dress uniform of the Soviet Procuracy.

Rogoff bowed slightly and came from behind his desk. He greeted us formally but not at all coldly. He inquired seriously, through Hutson who acted as interpreter, about the smoothness of our flight and the accommodations of our hotel. We smiled, and then he smiled, and it began to dawn on me that the Soviets might be as uncertain of what to expect of us as we were of them. We exchanged polite observations about the beauty of the city—in our brief exposure to it, Moscow seemed more heroic than beautiful, exactly, but I did not venture such distinctions at that point—and Rogoff seemed genuinely pleased that we should find it so. A wizened maid in layers of cotton dresses appeared from nowhere to take our overcoats and hats, and, loaded to the shoulders, she scampered way.

Rogoff cleared his throat. "Well, then," he said, "Shall we go?" Out of his office we went, Zhukov, then the four Americans, then

Rogoff, and back into the hall. Rogoff motioned us to the elevator behind the staircase. I had no idea how high we would go, but it was a major effort to fit six of us into the quaint contraption with its wood paneling and accordion gate. It inched slowly upward, creaking and shuddering. Rogoff smiled. Zhukov smiled. We smiled. After one floor, we got off.

It was clear now that we were indeed at the highest level. These were suites instead of single offices like Rogoff's, and there were carpets on the floor. It was not luxurious by Western standards, but the brass rails were polished and the carpets were spotless. It was a place that induced respect. There was no one in sight, but Rogoff and Zhukov did not seem concerned. We stood for a few moments without talking.

There were several doors from this room, all of them closed. After a moment or two, one of them opened from the other side and we saw a long table with four empty chairs on one side and a row of official- and serious-looking Soviets on the other. The man who had opened the door was quite clearly a man of some importance, in his fifties, wearing not a uniform but a gray wool suit that seemed tailored for him. He had not an ounce of fat on him. He could have been, in his youth, a weight lifter or a hammer thrower. He smiled, revealing even white teeth rimmed in gold, top and bottom. He bade us enter, and we did.

He introduced himself to us, through Hutson, as Aleksandr Mikhailovich Rekunkov, the First Deputy Procurator General of the Soviet Union. His handshake was firm, and I recall thinking that he probably could have broken several small bones in my hand if he wished. I gave him back my firmest handshake in return.

Rekunkov showed us to the four empty chairs on the near side of the long table. Rogoff and Zhukov went to the opposite side, amidst their colleagues, and Rekunkov took the chair at the far left as we faced him. For the first time I noticed that there was an empty seat at the head of the table. My spirits rose at once. That could only have been meant for General Roman Andreyevich Rudenko, the Procurator General of the Soviet Union, for he would be the only one who could outrank Rekunkov. As I placed my yellow pad carefully on the table, I thought that maybe, after all, we might get somewhere, for they would not bring out the Procurator General himself unless they expected some business to be done. I quickly put a check on myself, however. Maybe the Procurator General was the designated spokesman to give us, as official representatives of the United States government, a dressing-down that we could take back to Washington.

Rekunkov quickly confirmed my guess about Rudenko's presence, if not his intention. He told us, through a young woman from the Procuracy who spoke excellent English, that the Procurator General would indeed meet with us, although he would not spend the entire day with us because he was recovering from "an illness."

His illness was not a surprise to us. We had been briefed on General Rudenko before we had left Washington. He was quite an elderly man who, as a colonel in Nuremberg thirty-five years earlier, had been the chief Soviet prosecutor at the war crimes trials. Recently, we had been told, Rudenko had suffered a stroke from which he would probably never fully recover, and as a result he did not work for long periods of time and spoke only with difficulty. He seldom made public appearances, and indeed there was some question whether he was still administering the Procuracy or simply staying on as a figurehead until his death. He had been named Procurator General some years ago by Josef Stalin, and I marveled at the survival instincts of a man who stayed in Rudenko's high position from Stalin to Khrushchev to Brezhnev.

As we waited for Rudenko to enter, Rekunkov asked if we would care for some refreshment from the bottles of mineral water arrayed neatly on the table between the two rows of us. A burly white-haired man directly opposite me took the cue and broke into a gregarious smile as he lifted one of the bottles and an opener. Smiling and gesturing, he went through the exaggerated motion of opening the bottle before him, but the cap stayed on. He did it again, and still the cap stayed on. It suddenly struck me that he was demonstrating how one takes a cap off a bottle, and motioning me to give it a try. Slowly, and very seriously, I took a bottle and an opener and very carefully watched him as—presto!—I successfully uncapped the bottle. There were great smiles all around. The Americans could open a bottle of mineral water; maybe they wouldn't be such bad fellows after all. Mr. Gregarious slowly poured the contents of the bottle into his glass. I did likewise. He drank; I drank; we all drank. He offered me a Russian cigarette from a pack on the table. I don't smoke cigarettes, but I was not about to go into any long explanations of that. I lit up. He lit up; they all lit up. There we sat, puffing and sipping and smiling at each other, waiting for General Rudenko to join us.

"Very good," I said, gazing at the glass in my hand as if it held fine champagne. "Da, da," said Mr. Gregarious, and there were more smiles all around.

At the time, it was not at all as silly as it now seems. Neither side knew the other, or what to expect, and we both discovered that sharing some soda water and a cigarette gave us some common ground of hospitality. For the first time, I began to relax.

We had about exhausted our compliments on the mineral water, and I was wondering if I was going to have to praise the cigarettes too, when the door opened and General Rudenko walked in. Both sides became somber again. Rudenko was heavyset, like the others, with thin hair, and clearly an old man, but he made his way to the head of the table unassisted and looked at us with clear blue eyes. One side of his mouth drooped, and he did not offer his hand, yet he looked at each of us directly and with a polite nod. He wore the blue uniform, with several small ribbons arranged in military fashion over his left breast pocket. Even at his age, and with his evident disability, he had a commanding presence that came not from his physique but from his bearing. He was plainly a man who was accustomed to being in charge.

He spoke without notes, and his voice was strong without being loud. Thirty-five years had passed, he said, since World War II, a war in which the Soviet Union and the United States had fought as allies. The Soviets had suffered grievous casualties in that war, he said, pausing for emphasis. We nodded solemnly, for indeed there was no denying the enormous losses of that country. Many of them were Jews who were lost not to bullets or the cold, but Rudenko did not mention that fact.

And again at Nuremberg, he continued, the Americans and the Soviets, together with the British and French, had held trials of major Nazi criminals, and Rudenko noted that he had been privileged to represent the Soviet side as chief prosecutor. And yet, he said, his voice more measured now, there was still unfinished business in the prosecution of these "Hitlerites." Since the war, the Soviets had held many trials, but the United States had held none. Many Hitlerites were living in the United States.

I held my breath. Which way would Rudenko go—to pledge his cooperation or to excoriate us for having let the job slip by?

He paused, his hand shaking slightly from the effects of his stroke. The Soviet Union, he said, stands ready to render whatever assistance we might ask in this endeavor of prosecuting those responsible for the deaths of innocent people. We are, after all, allies still in this important work; whatever we can do together, we should do.

He would not be with us for the rest of the meetings, he said seriously. The task would be in the hands of his deputy Rekunkov and the Procuracy staff. But he was confident that we would successfully conclude the necessary arrangements.

As the young woman finished the translation, he nodded to each of us with a slight smile, official but cordial. And now, he asked, what had we to say?

Before leaving Washington, I had drafted a lengthy statement setting forth our requests. Walter now put this script aside and spoke to Rudenko as directly as he had spoken to us. He began by acknowledging that the United States had done little to investigate or prosecute these people since the war, but he followed up with a firm statement of our intention to do so now, however late the date. There was little time, he said, to dwell on the past. What was important now was what we would do in the future. Rudenko nodded slightly in agreement.

Walter emphasized that the bulk of the several hundred cases that the Office of Special Investigations had identified involved persons who had committed crimes on Soviet soil, and thus the cooperation of the Soviet Union would be particularly important. As General Rudenko would remember from the Nuremberg tribunal, American rules of procedure were complex, but, Rockler continued, the Americans and the Soviets could surely work together as the allies we were in the war so that the evidence that might be available in the Soviet Union could be produced in a form acceptable to American courts. That was what we had come to Moscow for, and we were ready to begin.

Rudenko nodded again, apparently gratified by the reference to the wartime alliance between the two countries. He stood up and extended his hand to each of us. I will go now, he said, and leave you to work out the details with my assistants. He turned and walked through the door, closing it softly behind him. We did not see him again.*

In the conference room, the mood became noticeably more relaxed. It was now official that Walter and I were no longer repre-

---

*Rudenko died several months later, and Rekunkov was appointed Procurator General.

senting the Soviet Union's 1980 adversary. We were representing Russia's wartime ally, the common enemy of the Hitlerites. We were over the hump.

Rekunkov looked at us across the table. What is it, he asked, that we would need from them?

We emphasized that the summaries of witnesses' statements that the Soviets had been sending were useful, especially in identifying which cases could be pursued by OSI in the expectation of arriving at tangible evidence admissible in United States courts. But the statements by themselves, we explained, were not enough. Under American law, no evidence could be heard unless the witness spoke either in the courtroom or in formal depositions, and the defense counsel had an opportunity to cross-examine.

Rekunkov interrupted. Why should cross-examination be necessary? If a man gives his statement, that is his statement and nothing further should be necessary. Would the American courts doubt the truthfulness of what a Soviet citizen was saying?

This was a critical moment. Rekunkov's question went to the heart of the matter. If the Soviets were unwilling to allow cross-examination, our whole trip might yet be for naught, and prospects of real cooperation would be doomed.

Walter took a deep breath and spoke calmly to an attentive Rekunkov. To understand the necessity for cross-examination, he said, we really must begin with the Magna Carta signed in England in 1215. That document established for the first time the concept that the powers of the sovereign were limited and that the people held certain rights against the government. To me, the irony of the moment was inescapable. Here we were in Moscow, setting forth the most elementary concepts of due process of law to the leading lawyers of the Soviet Union, with no hint that they understood what we were talking about.

Walter covered six hundred years of Anglo-American judicial development in about ten minutes, setting forth concisely the emergence of the adversarial process—two opposing sides presenting their evidence before an independent judge, each side entitled to probe the evidence through aggressive questioning, hostile if need be, of the other side's witnesses. It was an article of faith in the Anglo-American tradition, Rockler went on, that the most reliable way of getting at the truth was to allow the defendant to confront the witnesses against him and to question them through his attorney. For this reason,

American courts did not accept statements taken out of court without the opportunity for that questioning. Thus, it was not a matter of disbelieving Soviet witnesses. The statements could not be offered no matter who they had come from. The defendant had the right to deal with them face to face, and any procedure that excluded that opportunity would not produce admissible evidence for American courts.

Rekunkov smiled as the translation concluded, his gold-rimmed teeth reflecting the soft light of the room. Of course, he said. It is that way in Soviet courts as well. It will not be a problem. Proceed.

I was astonished. I had no idea whether Rekunkov had studied Western judicial systems and had any true idea of what cross-examination was, but it certainly could not be compared to anything that he was familiar with in the courts of his own country. And I was quite certain that, despite Walter's careful admonition that cross-examination could be quite pointed, Rekunkov could have no appreciation of what that meant in American practice, or that defense counsel would certainly ask these witnesses not only detailed but unfriendly questions about whether their testimony had been prepared, perhaps even dictated, by Soviet officials. Nonetheless, Rekunkov had accepted the requirement of cross-examination, at least in theory. We pressed on.

The normal means of assuring cross-examination, we continued, was to have the witness appear in the courtroom before the judge and testify, with the defendant's attorney carrying out his questioning immediately thereafter. But this was often impossible, because a witness might be ill and unable to appear in court, or he might live so far away that he could not appear without considerable inconvenience. To cope with these situations, a device known as the deposition had evolved.

Walter and I yielded to each other in turn, explaining to Rekunkov and the others how the deposition procedure worked, emphasizing again the importance of cross-examination, summarizing the advantages of videotape. Rekunkov occasionally interjected questions. Like Rudenko, he had a distinct command presence, but, unlike Rudenko, he fortified it with a physical bulk that could have quickly become intimidating had he chosen to turn it on his adversary. He did not do so with us; indeed, he was the model of civility and courtesy. But he would rise slightly in his chair to emphasize a point now and then, and it was not difficult to imagine that, in other circumstances, he might not only rise but spring. It was not an endearing thought.

Walter spoke to the interpreter on Rekunkov's right hand, and when he listened, he listened to her. I spoke directly to Rekunkov, and when he answered, I kept my eyes on him as well. Actually, I found the need for translation not a hindrance at all but an advantage. As Rekunkov spoke in Russian, a language that I spoke not at all, I could ignore his words and study his eyes and the tone of his voice without having to attend to the substance of what he was saying. The translator supplied that in good time. I found this opportunity to separate style and substance to be most helpful in appraising Rekunkov's statements. Like the judges we were talking about, I gathered much from observing the witness's demeanor.

Walter and I had already decided that we would settle for depositions if the Soviet would not allow their citizens to travel to the United States to testify. We half expected the Soviets to require, as a condition of travel, that no asylum be given in the United States to anyone who defected. While we thought it unlikely that these farmers and laborers would wish to defect, we had agreed that we could not accede to any such condition. As it turned out, the Soviets did not even raise the matter.

We concluded our presentation, therefore, by requesting that the Soviets allow witnesses to travel to the United States when feasible, but to allow videotaped depositions in the Soviet Union as an acceptable substitute. We stressed that documents could be important, but that it would take the testimony of witnesses to describe in detail what had happened and what the defendant had done or not done. The witnesses would supply the human perspective that documents could never do.

Rekunkov listened to our points intently, looking from Rockler to me and back again, posing questions and noting carefully our answers. When we had concluded, he drew himself up and spoke again. It would not be a problem, he repeated, to assist us under the conditions we had specified. Soviet witnesses had traveled to other countries to give testimony in war crimes cases, and there would be no objection to their traveling to the United States. But two conditions would have to be satisfied. First, they must be healthy enough to endure the rigors of extended travel and testifying in court, and second, they must be willing to do so. No one would be sent out against his will. But anyone who was unable or unwilling to travel could be de-

posed in the Soviet Union, in the presence of defense counsel, and
on videotape. Rekunkov stated candidly that, in his opinion, only about
one witness in ten would be both able and willing to travel; the rest
would have to be deposed. And because there was no formal legal-
assistance treaty between the United States and the Soviet Union, all
these arrangements would have to be made through established diplomatic channels, on a case-by-case basis. Perhaps, he said, we might
be able to provide them with the names of those witnesses whose testimony would be needed first, in the most pressing cases. I immediately answered that we could do so the next day.

The first day's session ended on that note. As the mid-afternoon
dusk darkened the windows, we all stood and shook hands, and made
arrangements to meet the following morning to discuss administrative
details. The four Americans left the room, with Zhukov escorting us
to the waiting embassy car outside.

As we drove away, we were both exhausted and elated. The day
had been an intense experience, uninterrupted by any recess or break
for lunch. I felt as if I had been on my feet in trial all day long. We
had emphasized the positive aspects of cooperation while dealing as
honestly as we could with the aspects of American procedure unfamiliar to our hosts, and we were immensely buoyed by the Soviet
response. With the car threading its way through the narrow streets
to the embassy, Tom Hutson, the consular officer and an experienced
Russian hand, shook his head in disbelief. He had never seen any
Soviet official discuss any matter with such directness and candor, he
said. It had been an extraordinary session.

Walter and I both knew that a promise was not a fact, and that
we would have to await concrete results to know whether we had truly
made progress or were simply providing grist for the Soviet propaganda machine. But these reservations dampened our enthusiasm only
slightly. We had made our points. We had been given full assurances
of cooperation. That had to count for something.

Back at the embassy, I commandeered a desk and a typewriter
and set to work composing a memorandum we could deliver to Rekunkov the next day, setting forth the names and addresses of those
witnesses whose testimony we wanted right away. We had come prepared for just such an eventuality, with case files and memoranda on
five or six cases that were closest to prosecution. By midnight I had
churned out a memo asking for the testimony of thirty-two named
witnesses in seven cases.

The second and third days were shirtsleeve sessions, almost literally. The tone had been set on the first day by General Rudenko's broad assurances of help among allies, and those assurances had been strengthened through the extended discussion that had followed. We spent the next two days working out the details, conscious that an unexpected obstacle, or the sudden emergence of a major misunderstanding, could cause either or both sides to pull away in apprehension. By themselves, the details were mundane, but several times during these two days it struck me that what we were actually doing was fashioning, for the first time in our two nations' histories, a single proceeding that could conform both to the American rules of evidence and procedure and the Soviet formalities of giving testimony. It was a wildly improbable marriage we were arranging, but as each detail was raised and resolved, we found ourselves coming closer and closer to final agreement.

We began by giving the Soviets the memorandum of important witnesses I had worked out the night before. They emphasized that they had given us statements of witnesses in the past and yet had heard very little about what use the United States had made of them. The answer, of course, was that very little use had been made. But we did not dwell on this point. Instead we promised that we would provide to them, through diplomatic channels, copies of the suits as they were filed in court, and periodic reports of the progress of the cases as they made their way through the legal system. They seemed satisfied at this.

Rekunkov raised the matter of oaths. We had mentioned the day before that testimony in depositions, like testimony at trial, was given under oath. There were, he informed us, no oaths in the Soviet judicial system. Would this be a problem?

This was a slow pitch right down the middle. While oaths were customary, I replied, no invocation of a Supreme Being was required. Under American law, any witness could, if he wished, dispense with the oath and substitute an affirmation—a solemn promise to tell the truth. Rekunkov told us that witnesses were warned, prior to testifying, of the penalties for false testimony and were made to promise that they would testify truthfully. This would be fine, I told him; our witnesses did the same thing when they took an oath.

We asked Rekunkov whether original documents could be forwarded for use in American trials. No, he said, these were valuable documents that could not leave the Soviet Union. Well then, we responded, could the Office of Special Investigations—and equally important, the defense—send handwriting experts or document analysts to the Soviet Union to examine the originals to determine their authenticity? Yes, said Rekunkov, that would not be a problem.

In fact, the Soviet Union was later to relent in their refusal to send original documents to the United States. As our cases came to trial, it became apparent that sending experts to Moscow or Riga or Lutsk to examine documents would be a cumbersome and expensive procedure. In response to our requests, the Soviets agreed to forward the original documents to their embassy in Washington, where an embassy official would convey them personally to the place of trial. There, they would be examined by our experts, the defense experts, and the judge. In none of our trials has there been any finding that these documents were anything other than what they appeared to be—records produced for administrative purposes during the war, undoctored, unchanged. I am convinced that the opportunity to lay these actual documents before the judges was not only significant in many of our victories, but assuaged the suspicion with which some judges might have treated photocopies from behind the Iron Curtain. It was a good example of the spirit of the Moscow negotiations—we had the use of original documents for trial, and the Soviet Union kept possession of them by having an embassy official act as courier.

We had another question to put to Rekunkov, and an important one. If the defense wished to call Soviet citizens to testify, either at depositions or at trial, in an effort to support the defense version of the case, would the Soviet government allow this? Although we did not say so explicitly, we were seriously concerned that any arrangement that provided witnesses requested by the prosecution but not those requested by the defense would be viewed with considerable skepticism by the courts, no matter how much cross-examination there might be of the government's witnesses. And courts aside, I was not at all sure that we would be willing to accept it ourselves.

Rekunkov waved the question away. The Soviet government would make the necessary arrangements to produce any witness we requested. If defense counsel told OSI whom they wished to call, we could tell the Soviets, and it would be done.

I pointed out that OSI could not require defense counsel to make their requests through us, but that I did not think any defense counsel would object to proceeding in that reasonable way to obtain witnesses. It was a minor point to make, but I wanted to miss no opportunity to demonstrate to the Soviet officials that, in the United States, defense counsel was entirely independent of the prosecution, the government and the court. It was a point that the Soviet witnesses would face head-on when defense attorneys began their cross-examination, and the Soviets might as well get used to it, even in such minor contexts as requesting witnesses.

Beyond this, I felt myself subtly coming to speak for defense counsel—and more significantly the rights of the defendant—in these negotiations with representatives of a totalitarian regime. Recognition of an individual's rights against the government is the keystone of the American legal system, and the independence of defense counsel was an integral part of a system of justice whose integrity I deeply believed in. I had been a defense attorney in the Marine Corps and later in private practice before I joined the Justice Department, and there was no doubt in my mind that representing a defendant carried with it an obligation to challenge the prosecution at every turn, lest some right of the client be lost or some tactical advantage overlooked. I wanted Rekunkov to understand that too. As we sat in the center of the Soviet legal system, I became conscious of the fact that, as representatives of the United States government, we were speaking not only as prosecutors—though prosecutors we surely were—but as spokesmen for a legal system that placed due process of law above every other consideration. By the end of our sessions, I realized very clearly that, no matter how guilty or contemptible our defendants might be, I would not let my zeal as a prosecutor lead me into any arrangement that would impair the exercise of their rights under American law, whether or not that impairment might later be apparent to a court. It was a conviction that I held through my last day at OSI, and it was shared as a matter of faith by every attorney in the Office.

Finally, the Soviets raised a delicate question, and one that had been almost conspicuous by its absence thus far. They understood that we did not have jurisdiction to place these accused people on trial for war crimes, but could only take action to have their citizenship revoked and to deport them. Could they be deported to the Soviet Union?

Under American law, there was nothing to prevent it or to require it. A defendant who was ordered deported could be sent to nearly any country of his choosing, or could be ordered to return to the country of his birth. We gave the Soviets a noncommittal answer. It was possible, we said. Possible, but we could not guarantee anything. They nodded silently. I felt that they believed, as we did, that such questions would probably be better raised when the trials were over.

We ended with Rekunkov's suggestion that there be no formal communiqué concerning our negotiations or our agreements. We would simply work together, and do what had to be done.

The absence of a formal statement of agreement suited Walter and me. Although we intended to be candid with the American press and the public about what had gone on in Moscow, we did not wish to raise false hopes or fears. A formal communiqué may have given the negotiations a higher profile in the press or in the diplomatic community than subsequent events might warrant. But Rekunkov's suggestion implicitly underscored the fact that with no mutual statement of what had been agreed to, the Soviets would be free to discontinue the arrangements at any time. We had simply agreed to cooperate until either side no longer wished to cooperate. In fact, cooperation was rather a misnomer, since the Soviets had asked nothing of us in return for their assistance. I wondered whether we might not hear from them about something they needed, several months down the road. (We never did.)

But such concerns were far in the back of my mind. When we stood at the table to exchange our final handshakes—each of the four Americans shaking hands with each of the eight or nine Soviets, like the end of a hockey game—the mood was far different from the uncertainty and doubt I had felt only three days before. That time seemed weeks in the past. We had spoken our minds freely, making clear our requirements and seeking the Soviets' help if they could give it on terms acceptable to us. They had agreed to cooperate. It had been a frank, candid, and constructive session, not in the sense that those words are often used among diplomats as synonyms for halting progress, but in their full literal sense.

We filed out of the room and down the stairs in knots of twos and threes, discussing the weather, exchanging cards, making tentative arrangements to meet again at some future point to review the progress that we hoped would follow. We shook hands again in the lobby of the Procuracy's little hotel and headed out the door, buttoning our coats against the ever-present cold.

As we sat in our rooms, sipping from a bottle of cognac, we were both drained and excited. The three days in Moscow had been an unqualified success, so far as we could tell, and yet we knew that the onus was now on us to follow up our memorandum with formal requests for attendance at trial or depositions, and to await the formal Soviet response.

There was one striking and discomforting epilogue to our Moscow negotiations. When we arrived at Zurich, I picked up the international edition of *Newsweek*, which had on its cover Andrei Sakharov and, inside, the story of his abrupt banishment to the closed city of Gorky, far from the scientific and academic circles of Moscow. I took the magazine to a lounge chair and leaned back, but as I opened to the story, I sat up quickly. According to *Newsweek*, the Soviet official who had ordered Sakharov summoned to his office, and who had read him the decree of exile, was the First Deputy Procurator General of the Soviet Union, Aleksandr Mikhailovich Rekunkov.

Over the following years, the marriage we had arranged in Moscow worked out surprisingly well. OSI took the testimony of over one hundred Soviet citizens in somewhat over half of the two dozen cases we filed from 1980 through 1983, and the process is continuing today. In the first few cases, we requested that the witnesses be allowed to travel to the United States for trial, but if that was not possible, we would take depositions. The Soviets responded by scheduling depositions. After a while, we decided to request depositions at the outset.

The depositions were held not in Moscow but in provincial cities where the crimes had taken place, and where the witnesses generally live today; consequently, OSI attorneys, and defense counsel, often found themselves in cities where Americans had never been before, at least to anyone's memory: places like Zaporozhe and Lutsk in the Ukraine, as well as more cosmopolitan places such as Riga, the handsome Hanseatic city that is the capital of Latvia, and Tartu, a university city in Estonia, just across the Baltic from Helsinki.

The deposition proceedings were usually models of correctness, although they often went very slowly because the witnesses testified in their native language (Ukrainian, say, or Latvian), which then had to be translated into Russian for official purposes and into English for the benefit of the attorneys. A simple question and answer thus involved six statements.*

Because these proceedings were taking place on Soviet soil, a Soviet procurator (prosecutor) was officially in charge. When the witness came into the room, the official formally notified him of the purpose of the testimony, ascertained his identity from his papers, and informed him of the penalties under Soviet law for giving false testimony. Usually, the procurator then asked the witness to recount the events in question. When this was finished, the OSI attorney conducted direct examination, which meant going over the same ground the witness had just covered, usually in more detail. After this questioning was finished, defense counsel conducted his cross-examination.

From the moment the witness sat down at the table until he left the room at the conclusion of his testimony, an OSI technician recorded the entire process on videotape, which remained exclusively in our hands until trial. Nothing that happened in the depositions was kept from the judge.

In a typical case, we had six to ten witnesses, who generally fell into three categories. Some witnesses had grown up with the defendant and knew him well, and recalled clearly that when the Germans invaded in 1941, the defendant had joined forces with them, as an auxiliary policeman or whatever. They saw him in uniform, they knew of his new importance under the occupation forces. These witnesses may not have seen any atrocities, but their testimony was valuable because there was little chance of mistaken identity. Usually these witnesses testified that the defendant disappeared with the retreating Germans in 1944 and they had not seen him since.

The second category of witnesses were those who either did not know the defendant or had not seen him at the site of any crimes, but could testify that the local collaborators had been instrumental in carrying out the mass killings of Jews. These witnesses were helpful in

---

*One of the benefits of videotaping was that every word was recorded; if the defense believed that something may have been mistranslated, it could play the tape back at trial and explain for the judge what the problem was. In practice, this seldom happened; the translators, provided by the Soviets, were remarkably good. On several occasions, defense attorneys brought their own interpreters from the United States. In our Moscow negotiations, the Soviets had agreed that any defendant who wished to attend the depositions would be allowed to do so, with no interference coming or going from Soviet authorities. No defendant chose to go to the Soviet Union.

supplementing our case, usually made by Professor Raul Hilberg of the University of Vermont or other experts, that, in general, local auxiliaries had been essential to the Nazis' implementation of the Final Solution. What Professor Hilberg could state as a general matter these witnesses could apply to the very situation in their town.

The third category of witnesses was normally the smallest but the most valuable. These were the men and women who knew the defendant and had seen with their own eyes the atrocities he had committed against innocent people. Very often these witnesses were themselves Nazi auxiliaries who had been at the killing sites with the defendant but, unlike the defendant, had not retreated with the Germans. Most of them had been tried after the war by local Soviet tribunals on collaboration charges, had served sentences in jail (generally, three to eight years), and had long since been released and had resumed their lives.

My suspicions that the Soviets had no real idea of American cross-examination proved correct. In the early depositions, Soviet officials took OSI attorneys aside during recesses or lunch breaks and demanded to know why defense counsel was attempting to embarrass the witnesses by insinuating that they were not telling the truth or by trying to get them to change their testimony. We explained that the whole purpose of cross-examination was to test the truthfulness of the witness's statements, and that if the Soviets interfered with the process by precluding hard questions, the entire deposition would be thrown out of court and the trip would have been for naught. The procurators would simmer down, and cross-examination would continue without interference.

In arranging the depositions, we notified defense counsel that the government would pay all travel and living expenses and would handle the paperwork involved in securing reservations, visas, and other details. Invariably, defense counsel went to the judge to request an order prohibiting the depositions, usually on the grounds that Soviet witnesses could not be trusted to tell the truth. Just as invariably, such requests were denied; the judge ruled, quite correctly, that at trial he would decide whether the witnesses were telling the truth and what weight ought to be accorded their testimony, which is what judges do with all witnesses, live or on tape, American or foreign.

In one case, involving a Lithuanian immigrant in Florida, the attorney decided that her tack would be to make herself as obnoxious as possible to Soviet officials, in the hope that the depositions would be angrily terminated. It almost worked. In an embarrassing display of personal vulgarity, she insulted every Soviet citizen in the room, official or witness, harangued the Soviet system ostensibly under the guise of "cross-examining" witnesses, and refused to cooperate in such mundane matters as scheduling lunch breaks. After two days of this, the Soviet procurator took OSI deputy director Neal Sher aside and told him that such crudeness could not be tolerated. Sher patiently agreed with him but emphasized that to cancel the depositions would be to play into the hands of the shrew and her client. After a while, the Soviet official gave in, and the depositions continued.

My conclusion, after seeing scores of such depositions, was that Soviet witnesses, on the whole, were about as truthful and reliable as American witnesses; that is to say, most of them told the truth to the best of their recollection; some were vague and not helpful one way or the other; a few were probably liars.* I became firmly convinced that the witnesses had not been "programmed" or rehearsed by the Soviets. An attempt to show the contrary was a common tactic in cross-examination, which is fair enough, but it never succeeded. More importantly, the judges who saw the videotapes at trial were impressed with the truthfulness and candor of the witnesses and often cited their testimony in the course of explaining the verdicts.

There is no doubt in my mind that the agreement we forged in Moscow in January 1980, and, more importantly, the testimony that resulted from it, has made an enormous contribution to getting the truth about Nazi criminals in America. Through this means, judges in Philadelphia and Chicago and New York have been able to hear testimony directly from Riga and Lvov and Tartu, and to study the witnesses with their own eyes, to judge for themselves the credibility and reliability of the witnesses, and to base their conclusions on this evidence.

Throughout this time, the Office of Special Investigations was subjected to unrelenting attack from the defendants, their lawyers, and their sympathizers. The best they said was that we were naive, the

---

*In those few cases where we felt the witness was not being truthful, we did not offer the depositions into evidence at trial. There was no pattern to these, as there would have been if the witnesses had been rehearsed by Soviet officials beforehand. I think personal animosity of the witness toward the erstwhile collaborator was the motivating force in such instances.

worst was that we were knowingly and intentionally subverting the Constitution, the Bill of Rights, and the American flag. We were using "Soviet evidence" invented by the KGB to embarrass anti-Communist activists in America. Letters flowed week after week from ad hoc defense groups and Ukrainian and Baltic organizations to the president, Congress, and the attorney general, all with one message: call off OSI. Forbid them to go to the Soviet Union for evidence.

Most of these letters came from people who obviously did not know the facts. They said that lawyers for the accused could not attend the depositions; cross-examination was not allowed. One group who sent a petition to the president claimed that the videotapes we were showing in court had been prepared by the KGB and delivered to OSI for exhibition in court.

I prepared a fact sheet setting forth the Moscow agreement and how it was being implemented, and sent it to every writer who expressed concern. My points were always the same: the safeguards that we had insisted upon in Moscow—confrontation, cross-examination, and other rights secured by the Constitution—were being fully honored by the Soviets; we as prosecutors were constantly alert to the possibility of false or perjured testimony from any witness; and, most importantly, the judges who had seen these witnesses testify on videotape had been persuaded, without exception, that their testimony, on the whole, was reliable. But the final responsibility for the rights of the defendant in court rested where it had since the Constitution was written: on the attorney representing the defendant. Through cross-examination, through the power to call his own witnesses, through the power to examine and attack the government's evidence, whether documentary or spoken, the rights of the defendant were protected. Our obligation as prosecutors was to ensure that those rights were exercised with no interference, and they were.

I routinely offered all writers the opportunity to come to OSI's offices and watch the videotapes to their heart's content to draw their own conclusions; no one ever took me up on this. I also expressed my willingness to meet with concerned citizens. I did meet once, with a delegation from the Ukrainian and Baltic communities at the Justice Department, and I spoke once in New Jersey to a meeting of the Ukrainian-American Bar Association. In both cases, I think the participants came away with a greater understanding of the process, and their more extreme fears were neutralized. But it was like trying to contain an underground fire; no matter where it was treated, it flared up somewhere else.

The explanations of our procedures satisfied the congressmen and the judges, but I doubt that it satisfied the letter-writers. To them, nothing that happened within the borders of the Soviet Union could be trusted, period, and they were not interested in explanations about safeguards and rights. Some of these people, however obstinate, were acting in good faith; others, I'm sure, were desperately trying to derail the prosecution of their countrymen in America. To them, my message was simple: I was determined that the Department of Justice would have no part in any process that infringed the rights of the defendants, but I was equally determined that we would seek evidence against the guilty wherever it was to be found.

The theory that Soviet cooperation was a KGB plot to undermine emigré activities in the West simply does not square with the facts. The Soviets have never attempted to tell OSI who to investigate. They do not send us unsolicited information; they respond to our inquiries. Moreover, there have been many cases where the Soviets had no incriminating information on a person about whom we inquired, and other cases where they sent some lukewarm statements from witnesses that fell far short of the amount of evidence we need. If we could not develop sufficient evidence from other sources, the file was closed and the case never went to court.

Moreover, our defendants, almost without exception, were not outspoken anti-Communists or leaders in their American emigré communities. For obvious reasons, they have stayed out of the public eye and have avoided drawing attention to themselves. Conviction of these people does little to discredit the leaders of the Ukrainian and Baltic communities in America, or to sow discord among them.

Why, then, have the Soviets cooperated with us, particularly at a time when U.S.-Soviet relations in nearly all other respects have been crumbling?

One must first understand the enormous significance of World War II, "the Great Patriotic War," as it is known in Russia, in present-day Soviet affairs. We are not talking about history here. As David Shipler said recently in his perceptive book, *Russia: Broken Idols, Solemn Dreams*, "The memory of the war is fresh, both because it is kept that way by a leadership seeking to bolster national pride and cohesiveness, and because it was a genuine trauma that left scarcely

a family untouched. . . . The recollections now stir authentic patriotic emotions, truer than the placard declarations of fidelity that hang
across city streets.''[1]

World War II might have ended yesterday in the Soviet Union.
There are monuments, eternal flames, bronze plaques wherever one
turns. Paperback books devoted to this or that battle are cheap and
plentiful. Pensioners taking the sun on a park bench proudly display
tiny battle ribbons over the breast pocket of their suitcoats. I have
talked to few Soviet officials, in Moscow or Washington, who did
not sooner or later tell me, with obvious sincerity and pride, of the
role played by a father or brother or uncle (or all three) in the Great
Patriotic War.

But, as Shipler points out, this pride is both natural and augmented: it reflects not only the genuine trauma of the war but a political reality of the seventies and eighties. Keeping the war alive is
part of the way the Soviets explain the world to themselves and others: the motherland must maintain its defenses in a hostile world lest
it be set upon again by brutal forces.

The motivation for cooperation, however, is more specific, I think;
it lies in a question that was raised almost casually in the original
negotiations and has surfaced from time to time since then. The Soviets view those who collaborated with the Nazis as traitors, and Russian memories are long. They want these people back, and when they
get them, trials will be held.

To date, no one has been deported from the United States to the
Soviet Union, largely because the endless rounds of appeals and delays has protected them here. For trials that began in earnest only in
1980, final decisions on deportation are still in the future. Yet that
time will come, and indeed in several of our cases deportation to the
Soviet Union has been ordered for those born there. Those decisions
are now on appeal.

The Moscow negotiations of 1980 were concerned primarily with testimony: witnesses recalling events in their own words. But the Soviets also promised to make available, for use as evidence, original
documents in their archives. That arrangement was to play a crucial
role in one of OSI's most important cases, and certainly one of its
most chilling: *United States* v. *John Demjanjuk.*

4

JOHN DEMJANJUK:
Ivan the Terrible

1942: At first, the tidy little railway station standing in the still morning air was a welcome sight. The night before, in Warsaw, the families had been crammed into boxcars, and the boxcars had been sealed shut, with only a tiny grate for ventilation and a single bucket for a toilet. There was little room to breathe, none to move around. Children whimpered in the arms of their mothers. Fathers craned their necks to find their families, until they fell into a stuporous sleep. In almost every car, some had died of suffocation, exhaustion, or fright.

Yet as the train chugged slowly across the flat Polish countryside, headed east, there was, as always, hope. Rumors had been circulating in the ghetto for weeks that the Jews of Warsaw would be sent to a mass-extermination site, but that was preposterous. There were over 300,000 Jews in Warsaw.[1] How could the Germans kill them all? And besides, the SS men who had rousted the Jews out of the dismal ghetto had ordered them to take their clothing and possessions with them. Doctors were to bring their bags, workmen their tools. They were being sent to the East, for resettlement. And so, jammed into the boxcars were suitcases, satchels, bundles of clothes and letters and photographs, a few tools, the manifestation of their hope. Why would the Germans have required clothing and tools, if not to be used in the East? Why allow papers and scrapbooks, if not to be kept?

When the train stopped, apprehension grew. Where were they? This could not be the East, not yet. It was too close to Warsaw. Was this a killing place? Were the rumors true? When the doors were pried open and the families pushed out, eyes smarting in the bright sun, they saw no camp, no killing place. This was only a railway station, for a village that must be just out of sight. It was too small to be anything else. Signs on the platform read "Stationmaster," "Cashier," "To Bialystok," "Transfer here for Eastbound trains."

For the observant, however, there were omens. If this was a transfer station, why was there only one track? And the clock. Every railroad station had a clock. But in this station, the hands did not move. They were painted on the face.

But few passengers had the time to notice tracks or clocks. The SS was here, and the detested Ukrainians, as brutal as their counterparts in Warsaw, shouting orders. Men to the left, women and children to the right. "Women and children are to take their shoes off at the entrance to the barracks. The stockings are to be put in the shoes. The children's socks are to be placed in their sandals. When going to the baths, take along your valuables, documents, money, a towel, and soap."

Was that it? A bath, a change of clothes, a chance to move around before continuing the journey eastward?

Mothers lined their suitcases and clothing bundles on the neatly swept ground next to the track, to be reclaimed after the baths. At the "cashier" window, they handed in their valuables. They went through the door marked "To Bialystok." They found themselves not in a train station, but in a barracks. They were told to take off their clothes, and they did. They filed into a large room. Several women, pale and weary, were standing by a row of benches, shears in hand, to give the arrivals haircuts.

What was this? Why haircuts? Why did the door say "Bialystok" when it led only to this room? Where did the other door—the door out—lead? There was no sign there.

Whatever hope had survived the grueling train ride was strangled in the haircut room. When the barbers were through with their work, when the room was full of shorn, naked women, the other door opened. The Ukrainians came in, with whips.

"Out! Out! Run!" they screamed, whips flailing the air. Panic swept through the hall. Crowds at the door, shoving and pushing, naked bodies forced through the door. "Run! Faster!" A path, lined by more guards with whips, some with snarling dogs. More shouting, more frenzy; the panicked women stampeded onward. Children fell and were trampled.

At the end of the path, ninety meters long, frightened and winded, they made a sharp right turn and came upon a strange and unnerving sight: a low stone structure, trimmed with wood. Five wide concrete steps, decorated with potted plants, led to a wide, massive door.

A man who spent a year at this place, writing even before the war ended, recalled the process that began at the stone building:

> A motor taken from a dismantled Soviet tank stood in the power plant. This motor was used to pump the gas which was let into the chambers by connecting the motor with the inflow pipes. The speed with which death overcame the helpless victims depended on the quantity of combustion gas admitted into the chamber at one time.
>
> The machinery of the gas chambers was operated by two Ukrainians. One of them, Ivan, was tall, and though his eyes seemed kind and gentle, he was a sadist. He enjoyed torturing his victims. He would often pounce upon us while we were working; he would nail our ears to the walls or make us lie down on the floor and whip us brutally. While he did this, his face showed sadistic satisfaction and he laughed and joked. He finished off the victims according to his mood at the moment. The other Ukrainian was called Nicholas. He had a pale face and the same mentality as Ivan.
>
> . . . Suddenly, the entrance door flew open and out came Ivan, holding a heavy gas pipe, and Nicholas, brandishing a saber. At a given signal, they would begin admitting the victims, beating them savagely as they moved into the chamber. The screams of the women, the weeping of the children, cries of despair and misery, the pleas for mercy, for God's vengeance ring in my ears to this day, making it impossible for me to forget the misery I saw.
>
> Between 450 and 500 persons were crowded into a chamber measuring 25 square meters. Parents carried their children in their arms in the vain hope that this would save their children from death. On the way to their doom, they were pushed and beaten with rifle butts and with Ivan's gas pipe. . . . The bedlam lasted only a short while, for soon the door were slammed shut. The chamber was filled, the motor turned on and connected with the inflow pipes and, within 25 minutes at the most, all lay stretched out dead or, to be more accurate, were standing up dead. Since there was not an inch of free space, they just leaned against each other.
>
> . . . Even in death, mothers held their children tightly in their arms. There were no more friends or foes. There was no more

jealousy. All were equal. There was no longer any beauty or ug-
liness, for they all were yellow from the gas.[2]

The place was Treblinka, and it was the most horrifying place on
earth. In the entire Third Reich, there were only four places designed
exclusively for death, all on the broad plains of Eastern Poland:
Chelmno, Sobibor, Belzec, and this place, the largest of the four.*
Treblinka was no more a concentration camp than the gas chambers
were baths. No people were concentrated here; there were no barracks, no latrines, no living quarters, except for those who operated
the camp. Everyone was sent here to be killed.

"It was Dante's Inferno," confessed Franz Stangl, Treblinka's
commandant, in 1971. "It was Dante come to life. The smell was
indescribable; the hundreds, no, the thousands of bodies everywhere,
decomposing, putrefying. All around the perimeter of the camp, there
were tents and open fires with groups of Ukrainian guards and girls—
whores, I found out later, from all over the countryside—weaving
drunk, dancing, singing, playing music. . . ."[3]

The Inferno operated from July 1942 until the fall of 1943, little
more than a year. Three hundred thousand Jews from the city of Warsaw alone were gassed here. Others came on the single track from
Germany, Austria, Czechoslovakia, Holland, Belgium, Greece, Bulgaria. How many in all? Seven hundred fifty thousand by a conservative estimate; nine hundred thousand by postwar German reckoning.[4]
But the most accurate figure may have come from a railway worker
in the yard outside the camp, a member of the Polish resistance who
counted the railway cars as they came in: "I stood there in that station day after day and counted the figures chalked on each carriage,"
he said later. "I have added them up over and over and over. The
number of people killed in Treblinka was 1,200,000 and there is no
doubt about it whatever."[5] In four hundred days.

October 1942 to January 1943 was the peak period. On some
mornings, twenty thousand Jews arrived; twenty thousand were dead
by noon. Afternoons were for burning the bodies. No furnaces here;

---

*The other killing centers were Auschwitz and Maidanek, each of which also housed large
numbers of forced laborers for German industry. Hundreds of other concentration camps, including Dachau, Theresienstadt, Gross-Rosen and Sachsenhausen, were built throughout the Reich.
Thousands of Jews, gypsies, Poles, and political prisoners died in these camps from starvation,
exposure, overwork, and brutality.

open pits were used. Night was to let the flames bank, to let the smoke waft into the pine forest, so that by daybreak the low haze over the pits could not be easily seen from the make-believe train station and the newly arriving transports containing more families for the fire.

The chances for survival were nil. At Auschwitz, the enormous complex of camps far to the south of Treblinka, a million Jews were murdered; perhaps 150,000, put to work as slaves to maintain the Nazi war machine, survived until liberation in 1945.[6] Of the million or more people who were sent to Treblinka, the number who left it alive was fewer than fifty.[7]

Treblinka was not only murder's main factory but its first research and development center. By 1942 the Nazis had concluded that the method of the Einsatzgruppen in the East—killing Jews by rifle fire—was far too primitive, too costly, too time-consuming. The Jews of Europe simply could not be killed one at a time; there were too many of them, and not enough bullets.

The Einsatzgruppen in the Ukraine had experimented with mobile killing vans in 1941: in pilot projects, Jews were loaded into the backs of closed trucks, a hose was connected from the exhaust pipe to a porthole in the side, and the trucks were driven until everyone inside was dead from carbon monoxide poisoning. But the vans were small— they held thirty or forty Jews, no matter how tightly packed—and running their engines for hours at a time consumed a lot of gasoline.

Yet the idea itself showed promise. If only it could be made more efficient, more cost-effective, it might be the answer, the solution to the Jewish question.

The Germans chose a desolate spot no more than fifty acres, some fifty miles east of Warsaw, as the site of the prototype. Construction began in 1941; it was completed by the spring of 1942. There were two sections: Camp I was the receiving area—the phony railroad station, the assembly area, the haircutting hall. From there, a ninety-meter path—dubbed Himmelweg ("The Road to Heaven")—led to Camp II, the gas chambers and the burning pits.

Camp II was camouflaged by tree branches woven into the high fence that divided it from Camp I. Thus it could not be seen until one actually entered it. The idea was not to panic the arriving victims too early. Panic was introduced at the haircutting area, as the men and women and children began the stampede down the Himmelweg. In this way, they would be out of breath from exertion and terror when they reached the gas, the quicker to inhale the lethal fumes.

As with any industrial enterprise, there was a certain period of trial and error before maximum efficiency could be achieved. In the beginning, it sometimes took three hours to kill everyone inside the chambers. That would not do. Different engines were moved in and out, various fuel mixes were tried. Consultants, engineers, designers all worked to solve the problem. Killing time was gradually reduced to ten to twenty-five minutes when all went well. If there was a malfunction in the process, the naked victims inside the gas chamber would scream for hours before the air was sucked out of their lungs.*

Disposal was a big problem. At first, the bodies were simply dumped into pits and covered with layers of sand or lime. After a few months, however, the Germans realized that there would simply not be enough earth to hold everyone, and so the bodies were dug up with a steam shovel and burned on the "grill"—a latticework of railroad tracks suspended over a pit.

One Jew put to work here remembered: "There were corpses all over the place, corpses by the tens, hundreds, and thousands. Corpses of men, women and children of all ages. . . . Heaven, earth and corpses!"[9] The burning went on night and day, summer and winter, creating a permanent haze over the land, even on the clearest days— "an almost sulphuric darkness," recalled the Polish railway worker, "bringing with it this pestilential smell."[10]

The work force at Treblinka was of three very distinct types. First were the SS, the Germans, no more than twenty at any given time, responsible for overseeing the entire process of slaughter. Many of them, including the commandant Stangl, had been drawn from the very successful euthanasia project that had put to death hundreds of thousands of Germany's "mental defectives" lest they be a burden to the master race.

Beneath the Germans were the Ukrainians, eighty of them, selected from the staggering numbers of prisoners captured by the Wehrmacht in its sweep across Russia. The Ukrainians were chosen for their brawn, their viciousness, their willingness to exchange the hard life of a POW for three meals a day in a death factory. The

---

*Rudolf Hess, later to be the commandant of Auschwitz, studied Treblinka's methods and decided that efficiency could be increased yet again by substituting fast-acting hydrogen cyanide gas for the diesel engines with their carbon monoxide fumes. Manufactured under the commercial name of Zyklon ("cyclone") B, cyanide gas was used to kill one million Jews at Auschwitz.[8]

Ukrainians were sent to Trawniki, a converted sugar factory commandeered by the SS to train death camp guards for Sobibor and Belzec and Treblinka, all nearby.

At Treblinka, some Ukrainians guarded the camp's perimeter, others rousted the Jews down the Himmelweg and to the doors of the gas chambers so that Ivan could drive them in, close the doors, turn on the engines.

Finally, far beneath the Germans and the Ukrainians, were the work-Jews: several hundred on any day, pulled at random from the arriving transports, to do the ghastly work that even the Ukrainians considered beneath them. Some work-Jews sorted the possessions at railside: good clothing, fountain pens, eyeglasses, tools and instruments, valuables, money—all to be sent back to Germany. The photographs and scrapbooks were burned.

Other work-Jews dragged the bodies out of the gas chambers and carried them at a run to the burning pits. Some were the barbers, cutting hair to be made into felt, others "dentists," who pulled the gold teeth from corpses with pliers. "Everything the Jews left behind had its value and its place," one survivor said later. "Only the Jews themselves were regarded as worthless." [11]

The work-Jews traded immediate death for a living hell, yet periodically they too were loaded into the gas chambers and replacements were selected from the day's arrivals.

In August 1943 the impossible happened at Treblinka. The Jews on the work crews staged an uprising. With crude weapons they had made or stolen, they overwhelmed the startled Ukrainians and SS, killed some of them, and made for the woods surrounding the camp. Some made it past the fence, but most of them were mowed down by gunfire before reaching the trees. Perhaps fifty made it to safety, plunged into the dark forest, and disappeared.

Treblinka was shut down soon afterward—its job was nearly completed anyway, since most of the Jews of Poland were dead, and Auschwitz with its Zyklon B canisters was fast making the carbon monoxide system obsolete for the other European Jews still alive. The Soviets were already pushing the Germans out of Russia. The SS razed Treblinka—gas chambers, barracks, railroad station, and all—and bulldozed everything into oblivion.

They installed a hapless Ukrainian farmer on the site and instructed him to tell the Russians when they arrived that he had been there since 1939 and had not noticed anything unusual. It was a poor ruse. The bones of a million men, women, and children could not be hidden for long. The eventual liquefaction of imperfectly burned bodies caused the earth to shift, and the gases released by putrefaction blew the topsoil off the burial pits. Whether the farmer stayed long in this haunted place, or what he told the Russians if he did, we will never know.

The human mind cannot comprehend the murder of a million people; it grapples with the horror by reducing it to recognizable terms. In 1970 two women, a British journalist and her Polish interpreter, traveled to the spot where Treblinka had been and walked through the bushes and pine trees planted there:

> It was a bitingly cold day—in spite of fur-lined boots my feet were soon freezing. After thirty minutes or so of walking around on our own Wanda and I came face to face among the trees. "The children," she burst out, with exactly the words which were dominant in my mind: "Oh my God, the children, naked, in this terrible cold." We stood for a long moment, silent, where they used to stand waiting for those ahead to be dead, waiting their turn.[12]

Of all the functionaries at Treblinka, few stood out in the minds of the surviving Jews as clearly as Ivan, the man who operated the gas chamber. They did not know his last name, of course, but they called him "Ivan Grozny"—Ivan the Terrible. He was stocky, with close-cropped blond hair and gray eyes. And he was brutally strong, capable of wielding a pipe six feet long as a club. The work-Jews, whose crude barracks were built next to the gas chamber, quickly learned one rule: one did not look into the eyes of Ivan. The price of that was a swift blow of the iron pipe and a shattered skull.

One man who escaped in the uprising of August 1943 made his way back to Warsaw, where he hid in a cellar until the Red Army marched into that destroyed city in January 1945. As he hid, Chiel Rajchman wrote down the story of Treblinka, and he remembered Ivan.

> On a hot day the Ukrainian helpers feel very good. They work with their whips from right to left, in all directions. Nikolai and Ivan, who work as machinists at the motor from which the gas

goes into the chambers, which also serves the generator that lights Treblinka, they feel very good and happy on such a hot day.

Ivan is about 25 years old, looks like a strong, big boss. He is pleased when he has an opportunity to expend on the workers his energies. From time to time he gets an urge to take a sharp knife, stop a worker who is running by, and cut off his ear. The blood spurts out, the worker screams, but he has to keep running with the carrier [a stretcher-like device to carry corpses]. Ivan waits patiently until the worker runs back. He tells him to put the carrier down, tells him to get undressed, to go over to the pit where he shoots him.

Ivan came over to the well once with a tool with which to bore holes in wood where I and another dentist named Finkelstein were washing the teeth [extracted from the corpses, to remove the blood and tissue from the gold crowns]. He told Finkelstein to lie down on the ground and he drilled the metal into his [anus]. This was just a joke. The unfortunate man didn't even scream out loud. He only groaned. Ivan laughed and kept yelling, "Lie still or else I will shoot you." [13]

But neither Chiel Rajchman nor anyone else knew what happened to Ivan the Terrible after Treblinka. The Treblinka Ukrainians went to various menial posts in Germany in the closing months of the war— they guarded warehouses or rail lines in the shrinking Reich—and when the war finally ended, they foundered there, like so many others from so many different places.*

Today, we know what happened to Ivan. He came to America as a displaced person in 1952 and went to Cleveland, Ohio, where he resumed his livelihood as a motor mechanic, this time for the Ford Motor Company. He and his wife, whom he married in a DP camp, raised three children in Cleveland, and became American citizens in

---

*There were two Treblinka trials in West Germany. In the first, in 1964, several German SS staff were convicted and sentenced. In 1967 Franz Stangl, the commandant, was located in Brazil and returned to Germany, where he was convicted in 1971 and sentenced to life imprisonment for his crimes. He died of a heart attack soon afterward, but not before giving a series of interviews to journalist Gitta Sereny, which she recounts in her remarkable book *Into That Darkness*.

The judgment of the German court in the Stangl trial described the operation of the gas chambers: "When it was no longer possible to squeeze additional people into the chambers, the doors were sealed and the German squad leader ordered the Ukrainian in the engine room (he might say, "Ivan, water!") to switch on the engine, whose exhaust fumes were then conducted into the chambers." [14]

1958, when he changed his name from Ivan to John. He saved his money and bought a nice ranch house on a pleasant street called Meadow Lane in the Cleveland suburb of Seven Hills. He cultivated a large garden in the back yard.

He lives there today, still strong and fit at sixty-four. He is active in the affairs of St. Vladimir's Church in Parma, which serves Cleveland's large Ukrainian Orthodox community. He is well liked by all who know him—in the neighborhood, in the church, at the plant—none of whom knew, until recently, what he had done in the war.

But the placid life of John Demjanjuk in the United States is over, very likely forever. On February 10, 1981, he went on trial before the chief judge of the federal court in Cleveland on charges that he was the same Ivan who had run the gas chamber at Treblinka thirty-nine years before, and that he had lied when he told DP officials that he had been a Ukrainian farmer during the war. On June 23, 1981, the court rendered its verdict: John Demjanjuk of Cleveland is Ivan of Treblinka.

For John Demjanjuk (pronounced "dem/yan/yook"), the lie started to unravel in 1975, although he did not know it then. Wasyl Yachenko (his name is changed here to protect his privacy), a Ukrainian living in America, sent a list of names to the Immigration and Naturalization Service. Yachenko's list was longer than Dr. Karbach's: seventy-three names of Ukrainians who had allegedly taken part in Nazi persecution, all reportedly living in the United States. Some names on Yachenko's list had American addresses, others had none.

An investigator working with Sam Zutty on INS's Nazi project interviewed Yachenko. Yachenko told him he had traveled to the Ukraine in 1974 and had gathered about half the names from documents in Soviet archives, the other half from Ukrainian newspaper editors or witnesses. Yachenko had no independent knowledge of whether the allegations were true, and he knew of no witnesses in the United States who might know.* [15]

---

*Unlike the great majority of Ukrainian-Americans, Yachenko is not a staunch anti-Communist, and some who know him consider him a Soviet sympathizer. Soviet archives on World War II are generally closed to outsiders, and if Yachenko had access to them, he was granted a highly prized privilege unavailable to most Western journalists and historians. Some Ukrainian-Americans believe, therefore, that Yachenko's list is part of a Soviet campaign to target

Yachenko's list, with its brief statement of the allegations against Demjanjuk, did not mention Treblinka. According to Yachenko's information, Demjanjuk had been a guard at Sobibor, a hundred miles south of Treblinka. Sobibor and Treblinka had much in common. They were both death camps operated by the SS in eastern Poland, under SS General Odilo Globocnik, to kill the Jews of Europe, Poland first. They were both manned by a small SS force and Ukrainian guards trained at Trawniki. Franz Stangl had been the commandant at Sobibor before being given command at Treblinka.

But Sobibor was not Treblinka, and when INS opened a file on Demjanjuk in the New York "project control office," it placed him at Sobibor.

In 1977 INS investigators prepared a photospread for Israeli police to show Treblinka survivors in the case of Feodor Fedorenko, a former Treblinka guard living in Waterbury, Connecticut. Along with Fedorenko's photograph, they needed others to include in the spread, and they stuck Demjanjuk's photo, from his 1951 visa application, in the folder.

Photospreads—an array of wallet-sized black-and-white photographs, with no identifying information, usually fastened into a manila folder—were important in the investigation of Nazi criminals. Under American law, a witness cannot normally be shown a photograph of a single suspect and be asked, Is this the man who committed the crime? The Supreme Court has held that such a procedure is suggestive; it subtly encourages the witness to identify the person in

---

Ukrainian-Americans for smear charges of Nazi collaboration, and that the Office of Special Investigations is a witting or unwitting dupe of the Soviets.

This belief is simply erroneous, and it overlooks several important facts. No case is brought based on the charges of a single source, particularly when the source has no independent knowledge of whether the charges are true. Yachenko has never been a witness (or, for that matter, a consultant or assistant) in any case; I've never even met the man. His list has never been introduced into evidence, because it is not evidence. As this chapter shows, the case against Demjanjuk was based on documents and witnesses that Yachenko had no part in obtaining.

Of the seventy-three names on Yachenko's list, seven persons, including Demjanjuk, have been formally charged. Two of them admitted the facts to be true and their citizenship was revoked by a federal court; Demjanjuk contested the facts but was found to be lying. Two others committed suicide shortly after charges were filed. The cases against the other two are in progress.

In short, in Demjanjuk's case as in every other case, the original source of the allegation is almost irrelevant. If proof can be assembled from documents and eyewitnesses, the case is filed and tried; otherwise it is not. The reliability of the original informant plays no part in this process, unless he happens also to be an eyewitness.

the photo as the suspect. A suspect's photo must appear as part of a "non-suggestive" spread of photographs: no bigger, brighter, or more prominent than the others. No names.* And the photospread must be presented to the prospective witness objectively, with no hint from the investigator calling attention to the photo of the true suspect. So a spread of eight photos—Fedorenko and seven other male Ukrainians of similar age, including Demjanjuk—was assembled and sent to the Israeli police.

In Israel, an investigator from the Nazi War Crimes Unit of the Israeli National Police took the Fedorenko photospread to the office of Elijahu Rosenberg, a warehouse manager who had escaped from Treblinka in the 1943 uprising. The investigator showed the photospread to Rosenberg, asking him if he "recognized anybody" in the folder.

Rosenberg looked at the spread carefully. He identified Fedorenko, although he did not know his name. Then he pointed to Demjanjuk. That man, he said, was Ivan, and he was at Treblinka too.

No, said the investigator, from what we know this man was not at Treblinka. Rosenberg looked at the investigator, then at the photo again. "I'm identifying him," he insisted. "He was at Treblinka." But, he told the investigator, "The picture is not precisely the way I saw him in Treblinka; it seems to me this photograph is—more mature."

Rosenberg was right. The photo he had seen was taken in 1951, eight years after he and Ivan had been at Treblinka. Rosenberg recalled the event later: "In my heart, I saw his appearance, the build of his head, and inside of me I was certain that that was [Ivan]."

Another Treblinka survivor, Pinchas Epstein, was summoned to police headquarters. The spread of eight photos was laid in front of him. Did he recognize anyone from Treblinka?

---

*In OSI, we took this procedure very seriously. If the suspect in the photo, for example, was a young Latvian with blond wavy hair, our photospreads usually contained eight pictures of young Latvians with blond wavy hair.

In one case, our investigators prepared such a spread and submitted it to me for approval of its "non-suggestivity" before they showed it to potential witnesses. The photos were remarkably alike. I sent it back—reluctantly approved—with my comment that "[The suspect's] mother would have a hard time picking him out of this spread." The witnesses who later saw it, however, identified the man. Every OSI photospread has been upheld by the courts as being wholly non-suggestive.

Slowly, carefully, Epstein looked at each photo. His eyes returned to the second to last in the folder. He studied it. Then he raised his eyes. "The person shown here"—he pointed to Demjanjuk—"reminds me a lot of Ivan. The picture is not completely in focus." He studied it again. "The age differential must also be taken into account [no one had told Epstein the date of the photo]. The general shape of the face," he went on, "especially the curvature of the forehead, strengthen[s] my opinion that it is Ivan." Epstein traced his finger on the picture. "The short neck is characteristic, on the broad shoulders. Exactly what Ivan looked like."

A third survivor, Chaim Rajgrodski, came to the headquarters. Like Epstein, he was not told that others had looked at the photos. Rajgrodski had no doubt. He pointed to Demjanjuk. "That is Ivan who was in camp 2 at Treblinka," he said.[16]

The news was cabled back to Washington. Yes, Fedorenko had been identified. But this other man was also at Treblinka, and his name was Ivan.

In Washington, nothing happened. INS wanted Fedorenko; it was not ready to go to trial against Demjanjuk, and the case languished.

In the summer of 1979 the newly assembled attorneys of the Office of Special Investigations went through the boxes of files we had inherited from INS, one by one, to see which cases showed promise of a successful prosecution. Norman Moscowitz was assigned the Demjanjuk case. The three photo identifications by the survivors in Israel were helpful, but more evidence was needed.

Moscowitz knew that there were no documents known to exist anywhere in the world from Treblinka; the Germans had destroyed them all when they razed the camp after the 1943 uprising. But what about Trawniki—the training facility for the guards of the death camps? Trawniki had been near Lublin, Poland, and Lublin had been captured by the Red Army in 1944. Anything linking Demjanjuk to Trawniki would strengthen the case that he had moved on to Treblinka.

Moscowitz sent a cable to our embassy in Moscow. Did the Soviets have records of Trawniki? Did any mention a man named Ivan Demjanjuk?

In January 1980 an envelope arrived at OSI from the embassy. The Soviet archives had sent the embassy one document in response to our request. Inside the envelope was a photocopy of an identification card issued by the SS authorities at Trawniki. It bore a clear photograph of a serious young man with close-cropped hair. The card had a wealth of information on it, seemingly mundane but the stuff of which prosecutors build cases. The man in the photo was born on April 3, 1920, in "Duboimachariwzi" in the Ukraine. "Face: oval; hair: dark blond; eyes: gray. Scars: on his back." His father's name was Nikolai. And the name on the card was Ivan Demjanjuk (see pages 346–47).

We compared the card to the 1951 visa photograph of John Demjanjuk of Seven Hills, Ohio. The resemblance was striking, considering the difference of nine years between photographs. Demjanjuk was born April 3, 1920. His father's name was Nikolai. And he had a scar on his back.

I looked at the card, over and over. There was no doubt that the two photos were of the same man. The man in Cleveland had been trained at Trawniki in 1942. And we had eyewitnesses who would place him at Treblinka. I put the two photos side by side and studied them for a long time. You son of a bitch, I thought. We've got you.

A prosecutor's gut is a long way from an airtight case, and we had a lot of work to do before we could go to trial. The authenticity of the Trawniki ID card would have to be established beyond question—by scientific analysis of the original (if we could get it from the Soviets), by testimony of expert witnesses, by those who had issued such cards at Trawniki, if they could be found.

We would have to make up a new photospread to include this picture, and show it to survivors of Treblinka. We had to learn all we could about that appalling place—and what Ivan had done there—to present an accurate, cohesive picture to the judge who would decide the case.

The case would be handled by Moscowitz and by John Horrigan, a federal prosecutor in Cleveland, under my supervision and that of my deputy, Neal Sher. Moscowitz and Horrigan made a good pair. Moscowitz, an intense young attorney with a quick sense of humor, was a Harvard Law School graduate who had come to OSI with a background in federal labor relations litigation. (I never looked for "Nazi hunters" in hiring lawyers. I wanted smart, hard-working trial lawyers, regardless of their specific background. A good litigator can litigate anything.) Jack Horrigan was a prosecutor with broad criminal experience. Only rarely in OSI did we delegate responsibility to federal prosecutors outside the office. But Horrigan, like Moscowitz, was good, and he worked long hours.

Over the following year the case against John Demjanjuk took shape, as all OSI cases did, a piece at a time. Treblinka survivors— the original three augmented by others—identified the 1942 Trawniki photo as Ivan from the gas chambers. Former staff men from Trawniki were located and interviewed in Germany. A professor from Berlin who had been an adviser to the German court in the Stangl trial worked with us to prepare an overall picture of how Treblinka operated and how it fit into the Nazis' plan to annihilate the Jews of Europe.

We took the pretrial testimony of Demjanjuk himself. To our surprise, he admitted that he had lied on his immigration papers. He had not been a farmer after all, he conceded. He claimed now to have been captured by the Germans in the Crimea in 1942 and to have spent the entire war in various German POW camps. He had made up the farmer story in order to avoid repatriation from the DP camp to the USSR; he feared that anyone careless enough to have been captured by the Germans would be shot by the Russians upon return after the war.

He denied that he had ever been at Trawniki, Treblinka, or any other death camp, but he had shown a side of himself we could use to full advantage. He admitted that he had perjured himself once to come to America. Could a judge believe that, with his POW story, he was not now perjuring himself to stay here?

Throughout our preparation, we were alert, as we were in every case, to the possibility that something, anything—a POW record, a discrepancy in photo identification, a fact that jarred—might arise and cast doubt on our case, to cause us to wonder, in the privacy of our offices late at night when everyone else had gone home, if we had the right man. But it didn't happen. The more we found out, the stronger the case became. And when we investigated Demjanjuk's POW alibi, we knew we had nailed him. Demjanjuk was lying again, and we could prove it in court.

The trial began on February 10, 1981, a cold, raw day in Cleveland. Two days before, 450 Ukrainians had attended a rally at St. Vladimir's Church, denouncing the use of "Soviet evidence"—the Trawniki ID card—and dropping cash and checks for Demjanjuk's defense fund into a cardboard box.[17] The protests continued on the morning of the trial, as a knot of Demjanjuk's supporters gathered in Cleveland's Public Square to burn a Soviet flag and to picket the courthouse with anti-Soviet signs. Inside the courthouse, twenty federal marshals stood guard against incidents and screened the audience as it wended single file into the courtroom.

To accommodate the crowds, Chief Judge Frank Battisti reserved the ceremonial courtroom, a spacious chamber whose high ceilings, intricately carved and painted in deep greens and golds, imparted a cathedral-like solemnity to the audience and participants. Ukrainians and Jews filled the rows of pews—Ukrainians on one side, Jews on the other.*

About midway through the trial, during a recess, I stood making small talk with a marshal, and we admired the dignity and beauty of the woodwork, the friezes, the expanse of the ceiling high above. "Yeah, it's a beautiful place," the marshal said. "Whenever the judges are going to swear in new citizens, they hold the ceremonies here. Sort of impresses on them what citizenship is all about, you know?"

In front of, and beneath, Judge Battisti's massive mahogany bench, Norman Moscowitz and Jack Horrigan sat at the prosecution's table, whispering occasionally to Nancy Kramp, an OSI paralegal assistant responsible for keeping the boxes of documents in the evidence file organized. A few feet away, on Judge Battisti's right, Demjanjuk sat impassively, dressed in a neat blue three-piece suit, with his two lawyers, John Martin and Spiros Gonakis. (On the first day, several observers mistook Demjanjuk for one of the lawyers and scanned the courtroom, looking for the defendant.) Behind him, in the front row of the spectators' pews, sat his family: his wife, Vera, their two grown daughters, and an adolescent son. Reporters and sketch artists took over the empty jury box; camera crews waited on the courthouse steps to film the comings and goings of the witnesses for the evening news.

Moscowitz called Professor Earl Ziemke of the University of Georgia as the first prosecution witness. A leading authority on the military campaign between the Nazis and the Soviets, Ziemke briefly

---

*Despite the latent hostility and suspicion on both sides, the trial was held without incident, due largely to the leaders on both sides who urged their communities to observe but not to disrupt the solemn atmosphere. One Ukrainian spokesman charged that the trial was a Soviet effort to create enmity between Ukrainians and Jews—"the two most formidable forces that can stand up to the regime there."

described the invasion of the Soviet Union in June 1941, and the capture by the Germans of large numbers of unprepared and ill-equipped Soviet soldiers. Here, as in all our trials, our plan was to assume that the judge knew nothing of history. One could not understand the workings of Treblinka without knowing about Trawniki, and to understand Trawniki one had to know about the Soviet POWs who were recruited to be trained there. So we started at the beginning. Professor Ziemke was on the stand only a short time, but he was to return later.

The star witness of the first day was Professor Wolfgang Scheffler, one of Europe's best-known scholars on "Aktion [Operation] Reinhard"—the Nazi plan to kill the Jews of Poland, named for SS leader Reinhard Heydrich.

Scheffler, a Berliner whose thick black-framed glasses and carefully chosen words gave him an owl-like demeanor on the stand, described the preparation and execution of the plan—how the Jews who were not shot outright were forced into ghettos, later to be deported to the killing centers of Treblinka, Sobibor, and Belzec. The killing centers were staffed by euthanasia experts from Germany and Trawniki-trained Ukrainian recruits: strong, healthy volunteers.

Scheffler traced the chain of command from Himmler, the Reichsführer of the entire SS, to SS General Globocnik, the head of Aktion Reinhard, to Franz Stangl, the commandant of Treblinka. He recounted the staggering success of the Nazis in achieving their goal—900,000 Jews killed at Treblinka in chambers poisoned by motor exhaust fumes.

Moscowitz handed Scheffler the photocopy of the Trawniki ID card. Yes, Scheffler said, it gave every appearance of being genuine. And it was signed by Kurt Streibel, the commandant of Trawniki. "On the basis of other documents, particularly his personal files, I know that this is the signature of Streibel," Scheffler said.[18]

Once Scheffler had shown where Treblinka fit into history, and had authenticated the ID card from the Trawniki training school for death camp guards, we were ready to move into the second phase of our case—Treblinka from the eyes of those who had been there.

We began with a most unusual witness. His name was Otto Horn, and he was a seventy-six-year-old retired German nurse who had been assigned to the Treblinka staff in October 1942, three months after it had begun operations. Of the twelve former Treblinka staff members tried in Düsseldorf in 1964, Horn was the only one to have been acquitted of participation in crimes against humanity. Speaking through an interpreter, occasionally toying with his glasses, Horn answered Moscowitz's questions clearly and concisely, without emotion.* He provided the courtroom in Cleveland a detached, clinical view of Treblinka, and of Ivan:

"Mr. Horn, what kind of a place was Treblinka?"

"It was an extermination camp. People were exterminated there, were gassed."

"[On] the first day of your arrival, were you met by anybody?"

"Yes. The Deputy Commander of the camp [Kurt Franz]. He showed us around—I mean the outside of the camp—fast."

"What happened then?"

"And then within the camp, we were divided up and I came into the upper camp."

"Was that where you were assigned to duty?"

"Yes."

"Was there another part of the camp as well?"

"Yes, the lower one."

"What took place there?"

"That was the unloading and undressing. Jews mainly."

"Where did these Jews come from?"

"One doesn't know. One didn't know what area they came from."

"What was located in the upper camp?"

"The people were gassed there and then burned."

"By what means were they gassed?"

"I don't know. There was an engine somehow."

"Were these people all men?"

"No. No. Just anything—men and women."

"Were there children as well?"

"Yes."

---

*Horn, who lives in Germany, could not be subpoenaed to appear in the United States and so his testimony was videotaped in Germany prior to trial. Demjanjuk's attorneys traveled to Germany at government expense and cross-examined him. The videotape was played back in the courtroom for Judge Battisti and the spectators.

Here, as elsewhere in this chapter, testimony has been compressed where necessary to eliminate repetition, objections, and discussions between the attorneys. In no case have the words of the witnesses been altered in any way. Clarifying material has been added in brackets.

"Were there other Germans, aside from you, stationed in the upper camp?"

"Yes, there were some. Perhaps eight."

"Aside from the Germans stationed in the upper camp, was anyone else stationed there?"

"Yes, there were Ukrainians there."

"Generally, what were the duties of these Ukrainians?"

"They were guards on the towers, and when transporting the corpses away."

"Was there anyone else present or stationed in the upper camp?"

"Yes—200 approximately, who had to work there. Mainly Jews."

"What were the duties of these Jewish people who lived in the upper camp?"

"Transporting away the corpses from the gas chamber and burning them."

"And to where would they bring the corpses?"

"To the pit, and then burned right away."

"Was there anyone in charge of the gas chamber?"

"Yes, Mathes and Schmidt. Mathes, as the commandant [of the upper camp], and Schmidt was with the gas chambers always; operating the engines, Schmidt was."

"Did anyone assist Schmidt at the gas chamber?"

"Yes. There were always two Ukrainians there. They were always the same."

"Do you recall the names of these two Ukrainians?"

"One was called Ivan. The other I don't know."

"Would you describe the physical appearance of this Ivan?"

"He was tall and mighty. Staunch, corpulent."

"What did his face look like?"

"It was round, full."

"Was he armed?"

"With a pistol, yes."

"Why is it you remember Ivan?"

"He was always there. He was Schmidt's right hand man. He was always present there when a transport [of Jews] came. He was on good terms with this Mathes and Schmidt."

"Was that unusual, for the Ukrainians to be on good terms with them?"

"Yes, yes."

"Do you recall seeing him at the gas chamber?"

"Yes. The anteroom to the gas chamber. The entrance. Inside."

"You were able to see him inside the gas chamber?"

"Yes."

"What was he doing there at that time?"

"He directed the prisoners, or he co-directed the prisoners, into the cells, into the chambers."

"Did there come a time when you saw him at any other part of the gas chambers?"

"At the place where the engines were. They were inside. Everything was built in[side]. I didn't go in there. I only saw him going in."

"Was Schmidt with him at the time that he would go into that entrance?"

"Yes. They were always in there. They were always there. They were always there."

"And what if anything did they do in the engine room?"

"They certainly turned on the engines and gassed the people."

"How long would the process of gassing last?"

"Perhaps an hour. Then after one hour only, the chambers were opened. And then the corpses were carried away into the pit and partly for burning."

Moscowitz put a folder of eight pictures before Otto Horn. Horn looked them over, pointing to one. "This looks like Ivan." The folder was taken away, a second one placed on the table. Horn studied it, then pointed again. "As far as I recall," he said, "Ivan looked like this."

The first photograph Horn had picked out was from John Demjanjuk's 1951 visa to America. The second was the serious-looking young man from the Trawniki ID card.

As the spectators watched Otto Horn testify on the cameras placed throughout the packed courtroom, two pickets walked slowly back and forth in the chilly Cleveland air outside the courthouse. One identified himself as the Imperial Wizard of the Ku Klux Klan in Ohio. He carried an American flag and a crudely lettered sign. "Jews Killed Christ," it read. "I've worked next to John Demjanjuk for twelve years at the Ford plant," he told a reporter. "He's a kindhearted person and well-liked at the plant."

The other man was from Toronto. His sign read, "Communism is Jewish." "There were no gas chambers," he told anyone who would listen. "The entire thing was a fabrication." [19]

On February 18, the sixth day of trial, we were ready to move into the next stage of the case against John Demjanjuk: the testimony of survivors of Treblinka. There were five: four men and a woman. They had come to Cleveland from their homes in Israel, Germany, and Uruguay. Each of them had been "work-Jews" at Treblinka, plucked by fate from the arriving trainloads, still alive on August 2, 1943, when the breakout took place. And each, prior to the trial, had identified Demjanjuk's photographs from the spreads we had shown them.*

Chiel Rajchman, the man who had written his memoirs of Treblinka while hiding in the Warsaw bunker in 1944, was the first. A sixty-six-year-old textile merchant from Lodz, Poland, he had resettled in Montevideo, Uruguay, in 1948. He gave his testimony in Yiddish, through an interpreter.

Rajchman was tall, white-haired, distinguished-looking, and well-dressed. But his eyes, fixed on the floor in front of him, betrayed his anguish as he testified. His voice often dropped to little more than a whisper, yet the courtroom, still packed, became shrouded in utter silence, and his whispers carried to the farthest pews.

Under gentle but thorough questioning by Jack Horrigan, Rajchman described how, on September 9, 1939, eight days after the Germans invaded Poland, they came to the city of Lodz and "Lodz became a hell." Rajchman and his family were sent to Warsaw, forced into the overcrowded ghetto the Germans had created there, and later sent to another ghetto in a little town called Ostrowlubelski. In Ostrowlubelski, the Germans and their Ukrainian helpers rounded up all the Jews and herded them to a train station.

Chiel Rajchman gave his testimony:

---

*We had interviewed an additional twelve survivors of Treblinka who had not been able to identify "Ivan" from the photographs they were shown. Many of these survivors had worked in the lower portion of the camp (also known as "Camp 1")—the receiving and undressing area—and would not have had much, or any, opportunity to see Ivan, who worked in the closely guarded upper camp ("Camp 2") where the gas chambers were. Others simply could not remember "Ivan" after nearly forty years, or were unwilling to commit themselves to an identification.

•   The names and addresses of all twelve were supplied to Demjanjuk's attorney well before trial. He did not call any of them to testify in Cleveland.

"What kind of train was it, sir?"

"A cattle car. My sister was with me. We were packed in there full. Men and women had to perform their bodily excretions on the place where they were. We did not have anything to drink.

"We established contact with the Ukrainians who came in from time to time with us and they greeted us with blows and with hitting. They sold us a little water from time to time if we gave them a watch or other things. A lot of them took away the watch and didn't even bring any water.

"The train began to move and it drove throughout the whole night and very early in the morning it stopped on a station. When the train stopped, we saw 'Treblinka' written.

"We assumed that we were riding to Russia and that the trip would take a few days. My hungry sister, I told her, 'We still have to travel a few days,' and she did not eat the food [she had brought from the ghetto].

"When they opened up the doors, they said, 'Get out, dogs,' and they gave an order, the men to go to the right, the women and children to the left.

"When we got out, the last minute I parted with my sister. This was the last time I saw my sister."

"Now, after the men and women were separated, where did you go?"

"They immediately gave us an order to get undressed; we should tie our shoes together in pairs; whoever has any valuables should hand them over, and everybody was beaten.

"I heard a German scream, 'Who's a barber?' I saw four naked men and I ran over. I was the fifth one. I was also naked. He asked me if I was a barber and I said yes. The five of us he took, no more.

"They led us over to a barracks where there were all the clothes that had been lying on the ground, and the German said to the one who was working [there] that this group is supposed to work as barbers, but when there would be no work as a barber, we would help in sorting the clothes.

"The work of sorting the clothes consisted of to separate pants, shirts, coats, gold, glasses, everything separately. If we found anything hard inside, we opened it up and we threw it out.

"That night, there were several people, everyone who had lost everyone in his family. We said Kaddish, a memorial prayer for the dead, and we cried; and we laid down on the earth and we slept."

"Mr. Rajchman, did you ever have any indication as to what happened to your sister?"

"On the second day I worked again sorting the clothes and, among the bundles, I found my sister's dress.

"I tore off a piece of the dress and kept it with me the whole time I was in Treblinka.

"On the second day, as we were working at sorting, a German came, and he screamed, 'Barbers step forward.' He took us to a place. There were benches lined up and we began to hear the screams and yells.

"The naked women started coming in. They told the women to sit down, and they gave us an order that, with five cuts, we had to cut off the hair of the women.

"A woman came in, grabbed my hand and asked me: 'Tell me, will the young children be left alive? Because I know that I'm going to my death. I want to go to my death in the belief that my son will take revenge for me.'

"A young girl came in and she heard the screams and the yells and she started to scream: 'Why are you screaming; why are you crying? Your enemies are satisfied. Let us laugh.' And she began to laugh hysterically."

"Mr. Rajchman, how long did you remain in the area of camp 1?"

"Three days."

"From there, where did you go?"

"One day when I was working, I heard a German yell, 'Come with me!' He took us to Camp 2 [the fenced and camouflaged area that held the gas chambers and burial pits].

"The reception in Camp 2 was blows across the head, all over the body. Two of us had to grab a carrier. We had to put sand in it, we had to run with the sand in the direction where a big pit was dug up; and there we had to spill out the sand, to turn over the carrier and spill it out.

"In that pit was laid out the gassed people, a layer of people one next to the other, so that more could get in; and on this layer we had to pour sand.

"Next time I had to carry a sort of stretcher, and on this stretcher we carried the gassed people who were thrown out of the gas chambers. We took them to the pits and we threw them in. At the bottom there were people who had to lay them out one next to the other.

"I was not experienced in this work, so when I carried the first corpse, the head of the dead person got stuck between the boards of the carrier and when I turned it over it couldn't fall off because the head got stuck; and until we pulled out the head, we got beaten terribly [by] Germans and Ukrainians.''

"Did there come a time while you were at Camp 2 that you became a 'dentist?' ''

"Yes. About a month after I arrived at Treblinka, I asked a dentist whether he could not give me poison because there in Treblinka many times people hung themselves with their belts. I couldn't do it. He said, 'Wait a little. Have patience.' He [took] me into his group. There were 19 [dentists]; I was the twentieth.''

"What was the work of the dentist at Treblinka?''

"As the carriers were carrying the corpses, we had to tear open the [corpses'] mouths with pliers and when we saw any dental work we had to pull out the teeth and drop them into a bowl.''

Horrigan paused, reviewing his notes at the lectern, facing the judge and the witness. On the stand, Rajchman did not move, his eyes still downcast, waiting. The stillness of the courtroom was absolute until someone in the audience sobbed, then someone on the other side, then two or three in the rear. An elderly woman, covering her face with a handkerchief, made her way across the floor and pushed open the leather-covered swinging door to the hallway. A man followed her out, and as the door swung back, one could for an instant see them in the hallway, embracing, each head buried in the other's shoulder.

As in a symphony hall at the end of the first movement, a low murmur rippled through the audience as purses were opened, throats were cleared, noses were blown. Horrigan began to ask his next question, but Judge Battisti raised his hand slightly to still him. When the audience grew quiet again, Judge Battisti nodded almost imperceptibly, and Horrigan resumed.

"Would you describe Camp 2, please, at Treblinka?''

"Yes. Treblinka was isolated. There were two gas chambers there. One gas chamber had three gas [sub]chambers. Near the gas chamber there was a sort of garage and in there there were two machines [engines]. One machine was to send the gas into the gas chamber and the second was to light the gas.*

---

*This may be a slight mistranslation of Rajchman's words, as the gas used to kill the victims was not ignited. The engines at the gas chamber did, however, generate electric power for the camp, and Rajchman may have meant "light the electricity.''

"The second gas chamber consisted of ten gas [sub]chambers. There were five at one side and there were five on the other side. These were bigger [sub]chambers and it took more time there until the people were dead."

"Do you remember the names of any Ukrainians in Camp 2?"

"I remember them. I remember them well."

"What were their names?"

"The biggest devil, who engraved himself in my memory, about whom I wrote 30 years ago, was called Ivan. His assistant was called Nikolai."

"This Ivan and Nikolai, in what area of the camp did they work?"

"They had the privilege to send gas into the gas chambers."

"Did you see them in any other parts of the camp besides the gas chambers?"

"Often. Near the small gas chambers there was a well. We dentists, when the transport finished, we went there to wash the teeth so that we should wash away the blood."

Rajchman, briefly consulting the notes he had made while hiding in the Warsaw cellar after his escape, recalled that Ivan's "greatest pleasure" was cutting off his victims' ears. And he recounted the grisly episode when Ivan had drilled an auger into a prisoner's anus. But Ivan's scimitar had been the pipe:

"I remember one time of Ivan when I stood and was doing my work as a dentist, he came over with a wagon with a horse with food for us. At the very moment when he was coming with the wagon, we heard the screams as they were driving the people into the gas chambers. [Ivan] left the horse, he ran, he grabbed his pipe, a long pipe, and he ran to the schlau to have the privilege of beating the ones who were going to their death."

"What was the schlau?"

"The schlau was a path over which all the victims were chased to the gas chambers. The schlau was beautified, and after each transport fresh sand was poured on it so that the blood should not be seen."

Horrigan then handed Rajchman a set of photographs that Rajchman had first seen a year earlier when he had identified the 1951 visa

· photo as being that of Ivan. In the courtroom, Rajchman looked at the photographs again and pointed to the photo of Demjanjuk.*

> "This is the man you identified as Ivan?"
> "Yes."
> "Mr. Rajchman, how long did you remain at Treblinka?"
> "Eleven months."
> "And you escaped [in the August 1943 uprising], is that correct?"
> "Yes."
> "Thank you. Your Honor, I have no further questions at this time."
> "I still have a request."
> Judge Battisti: "Let him make his request."
> "I always begged God that I should have the privilege to tell the world how they annihilated us; and to you, the authorities of America, the American people, I want to thank you."

Rajchman still had to face cross-examination by John Martin, Demjanjuk's attorney. But Martin's questioning simply strengthened Rajchman's testimony. He began with a long line of questions evidently designed to suggest that when Rajchman had been shown the photospread in Uruguay a year earlier, American officials had told him that they needed his testimony for a case against "Ivan." Rajchman put an end to that theory when he testified that he did not know what the case was about, or who the defendant was, until months after he had seen the photospread.

Stung, Martin pushed into a new area:

> "When you arrived [at Treblinka] in October of 1942, was this person by the name of Ivan at Camp 2 at that time?"
> "I didn't know whether he was there because I didn't know anybody there."
> "When you were transferred to Camp 2 about three days after arriving at Treblinka, did you observe this fellow you call Ivan?"
> "No. I was blinded then."

Martin paused, evidently taken aback by this characterization.

---

*We never asked witnesses to point out the subject in the courtroom. The change in one's appearance over forty years makes such identifications (or failures to identify) of little value.

"When you say 'blinded,' did you have some problems with your eyes?"

"No. Only that they murdered us."

"When you say you were blinded, would you explain that, please?"

"Yes. No person cannot imagine [*sic*] what Treblinka was. It's possible that a normal person can see with his eyes. These bandits came over to a mother when she was naked and had her naked child, and one of them tore the child out by its legs and killed it by smashing it in the wall.

Rajchman looked at Martin. "Can you be blind?" he said.

Martin immediately changed the subject, asking Rajchman to describe the "Ivan" he knew at Treblinka.

"Can you tell us how tall he was?"

"Taller than [you]."

"And about how much did he weigh?"

"I never weighed him."

It was one of the very few times in the long trial that laughter rippled through the courtroom. Rajchman, not intending to make a joke, did not smile. Nor did Demjanjuk.

"How can I know what he weighed? I know that he was strong like a horse; he carried a long pipe and he split people's heads with it, that I know."

Martin then made a serious blunder. As he knew, Rajchman had been shown two photospreads prior to trial: one containing Demjanjuk's 1951 visa photo, the other containing the 1942 Trawniki ID photo. Rajchman had picked out Demjanjuk from the first spread—the identification he had repeated in the courtroom earlier in the day—but he had not been certain enough of the photos in the second spread to make any identification. We had routinely informed Martin and the judge of this before the trial began.

Rather than leave well enough alone and point out to the judge in his final argument that Rajchman had been unable to pick out the 1942 photo, Martin now apparently wanted to see Rajchman fail again. He placed the second photospread in Rajchman's hands. In full view of the judge, Rajchman studied the photospread. He jabbed his finger and began to speak to his interpreter.

Judge Battisti interrupted: "In those photographs you have before you now, can you indicate whether there is a photograph of the man [you] refer to as Ivan?"

"Yes," said Rajchman.

We were surprised. Martin must have been appalled.

"Select it," said the judge.

Rajchman put his finger firmly on the photograph of Ivan Demjanjuk.

Martin was in trouble. His effort to contain Rajchman's testimony, to cast doubt on the identification of Ivan, had blown up in his face.

Martin tried to backtrack:

> "Mr. Rajchman, when were you first aware of this person named Ivan in Camp 2?"
>
> "Our barrack where we slept was closed with barbed wire, and there was a little area where you could walk out of the barrack.
>
> "Opposite that, there was the small gas chamber where his residence was, Ivan's residence; and where we went after work and we looked across, and it was not at all—we saw him because he was sitting, usually outside, resting from his hard work."
>
> "Can you give us a date, if you can, that you first became aware of this person you call Ivan?"
>
> "When I came to Camp 2, everyone was crying over his fate. One told the other, 'This is Ivan.' He didn't present himself, introduce himself to me."

Rajchman raised his eyes and turned slightly to the judge on his left.

> "Because, if he did, the judge would not have me here today as a witness."

For two days Rajchman had been sitting only ten feet from John Demjanjuk, and he had never once glanced up. Thirty-eight years after his escape from Treblinka, the instincts that had enabled him to survive had returned. At Treblinka, eye contact had been forbidden. Sitting in a courtroom in the United States of America, Rajchman could not bring himself to look at Ivan the Terrible.

Our next witness was Elijahu Rosenberg, the fifty-nine-year-old warehouse manager who had first identified Demjanjuk from the photospread in Israel. Rosenberg had been a man of twenty in Warsaw when the Germans forced the Jews of that city into the ghetto. His testimony was crucial because he, of all the witnesses, worked at the gas chambers themselves. Few Jews who survived the Holocaust were as constantly exposed to its horrors. Norman Moscowitz led him quietly through his story, beginning in the Warsaw ghetto of 1942.*

> "Before the morning, Germans appeared [outside the building where his family had been confined] with screams that we should all go down. My mother said, 'I have no more strength. Let's all go down, and whatever happens to everyone will happen to us.'
>
> "I saw many Jews lined up in rows. After a little time we started to walk in the direction of the Umschlagplatz [literally, 'distribution center'; the open space near the railroad tracks in Warsaw where the Jews were put onto the trains]. We all sat down in that place, until the evening. Cars arrived for cattle or for horses and we started to enter with screams. We started to move."
>
> "How long did you continue moving?"
>
> "All through the night. In the morning the train was halted. The door was opened. Terrible cries began. I saw before me Germans, Ukrainians, also civilians. Screams were, 'Men to the right, women to the left,' or opposite that. My mother said to me, 'When we get to a place, you will write a letter and I will write a letter' to a Christian Polish man who was known to us, 'and in this way we will know where [each other is].' From then on I never again saw my mothers or my sisters.
>
> "A German came along and with a whip he began to choose people. I instinctively joined that group and I remained standing there. Two Ukrainians stood near us. They started to push us with their guns and they brought us over to another place where there was a big pile and according to their order we started to sort the things of the victims.

---

*None of the government's witnesses were present in the courtroom when another was testifying.

"I saw one gentleman who was walking with a valise that was hanging on him. He was a neighbor of ours from the house where we had lived. With difficulty I recognized him. His face was swollen. He was calling out, 'Gold, money. Gold, money.' If anyone found anything like this, he was supposed to throw it into his valise.

"As he circulated about, I asked him, 'Where is my mother?' He was afraid to answer me. When he returned again, I asked him: 'Please tell me, where is my mother.' He pointed with his head over there. 'You will not see her any more.'

"[The next day] a German arrived and he called 30 people to volunteer for easy work. Out of fear, since he stood next to me, I stood next to him with several other people. After they were all there, he began to lead us in the direction from which one does not return."

"Where did he take you to?"

"I arrived at the place where there was a gate which was covered with camouflage. This German opened the gate. I entered. Before me piles of corpses. Screams. Ukrainians, Germans, everyone with his whip, were beating, screaming. From the screams I understood that I was supposed to grab a litter and drag the corpses."

"Did you do that?"

"Yes. From right near the gas chambers, we brought them over to the wagons and there other people threw them into the wagons, and they pushed them over to a very big pit."

"How long did you continue to perform this duty?"

"More than a few weeks. [Then] I was chosen to work inside the gas chambers."

"What kind of work was this?"

"The removal of the bodies after they were killed."

"What was at the entrance to this gas chamber?"

"There was a big opening and above was written in letters that are holy to the Jews, 'This is the gate of the Lord. The righteous shall enter through it.' The letters were in gold and above was hanging a parochet—a cloth that is made out of satin that is found in the synagogue where the holiest books of the Jews are kept."

"Mr. Rosenberg, were you ever present at the gas chambers while they were in operation?"

"Yes. When there were transports, the outside doors of the gas chambers were closed. I stood on the ramp and we waited until the victims had been choked. I heard and I saw how they

entered the gas chambers. I heard the screams, the crying of the
children. 'Mama, daddy!' 'Hear Oh Israel!'

"After a short period, about a half an hour, approximately,
everything was quiet.

"A German went up, he put his ear to the door, and he said,
in German, 'They are all asleep. Open the door.' We opened the
door and we started to remove the corpses, we threw them down
on the ground, everybody practically still groaned."

"Who was it who operated these gas chambers?"

"Two Ukrainians."

"Do you know what their names were?"

"Yes."

"What were they, sir?"

"Ivan and Nikolai."

"Did you yourself see them, this Ivan and Nikolai, at these
gas chambers?"

"Every day, whenever there were transports. They beat people. Ivan had—he had a weapon of destruction; he had a pipe, a
sword, a whip, and he tortured the victims with this before they
entered the gas chambers, especially the women. He cut pieces
between their legs. I saw this with my very eyes."

"Now, after they entered the gas chamber, what if anything
did Ivan and Nikolai do?"

"They returned to the room where the motor was, and they
activated the motor."

"Can you describe Ivan?"

"He was a tall man, about 23, 22, 24; he was broad shoul-
dered, round face; he had gray eyes, his ears stuck out a little,
short hair, not especially light."

"Do you remember any other particular incidents of mistreatment of the victims by this Ivan?"

"Yes, sir. It wasn't anything special. These things happened
every day."

Rosenberg bowed his head, his hands folded tightly in his lap.
After a moment, his head and shoulders began to shake in short, silent sobs. After a full minute, he grew still. He raised his head, took
a deep breath, and continued his testimony.

"I saw that he brought a Jewish man with a long beard and
ear locks, naked. [Ivan] appeared behind the gas chambers, he

pulled apart with his own hands the barbed wire in the fence and he pushed the Jew's head inside and he beat him with his whip.

"The Jewish man screamed; he threw himself—it looked as if the barbed wire had cut his throat, and he choked after a little while."

Rosenberg had identified Ivan's photo from both photospreads in Israel, and Moscowitz handed him first one folder, then the other. Again, Rosenberg picked out Demjanjuk's 1951 visa photo from the first folder, the 1942 Trawniki ID card from the other. These pictures, he said, are the same man, and they are Ivan.

Martin confined his cross-examination of Rosenberg to a long series of rather disjointed questions about his identification of the photos. This accomplished little except to strengthen the certainty of Rosenberg's identification, and after a while Martin let him go.

By the end of the seventh day of trial in Cleveland, we knew we were ahead. The witnesses had been strong, their testimony delivered with such simple strength and dignity that no one sitting in the courtroom could fail to believe it. I had always believed, as many trial lawyers do, that success in the courtroom depends on preparation before trial; Horrigan and Moscowitz had spent long days and nights preparing the case, and it showed. They had easily overcome all of Martin's objections to placing the photospreads in evidence, and we were convinced that Judge Battisti, who had studied them carefully, was impressed with the certainty that each witness had showed. After all, unlike a bank teller who has a fleeting glimpse of an armed robber, these survivors had seen Ivan almost daily over a period of several months.

But our case was not yet won—we had three more survivors waiting to testify, each of whom, like Rajchman and Rosenberg, had selected Demjanjuk's picture from our photospreads. No matter how repetitive their testimony might be, five identifications were always better than two.

The other leg of our case was the Trawniki identification card—the simple, two-sided document with the photograph and the name of Ivan Demjanjuk, and his date of birth, and his father's name. There was no doubt that the Trawniki card, if genuine, was a highly incriminating piece in the mosaic of evidence against John Demjanjuk. But we knew that Martin's tack, when he presented his defense, would be to claim that the card was a forgery engineered by the Soviets to nail his client. We had no reason to think the card was a forgery, and there would seem to be little reason for the Soviets to pick Demjanjuk as a target for anything. He was not an active anti-Communist; as far as we knew, he belonged to no political organizations, nor had he ever spoken out against the Soviet regime. To be sure, Ukrainian-Americans as a whole were decidedly unsympathetic to the Communist regime that ruled their homeland, but there were hundreds of Ukrainians in this country who regularly spoke at rallies, or published tracts in newspapers, or wrote books attacking the Soviet Union. Why would the Soviets single out Demjanjuk?

Still, we had only a certified photocopy of the Trawniki ID card to work with, and thus we could not subject it to the ink and paper tests that would prove its authenticity as a 1942 document. Despite several requests we had made to the Soviet government to let us borrow the original for this purpose, we had received no answer. We expected that Martin would seize on this silence to argue to Judge Battisti that the Soviets had produced a forgery which they obviously could not afford to release.

Then, halfway through the trial, we received a phone call from the Soviet embassy a few blocks away from our office in Washington. They had the original of the Trawniki ID card, flown in from Moscow. Would we like to examine it?

We notified Martin immediately, and the trial in Cleveland recessed so that he could come to Washington with his document expert to examine the Trawniki card. The Soviets readily agreed to our suggested procedure: Our document expert, with his equipment, would examine the Trawniki ID card in the embassy to test the ink, the paper, the signatures, and the photograph. Then the document would be turned over to Martin, who would have his expert examine it by whatever means he wished. The Soviets would not take part in the process, or even be present when it was taking place. When the trial resumed, the original would be flown to Cleveland so Judge Battisti could see it with his own eyes before returning it to the Soviets.

In the baronial mansion that is the embassy of the Soviet Union in downtown Washington, our expert, Gideon Epstein of the Immigration and Naturalization Service, studied the document, extracting pinprick ink samples and a tiny corner of the paper for microscopic testing to determine age. He studied the signatures and photographed them for analysis of pressure, stroke, and other peculiarities. He also looked closely for evidence of erasures—the disruptions in the paper that would inevitably have occurred if the Soviets had taken a real 1942 document and substituted Demjanjuk's name for that of the original bearer. For a questioned-document examiner as experienced as Epstein, armed with the latest technology, this single piece of paper could conceal few secrets. He pored over the paper as if he were a building inspector walking through a huge and complex structure, alert to everything.

When Epstein had finished his examination in the embassy, he told us that he had seen nothing that would cast any doubt on the authenticity of the document. But he could not give us a definitive answer until he had developed and blown up the photographs taken through the microscope.*

We turned the document over to Martin and his examiner and left them to study the paper as we had. If there was any indication of forgery, Judge Battisti would hear it all from the witness stand in Cleveland, and so would we.

Although there were still several survivors of Treblinka waiting to testify, Horrigan and Moscowitz decided that it would be an unnecessary ordeal for them to describe Treblinka in the detail that Rajchman and Rosenberg had done. We had made the point. The judge was well aware, now, of the place where one million Jews had been annihilated in the thirteen months of 1942–43.

Moscowitz called Georg Rajgrodzki, a seventy-one-year-old retired architect from Warsaw, and one of the few Holocaust survivors who had decided to live in Germany after the war. Rajgrodzki had carried corpses from the gas chambers to the burning pits; he had seen Ivan often and had readily identified Demjanjuk's photograph.

But Rajgrodzki had one opportunity to see Ivan that no other witness had. At the end of November 1942, one of the bundles that came off the train at the little Treblinka station contained a violin—the manifestation of some musician's forlorn hope for a new life in the East. One of the guards demanded that someone play it, and Rajgrodzki volunteered:

---

*Epstein later testified that, by every test, the document appeared to be genuine and unaltered.

"I played, and then the chief foreman told me to come to work in the kitchen, and I played Viennese songs for him. He was Viennese. And he said, 'You'll stay here and work in the kitchen.' "

"Did you ever play the violin for the guards?"

"This was in the summer of 1943. We were shut up in our barracks area behind the barbed wire fence, and the guardsmen came over to listen, and Ivan was with them. There were three of us; there was a clarinetist, and the harmonica player, and myself. We played for them, and I do remember that [Ivan] turned around and wiped tears away from his eyes."

Had Ivan the Terrible such an ear for music that he was moved to tears by the strains of this pathetic little trio? Or did he, just for a moment perhaps, come to understand that Rajgrodzki could have been any of the hundreds of thousands of Jews who were perishing every day in Ivan's little fiefdom of gas, together with God knows how many other violinists? It is a question only Ivan could answer. Ivan never did.

Sonia Lewkowicz, a thin, pale woman of fifty-nine, testified next. When she had arrived at Treblinka, confused and frightened, someone told her to say that she was a laundress. She was put to work washing the Ukrainians' clothes, one of the few women who worked at Treblinka, one of the very few who survived.

The ordeal of reliving and recalling the time of Treblinka was hard on all the witnesses, but it seemed hardest on Sonia Lewkowicz. Her testimony came in short sentences, almost in gasps.

"What do you remember about this Ivan?" Norman Moscowitz asked.

"Terrible fear. He was always busy. He screamed and he ran about. He adopted the style of the Germans. He beat very much and he always threw fear on everybody. We were all terribly afraid of him.

"He was young. He was light. He had light eyes and protruding ears."

She picked Demjanjuk's picture out of the spreads, now the fourth witness to do so.

Our fifth and final witness was Pinchas Epstein, at fifty-six the youngest of the witnesses, a native of Czestochowa in Poland. Testifying in Hebrew, he told what had by now become a familiar story to those attending the trial: driven out of his ghetto quarters with his family in 1942, crowded on a slow-moving train, confronted at the little Treblinka station by German and Ukrainian guards, selected to live while his family, and almost everyone else on the train, died.

After three days in the lower camp, Epstein was taken through the fence to the upper camp—the death camp:

> "We saw a terrifying sight. Right near the gas chambers, a heap of dead bodies, and we were immediately beaten and screamed at and they order us, two people should take a stretcher and pile up corpses on it and to run in the direction of a pit and there to throw down the corpses and to return. And in the course of running we were beaten and they even wounded us.
>
> "One time, a new unit of SS men arrived and I remember one of the SS men who saw what was being done there in Treblinka and I heard him say, 'Mein Gott, was kommt hier vor?' ['My God, what is going on here?']"
>
> "Mr. Epstein, did there come a time when your duties at Camp 2 changed?"
>
> "Yes, sir. After they emptied out the pit with a crane, this is a digging machine, and some bones were left down in the bottom in the pit, I and another young man were let down into the pit and, with our hands, we gathered up the bones and put them into the crane and they raised it. They burned these bones like all the other corpses.
>
> "I worked at this until the second of August, 1943. That was the day of judgment, the day of the uprising, and then I escaped."

Jack Horrigan led him into the crucial part of his testimony:

> "Mr. Epstein, did you ever have occasion to be in the area of the gas chambers when the motors were turned on, to see this area clearly?"
>
> "Yes, sir."
>
> "And do you know who operated the motors?"
>
> "The motors were activated by two Ukrainians. One was Ivan and the second was Nikolai. At the time they were killing the

people in the gas chambers and the gas chambers were still closed, they told us to sit down; and I had an opportunity to sit right near the entrance of the room where the motor was, and there I saw very clearly who was activating the motor."

"Mr. Epstein, did you have occasion to observe Ivan's treatment of the Jewish inmates of Camp 2?"

"Yes, sir. In a very brutal fashion. I cannot find words to describe it."

"Do you recall any specific instances?"

"One day Kurt Franz, he was an SS man [the deputy commandant of Treblinka], attacked one young man whose name was Konrad. He smashed up his whole face and he said to him: 'You know who's getting ready to escape.' This young man, Konrad, did not know what he was doing and he indiscriminately pointed to a group of people, and [Franz] ordered these people to go over to the side and lie down. Ivan, with an iron pipe, and other Ukrainians with the handles of their pistols and the Germans with shots . . ."

Epstein paused, then took a deep breath and went on.

"Ivan split one skull after another. Every blow of his arm with an iron pipe split the person's head.

"Another night, it was winter, a group of people managed to escape, and on that very night the first snow fell of that winter and that snow betrayed them. They brought three back alive. They tied them up, their hands and their feet. They kept them outside until the evening. Ivan with his metal pipe tortured them all day. He broke their hands and their feet before nightfall. They had a roll call and they indicated anyone who tries to escape, his end will be just like this. And then they hung them."

Horrigan handed Epstein the photospreads, and Epstein picked out both photos from the folder, as he had done in Israel several months earlier. These pictures, he said, were Ivan.

Epstein concluded his direct testimony by describing the uprising in which he escaped:

"Many were killed. Many remained hanging on the barbed wire. My fate was to remain alive."

On the cross-examination both of Sonia Lewkowicz and Pinchas Epstein, defense attorney John Martin, now seeming to grow more dispirited with each day, had each witness describe the circumstances of the first time he or she had seen the photospread in Israel. He was searching for some fact, some suggestion, that the Israeli police had coached the witnesses in the process, or that the identifications might have somehow been less than certain. Each witness answered the questions patiently, but the result, as it had been with the first three witnesses, was to strengthen the conclusion that the photospreads had been presented fairly, and the witnesses were firm in their belief that they were looking at Ivan, the man who "threw fear on everybody." *

We had now completed, after eight days of trial, the first two phases of our case: the overall role of Treblinka in the annihilation of Europe's Jews, and the identification of Ivan Demjanjuk by those who had been there. We were ready for the third and final phase: to establish that a man who had run the gas chamber at Treblinka was ineligible under the Displaced Persons Act to come to America, and that if such a man had told the truth about his background, he would have been denied a visa. Although the anguished testimony about Demjanjuk's role, and his gratuitous brutality against individual victims, had made the case appear very like a war crimes trial, the legal issue here was whether his citizenship must be revoked.

Over the next two days, Moscowitz and Horrigan put on the string of witnesses who had been responsible for screening and admitting displaced persons in the years after the war: the former chief eligibility officer for the International Refugee Organization, the case analyst for the Displaced Persons Commission who had prepared Demjanjuk's papers (the man to whom Demjanjuk had given the phony story that he had been a farmer in Poland during the war), the vice-consul who had issued the visa, the naturalization examiner who had approved Demjanjuk's petition for citizenship in 1958.

After the dramatic week of testimony from the Treblinka survivors, the testimony of these men on the rules and regulations of postwar immigration was of little interest to the press and spectators, who

---

*Martin could have subpoenaed the Israeli investigator who had shown the spreads, and who was in Cleveland to observe the trial, but he did not.

dwindled to a handful. None of the witnesses recalled Ivan Demjanjuk by name or photo; he had been just another Ukrainian in the thousands of cases they had handled thirty-five years before. But their
testimony was clear: no one, German or Ukrainian or anyone else,
who had been on the staff of Treblinka or any other death camp could
possibly have been eligible for a DP visa to come to America.

On February 25, 1981, the prosecution rested.

Many years ago, the Supreme Court ruled that, in cases where the
government seeks to revoke naturalized citizenship, its proof must be
"clear and convincing, and not leave the issue in doubt."[20] This is a
higher standard than that applied in other civil cases; it is, as a practical matter, the same as a criminal case: if there is any doubt, the
government loses.

This is the way it should be, and in none of OSI's cases did we
ever argue that the standard should be weakened or loosely applied.
American citizenship is a precious right. It should not be lost under
rules of proof that govern ordinary cases. If we could not prove to
Judge Battisti, clearly and convincingly, that John Demjanjuk was who
we said he was, then he should win and we should lose.

So the task facing the defense in this case was clear: create a doubt
in the judge's mind that John Demjanjuk was Ivan the Terrible, the
man at Treblinka.

Only one man could do that—the only man in the courtroom who
knew, beyond any doubt, whether John Demjanjuk had been at Treblinka.

The courtroom was full again on the day Demjanjuk took the stand
in his defense. The marshals were back in force to put the spectators
through the metal detector; the reporters and artists filled the jury box
as Demjanjuk, dressed in a conservative gray suit, took an oath before God to tell the truth.

As he stepped into the witness chair, I was struck by the bulk of
the man. At sixty-one, there was no fat on him. He was fit and strong.

Despite living in the United States for twenty-nine years, Demjanjuk
told the judge that he spoke very little English; he testified in Ukrainian, through an interpreter. His face showed no emotion as he answered his attorney's questions.

He had been drafted, he said, in 1940, and had received a back
wound in combat in 1941. He had been hospitalized, then released

and sent to the Crimea, where he was taken as a prisoner of war by the Germans following a battle. He worked for a while repairing railroad tracks, then was taken to a POW camp in Rowno, Poland—"in '42 or '43, I don't remember exactly"—then to another camp at Chelm, where he was interred "until about 1943 or 1944."

Demjanjuk said that the Germans sent him next to Graz, in Austria, then a town called Oelberg, finally to a place called Bischofshofen, where he was liberated by the Americans and sent to Munich.

> John Martin: "Mr. Demjanjuk, at any time during the war years did you ever serve as a concentration camp guard at any location?"
> "No."
> "At any time during the war years, were you in any concentration camp where civilian populations were kept?"
> "No."

Rosenberg had testified that Ivan had gray eyes. Martin now asked Demjanjuk:

> "What color are your eyes?"
> "Blue."
> "What color were your eyes in 1942?"
> "Blue."

Martin handed him the Trawniki ID card.

> "Have you ever during the war years been issued documents similar to this, at any time period?"
> "Never."
> "The photograph on there, is that a photograph of you?"

Demjanjuk hesitated.

> "I cannot say. Possibly it is me."
> "Well, why can't you be sure?"
> "Because I never had such hair as the man in the photograph except in the Russian Army."
> "Then if this photo is yours, it would have to have been during an era that you were in the Russian Army?"
> "Yes."

Martin moved on:

"During the time you were in the [DP] camps, were you or did you have a fear of being forcibly repatriated to the Soviet Union?"

"Yes. '45, '46, '47 were the most terrible years."

"After '47, did you fear being repatriated to the Soviet Union?"

"There was still fear, but it wasn't as bad as before because Soviet officers weren't going around [to the DP camps] any more."

"Would you tell us why you were afraid of being repatriated to the Soviet Union?"

"Because I had been a soldier of the Red Army and there was a regulation that if you were going to be taken prisoner of war, you had to shoot yourself, and I hadn't done so."

"Was it out of this fear that you made certain misrepresentations on your IRO application and visa application that you were a farmer from 1934 to 1943?"

"Yes."

"Now the travel that you did between the various POW camps—were you being forcefully taken to these different locations by the Germans?"

"Yes."

"So you had no choice in your movements during this era; is that correct?"

"Yes. There was no choice."

Martin sat down. "Nothing further," he told the judge.

That was it. Demjanjuk's entire testimony in his own behalf had taken about thirty minutes. Moscowitz and Horrigan, somewhat taken aback by the brevity, conferred quickly, then Jack Horrigan stood to begin his cross-examination. Horrigan had been waiting for this for a long time.

Horrigan went first for Demjanjuk's most exposed flank. He handed Demjanjuk a copy of his application for a visa.

"This application indicates that from 1934 to 1943 you were [a farmer] in Sobibor, Poland. Mr. Demjanjuk, were you in Sobibor, Poland, from 1934 to 1943?"

"No."

"And it so indicates that from 1943 to 1944 you were in Pi-

lau, Danzig. You were not in Pilau, Danzig, during that period
of time.''

''No.''

''This application, Mr. Demjanjuk, is under oath, isn't it?''

''I don't remember whether it was under oath.''

The oath had been in writing. The judge could see Demjanjuk's
signature underneath it.

Horrigan: ''Didn't you testify that you were only afraid in 1945,
1946 and the beginning of 1947?''

''I said, when my attorney asked me, that the strongest fear
was in '45, '46 and '47.''

''Thank you.''

The visa had been granted in 1951.

Horrigan had drawn first blood quickly: Demjanjuk had admitted
lying under oath to gain entry to the United States. His asserted excuse—fear of repatriation—had been blown away.*

Horrigan went over Demjanjuk's tale of being moved from one
POW camp to another. We believed that Demjanjuk had been captured in the Crimea in May 1942 and sent to the POW camps at Rovno
and then Chelm, and had been recruited by the Germans at Chelm in
the summer of 1942 to go first to Trawniki for training and then on
to Treblinka. Demjanjuk was claiming that he got as far as Chelm
and stayed there as a POW until very late in the war, when he was
moved to Austria and ultimately was liberated by American troops.

The critical time period was the summer of 1942 to the early fall
of 1943—the time when Treblinka had been in operation. Horrigan
tried to pin Demjanjuk down as closely as possible to the dates he
moved from one camp to another.

Demjanjuk was evasive: ''I don't know''; ''I can't say exactly.''
Under sustained attack from Horrigan, he dropped his voice to a
whisper, and Judge Battisti had to interrupt twice to tell him to speak
up so that he could be heard. Gradually, reconstructing seasons and

---

* As noted previously, repatriation as a factual matter had ended long before, in late 1945. The
refusal of American authorities to repatriate DPs to the Soviet Union against their will had contributed heavily to the overcrowdedness in the camps and was one of the strongest arguments
leading to enactment of the DP Act.

travel times, Horrigan got Demjanjuk to testify that he had been held as a prisoner at Chelm until October, 1944.

Horrigan returned to the Trawniki ID card:

> "Is that you, Mr. Demjanjuk?"
> "Looks like me, but I am not 100 percent certain."
> "But it looks like you, doesn't it?"
> "Possibly."
> "Very similar to you, isn't it?"
> "Yes. Possibly."
> "This card indicates that the Ivan Demjanjuk [described on the card] has gray eyes. You indicated to your attorney [on direct examination] that you have always had blue eyes, is that correct?"
> "Yes."

Horrigan put aside the Trawniki card and handed Demjanjuk his visa application.

> "Do you see the color of the eyes in this visa application?"
> "I don't see it."

"Let me help you," said Horrigan, pointing to the application that Demjanjuk was holding in his hands.

Demjanjuk studied it.

"Would you tell us the color of the eyes in this visa application?"

Demjanjuk looked up. "Gray," he said.

Horrigan pressed, keeping Demjanjuk off balance. He picked up the Trawniki ID card again.

> "This Ivan Demjanjuk that was trained at Treblinka has a scar on his back. Do you have a scar on your back?"
> "Yes."
> "This Ivan's father's name was Nikolai. Was your father's name Nikolai?"
> "Yes."
> "This Ivan Demjanjuk was born on April 3, 1920. When were you born?"

"The same."
"In what language is this signature?"
"Ukrainian."
"What does it say?"
"Demjanjuk."
"Is this your signature?"
"I don't think so."
"But you are not sure?"
"I never wrote the letter 'ya' the way it is written here."

Horrigan had made the points he needed to make. He sat down. "Your honor," he said, "we intend to present tomorrow in rebuttal a witness who will be here this evening. In fact he's already on his way."

The witness was Professor Ziemke, the authority on the war's Russian front, who had testified three weeks earlier at the outset of our case. We had called him to demolish Demjanjuk's latest alibi, and he did.

> Moscowitz: "Is it possible for the defendant or any other prisoner of the Germans to have been in a prisoner of war camp in Chelm, Poland, in October 1944?"
> "No."
> "Why is that not possible, sir?"
> "Because Chelm, Poland, was at that time in Soviet hands."

Ziemke explained that, early in 1944, the Red Army had pushed to within fifty-five miles east of Chelm, sucking Chelm into the zone of operations of the fast-retreating German army. All POW camps and other installations not essential to combat were moved. At the very latest, said Ziemke, the Chelm camp had been abandoned by January 1944.

Demjanjuk's alibi was ten months wide of the truth.

John Martin asked Judge Battisti for a five-day recess so that he could confer with his expert who had examined the original Trawniki ID card at the Soviet embassy in Washington.

When the trial reconvened the following week, Martin made a stunning announcement. He had no further evidence to present for the defense. This could mean only one thing: his expert had found no evidence that the Trawniki ID card was a forgery.

The trial of John Demjanjuk was over.

In criminal trials the jury is locked up until it delivers its verdict. No such rule applies to denaturalization cases, which are decided by the judge. After hearing final arguments from both sides, Judge Battisti thanked the attorneys, gathered up his notes, and left the courtroom.

Three and a half months later, in June 1981, the verdict arrived in the mail, a detailed, forty-four-page exposition of the facts of the case and the law that applied. Judge Battisti discussed the Trawniki ID card in detail, noting that every element of it suggested its authenticity and that the information it contained corroborated Demjanjuk's appearance and life history. "Throughout the trial," Judge Battisti noted, "the [defense] contended that [the card was] not authentic and suggested the possibility of forgery. However, at no time during the entire course of the trial was *any* evidence introduced to substantiate these speculations." Judge Battisti concluded that Demjanjuk had been transferred to Trawniki in the summer of 1942.

He turned to Treblinka: "The ghoulish, diabolical operation of Treblinka, resulting in the almost incomprehensible annihilation of 900,000 Jews, is indelibly stamped on the human conscience, and unfortunately is now part of the human experience." He noted that each of the witnesses who had testified—the German nurse Otto Horn and the five survivors—had had ample opportunity to see what had gone on at the gas chambers. Because "the length of time between the events in question and the witness identifications is an extraordinary 34–35 years," he said, "the Court [has] a duty to scrupulously examine the eyewitness identifications."

Battisti found that, despite the passage of time, it remained true that each of the witnesses had had ample time at Treblinka to observe Ivan, that the photospreads had been in no way suggestive, that they had been presented fairly to the witnesses, that each identification had been unequivocal, and that "[t]horough cross-examination of each witness failed to depreciate in any way the certainty of the identifications." "[T]he Court must conclude," Battisti wrote, "that defendant was present at Treblinka in 1942–1943."

As for Demjanjuk's alibi, Judge Battisti noted that it had been "severely undercut" by the prosecution evidence from Trawniki and

Treblinka and the fact that the POW camp at Chelm had been abandoned long before the time Demjanjuk insisted he was still there.

Threading his way through the law, Battisti concluded that Demjanjuk had been ineligible for a visa under the Displaced Persons Act and that his citizenship had therefore been illegally procured. "Accordingly," the judge concluded, "judgment will be entered in favor of plaintiff United States and against defendant John Demjanjuk." Demjanjuk's citizenship was formally revoked.[21]

Thirty-seven years after the death camp Treblinka was bulldozed into oblivion in the Polish countryside, Ivan the Terrible had been brought to justice.

Yet what sort of justice was it? Demjanjuk did not go to jail—he lost his citizenship. Twelve months later, the court of appeals upheld Judge Battisti's ruling; a few months after that, the Supreme Court declined Demjanjuk's request for review. Deportation proceedings are now under way.* Demjanjuk continues to live as a free man while all this goes on.

But in the months following the verdict, we had come to expect the delays of the appellate process; in OSI's cases, a judgment of denaturalization is seldom the end of the battle. There was something more profound that disturbed me about John Demjanjuk.

Certainly I detested him and everything he had done in his life. He was a coward who had volunteered to sign on as a cog in the machinery of murder. He had delivered death to hundreds of thousands of children and their mothers and fathers. In doing so, he had gone out of his way to degrade them, making the last moments of their lives as terrifying as he knew how. He was a bully who had brutalized for sport the work-Jews, devastated by fear and hunger and impotence. Not one witness could recall a single act of mercy or decency or even simple human forbearance from this beefy thug.

He had perjured himself to come to America. He had taken everything America had to offer. Faced with the overwhelming evidence against him, he had not even spared his family the ordeal of the trial. Every day they had listened in the courtroom to the agony of those

---

*In what might prove to be a major development, Israel requested Demjanjuk's extradition in November 1983. If extradition is granted by the courts, Demjanjuk would be sent to Israel to face criminal charges there, with the possibility of life imprisonment or death.

whose fate, in one survivor's words, had been to live. At one point, Demjanjuk's wife had collapsed under the strain and was taken from the courtroom unconscious on a stretcher. Yet Demjanjuk pressed ahead with his bland assertions of innocence.

A trial is every man's right. What gnawed at me about this man had nothing to do with the law. It had nothing to do with the fact, as contemptible as I found it, that at every point in his life when his own security and well-being had been threatened, he had shown no feeling for the lives of others, whether they were innocent and defenseless strangers or his own family.

I wanted to know what had gone through his mind as he sat in the courtroom day after day, reunited against all odds with those whose lives he could have snuffed out with one whistling swing of his gas pipe. Had he seen again in his mind's eye, as they had, the camouflaged fence, the squat little gas chamber, the bodies so closely packed that even in death they could not fall, the burning pit crackling with melted fat, the chronic haze? Did the pestilential smell return? Could he see again Georg Rajgrodzki playing on his violin?

If he did, he gave no sign. He was alert and attentive, but he showed no emotion whatever at any point in the trial, not even when he took the stand, supposedly an innocent man—a prisoner of war— accused of the most grotesque crimes in a place he had never been. Had he been at Trawniki? "No." Had he been at Treblinka? "No."

I came to realize that, as much as I loathed John Demjanjuk, I resented him more, with his impassive silence, his callous, almost bored, demeanor as he faced his accusers, his careless and demonstrably false alibi. It was as if the most important thing to Demjanjuk was not that he might be found guilty of being Ivan the Terrible, but that he reveal as little as possible about himself. He was cheating us, and much more than us, he was cheating history by his utter refusal to acknowledge his past. His guilt could not be disputed by any objective observer—and Judge Battisti was as objective and fair a judge as any I had ever seen—yet Demjanjuk sat there, day after day, showing nothing.

Even the Ukrainians in the courtroom—united in sympathy for their countryman, willing to believe in his personal innocence—had been visibly moved by the testimony of the victims and the horrors they had suffered. During those long hours of testimony, witness and spectator were joined, however fleetingly, by a human bond of the most elemental nature that transcended religion, culture, politics, and trials. Demjanjuk, on the other hand, had gazed at the victims as if they were discussing something wholly alien to him, and to the human condition.

In this perverse way, Demjanjuk had lost the case but the Nazi mind had won. It had won by refusing to reveal itself. It had won by answering the agony of the survivors with a monosyllabic denial and a mockery of an alibi. The Nazi mind had won by not even acknowledging its own existence—no explanation, no defense, no excuse, no emotion, nothing.

Demjanjuk stands convicted, but he is an insignificant character. Had he been killed in action in the Crimea, another would have done what he did at Treblinka. He was no more unique than a cockroach. But the Nazi mind that he represents is not insignificant. In his smug silence, Demjanjuk is the Nazi mind, telling us something: I did it once, and got away with it. I won't explain how or why, for if I did, you might understand it a little better than you did before, and learn to recognize it when it rears its head again.

He is cheating us; let us at least recognize that. And he is cheating the dead of Treblinka. He is cheating those Jews whose voices joined in elegies in the drafty barracks at night, when the gas chambers had been emptied and the hump-backed little transports rolled across the countryside with the next morning's cargo.

5

ANDRIJA ARTUKOVIC:
The Dean of
America's Nazis

In the wretched story of genocide and barbarism that took place throughout Europe under cover of World War II, few chapters are as tragic as that of Croatia, in Yugoslavia. From its capital, the ancient and cosmopolitan city of Zagreb, an official reign of terror spread through its hills. At times small rivers literally ran red with blood. Under the patronage of Adolf Hitler, a crude and merciless thug named Ante Pavelic was installed as chief, and for four years he oversaw the slaughter of hundreds of thousands of Serbs, Jews, and gypsies in the cruelest imaginable fashion. He became the only European Axis head of state to escape the war, and the war crimes trials that followed, alive.

Croatia produced, as well, the highest-ranking Nazi puppet ever to set foot in the United States—the minister of the interior, Andrija Artukovic. This man, later judged by an American tribunal to have been second only to Pavelic in his control of the machinery of genocide and torture, stepped off a plane in Los Angeles in the summer of 1948 and has never left. He lives today in a home on the Pacific shore in Orange County.

For more than eight years, from 1951 to 1959, Artukovic waged a nonstop legal battle to resist both extradition and deportation. Aided by court decisions that seemed blind to the lessons of Nazism and by a conspicuous reluctance of the United States government to take decisive action, he won.

The people of Belgrade, Yugoslavia, took a courageous and futile step in March of 1941—they defied Hitler. Two days after a delegation sent by their regent Prince Paul signed an accord with Nazi Germany on March 25, they overthrew the prince and installed a determined anti-Nazi government headed by a group of Army and Air Force officers.

They were to pay grievously for their refusal to appease the Führer. When news of the coup reached Berlin, Hitler flew into a savage rage. "To treat the German Reich in this way is impossible," he stormed, and he had plans drawn up that very night for "Operation Punishment," a blitzkrieg of unrestrained armed force against the Yugoslavs.[1] Belgrade fell defenseless to the Luftwaffe; 17,000 civilians were killed as the city was razed from above. After eleven days of pummeling, the Yugoslavs surrendered and watched as Hitler carved up their country; he took some for himself and gave chunks to Italy, Hungary, Albania, and Bulgaria. Yugoslavia as a state ceased to exist.

The biggest chunk went to the biggest hounds. The German Foreign Ministry, assisted by Mussolini, hustled a group of Croatian nationalists out of exile and installed them as a puppet government to control nearly half of prewar Yugoslavia, from the Adriatic to the Hungarian border. Ante Pavelic, grim-faced leader of the Croatian separatist group known as the Ustashi (or Ustase), was made chief of state and prime minister. Germany had its Führer, Italy its Duce, and Croatia now had its Poglavnik. The "Independent State of Croatia," as Pavelic's government called itself, began preparations for a bloodbath.

In dividing Yugoslavia, Hitler was shrewdly playing on ancient hatreds. Since its birth in 1918 from the remnants of the Austro-Hungarian and Ottoman empires, Yugoslavia had been an uneasy coalition of nationalities—Macedonians, Montenegrins, Bosnians, Slovenes—each with its own religion—Roman Catholic, Orthodox, and Moslem—each with its own culture, each suspicious of the others. But no enmity surpassed that between the Serbs and the Croatians. The Croatians, or Croats, were Roman Catholic, European, Teutonic, and proud. The Serbs were Eastern Orthodox, Slavic, Byzantine, and proud. Each despised the other. The Serbs had dominated the postwar Yugoslav government, and the Croatians had been restive in their subordinate role. Though neither people was particularly fascist by tradition, Pavelic's fiercely nationalistic Croatian Ustashi movement seized upon fascism and terrorism during the thirties to harass the fragile Yugoslav government from exile outposts in Mus-

solini's Italy. With an avowedly anti-Serb and anti-Semitic tradition
dating back eighty years, the Ustashi were the perfect tools in Hitler's
design to keep the Balkans in ferment while he sent his armies toward
Moscow.[2]

The Independent State of Croatia, in the words of one scholar,
"was not independent, it was hardly a state, and it was only 50 percent Croat."[3] It mortgaged its independence to Hitler and Mussolini,
at whose pleasure it existed. Three days after they declared war on
the United States, the Poglavnik and his cabinet did so as well. As to
being a state, although it sprawled through most of northern Yugoslavia, no one was ever quite sure of its exact boundaries. And only
three million or so of its six and a half million inhabitants were Croatian; two million were Serbs, the rest Moslems or other groups, including 45,000 Jews.[4]

The driving force of the Croatian government was blood lust, under the leadership of men who brought about a twentieth-century In-
quisition. Pavelic and his cohort, possessing absolute power despite
a shaky base of popular support, ruthlessly subjugated the Serbs and
the Jews in their midst. Those who were not to be slaughtered were
to be deported; those who were not deported were to be forcibly converted to Catholicism. The Cyrillic alphabet of the Serbs was out-
lawed; the Eastern Orthodox Church, to which nearly all Serbs
belonged, was banned, its churches destroyed by fire. Officials of the
overthrown Yugoslav government were forced to surrender their "illegally acquired" property.[5] It was a policy of purification, and only
the Croats were pure.[6]

Yet the greatest subjugation of the Serbs was not by the law but
by the knife. Pavelic was a hoodlum, utterly without mercy or compassion. He was both chief of state and the "supreme head" of the
Ustashi, and the "principles of the Ustashi" were officially declared
to be "the actual needs of the Croatian nation." In theory, this meant
"the virtues of ancient heroism and courage," summoned to protect
"the national characteristics of the Croatian people." In practice, it
meant that the slaughter of Serbs and the deportation of Jews to the
Nazi SS was official state policy, carried out by vigilante bands of
Croatian terror squads who traveled the hills and valleys in search of
families.

The Ustashi were not content merely to kill Serbs; they mutilated
them. "A good Ustashi," Pavelic declared, "is one who can use his

knife to cut a child from the womb of its mother."[7] A captured photograph shows Ustashi militia mugging for the camera as they dangle a severed head.[8] Another photo shows one technique of "ancient heroism and courage"—the panicked victim on all fours, while one Ustashi holds his hair and two others saw through his neck. These and similar techniques of death by mutilation—and the inhuman disposal of the remains—sickened even the Germans, not to mention the more moderate Croatians excluded from power.[9]

"The widespread use of the knife as an instrument of death," wrote one journalist, "revealed at what depth their tribal animosities were rooted. Although most of the impersonal instruments of death produced in our age were available to them, the extremists sought a personal involvement in the administration of death."[10]

Fitzroy Maclean, chief of Britain's military mission to Tito's partisans, who were fighting their own guerilla battles in the hills of Yugoslavia against the Germans, starkly described the Ustashi horror of 1941:

> The massacres began in earnest at the end of June and continued throughout the summer, growing in scope and intensity until in August the terror reached its height. The whole of Bosnia ran with blood. Bands of Ustase roamed the countryside with knives, bludgeons and machine guns, slaughtering Serbian men, women and little children, desecrating Serbian churches, murdering Serbian priests, laying waste Serbian villages, torturing, raping, burning, drowning. Killing became a cult, an obsession. The Ustase vied to outdo each other, boasting of the numbers of their victims and of their own particular methods of dispatching them. The aged [Serbian] Orthodox Bishop of Plaski was garroted by his assassins. Bishop Platon of Banjaluka was prodded to death in a pond. Some Ustase collected the eyes of Serbs they had killed, sending them, when they had enough, to the *Poglavnik* for his inspection or proudly displaying them and other human organs in the cafes of Zagreb. Even their German and Italian allies were dismayed at their excesses.[11]

The chief of the German Secret Service in Zagreb put it more succinctly. "Efforts to educate the Ustase bands to civilized warfare," he wrote, "were quite useless."[12]

Catholic churches in Croatia were overrun by Orthodox Serbs

seeking instant conversion to protect themselves against the frenzy of
Ustashi death. The situation grew so chaotic that even the bishops
cried "enough." "Even the Orthodox Church has its genuine adher-
ents," wrote one bishop to Pavelic, "who cannot automatically change
their views or their nature overnight." Another bishop reported in
disgust that six railway cars of women, girls, and children were shipped
to a mountaintop and "thrown over a precipice"—all killed.[13]

Accurate figures of this revolting campaign will never be known,
but reliable estimates are that 400,000 Serbs, including children, were
killed by the Ustashi.[14]

To protect "the national characteristics of the Croatian people"
there was as little need for Jews as for Serbs. Although Jews comprised less than one percent of the population in the area controlled
by the Independent State of Croatia, the government was only two
weeks old when it issued an elaborate legal definition of a Jew—even
more detailed than Hitler's infamous Nuremberg law of 1933. In the
Ustashi scheme, a Jew was any person with at least three Jewish
grandparents, or who had two Jewish grandparents and belonged to
the "Jewish community," or who was defined as a Jew by the minister of the interior.[15]

Just as in Germany, once the Jews were defined, they could be
oppressed. Jewish businesses were expropriated and Jews were sent
to concentration camps, to the salt mines, and ultimately were "deported to the East"—the odious euphemism for the gas chambers of
Nazi-occupied Poland. The Ustashi did little of this themselves; the
Pavelic government simply contracted out the work to its German patrons, paying them thirty reichsmarks per Jew for transporting the Jews
from Croatian concentration camps to Auschwitz. By April 1944, the
German Foreign Office representative in Zagreb reported to Berlin that
the Jewish question in Croatia had been solved.[16]

If Pavelic was Croatia's Hitler, Andrija Artukovic, short, burly, square-
faced, was its Himmler. Born in Croatia, then part of Austria-
Hungary, in 1899, he took a law degree in 1923, joined a small Croatian separatist party, and soon hooked up with the Ustashi. He fled
Yugoslavia in 1932 for London and Paris following a provincial
Croatian uprising; the French extradited him back to Belgrade in 1934
to stand trial for the assassination of Yugoslavia's King Alexander—
a crime of which Artukovic was acquitted but which is now believed
to have been engineered by Pavelic, who was never apprehended.

Artukovic left Yugoslavia quickly after his trial and spent the rest of the thirties as an Ustashi agent, stoking the separatist fires from Budapest, from Austria, and from Germany, where he was apparently subsidized by the Abwehr, German military intelligence, then busily compiling its own dossier on these Croatian terrorists for future use. He returned to Belgrade in 1941 under the protection of the German army when it overran his native country. When the Germans installed Pavelic as chief of state, Pavelic immediately appointed Artukovic his minister of the interior.[17]

Pavelic and Artukovic wasted no time in issuing a series of decrees placing the machinery of terrorism in Artukovic's hands. Just one day after the government was formed in April 1941, Pavelic made terrorism legal by dashing off a "law" providing the death penalty for anyone guilty of treason, which he defined as doing "harm to the honor and vital interests of the Croatian nation." He immediately gave Artukovic the responsibilities of "commissioner of the entire public security and internal administration." When Pavelic handed out the constitution of the Independent State of Croatia two months later, it vested in Artukovic's ministry the "care of public peace and order, of personal and property safety, of public morals," and of "racial policy."

In his new role, Artukovic created the "Directorate of Public Order and Security" whose chief, Eugen "Dido" Kvaternik, had "supreme control over the activity of all police authorities" and "supreme control over all police employees of all kinds." Kvaternik's control was not quite "supreme," however. Kvaternik would be "directly subordinated to the Minister of Internal Affairs—Artukovic himself, who also retained the power to appoint all of the directorate's personnel.[18]

As Hitler's Holocaust spread across occupied Europe in 1941 and 1942, Artukovic, now secure in his supreme control over the security apparatus, took charge of "[a]ll questions which relate to Jews," including the power to define Jews who might not otherwise qualify by ancestry. Soon afterward, Pavelic authorized Artukovic to establish a system of concentration camps. Into these camps went the families of anyone who dared to "threaten the peace and quiet of the Croatian people" or even to "fle[e] from their homes." The opponents themselves had no need for concentration camps; they were to be killed. The Interior Ministry would decide who would be sent to the camps and would control how the camps were run. And anyone who was sent to the camps—that is, any enemy of the government—would forfeit all their property to the state, to be disposed of as Artukovic deemed fit.

Those who fled Croatia or who left for "racial or politico-national reasons"—a nice term for Jews, Serbs, and political opponents—lost their citizenship and with it the "protection" of the government. And since those who "fled from their homes" were lumped into the same category as those who threatened the "peace and quiet of the Croatian people," Artukovic was given authority to inter their families and seize their property as well. No courts were set up to hear the claims of the opponents or to interpose the rule of law against the government. Artukovic's authority was unrestrained.

Croatia was not, of course, a government of laws. The legal-sounding terms—"public security," "peace and order," "police authorities," "protection of the government"—were nothing more than euphemisms for utter political power justifying the acts of terrorists. Sentences to concentration camps were meted out in back rooms, not courts. Once the camps were in operation, they could and did become the final destination of any person and any group deemed an enemy of the government, which is to say primarily Serbs, Jews, and gypsies. The state was Pavelic, and Artukovic, and those who answered to them.

Of the dozen or so concentration camps thrown up in Croatia, the most notorious was that at Jasenovac. It did not have the gas chambers and smoking ovens of Auschwitz, but it hardly needed them. By one conservative estimate, 200,000 persons died there through exposure, starvation, bullets, and blunt instruments; another scholar puts the figure at more than four times that number: 830,000 persons put to death.[19]

Beyond a certain point, numbers lose their meaning when applied to fathers, mothers, sons, and daughters. One can envision one hundred dead, or perhaps five hundred or even a thousand, but 100,000 or 200,000 is incomprehensible. The fact is more compelling: people at Jasenovac were murdered for any reason, or for no reason; people were murdered singly and by the thousands; instantly and slowly; by iron pole, by machine gun, by boots, by sledgehammer, by being set afire, by being cut into pieces. Children were murdered by ways that need not, and perhaps cannot, be described.

Of the hundreds of thousands of Jews and Serbs at Jasenovac, probably fewer than one hundred survived. These are the words of four of them:

> "We slept in the mud. Whoever found a piece of wood board to lay on felt like a king."

> "The Ustashis would laugh while they hit the prisoners and they would compete with one another to see who could do it the fastest. The prisoners could not contain their pain and would shriek like animals."

> "Since the Ustasha thought that the work [of building a dam to protect the camp] was proceeding too slowly mass executions were begun to instill terror, so that one can say this dam was built with the bones of the Jews and Serbs."

> "Once a group of ten young Ustasha guards came. We saw that they had just joined up. They came from Bosnia. They were young people and knew absolutely nothing about Jews. They began to ask us who we were and why we were imprisoned. After a couple of months . . . one member of this group boasted . . . that he killed the Jews with a piece of wood three centimeters long. He sharpened it on both ends and drove it into their mouths."[20]

The laws establishing these camps were signed by Ante Pavelic and Andrija Artukovic.[21]

In the end, the Ustashi government defeated itself. Unable to mount an effective military campaign, particularly against Tito's well-disciplined insurgents; hemorrhaging from the defection of moderate Croatians as well as Jews and Serbs who managed to elude the Ustashi terror squads; and losing the support of its patrons in Berlin and Rome, who had more pressing battles to fight, the Independent State of Croatia saw the territory it controlled shrink inexorably until, in the final days, it encompassed little more than the city of Zagreb.[22] A gutted and weakened shell, devoid of any popular support or legitimacy, the government lasted precisely as long as its creator and benefactor, the Third Reich. In early May 1945, as the world learned of Hitler's suicide, and as the Red Army met the Americans at the Elbe, Pavelic fled Zagreb for Austria, where he remained for two years in secrecy. In 1949 he fled to Italy, disguised as a monk, where he lived for another two years in a monastery until he flew to Buenos Aires.

On April 10, 1951, the tenth anniversary of the founding of his government, he announced over a Montevideo radio station the "reconstruction" of the "Independent State of Croatia." He never saw Zagreb again. In 1957 he left Argentina for Madrid, where he died in 1959.[23]

Artukovic took a different route, one that ended far from Zagreb and far from Buenos Aires. On May 5, 1945, with thousands of other Ustashi and their sympathizers, he fled with Pavelic and the German army to Austria, where British authorities later found him and detained him for a month of interrogation. Inexplicably, he was released, his Croatian passport stamped "No security objection." Fearful nonetheless of being returned to Yugoslavia, he went to Salzburg in August 1945, where the local authorities endorsed his passport as a Yugoslav citizen—a keen irony. He stayed in Austria a year before fleeing once again, this time to Switzerland, where he entered—illegally, the Swiss later claimed—as a "political refugee." Here he adopted the alias "Alois Anich." The Swiss allowed him to stay for eight months on condition he make arrangements to go elsewhere in that time, and on July 15, 1947, he departed for Ireland under the false name of Anich.

The Irish were apparently no happier to have him than the Swiss, although it is doubtful that they knew who he was. They allowed him to stay for one year on condition that he leave when the year was up. In June 1948, shortly after the birth in Ireland of his third child, his first son, he applied at the American legation in Dublin for a tourist visa to come to America, stating under oath that his name was Anich. The visa was granted, allowing Artukovic and his family to enter the United States. On July 16, 1948, they arrived in New York. The visa was valid for ninety days.

Artukovic and his family flew immediately to Los Angeles, where they joined his brother, a naturalized American citizen who had built a prosperous contracting business after entering the United States in the thirties. His brother supported the family, putting them up rent-free in an exclusive enclave in Surfside, California, south of Los Angeles, where John Artukovic owned several houses and apartment buildings. He gave Andrija a job as a bookkeeper in the family business.

On September 15, 1948, a few weeks before his "tourist" visa was to expire, Artukovic—still using the name Anich and boldly denying under oath that he had been known by any other name—applied for an extension of his permit, which was granted to February

3, 1949. On January 25 he applied for another extension, and for the first time revealed that his true name was Andrija Artukovic. That extension was routinely granted—the name Artukovic meant nothing to immigration clerks—and expired April 17, 1949, some nine months after Artukovic had come to America. April 17 came and went, and Artukovic stayed.

In the meantime, Artukovic applied to become a permanent resident of the United States under the Displaced Persons Act. Nothing ever came of Artukovic's application, because the act's cutoff date for entry was April 1, 1948, some three months before Artukovic had arrived.

But John Artukovic had influential friends in California, and in March 1949 his congressman introduced a seemingly routine "private bill" that would have given Andrija Artukovic and his family the status of legal residents, wiping out the illegality of their phony-name entry into the United States. At that time private bills were little favors that congressmen gave their alien constituents to avoid all the troublesome red tape of lawful immigration: a sort of legal end run around the requirements of the law. But when the Justice Department referred the bill to the Immigration and Naturalization Service for a routine investigation of its intended beneficiaries, it was little prepared for what it would find.

In April 1949, the INS office in Los Angeles called Artukovic in for an interview. He told his story, and INS realized for the first time that they were not dealing with just another wandering refugee who had washed up on the shores of California. Artukovic, the Los Angeles office reported back to Washington, had been the minister of the interior for the Independent State of Croatia and, while he claimed to be fleeing Communism, the INS interviewer was not so sure. "From such histories as are available locally," he reported, "it would seem that this Croatian government was one of the Axis dominated governments set up after the Germans overrun [sic] that area, and was the government headed by Ante Pavolic [sic], an anti-Communist but pro-Nazi dictator."

The Immigration Service had stumbled upon a Nazi in Los Angeles.

When the report reached Washington, INS headquarters called in the State Department. State checked its files and tossed INS a bombshell. It discovered that as early as July 1946, when Artukovic was hiding out in Austria, Yugoslavia had notified the United States that it was looking for him: "as Minister of the Interior, the subject gave orders for the arrest and complete extermination of Serbs and Jews in the independent state of Croatia and ordered the establishment of concentration camps where masses of Jews and Serbs of Croatia were deported, kept under the most inhuman conditions, ill-treated and eventually exterminated." The State Department also reported that the Yugoslavs had made a similar request to Great Britain but that, of the hundreds of people named by the Yugoslavs, the British had considered only nineteen to be worth looking for. One of the nineteen was Artukovic.

Britain's parliamentary undersecretary of state for foreign affairs, the State Department told INS, had addressed the House of Commons on July 26, 1948, only ten days after "Alois Anich" had landed in America. Thinking that Artukovic might be in Britain, the undersecretary had declared that Artukovic and his eighteen fellow fugitives wanted by the Yugoslavs "are all persons who by the nature of their official positions rendered such signal service to the enemy that it would be difficult if not impossible for us to justify refusal to consider surrendering them."

The State Department also told INS that Artukovic would never have made it into the United States under his own name. Had he used his true name when he applied at the American legation in Dublin for his visa, the investigation—which had of course turned up nothing for the name "Alois Anich"—would "in all probability have disclosed that Mr. Artukovich [sic] had been a high-ranking official of the Nazi-inspired Independent State of Croatia, and that he had been active in promoting the Nazi ideology." Such a discovery would have been "ample grounds" to bar Artukovic's entry into the United States.*

The State Department report, which told INS everything it needed to know about Artukovic's past, was delivered to INS on November 14, 1949. On February 6, 1950, INS sent its report not to the congressional liaison at the Justice Department, which was handling

---

*There is little doubt that Artukovic intended to deceive American authorities. Not only did he use a phony name, he said he was coming to visit his "sister-in-law" Lucille Artukovic. Lucille was the wife of Artukovic's brother John, but American officials would have assumed, since the applicant's name was "Anich," that he meant his wife's sister. Had "Anich" disclosed that he was visiting his brother John Artukovic, his deception might have come unraveled when American authorities inquired as to why his name was different from his brother's.

the private bill question, but straight to the number two man at Justice, Deputy Attorney General Peyton Ford.

At this point, two things were absolutely clear. First, Artukovic's status in the United States was as illegal as could be, regardless of his past. His visa and the two extensions had expired a year before, in 1949; the private bill, which might have saved him, was doomed;* and Artukovic's application for permanent residence under the Displaced Persons Act was stillborn, because he had arrived after the act's cutoff date. On top of all that, it was undeniable that, by using a false name, Artukovic had never entered the United States legally to begin with. Second, the Immigration and Naturalization Service, and indeed the deputy attorney general, who supervises INS for the Justice Department, was by that time fully aware that Artukovic had been a high-ranking Nazi collaborator wanted by a foreign government. The State Department had told INS and Justice that, in effect, if the government had known in 1948 what it knew now, Artukovic would never have been allowed to come here. In short, Artukovic was a distinctly undesirable person to have around, and there was nothing standing in the way of his deportation.

Yet despite these undeniable facts—and whether Artukovic was responsible for concentration camps and mass murder was beside the point—the United States government did absolutely nothing to move against Artukovic. Without a legal leg to stand on, he went to work at his brother's construction company every morning and came home every night. For over a year the government's paralysis continued. No one said anything; no one did anything.†

In 1950 Congress extended the Displaced Persons Act cutoff date to April 30, 1949; anyone who entered the country before that date, as Artukovic had, could now apply for permanent residence—the first step to citizenship. Nazi collaborators, as well as those who had entered the United States under false names, were ineligible. Nonetheless, on October 19, 1950, Artukovic filed another application for permanent residence in the United States.

---

*The private bill was never brought to a vote and it expired when Congress adjourned in the summer of 1950.

†On February 14, 1951, the FBI reported to INS that "another government agency conducting intelligence investigations" had determined in 1943 that Artukovic was "head of the Croatian Gestapo." INS did nothing with this information.

Still nothing happened. Neither INS nor the Department of Justice acted on the application or took any action to deport Artukovic. But the secret could not be kept forever. Indeed, considering how many people knew of it—the INS office in Los Angeles, INS headquarters in Washington, the deputy attorney general's office, the State Department, almost everyone, it seemed, but the public—the question had to be not whether the word would get out, but when.

In March 1951 the tremors began in Los Angeles. Yugoslav consular officials, apparently onto something, contacted Yugoslav emigrés asking if they knew the "exact address" of Artukovic. Apparently they did. On March 31, more than sixteen months after INS had quietly pieced together the Artukovic story, the government of Yugoslavia delivered a formal diplomatic note through its embassy in Washington to the State Department. It provided Artukovic's precise address in California and reported that he was living "unhidden, under his true name." Yugoslavia firmly requested that "immediate steps be taken by American authorities . . . to hand over this notorious war criminal to the Yugoslav authorities and, thus, help put him on trial in the country where he committed his abominable crimes."

The State Department accepted the note and quietly tucked it inside its institutional vest. Weeks went by, and the State Department did not respond.

The Yugoslav embassy grew impatient. If the American government would not do anything, it would take its case to the American public, and it knew just how to do it. On April 29, 1951, the tremors ended and the story erupted.

Drew Pearson, the syndicated columnist, went on the air that Sunday evening and broke the Artukovic story on his nationwide radio broadcast. For the first time, the public learned that a high Nazi official—and very possibly a major Nazi war criminal—was alive and well and living in California. The Los Angeles *Daily News,* a clamorous tabloid, took it from there. Its reporters tracked down Artukovic at his home, and on Friday, May 4, its banner headline screamed, "ACCUSED WARTIME 'BUTCHER' IN L.A." On the front page were photographs of Artukovic's beachside home and of his brother's construction company.

Artukovic refused to be interviewed, and government officials had said nothing, but the Yugoslav embassy was ready. Artukovic was one of "the very worst war criminals," a Yugoslav spokesman told the *Daily News.* "We cannot understand why a man like Artukovich is allowed to have life and liberty in the United States when he has the blood of hundreds of thousands of our people on his hands and in his conscience."

Then as now, nothing galvanizes the government's bureaucracy into action faster than sensational publicity. The Los Angeles office of INS cabled Washington: the hearing on the second application for permanent residence, which had been languishing for six months, would start in four days. Letters and telegrams, for and against Artukovic, began arriving at INS offices.*

Artukovic's honeymoon was over. The Immigration Service, which had been ignoring him for fifteen months, could ignore him no longer. Nor could the State Department, which now faced the necessity of responding to Yugoslavia's note demanding that Artukovic be arrested. On May 7, a week after Pearson's broadcast, two State Department officials went to the INS commissioner's office and "suggested" that INS immediately begin deportation proceedings to return Artukovic—not to Yugoslavia, but to Ireland, from whence he had come to the United States, "or to some other country of [Artukovic's] choice." Clearly, the State Department had no intention of turning Artukovic over to the Yugoslavs, and was asking INS to get State off the hook by beginning the process of deporting Artukovic to anyplace else.

The deputy commissioner of INS went immediately to Deputy Attorney General Ford to ask him what to do, and the following day Ford's assistant, noting that he was speaking with Ford's approval, sent a remarkable handwritten note back to INS:

> Altho it appears that deportation proceedings should be instituted, [Artukovic] and/or his family should not be sent to apparently certain death at the hands of the Yugoslavia communists. Unless it can be established that he was responsible for the deaths of any Americans, I think that deportation should be to some non-

---

*Two letters will give a good idea of the passionate feelings that quickly arose when Artukovic was discovered. From the Akron, Ohio, chapter of the United American Croatians: "diabolically false charges . . . by the hateful Communistic representatives of the more hateful Communistic State of Yugoslavia." From the Butte, Montana, outpost of the Montenegrin Literary Society: "Andreija Artukovich, as Fascist Number One and one of the heinous criminals in history . . . should be extradited to Yugoslavia to stand justice before the people of that country where his dastardly, inhuman crimes were committed."

communist country which will give him asylum. In fact, if his only crime was against communists, I think he should be given asylum in the U.S.

Apparently, just to make sure the message came across, Ford himself called the INS commissioner, for two days later the commissioner told his deputy, "For your information, it is the feeling of Mr. Ford that we should not deport this man to put him into the hands of his enemies."

So, before any of the facts were in, before the deportation proceedings had even begun, the Justice Department was letting it be known that Artukovic, whatever his crimes, would not be returned to "Yugoslavia communists." And it left open the astounding possibility that Artukovic might even be given asylum in the United States, provided "his only crime was against communists."

The assistant who wrote that note, and the deputy attorney general for whom he spoke, were, one must dearly hope, not familiar with the slaughter that had taken place in Croatia ten years earlier, where Jews and Serbs, men, women, and children, were tortured and killed with little care whether they were "communists" or not. But their message reveals much about United States attitudes in 1951: it was no longer the victims who mattered, nor the crimes, nor even the criminals. It was the Communists. "Yugoslavia communists" would not get their hands on Andrija Artukovic.

Thus, barely a week after the press had made public the biggest Nazi war criminal story of the decade, the State Department and the highest levels of the Justice Department had quickly and firmly, and quite secretly, joined hands to stand between Artukovic and Tito's government. While something would now have to be done about this Nazi in California, at least for the public's sake, sending him back to the land of his birth and the scene of his crimes was simply not going to happen. This decision was not made public.*

The following day, May 9, 1951, the deportation machinery was set in motion when INS served Artukovic with a summons. The summons did not and could not order him deported forthwith. No alien can be deported from the United States without a hearing at which

---

*While this was going on in Washington, the hearing on Artukovic's application for permanent residence under the Displaced Persons Act was hurriedly convened in Los Angeles on May 7 and 8. Because Artukovic had entered the United States under a false name, he was ineligible for displaced persons status, and his application was denied.

the government must prove that he is here illegally. But serving the papers set that process in motion. And, indirectly, it set the process of extradition in motion as well, as we shall see. These battles, each fought on its own turf, would pit Artukovic against American law, though which side the government was on would never be quite clear.

Extradition and deportation are two quite different legal creatures, though they are often confused in the public's mind. Extradition begins when a foreign country—Yugoslavia—demands that the United States arrest and hand over a person wanted for crimes he committed in the foreign country. The formal process reflects the general belief among nations that a criminal should not be allowed to escape justice in one country by crossing over to another. Deportation, on the other hand, begins when the United States government itself moves to evict an alien because he was never legally admitted in the first place, or because something he has done since he entered—staying too long, committing a crime, failing to register, or whatever—has made him ineligible to remain. Where an alien goes when he is deported is usually a secondary concern, and that question is not even brought up, as a legal matter, until the hearing is concluded and the alien is found to be in residence illegally. Under American deportation law, an alien is entitled to pick the country he wishes to be deported to—a choice that American officials may or may not choose to honor—but if he does not make a choice, he may be deported to the country from which he entered the United States (Ireland, in this case), or the country of birth (Yugoslavia), or, failing that, any country that is willing to receive him. What happens to an alien once he is deported is solely a matter for the country that takes him.

Extradition and deportation thus have nothing to do with each other; they are two quite distinct ways of getting someone out of the country. An alien can be deported whether or not an extradition request from another country has been received (and indeed the vast majority of deportees are never sought by other countries for crimes), and an extradition request may be granted by the United States without ever cranking up the deportation machinery (and indeed someone can be extradited even though he might be quite immune from deportation, a United States citizen perhaps). Deportation can be sought only by the United States; extradition can be sought only by a foreign country.

Only once in a very great while are the two maneuvers brought to bear against the same person, as they were against Artukovic in 1951. Even then, the proceedings have entirely separate lives; what goes on in one case has nothing to do with the other. Extradition may succeed and deportation fail, or vice versa. This is not only because they are unrelated legally—extradition requires proof of a crime abroad, deportation requires proof of illegal presence in the United States— but because they are decided by two separate branches of the U.S. government: extradition by the federal courts, deportation by the executive branch through the Department of Justice and its wholly-owned subsidiary, the Immigration and Naturalization Service.

Artukovic thus found himself fighting two separate legal battles. Loss of the extradition fight would mean his return to Yugoslavia; loss of the deportation fight would mean his removal to any number of possible countries (any of which could, if it chose, then extradite him to Yugoslavia). Yugoslavia was the one place in the world he did not want to be. Whether the trial was fair or not, whether the world would proclaim it as justice for unimaginable crimes or as a political execution at the hands of a Communist dictator, would make little difference. Once in Yugoslavia, conviction and execution would be virtually certain. Artukovic was in California, and in California he was determined to stay.

When INS by its summons notified Artukovic on May 9, 1951, that it intended to hold a deportation hearing—which was still several months away—the State Department was indeed off the hook, as it had requested, and could reply at last to the Yugoslavs' request that he be summarily handed over. On May 14 State replied that "proceedings have been instituted in the United States with a view to his deportation." But, added State, "[i]f the deportation of Dr. Artukovic* is not effected the Secretary of State will be pleased to give consideration . . . to a request from the [Yugoslav] Ambassador for the extradition of the accused pursuant to the Extradition Treaty of October 25, 1901, in force between the United States and Yugoslavia." The State Department was telling Yugoslavia that it would not simply send out the FBI to arrest Artukovic and turn him over to Belgrade, but that Yugoslavia could invoke the traditional extradition process and leave the question to the courts. A week after this reply,

---

*Artukovic was thought entitled to use "Doctor" under the European tradition of awarding lawyers a Doctor of Laws degree.

State sent another, disavowing any implication that the Yugoslavs must await the outcome of deportation hearings before requesting extradition. "The formal request for the extradition of Dr. Artukovic may be filed at any time," it said.

The State Department's reference to "The Extradition Treaty of October 25, 1901, in force between the United States and Yugoslavia" was not nearly as innocuous or as technical as it seemed. American law prohibits extradition to another country unless a formal extradition treaty is in effect. The United States had no extradition treaty with the Tito government; indeed, we had held our diplomatic nose when we formally recognized Tito in 1945, noting that, while Washington might accept Tito's ambassador, this act "should not be interpreted as implying approval of the policies" of Tito's Communist regime. State Department archivists had to dig back to 1901 to find an extradition treaty between the United States and the "Kingdom of Serbia," a treaty that had been signed, no doubt with marvelous Victorian ceremony, with "His Majesty King of Servia, M. Michael Vouitch, President of His Council of Ministers, Minister for Foreign Affairs, Senator, Grand Officer of the Order of Milosh the Great, Grand Cross of the Order of Takovo, Officer of the Order of the White Eagle, etc. etc." And the Kingdom of Serbia, which had never included Croatia anyway, had disintegrated in World War I, to be replaced by the Kingdom of the Serbs, Croats, and Slovenes in the 1918 restructuring of the Balkans at Versailles. That government, in turn, had dissolved in 1928 when Yugoslavia became a monarchy, and the monarchy had gone under as a practical matter when Hitler dismembered Yugoslavia in 1941 and as a legal matter when Tito declared it abolished on assuming power in 1945. The 1901 extradition treaty had long since been lost in the shuffle, and in fact no one had ever been extradited under it from the day it was signed. The State Department's bland note to the Yugoslav ambassador was an invitation to resurrect this treaty concluded with a long-forgotten Balkan monarch.

Yugoslavia took the State Department up on its invitation. On August 29, 1951, the Yugoslav consul general in San Francisco filed a formal action in the federal court in Los Angeles seeking the extradition of Artukovic under the 1901 Serbian treaty, and Artukovic was arrested and taken to the Los Angeles County jail that same day on a federal warrant.[24]

There was one problem. The treaty, like all extradition treaties, required that the fugitive first have been charged in his home country with an extraditable crime. Artukovic had never been formally charged. So, a week after the extradition demand was made, the County Court of Zagreb handed down an indictment charging that Artukovic, as minister of the interior under Pavelic in 1941 and 1942, caused or ordered the murders of 1,293 named victims and more than 200,000 unnamed victims, including 17,600 children. The Yugoslav government forwarded the indictment to the federal court in Los Angeles, and the battle for the extradition of Artukovic was on.

Extradition is a fight between a foreign government and the defendant, using the United States courts as a battleground. The U.S. government is really a neutral party, entitled to turn over the defendant if the evidence is sufficient, not entitled to do so if it is not, but having no real voice in the way the contest is waged. Both the foreign government and the defendant are represented by American lawyers, retained by each, and the proceeding is before an American judge under American rules. The normal procedure, once an extradition request is filed and the defendant has been arrested, is for the foreign government to put before the federal judge what it hopes is sufficient evidence of the defendant's crimes. If the judge concludes that the charges are indeed valid and that the defendant ought to stand trial, he orders the defendant turned over to the foreign government. The judge does not decide the guilt or innocence of the accused. If he is satisfied that the defendant is not being charged unjustly, and that the treaty is being honored, he grants extradition.

Artukovic's extradition hearing was originally scheduled to begin on October 22, 1951, but on September 12, two weeks after he was arrested, Artukovic filed the first salvo in his counterattack. It was to open a legal battle that would delay the presentation of evidence for nearly seven years.

Artukovic's attorney, Robert Reynolds, of Washington, reached for the strongest and most venerable weapon in the American legal tradition—a writ of habeas corpus. This is, in its simple form, an order from a court to a jailer ordering that the prisoner be set free because he is being held illegally. By seeking such an order, Artukovic was serving notice that he did not intend to play Yugoslavia's game at all—arguing at an extradition hearing whether there was or was not sufficient evidence to justify his return. Instead, Artukovic was launching a frontal attack on the very notion that he could be extradited at all, regardless of what the evidence might be.

Reynolds' points were two: first, the 1901 treaty with the King of Serbia, the only conceivable legal means of extradition, had long since become obsolete; and second, even if it was still in effect, the Yugoslav charges amounted to nothing more than accusations of "political crimes," for which that treaty, and virtually every extradition treaty the United States has ever signed, precluded extradition. The federal judge would have to decide these questions before it could hear the evidence, and indeed if it decided either question in Artukovic's favor, it would not hear evidence at all.

First, however, there was the matter of getting Artukovic out of jail, where he had been since the extradition case was filed nineteen days before. The bail hearing was packed with Artukovic's supporters—there were thirty-two Croatian social organizations in Los Angeles alone—and a few opponents. Those who expressed anti-Artukovic sentiments "were pushed around a little and called Communists" by the others, one observer reported.

Bail is rarely granted in extradition cases, but federal judge Peirson Hall was more than willing to make an exception in Artukovic's case. In explaining his decision, he made out Artukovic not as a cabinet-level Nazi collaborator wanted for thousands of atrocities in Europe, but something very close to a model American citizen. In the first place, said the judge, bail was proper because he might never grant extradition; "if extradition treaties with various countries were carried out to the letter in connection with charges that might be made, [foreign countries] might demand the extradition of every person who was a member of any armed forces against them and charge them with having committed murder, because surely people who are members of armed forces do kill other people, and they kill them just as dead as they would if they privately did it and certainly with as much intention."

This logic, of course, missed the whole point, for not even Artukovic had been bold enough to claim that he had been merely a foot soldier, or even a general. And the judge's astonishing explanation blurring the distinction between combat and persecution seemed to apply more to an American trooper charged with killing Axis forces than to a member of a cabinet that had declared war on the United States.

But there was more. Judge Hall noted that Artukovic had disclosed his true identity "as early as January 1949" and since then had "lived openly" under his real name, "[s]o there has been no concealment of identity here." Never mind that Artukovic had been required under the law to disclose his true name when he had applied in Ireland to come here, and had not done so.

In addition, said the judge, "[f]rom seeing the petitioner on the witness stand, I am impressed with his sincerity and honesty." Plus he had a wife and four children, and finally, said the judge, "here, in this country, and in this proceeding, is his only chance for vindication of what he has conceived to be his efforts to advance his own ideas for the welfare of his native land." [25] Just what the judge thought that had to do with anything was not clear. Yet with those words, Andrija Artukovic—World War II vet, family man, patriot—walked out of jail on a $50,000 bond, which was immediately posted for him by local Croatian societies. Judge Hall's sympathetic portrayal and kind words for Artukovic could not have encouraged the Yugoslav government or those who wanted to see Artukovic stand trial for his crimes.

Their apprehensions would prove justified.

Artukovic's release from custody in September 1951 on the extradition charge was only the first step. His lawyers now faced two deadlines: to get in their briefs on the legality of the Serbian treaty, and to prepare their client for the INS deportation hearing, one month away.

The extradition proceeding pitted Artukovic against the Yugoslav government in federal court; the deportation proceeding was something else again. There, Artukovic's adversary, if that is the word, was the Immigration and Naturalization Service, a bureaucracy not known for its ability to deal with complicated cases or notorious defendants. Strictly speaking, Artukovic was not even in court; he was in the hearing room of a government agency. While Artukovic had his lawyer, the INS had an "examining officer," a sort of prosecutor, and a "hearing officer," a sort of judge, both employed by INS. There was no indictment listing thousands of innocent victims of Ustashi terrorists; there was a printed form, signed by an INS official in Los Angeles, charging that Artukovic was subject to deportation because he had come in without a passport or "other travel document showing his origin or identity"—the false-name charge—and because "after admission as a visitor, he has remained in the United States for a longer time than permitted." Both charges had been placed on the form with a rubber stamp.

Simple as these charges were, they presented Artukovic with a major problem. He could argue around the false-name charge by claiming that the Swiss government had conferred the name Alois Anich upon him legally—a charge the Swiss denied—but the one fact he could not argue around, the one fact that was documented for anyone to see, was that he had arrived in July 1948, his visa had expired in April 1949, and it was now September 1951. He had no right to be here.

On the other hand, the Immigration and Nationality Act has never been a model of simplicity and efficiency. Only the Internal Revenue Code can rival it as a layer cake of loopholes, escape clauses, and mysterious language. To say that an alien is here illegally is a long way from saying that INS can round him up and ship him out. First, there must be a hearing, complete with cross-examination, the right to call witnesses and present evidence. Then there are several layers of appeals. If those fail and the alien is ordered deported, there are several ways he can apply for "discretionary relief" by showing that deportation would result in some hardship to him or his family. "Discretionary relief" is official permission to remain in the country illegally.

It is no exaggeration to say that the Immigration Act seems designed not to remove illegal aliens from the country but to give them every opportunity to stay. In 1966 the Supreme Court added to this problem by prohibiting the government from deporting anyone unless it could prove its case by "clear and convincing" evidence, a burden not far removed from the criminal standard of proof beyond a reasonable doubt.[26] It has thus become almost as hard to deport someone as it is to put him in jail for murder, and if the alien has a lawyer, it takes a lot longer than most murder cases.

Faced with this situation, Artukovic, through his lawyers, admitted that he was deportable—he could hardly deny it—but asked that his deportation be suspended because it would result in "serious economic detriment" to his ten-month-old daughter, who had been born in California and thus, as a U.S. citizen, could not be deported at all.* The law does not make any allowance for the fact that an alien would never have had a U.S.-citizen child if he had not come here

---

*Artukovic had three older children—two daughters, ages nine and seven, born in Zagreb, and his three-year-old son born in Dublin. A fifth child was born in California in 1952.

illegally to begin with, and Artukovic seized on that oversight to stake his claim. A hearing was set for October 25.

The ostensible question for the hearing officer to decide at this hearing was whether Artukovic's deportation would so adversely affect his infant daughter economically that he ought to be allowed to stay as a matter of grace. But any mention of her in the proceedings seemed an afterthought. INS examining officer (prosecutor) James H. Busselle, an INS investigator charged with presenting the case against Artukovic, paid scant attention to his daughter and focused instead on Artukovic's actions in Croatia during the war. Since deportation could be suspended under the Immigration Act only if the little girl's father was of "good moral character," Busselle set out to prove that Artukovic's character was anything but good.

It was a sound strategy, because it would allow the hearing officer to consider evidence of Artukovic's record as minister of the interior—an opportunity that Artukovic was vigorously trying to deny the federal court down the street. But on this crucial matter the chief witness that Busselle called to lay out the truth of what happened in Croatia was Artukovic himself. If Busselle thought that Artukovic would confess his past and throw himself on the mercy of the INS, he soon learned otherwise. Artukovic had not gone from a declaration of war on the United States to a California beachside colony in seven years by being a fool.

Over a period of three days, speaking in broken English, Artukovic engaged in one of the most startling exercises in historical revision that any American courtroom has ever seen. The Independent State of Croatia, he maintained, was not a puppet government of Germany and Italy, or even controlled by those countries; in fact, he testified, "the very existence of the Independent State of Croatia was threatened" by Hitler and Mussolini. The anti-Jewish laws were enacted only at the insistence of the Germans; Artukovic himself opposed them and personally saved "hundreds and thousands" of Jews. The declaration of war against the Allies was "forced" on Pavelic by Hitler; "we Croatian people," he testified, "would have been the happiest people in the world if we could finally go with our real natural allies, our friends"—the United States and Great Britain. Artukovic even tried to sweep under the rug the animosities between the Serbs and the Croatians—the Ustashi government was "for all political parties, including the Serbs" and never sought a "pure Croatian government." In fact, said Artukovic, he never advocated ridding

Croatia of Jews, Serbs, and gypsies. Norway and Sweden were "puppet governments," according to Artukovic; Croatia was not. In fact, the Ustashi stood only "against tortures, against sufferings," and tried "to make life livable for a human being."

He admitted only what he could not possibly deny, and that, as it happened, was very little. The following exchange between Busselle and Artukovic was typical:

> "And on April 17, 1941, Ante Pavelich had arrived and taken over the government of the newly created Independent State of Croatia, is that correct?"
>
> "Yes."
>
> "And you were at that time appointed as Minister of the Interior in his cabinet?"
>
> "Yes."
>
> "Did you accept that position willingly?"
>
> "I accepted because of my friends that pressed so to such that I accepted this position."
>
> "And as Minister of the Interior, what were your specific duties?"
>
> "To begin establishing of a State . . . road building, the railroads, house building—all possible kinds of administration to organize—to organize power and order—to establish order in Croatia."

This was, in fact, a naked lie. The Croatian constitution, signed by Pavelic on June 24, 1941, gave all responsibility for public roads, railroads, private building, and power to the minister of communications and public works, a post Artukovic never held.

> "You were, in fact, Number Two man in the government, weren't you?"
>
> "I don't know. I was only Andrija Artukovic."
>
> "Weren't you the second-ranking man in the government under Pavelic?"
>
> "No. I was—my position was not that. [While] I was minister I was known as home or property and my moral qualifications were more official [than] my position."

Artukovic's boldness in rewriting history was breathtaking: Germany and Italy threatened the existence of Croatia, the Allies were the real friends, the Ustashi were nationalist patriots only, with a concern for all human life, the Jews were protected, the valiant state of Croatia resisted all attempts of Hitler and Mussolini to control it. His contradictions were obvious: Germany and Italy "forced" on Pavelic anti-Jewish laws and a declaration of war against the Allies, yet they never "controlled" the government; Artukovic saved thousands of Jews, even though Jews were protected from persecution; Croatia was a democratic government, yet the declaration of war was Pavelic's act alone.

Beyond its internal inconsistencies, Artukovic's account of wartime events in Croatia was wretchedly at odds with every objective account of events in the Balkans during those years. Yet Busselle did virtually nothing to refute Artukovic's version of the facts. The only other witnesses he called were some Yugoslav emigrés living in the United States who gave vague testimony that they had heard a man identified as Artukovic broadcast a radio appeal to Croatians on behalf of the invading Germans on April 9, 1941—a charge that Artukovic stoutly denied and that by its nature could not be documented. One of the witnesses that Busselle called on this point knew nothing about it. He wanted to talk only of his escape from Yugoslavia, until Busselle hustled him off the stand in embarrassment. The INS case consisted of Croatian laws, signed by Artukovic. No witnesses refuted Artukovic's well-rehearsed recital of wartime events.

Nevertheless, some eight months after the hearing began, on June 27, 1952, the hearing officer ordered Artukovic deported. He did not find Artukovic guilty of persecution—he did not have to. The question was whether Artukovic's admitted overstaying of his visa—he had now been in America four years on a ninety-day permit—was outweighed by the hardship that deportation would visit on Artukovic's American-born daughter, now a year and a half old. The INS officer had little difficulty on that question: Artukovic, he decided, "is a man of education, training and ability. It appears that he might support his family, including his United States citizen child, in some other country as well as the United States." As to good moral character, said the hearing officer, there were enough questions raised about Artukovic's activities during the war to conclude that his good moral character had not been firmly established. Artukovic was ordered deported from the United States.

At that point Artukovic might have been better off to pack his bags, slip across the Mexican border, and head for Argentina to join his old sidekick Pavelic. The deportation decree did not require him to go to Yugoslavia; the extradition proceeding then gaining speed in the federal courts would have, if he lost it, and if he lost it he would be very likely clapped in jail to await the next plane to Belgrade, with no opportunity to slip away. But he did not pack his bags. There were at that time four levels of appeal for a deportation order (today there are three), and Artukovic's attorneys filed their papers to take the first appeal to the Board of Immigration Appeals, a branch of the INS in Washington. This would stay Artukovic's deportation for the time being. It was only the first step in what would prove to be a very long involvement with the INS.

In the meantime, Artukovic's lawyers, and those for the Yugoslavian government, were putting together their briefs for Judge Hall in the extradition case. Artukovic was determined to delay the presentation of evidence as long as possible, and his lawyers urged Judge Hall to rule that no hearing could be held because the 1901 Serbian treaty had expired long ago.

Judge Hall handed down his decision on July 14, 1952, just two weeks after Artukovic had been ordered deported. It was carefully thought out; a lesson in law and Balkan history according to Hall.

The judge first rejected the Yugoslavs' argument that the 1901 treaty was valid just because the State Department, by its note to the Yugoslavs inviting them to invoke it, had declared it so. Reaching back nearly 150 years to summon forth concepts first established by Chief Justice John Marshall, Judge Hall declared, "It has been settled since *Marbury* v. *Madison*, 1803 . . . that the power to determine whether a law exists . . . and to interpret it, is a judicial power and rests solely in the courts with all the safeguards of review and does not lodge in the *ipsi dixit* of the Executive Department or any branch thereof. Any other conclusion flies not only in the face of the plain words of the constitution, but also in the face of the fundamental concepts of this government . . ."

With that question out of the way, Judge Hall stepped adroitly through the shifting borders and shifting politics of what he called "the unfortunate Balkans" with its conglomeration of nationalities— Slovenia, Herzegovina, Montenegro, Bosnia, Albania, Macedonia, Croatia, Serbia, and the rest—and its various governments: Austria-Hungary, the Ottoman Empire, the Turkish sultanate, various kingdoms and principalities. His conclusion was a simple one: "The Kingdom of the Serbs, Croats and Slovenes" formed after World War I was a new state, not merely a continuation, in new clothes, of the kingdom of Serbia. Treaties executed with the King of Serbia died with that kingdom, and no new extradition treaty had been signed with any subsequent government. Without a treaty there could be no extradition, and if there could be no extradition there was no point in holding a hearing on what Artukovic had done during the war. Artukovic was free, as far as Judge Hall was concerned.[27]

The government of Yugoslavia promptly announced it would appeal that decision to the United States Court of Appeals in San Francisco, and once again the lawyers turned to their briefs. Artukovic faced the fall of 1952 with an uncertain future—he had won one and lost one, but for him that could not be enough. He had to win both to remain in Surfside. Yet for the moment he was in no danger of going anywhere. The focus had shifted to the appeals process.

In April 1953 bad news for Artukovic came from Washington. The Board of Immigration Appeals upheld the deportation order of ten months before. It lit into Artukovic with a vigor unmatched by any court before or since in this long case. Reviewing the historical record, the board declared:

> The government of the new Independent State of Croatia promulgated a complete set of Nazi-type laws providing for establishment of concentration camps, imprisonment of Jews and Communists, summary execution, expropriation of property and expatriation of any inhabitant who fell into disfavor with the regime. Under these laws it was the duty of the Ministry of the Interior, admittedly Artukovic, to decide who should be thus punished, and to determine the disposition of the members of their families and of their property . . . There appears to be little doubt (1) that the new Croatian State, at least on paper, pursued a genocidal policy in Croatia with regard to Jews and Serbs; (2) that Artukovic helped execute this policy in that, as Minister of the Interior, he had authority and control over the entire system of Public Security and Internal Administration, and (3) that during this time there were massacres of Serbs and, perhaps to a lesser extent, of other minority groups within Croatia . . . [I]t is difficult for us to think of any one man, other than Pavelic, who

could have been more responsible for the events occurring in
Croatia during this period than was [Artukovic].

It was, really, quite a courageous opinion. The board minced no
words in assessing responsibility for Croatia's "genocidal policy," in
effect saying that it did not for a minute believe Artukovic's pious
statements that he had been a public servant in a freedom-loving
democratic state. And 1953, very near the apogee of McCarthyism,
was by no means the best year for a panel of Washington bureaucrats
to order deportation of a man for imprisoning and executing Communists. Still, for all its condemnation of Artukovic's actions, the Board
of Immigration Appeals was not prepared to see Artukovic actually
stand trial in Yugoslavia. It suggested that he be allowed to go to
South America.[28]

But the board had no power to enforce its own decision. That was
up to the commissioner of INS, and the Justice Department. And the
decisiveness of the board was not shared in those offices.

The question of what to do with Artukovic had been an uneasy matter
at Justice for some time. Soon after the original order of deportation,
both the Department of Justice and the Yugoslav government were
bringing pressure on INS not to deport Artukovic to Ireland or South
America—no one had yet dared mention deportation to Yugoslavia—
before the legality of the Serbian treaty could be decided in the federal courts. When the Board of Immigration Appeals handed down its
decision upholding deportation, INS and the Justice Department finally put on the brakes. They decided not to deport Artukovic. It would
be, they decided, "inappropriate to interpose the [deportation] processes in the case pending the outcome" of the extradition case. "[A]s
long as the extradition matter is still pending," said Assistant Attorney General Warren Olney III, "there is an obligation under the treaty
with Yugoslavia that it be brought to a final conclusion." He directed
that the deportation case be "held in abeyance until the request for
extradition is finally determined." A month later, INS dutifully notified Artukovic, but not the public, that the deportation case had come
to a flat halt.

Why were Justice and INS so solicitous of the extradition case?
Clearly, this was not one of those cases where the underlying principle is more important than the players involved. The validity of the

1901 Serbian treaty, at issue in the extradition case, was hardly a burning legal issue.

Nor does it appear likely that anyone wanted to be sure that Artukovic ended up in Yugoslavia. The 1951 directive from the deputy attorney general had expressed strong disapproval of sending Artukovic back to "Yugoslavia communists." Administrations had since changed—Olney was appointed in Eisenhower's administration—but there was no indication that the sentiments were any different. And since Yugoslavia was hardly an old friend of America, there was no danger that by shipping Artukovic to Ireland or Argentina we would be depriving an ally of its right to try him at home. In any event, the Irish, if not the Argentines, would no doubt have shipped Artukovic to Belgrade the minute he landed on their soil.

The most plausible reason seems to be that the government did not want to do anything about Artukovic because there was no safe way to handle him. The deportation case had gone as far as it could go short of actually putting Artukovic on a plane,* yet if he were deported to Ireland there would be an uproar from anti-Communists here (and in 1953 there were many anti-Communists here), and if he were deported to Argentina, there would be protests that the United States government had allowed a major Nazi collaborator safe passage to a new haven. Faced with this choice, the most attractive alternative was to do nothing, and the pending extradition case was a very convenient excuse to do nothing.

It could not last forever, of course; sooner or later the courts would either order Artukovic extradited or they would not. But if they did, then it would be the State Department, not the Justice Department, that would take the heat for delivering him—or refusing to deliver him †—to the "Yugoslavia communists," and Justice would be free of its dilemma. And if the courts did not order extradition, the situation would be no worse; the deportation decision would then have to be faced. But at least the decision to delay deportation gave Justice and INS a 50-50 shot at avoiding the ultimate decision altogether. In

---

*Inexplicably, Artukovic's lawyers did not appeal the BIA decision further, and it became final.

†Under American extradition law, the secretary of state may refuse to turn a suspect over even if the courts rule that the requesting government has proven its case and that extradition would be lawful.

fact, it was better than a 50-50 chance, because something else might always intervene in the meantime. Tito might be overthrown and replaced by a democratic government. Artukovic's congressman James B. Utt was regularly introducing private bills to protect Artukovic; none had gone anywhere yet in Congress, but if one ever did it would end any deportation possibility. Artukovic might head across the border to Mexico or Argentina or Switzerland—or anywhere—in the dark of night. For that matter, Artukovic might die. Stranger things have happened to a man with enemies.

Above all, there was no independent force pushing the case to a resolution. Like all deportation cases, INS had filed the charge, had heard the evidence, and had decided the matter. It was not like a court, with two opposing parties before it, one sure to be pushing the other. Here, there was no one outside the Justice Department involved in the deportation case. What INS had created, INS could neglect.

The decision to delay paid its first dividend the following year. On February 19, 1954, the U.S. Court of Appeals overturned Judge Hall's decision that the 1901 treaty with the Kingdom of Serbia was no longer valid.[29] The court ruled that the Kingdom of Serbs, Croats, and Slovenes formed in 1918, the forerunner of modern Yugoslavia, was not a new country at all; it was simply a union of Serbia with the Balkan elements of the old Austro-Hungarian empire, and thus the treaties of Serbia became the treaties of its successor. Artukovic could be extradited under the treaty. Judge Hall, the court intimated, had simply not understood his Yugoslavian history.*

It is worth noting that, by this point, the State Department had apparently reversed the opposition to Artukovic's extradition that it had expressed to INS when the Yugoslavs first filed their demand for

---

*It was the court of appeals that did not understand Yugoslavian history, however. The documents surrounding the 1918 birth of Yugoslavia were ambiguous; some implied that it was a new state, others seemed to preserve the old Kingdom of Serbia in a new form. To resolve the confusion thirty-six years afterward, the court of appeals sought some consistent thread of history. What it came up with, however, was a gross misreading of history: "The people of each of these combining countries [Serbia, Croatia, Slovenia] are preponderantly of Yugoslav or South Slavic blood and throughout a very, very long period of time they have been keenly conscious of their interrelation and have harbored an unabated ambition to live as part of a United Yugoslav state."

That crucial principle is simply not true. The Croats, Serbs, and Slovenes were mutually suspicious peoples of quite different cultures, histories, politics, and religions. The 1918 state was a "shotgun marriage," in one expert's words, arranged by the Allies at Versailles.[30] There had never even been a consensus on the constitution of the state, and the underlying animosities had festered for twenty-three years until they blew the country apart in 1941.

Artukovic in 1951. State had filed a brief with the court of appeals as a "friend of the court" urging it to uphold the treaty, not because State was concerned with Artukovic individually but because it was vehemently opposed to Judge Hall's overturning a treaty that State had declared to be valid. Apparently the prospect that courts might ignore State's interpretations of treaties was more abhorrent than the prospect of returning Artukovic to Yugoslavia, and State rushed to protect its institutional flank.

The court of appeals sent the extradition case back to Judge Hall to resolve the second matter in Artukovic's attempt to avoid the extradition hearing—the claim that he was being accused of merely "political" crimes.*

At this point, matters looked bleak for Artukovic, at least on paper. His deportation had been upheld, and his early victory in the extradition case had been snuffed out. But on the other hand, INS was leaving him alone, and he still had one more argument to make before Judge Hall. And 1955 was approaching; each legal step had taken months, and the months had become years. He had been in the United States now for six and a half years, living quietly, working for his brother, serving on a neighborhood civil defense committee, keeping out of public sight while his attorneys fought the legal battles. Surfside, California, had become the quiet eye of the storm.

It was by Judge Hall's grace that Artukovic was free on bail, and it was Judge Hall who had kicked the first legal underpinnings out of the Yugoslavian government's case. Now, on April 3, 1956, Judge Hall came to Artukovic's rescue again: he handed down his decision on the question of whether the crimes alleged by Yugoslavia were "political" and thus exempt from the terms of the treaty. In contrast to his first decision, the second was brief to the point of bluntness. "It appears from the face of the Indictment," he said, referring to the long list of victims whose deaths Yugoslavia had laid at Artukovic's hands, "that all of the asserted offenses for which extradition is sought were the result of 'orders' issued by [Artukovic], acting as [an] official of the [Croatian] government during the time of war." No further analysis would be necessary. "[T]he plain reading of the In-

---

*The Supreme Court declined to hear Artukovic's appeal, thus letting stand the court's ruling on the validity of the 1901 treaty.[31]

dictment here makes it immediately apparent that the offenses for which the surrender of [Artukovic] is sought, were offenses of a political character." No extradition.[32]

The decision was more than a victory for Artukovic and a defeat for Yugoslavia. It was a stunning perversion of American law. The political-offense exception, standard language in U.S. extradition treaties, is designed to protect true political refugees in this country from prosecution elsewhere simply because they had dared to oppose a ruling government or political party. But Artukovic had not been charged with acts constituting political opposition—pamphleteering, criticism of a regime, escape from a political prison; he had been charged with mass murder, and there was little doubt that if his role had been even close to what Yugoslavia had charged the crimes would hardly have been "political" ones. Judge Hall was saying, in effect, that Artukovic could literally get away with murder if it was committed simply by "order" and not by actually pulling a trigger.

Judge Hall went one step further. He released Artukovic from his $50,000 bond. As far as the judge was concerned, Artukovic was free to go anywhere in the country—or out of it—that he wanted to go.

Yugoslavia was certain to appeal the decision, but in the meantime the local INS office in Los Angeles was on the spot. There was an outstanding order for Artukovic's deportation, and, while it had been put on the shelf while the extradition battle was going on, that battle was now, at least temporarily, over. The INS supervisor in Los Angeles sent a cable to Washington asking what he should do: "Shall this office, subject to appeal of [extradition] action, proceed toward execution of outstanding final order of deportation. . . ?"

What happened next is not entirely clear, but apparently INS headquarters in Washington gave Los Angeles clearance to go forward; the Los Angeles office sent Artukovic a letter telling him he had thirty days "to depart from the United States at your own expense to a country of your choice under the outstanding order of deportation." But then, two days later, the Los Angeles office wrote to him again and handed him the gift of his life: if he did not depart, INS would order him deported—to Yugoslavia.

Why was this a gift? INS laid it out for him: "Section 243(h) of the Immigration and Nationality Act provides in substance that [INS] may withhold deportation of any alien within the United States to any country in which, in [INS's] opinion, the alien would be subject to physical persecution.'' In light of the fact that INS was proposing to send him to Yugoslavia, would Artukovic wish to apply for withholding of deportation under Section 243(h)?

Artukovic certainly would. Within five days, his attorneys filed the application. It would require a hearing, and pending the hearing, of course, he would not be deported.

It is not clear precisely who made the decision to ''deport'' Artukovic to Yugoslavia, but it was almost certainly done at INS headquarters—or at the Justice Department. The Los Angeles office was little more than a messenger service in this high-stakes case.

Without question, ''threatening'' Artukovic with deportation to Yugoslavia was the best thing INS could have done for him. By raising the specter of a return to the scene of his crimes, INS had given Artukovic a bright new hope.

The hearing on his application to withhold his deportation to Yugoslavia began two months later. Artukovic, his English much improved over his deportation hearing five years earlier, had lost none of his guile. The question at his deportation hearing had been whether Artukovic was of ''good moral character,'' and he had accordingly portrayed himself as a benevolent public servant who had tried to help everyone, working only for the freedom of his country. Now the question was different—whether the Yugoslav government would persecute Artukovic if he was returned there—and Artukovic accordingly took on new colors: those of a prominent and influential cabinet minister who had sworn eternal opposition to the ruthless Communists and had done everything in his power to oppose them.

The change was as devious as it was dramatic. For example, at his deportation hearing in 1951, Artukovic had been asked if he had signed a law on October 2, 1941, which had ordered ''the execution of ten persons from the ranks of Communist leaders'' for every victim of a Communist attack. Artukovic the benign public works administrator had answered, ''No—I couldn't remember—I couldn't remember.'' When pressed, ''Did you or didn't you?'' he testified, ''I think no, sir.''

Now Artukovic the outspoken anti-Communist boasted, ''I signed the law.'' There was no ''prosecutor'' now—just an INS hearing officer—and no one called attention to his earlier testimony. The ''law'' that he now boasted of signing was in fact nothing more than a legalization of terrorism. According to a 1951 State Department analysis:

This law provided a convenient outlet for the Independent State of Croatia to excuse its arbitrary executions. Anyone ordered shot by executive order, or who was slain by a punitive expedition, was conveniently labelled a "Communist." In this sense they followed the Nazi line that all opposition to the regime, armed or otherwise, was "Communist." It was the duty of the Ministry of the Interior to determine who was or was not a Communist.

Artukovic went on: the real enemy of the Croatian nation was "international Communism." "The most tragic question in world history," he mourned, was "what happened to noble Croatian people under these gangster rulers, whose real name is Communism." Tito was using "diabolical methods" to reach across the seas for Artukovic "because he knows too well all oppressed people all over the world today look on the United States of America as unique hope after God, who could help them that they could be liberated from this atheistic Communism."

All day long Artukovic swatted back the easy questions tossed up by his lawyer as he proclaimed the virtues of America—"this great country" on which he had declared war—and the dark evil of Communism.

In fact, of course, the Independent State of Croatia had fought Tito's partisans during the war, for if Tito prevailed, the wholesale slaughter of Jews and Serbs and the deliverance of a pure Croatian state would have come to a halt—as it did in 1945. But in 1956, international Communism was international Communism, and a very safe target in Southern California. Artukovic lost no opportunity to lay out his fervent opposition to all things Communist as the hearing officer listened.

At the end of the day, the hearing officer promised a decision on Artukovic's stay of deportation "as soon as it is practicable." Artukovic stepped down from the stand.

"As soon as practicable" turned out to be a very long time. On October 31, 1956, five months after the hearing concluded, INS granted a free ride to all aliens facing deportation to Yugoslavia; except for Artukovic, they were primarily crewmen who had jumped Yugoslavian ships while in American ports. "Official notice may be taken," the INS commissioner stated, "that Yugoslavia is under the control of a Communist government which operates as a totalitarian dictatorship. As in other Communist states, the authorities impose arbitrary restraints on the people when necessary to bolster their authority or attain their objectives.'' The commissioner professed uncertainty as to whether ''such persecution is directed indiscriminately against the populace as a whole or whether it is employed on a selective basis against particular elements,'' such as religious or political groups. Therefore, all Yugoslavs who had applied for stays would be granted them for the time being pending ''the collation of intelligence material being gathered by other agencies of the United States government,'' no doubt meaning the CIA. When all that ''intelligence material'' was in, INS would consider what to do next.[33] The stay was extended for fifteen months. In the meantime, fortune had smiled again on Artukovic, from a federal court.

Yugoslavia had appealed Judge Hall's ruling that the accusations against Artukovic were ''political'' to the United States Court of Appeals in San Francisco—the same court that had earlier reversed Judge Hall's ruling on the 1901 Serbian extradition treaty. This time, however, the appeals court upheld him, and ruled that Artukovic could not be extradited on these charges.

It reached this conclusion by reasoning that the ''common crime'' of murder, as alleged by the Yugoslavs, ''show[ed] a marked degree of connection . . . [with] a political element,'' because the crimes were alleged to have been committed only on Artukovic's ''orders,'' not by the man himself. ''Various factions representing different theories of government were struggling for power during this period in Croatia,'' the court of appeals observed; therefore, Artukovic's crimes, assuming for the moment that he had indeed committed them, ''were offenses of a political character.''[34]

It was an astounding ruling, for the court of appeals gave every appearance of legitimizing mass murder as a tool of political struggle: the United States, it ruled, could not legally hand over a man responsible for the deaths of thousands of innocent victims if those victims died as a result of ''orders'' that were part of a ''political'' offensive.

Under this principle, it is difficult indeed to find any distinction between the slaughter carried out by the Ustashi and that of Nazi Germany itself. Had Eichmann—had Hitler—escaped to the United States and settled in California, how could they have been extradited to Germany, or anywhere else, under this ruling? The deaths of six million Jews in the gas chambers of Auschwitz, Treblinka, and the other Nazi extermination centers were every bit as "political"—whatever the court of appeals believed that to be—as the deaths of hundreds of thousands of men, women, and children by Ustashi knives and gouges. Eichmann, after all, had not personally shot anyone or thrown the switch on any gas chamber; he had simply given the orders by which they died. And he, like Artukovic, was a high official in a government fighting against the supporters of "different theories of government," as the court of appeals so nicely characterized the Allies. There was simply no recognition by the court that genocide could be attempted under cover of a war or political strife. Twenty years earlier, such blindness might have been understandable; in 1957 it was stupefying.

To the great benefit of American jurisprudence, the ruling was short-lived. The Yugoslav government appealed to the Supreme Court and on January 20, 1958, that court, without even hearing argument, vacated the court of appeals' decision, thus stripping it of all validity or precedential value. It ordered that the extradition hearing go forward. Without saying why, the court rejected the claim that war crimes were "political offenses" exempt from American treaties. Even to that, however, Justice Douglas and Justice Black dissented, without comment.*

Nearly seven years after the Yugoslavs had filed their demand for extradition, all legal obstacles to the hearing had been removed. At long last, they would have their chance to put before a federal magistrate the evidence of Artukovic's crimes.

In the meantime, INS had lifted its blanket stay against all deportations to Yugoslavia and had determined to consider each one on its own merits, apparently satisfied that Tito was not engaged in "indiscriminate" persecution against everyone in his country. But when that decision was made, a familiar shadow had crept back over Artukovic's file. A handwritten note told the story: "4-17-58. Take no ac-

---

*The entire text of the Supreme Court decision is as follows: "The petition for a writ of certiorari is granted. The judgment [of the court of appeals] is vacated and the case is remanded to the United States District Court for the Southern District of California for the discharge of the writ of habeas corpus and the remand of [Artukovic] to the custody of the United States Marshal in order that a hearing be held under [the extradition law]. Mr. Justice Black and Mr. Justice Douglas dissent."[35]

tion on [application for stay of deportation] until extradition case now in courts is settled.'' The file was put back on the shelf.

June 16, 1958, was the date Artukovic had been fighting for nearly seven years. In a federal courtroom in Los Angeles, Artukovic and the government of the Federal People's Republic of Yugoslavia squared off at last to present their cases to United States Commissioner (Judge) Theodore Hocke.

The hearing was a tense affair. Croatian sympathizers and Serbian opponents, many of them survivors of wartime Yugoslavia, packed the courtroom alongside reporters and television cameras outside. Representing the Yugoslavs, Los Angeles attorney George E. Danielson, a thirty-five-year-old former FBI agent and federal prosecutor, promised Hocke evidence of the most horrifying crimes for which Artukovic, said Danielson, was responsible: innocent peasants murdered, their bodies mutilated and dumped into mines or caves, or over cliffs; three-year-old children beaten to death as they cried out for their mothers; families locked in their homes or stables and incinerated alive; pregnant women subjected to ghastly pain as they, and their unborn children, were slowly killed; forty-seven Serbian priests, by name; forty-eight rabbis and cantors, by name—page after page of names and dates, all victims not of warfare but of "pure simple, common murder," in Danielson's words. And Danielson promised proof as well that Andrija Artukovic, minister of the interior, was responsible for issuing the orders for their deaths.

But when Danielson stood to present his case he did not call a single eyewitness to these, or any other events. He lifted a stack of over one hundred affidavits of Yugoslav citizens who had, they said, seen or heard of these massacres, and he laid them on Hocke's bench. His case was over.

Artukovic's attorneys knew a sitting duck when they saw one. Over the next two weeks they brought before the court a parade of Croatian sympathizers from the United States and Argentina—exiles who had lived through the Independent State of Croatia, some as government officials. Almost to a man, they laid the blame for all Ustashi and secret-police activities on "Dido" Kvaternik, Artukovic's subordinate in the Interior Ministry, the man who headed the Directorate of Public Order and Security. They portrayed Artukovic as a popular but essentially powerless minister, a figurehead who had been drafted by

TOP: Andrija Artukovic (*extreme left*) and Ante Pavelic, the chief of the Independent State of Croatia, greet a visiting Nazi in ceremonies at Zagreb. BOTTOM: Andrija Artukovic carried by supporters in Orange County, California after being released on bail in his 1951 deportation case.

The three faces of Ivan Demjanjuk: At the Trawniki training camp, 1942; an immigrant to America, 1952; no longer a citizen, 1982.

Ivan Demjanjuk leaving the district court in Cleveland on November 18, 1983. *(UPI photo)*

Bohdan Koziy, Ukrainian policeman and murderer of a three-year-old girl, leaving the Federal Building in West Palm Beach. (*Stephen Crowley*)

Valerian Trifa, Romanian Orthodox Archbishop, denying charges in Southfield, Michigan, after he was served his deportation orders in 1982. (*AP/Wide World photo*) INSET: Archbishop Trifa in his robes.

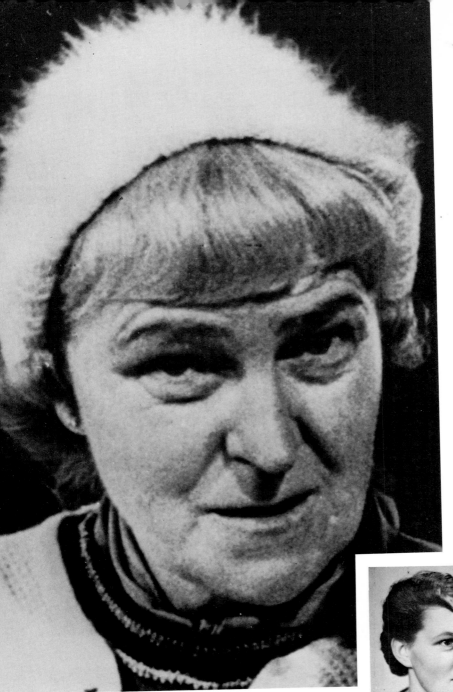

Hermine Braunsteiner, the "Stomping Mare of Maidanek," 1948 (*inset*) and 1975.

(*AP/Wide World photo*)

22. Based on the negotiation between ID, CIC, and DID, the ...... articles of 28 April 1950 can be interpreted as a malicious distortion of fact.

23. By virtue of the fact that this headquarters has had time to liquidate the net operating in the French Zone, CIC sees no reason for denying the French the extradition of BARBIE. However, it must be pointed out that never has there been a written request for the extradition of BARBIE on the part of the French. Secondly, no evidence has been presented to this headquarters in writing to substantiate the allegation that BARBIE is a war criminal. Also, prior to May 1949, this headquarters had had no indication that BARBIE was wanted by the French for war crimes but had always gone on the assumption that he was wanted merely as a material witness against HARDY.

PREPARED BY MR. VIDAL

4 May 50

Decided by Col Erskine, Lt Col Eckman. Majors Wilson and Daniels Mr. Vidal that Barbie should not be placed in hands of ench contrary to opinion here. DID (Col Ligon and Col. Johnson) cur in this viewpoint:

~~TOP~~ SECRET

Page 5 of 5

Copy 1 of 1 copie

The smoking gun in the Klaus Barbie case. When France requested Barbie's extradition in 1950, Joseph Vidal of the army Counter Intelligence Corps prepared a memo recommending that Barbie be turned over: "CIC sees no reason for denying the French the extradition of BARBIE."

The next day, May 4, 1950, Vidal was overruled. The handwritten note reads: "4 May 50. Decided by Col. Erskine, Lt. Col. Eckman, Majors Wilson and Daniels and Mr. Vidal that Barbie should not be placed in hands of French contrary to opinion expressed here. DID [Division of Intelligence, EUCOM] (Lt. Col. Ligon and Col. Johnson) concur in this viewpoint."

Barbie, preparing to go to Bolivia in 1951 (*inset*), and on the streets of
La Paz thirty years later.   (*AP/Wide World photo*)

Pavelic to give his government credibility with the Croatian people, a man of integrity, compassion, and deep religious faith who had no influence or control over the wily Kvaternik.

Once again, Artukovic's strategy was shrewdly designed to meet the question at hand. If Yugoslavia introduced affidavits of mass atrocities, then Artukovic would give the judge a villain. But it certainly would not be Artukovic.

There was one dramatic misstep in the defense case. On the fifth day of the hearing, Artukovic's lawyers called to the stand Father Stephen F. Lackovic, a forty-five-year-old Croatian priest then living in Lackawanna, New York, who had served during the war as the private secretary to Archbishop Stepinac, the primate of Croatia. Archbishop—later Cardinal—Stepinac had been an influential and well-connected man who had sympathized with the Croatian government while refusing to condone its more barbarous excesses. Lackovic, like the other witnesses, began his testimony by praising Artukovic as a great Croatian patriot who could do little to alleviate the suffering caused by the secret police under Kvaternik. But under cross-examination, he was at least honest enough to concede that the Jews and Serbs in concentration camps were there because they were enemies of the state and not, as one sycophant had testified the day before, because Pavelic wanted to protect them from harm and strife.

On further cross-examination by Danielson, Lackovic began to stray more and more from the defense profile of Artukovic. Archbishop Stepinac on one occasion had protested to Artukovic the internment of a Catholic priest in the concentration camp at Jasenovac, particularly since Stepinac had not been notified of his arrest or whereabouts. "I have waited patiently and kept silent for a year," Archbishop Stepinac wrote to Artukovic, "but this manner of treating priests causes me profound anguish. I ask you respectfully, Mr. Minister, to give orders that I be sent precise information." Artukovic replied to Stepinac that the priest had been sent to "forced detention" at Jasenovac for refusing to "celebrate a solemn High Mass on the anniversary of the founding of the Independent State of Croatia . . ."

On another occasion, Archbishop Stepinac pleaded with Artukovic to stop the internment of Jews in the camps: "I take the liberty, Mr. Minister, of asking you to prevent through your power all unjust proceedings against citizens who individually can be accused of no wrong. I do not think it can bring us any glory," he wrote, "if it is said of us that we have solved the Jewish problem in the most radical way, that is to say, the cruelest. The solution of this question must provide only for the punishment of Jews who have committed crimes, but not for the persecution of innocent people."

Still later, Archbishop Stepinac pointed out that priests had been barred from visiting the sick and dying in the concentration camps, and he employed Artukovic to "take all necessary steps with the proper authorities in the ministry under your direction" to remedy the situation.

To all of these requests, Lackovic testified, Artukovic had replied to the archbishop that there was nothing he could do. But the words hung in the courtroom: "give orders"; "prevent through your power"; "authorities in the ministry under your direction." Why would Archbishop Stepinac, who had by virtue of his ecclesiastic office access to any official in heavily Catholic Croatia, including Pavelic himself, repeatedly go to the supposedly powerless Artukovic to seek information, to plead for an end to persecution, to seek reforms in the camps? Why indeed, unless Artukovic was responsible for them, or at least had it within his power to end them? And did Artukovic tell Stepinac there was nothing he could do—or nothing he would do?

But this inroad into the defense case was by no means guaranteed to reverse the momentum of Artukovic's evidence. The fact remained that the defense had at least presented live witnesses to be heard, and they were unanimous in laying the power of the police state on Kvaternik and absolving Andrija Artukovic. The prosecution's case had not a single live witness, and its stack of affidavits had been taken by Yugoslav, that is of course to say Communist, officials. Artukovic's attorneys had not been present to cross-examine the speakers, a point they hammered home again and again to Commissioner Hocke.

The affidavits were not even particularly good ones; many of them simply recited stories the speakers had heard from someone else, making them double hearsay.* Only a dozen of the 119 affidavits even mentioned Artukovic, and none of them recounted Artukovic's words or actions firsthand. Even as to those, the defense met paper with witnesses. The prosecution presented an affidavit of a Yugoslav who claimed he was at the only session of the Croatian parliament that was ever held and that Artukovic had made a speech calling for the

---

*One affidavit, for example: "[A] group of Ustasha went to the village of Berkovici and continued killing the Serbs up there. I know because it was talked of in Stolac."

extermination of Jews and Serbs. The defense presented three witnesses who sat before Hocke and swore that they had heard Artukovic's speech and that he had never said any such thing. The motives of the three witnesses were certainly open to question—one was a "sworn Ustashi" who still believed, in 1958, in the principles of the movement; the second was an Ustashi supporter and former government functionary who claimed that the Communists were out to get Artukovic because he was a Croatian "martyr"; the third was the deputy foreign minister in Pavelic's government, an Ustashi who had come to testify from Argentina where, like Pavelic himself, he was living in exile. But at least they were flesh-and-blood witnesses. All Danielson had were affidavits.*

Artukovic himself, though he was present throughout the hearing, did not testify. Certainly he was experienced enough by this point— he had testified at his 1951 hearing to become a permanent resident, at his deportation hearing later that year, and at the hearing on the still-pending question of whether his deportation should be stayed because he would face persecution if returned to Yugoslavia. But the extradition hearing was the first proceeding where he would have been subject to cross-examination by a true adversary. Danielson had proven himself no slouch on Croatian history or on legal skills.† Faced with this prospect, and apparently confident that they could win the case without his testimony, Artukovic's lawyers did not put him on the stand to face Danielson. It was a smart decision.

Commissioner Hocke handed down his decision on January 15, 1959, exactly ten and a half years after Artukovic had stepped off the plane onto American soil. There was no evidence, Hocke held, that Artukovic had committed murder; Yugoslavia's affidavits established, at most, that the Ustashi committed murders on orders from Artukovic. But Hocke did not believe the Yugoslav affidavits. He was persuaded by the witnesses for the defense who had put the blame on Artukovic's underling. "Mr. Kvaternik was theoretically under the Minister of Internal Affairs," Hocke admitted. "But I am convinced that in fact Mr. Kvaternik was taking orders from no one."

Hocke likewise acknowledged that the orders establishing the se-

---

*The decision to go with the affidavits, rather than bringing the witnesses from Yugoslavia to California to testify, was made not by Danielson but by his client, the Yugoslav government.
† Nor in political skills. He entered politics in 1962 as a state legislator and served in Congress from 1970 to 1982.

curity apparatus, including the concentration camps, were issued by Artukovic. But this was not enough. To hold superiors responsible for the crimes of their subordinates "would probably result in failure to find any candidate who would accept the responsibilities of high office." It was a fatuous and shallow reason, but more importantly, Hocke seemed to be saying not that Artukovic was in fact powerless, but that Hocke simply would not hold him responsible for what he did lest future government officials—anytime, anywhere—shy away from public service on the precedent that would be established.

The Yugoslav government, Hocke concluded, "has not shown by sufficient evidence that there is reasonable or probable cause to believe [Artukovic] guilty of any of the crimes charged. I hope I do not live to see the day when a person will be held to answer for a crime in either the California or United States courts upon such evidence as was presented in this case on behalf of [Yugoslavia]." For good measure, he went on to hold that the affidavits established, at most, political crimes.[36] (The Supreme Court's decision had meant that war crimes could not be considered "political" simply by definition, but it left open the door to proof that specific crimes in specific cases might be considered political on their facts. Hocke said that these crimes were.)

It was clear that the defense had outmaneuvered the Yugoslav attack and had won Hocke over. His scorn for the affidavits was unreserved; they had, he said, been written by lawyers and simply signed by the witnesses (there was no evidence in the hearing that this was true, although the practice is common in American courts); there was no opportunity for Hocke to observe the demeanor of the Yugoslav witnesses (certainly true); much of the affidavits were hearsay, and they were drafted "to incite passion and prejudice" by referring to "newborn babies" and "cruel and inhuman" treatment (a curious suggestion that Yugoslavia's case might have been stronger if its evidence had been weaker). Finally, and perhaps most significantly in Hocke's eyes, "[t]he live witnesses were in the United States and under no fear, inducement or compulsion to testify falsely. History indicates," Hocke wrote without further explanation, "this might not have been true in Yugoslavia at the time the [affidavits] were taken."

What Hocke failed to mention, however, was also substantial. The eight major witnesses for the defense were all Croatians; six had held positions in the Pavelic government; at least six were present or former Ustashi members or avowed sympathizers, and all were bitterly opposed to the Tito government and all it stood for. This undeniably was strong evidence of bias in favor of the defendant—a Croatian, a Ustashi, a fellow official, and a foe of Tito. Moreover, Hocke had before him certified copies of Croatia's laws, signed by Pavelic and Artukovic, that explicitly gave Artukovic charge of all internal-security measures and just as explicitly made Kvaternik answerable to him. The witnesses before Hocke testified that, despite this, Kvaternik made his own liaison with Pavelic and cut the hapless Artukovic out of the bureacratic picture. Hocke believed them.

Hocke also failed to note that while those who signed the affidavits were unseen, the Ustashi record of terror was well documented, the orders signed by Artukovic were undeniable, and most important, Artukovic was not on trial, nor was the Tito government or Communism itself—at least not officially. The only question was whether there was sufficient evidence to bring Artukovic to trial in Yugoslavia. But Hocke was having none of that. He was not going to send Artukovic back to Belgrade on the basis of affidavits and documents, no matter what they said.

Lawyers know that affidavits don't win cases; witnesses do. By sending over a box of paper rather than a roomful of eyewitnesses, Yugoslavia had made a fatal misstep, and Artukovic's attorneys took full advantage of it.

Yugoslavia could not appeal Hocke's decision. After eight years, they had to give up. The extradition battle was over.

In the meantime, INS was keeping a close and uneasy eye on the proceedings. It no doubt would have preferred to see Artukovic extradited so that it could close the case without having to make a decision. But with Hocke's refusal to extradite, INS was forced to do something. The 50-50 gamble taken in 1953 had bought Justice and INS six years, but now it was time to do something.

The hearing on Artukovic's application to remain in the country on grounds of political persecution had ended nearly three years before, while INS considered the blanket stays and then shelved the case while the extradition proceedings were played out. Hearing examiner Michael Leone reopened the hearings in April 1959, three months after Hocke's extradition decision, to see what had happened in the interim.

The extradition hearings had made Artukovic a notorious—heroic, to some—figure, and INS had no desire to deal with throngs of

Artukovic's friends and enemies, or with the press. It posted guards
at the door and allowed only Artukovic and his lawyer into the hearing room with Leone. There was no one, not even an INS investigator acting as prosecutor, to challenge what Artukovic was about to
say.

Artukovic took the stand and promptly bolstered his claim of
probable persecution by reciting all the anti-Tito speeches he had given
since the hearings had adjourned in 1956: to the Knights of Columbus
(a Catholic layman's group, of which he was a member) in Long Beach
and Anaheim; to the Holy Name Societies of local parishes in Los
Angeles and Downey; even a speech to a GOP women's group two
weeks after the denial of extradition. These speeches, of course, were
a perfect way for Artukovic to bootstrap his own case before Leone.
The more speeches he gave, the more anti-Communist his image; by
attacking Tito from Southern California, he was making his "fear of
persecution" all the more prominent.

Leone put the question to him anyway: "Do you believe that you,
individually, would be persecuted by the present government of Yugoslavia if returned to that country?" Of course, replied Artukovic:
"Because as a staunch opponent against Communism and at the same
time, living free in this great country, and having an opportunity to
freely express my thoughts about this international cancer, they see
in me the most potential enemy against them." All prominent Croatians, Artukovic claimed, were branded by the Yugoslavs as war
criminals and "I should expect, as I said before, the most tragic death,
if I should be returned to Yugoslavia."

The hearing closed after a few hours, and a month later, Leone
issued his decision. Reviewing all that had gone before, he ruled that,
as a Croatian, as a minister of the puppet government, as an anti-
Communist, as a Catholic, and as a speechifyer against Tito, Artukovic "has a reasonable basis to fear physical persecution in Yugoslavia if deported to that country." Leone stressed that he was not
finding that Artukovic had "good moral character" or "whether he
is desirable as a lawful resident." Artukovic's presence in this country, Leone noted, was unlawful. But he could stay.

The long battle was over. Artukovic had won, again.

As with the extradition decision six months earlier, public opinion was
divided. But the president of the Association of Yugoslav Jews in the

United States sounded the most dignified—and the most plaintive—note, in a letter to INS:

> . . . [T]he position taken by the Department of Justice in handling this case caused great surprise among the members of our community.
>
> On various occasions, when persons who were truly refugees from oppression came to this country without proper visa[s], it proved impossible to induce the Immigration and Naturalization Service to withhold deportation for so many years, and in many cases such refugees were held in custody.
>
> Andrija Artukovic entered the country under a false name from Austria [sic], and it is not clear why he could not be returned to the country from which he arrived in the United States.
>
> There are members in our community who came from the Jasenovac concentration camp, which had been established through Mister Artukovic's decree and where they had been subjected to most inhuman treatment. These people simply cannot understand the protection accorded to a man who is responsible for the killing of many thousands of innocent victims, while refugees from communist oppression still have to languish in [displaced persons] camps in Germany for years and years without any possibility of coming to this blessed country.

In fact, INS did make two subsequent efforts to seek another place for Artukovic, but they were halfhearted. On June 2, 1959, the local INS official in Los Angeles wrote to the Consul of Ireland in San Francisco and the Consul of Switzerland in Los Angeles, asking that they "consider" taking Artukovic back on a deportation order. Both gentlemen checked with their governments and declined—Ireland on June 15, Switzerland on October 1.

INS made no further inquiries. It canceled Artukovic's bond, thus freeing him from any official restraints. Yet for years thereafter, in response to letters from citizens and congressmen inquiring as to the status of the case, INS implied that it was still seeking places to send Artukovic. In July 1962 INS in Los Angeles was replying that deportation would be accomplished "as soon as a country can be found which is willing to accept him into its territory and in which he will not be subject to physical persecution." And as late as February 1963—nearly three and a half years after the only requests had been turned down—INS in Washington was giving a distinctly misleading response to inquiries: "This Service has continued its efforts to obtain a travel document for deportation to some other country, but to date has been unsuccessful."

In 1961 the Long Beach *Press Telegram* phoned Artukovic to see what his plans were. His plans were to stay right where he was, in his house on the beach. "It's so beautiful," Artukovic told the reporter, "and the children love it so."[37]

What might have been the epilogue to this twelve-year episode came in the form of two very obscure pieces of paper in May 1963. An INS investigator in Los Angeles noticed that nothing had been done in the case of Artukovic's wife and three eldest children, all of whom were technically illegal immigrants because they had entered the United States in 1948 with Artukovic under the false family name of "Anich." But his superior told him to forget it: "Any move on our part [to consider legalizing their status] will undoubtedly arouse a great deal of public clamor and accusations against the Service from each side. . . . [L]eave these cases dormant for the time being as it is unlikely that the wife and children could be decided without bringing the case of [Artukovic] into the limelight."

Two days after that decision was made, the associate commissioner of INS replied to an Iowa businessman who had written to Attorney General Robert Kennedy to complain that "little [or] nothing is being done about deporting this individual." "You may be assured," the associate commissioner wrote back, "that the case has received and is receiving full consideration in all its aspects."

What this saga tells us about ourselves and our government is more valuable than what it tells us about an aging Croatian leader in California, but let us consider Artukovic himself first. He knows what he did in the four chaotic years of the Independent State of Croatia; others do too, but few were in a position to know the whole story and fewer yet are still alive. One cannot place much reliance on what Serbs have to say about Croatians during that time, nor on what the Croatians have to say about themselves. Serbs, and Jews to a certain extent, were understandably willing to believe the worst about Artukovic's guilt when he was before American courts, and for most Croatians, particularly outside Yugoslavia, any objective inquiry is quickly submerged by the larger but essentially irrelevant issues of Communism and of Croatian nationalism and independence.

But of the horrors committed by the Independent State of Croatia there can be no doubt. It has been too well documented by too many objective witnesses and researchers to be open to question, and indeed the defense witnesses in the 1958 extradition trial abandoned Artukovic's rosy account of the Croatian government in the 1951 deportation hearing and simply tried to point the finger of blame elsewhere. There is little reason to believe their testimony that Kvaternik was responsible for the carnage and the hundreds of thousands of victims, and that Artukovic was a well-meaning but powerless figurehead. That version of history requires one to believe that the many laws, decrees, and regulations that explicitly placed Artukovic in control of the concentration camps, the racial purity laws, and the secret police, and explicitly made Kvaternik subordinate to Artukovic, were set aside by a scheming Kvaternik with the acquiescence of a passive and timid Artukovic. That is highly unlikely. The record that Artukovic has compiled in America hardly suggests a weak or passive personality. What emerges from this long involvement with the law is a picture of an intelligent, disciplined, and supremely shrewd individual who sensed danger like a mountain cat and who placed himself in the position of maximum strength when danger approached. Throughout his hundreds of pages of testimony there is not a single false step. There is demonstrable perjury, but never when he was in danger of being caught at it. It is not difficult to believe that this man could have maneuvered himself into a position of tremendous power in the control of terrorism, reprisal, and persecution. What is difficult to believe is that he could have let himself be maneuvered right out of it by an underling. The evidence simply does not support Commissioner Hocke's benign portrait.

The record of our own government in responding to the situation it discovered in 1949 is another matter altogether. Regardless of whether the day-to-day supervision of butchery was in fact overseen by a subordinate, Artukovic was a cabinet minister in one of the most murderous governments of modern times; he was at least officially responsible for the concentration camps in which hundreds of thousands died and for a public-security network that operated with bestial cruelty. He entered the United States by swearing that his name was not Andrija Artukovic. And he had no conceivable right to be here when those papers, false as they were, expired in 1949. The United States government knew all of this no later than 1950. Yet he is still here. Why?

First, the Department of Justice and the Immigration and Naturalization Service simply abdicated their role of enforcing the law against Artukovic. The hearing officer who ordered his deportation and the Board of Immigration Appeals that upheld it presented the enforcement side of the bureaucracy—the Attorneys General and their subordinates, and the INS commissioners and their subordinates—with a clear responsibility to act. They refused. At first they simply ignored Artukovic; when they could no longer ignore him, they offered to send him back to the one country that posed a threat of "persecution"—and then allowed him to stay here lest he be persecuted.

Like all bureaucracies, Justice and INS reflected the political tenor of the government, which is to say the political consensus of the American people. No government can consistently operate outside, much less at odds with, the broad perceptions of the people who elect it. In the 1950s, Communism—international and, at least by perception, domestic—was proclaimed the greatest threat to United States interests at home and abroad. Nazism was not. The war was over; Nazism was defeated.

In the matter of Artukovic, there was no clear political consensus of the American people. For every letter and newspaper column demanding that the United States not be a haven for Nazi butchers, there was another demanding that the United States not deliver up a nationalist patriot to the hands of Communist thugs. Faced with this dilemma, the Justice Department passed the buck to the courts, declaring that it would not deport Artukovic anywhere until the extradition request was decided—a resolution that was a product of expediency, not of law. And when that gambit seemed to be near the end of its usefulness, they thrust Artukovic in front of the bear cage and asked if he wanted protection from the bear. In that way, they could appease the anti-Communists while telling the anti-Nazis that the decision was reached in accordance with the law.

The Justice Department was simply a government agency that chose to follow the weak but safe course rather than the strong but controversial one, figuring, correctly, that it would get in less trouble that way. And so, as is usually the case, we got exactly the kind of government that we deserved.

The troubling and mystifying position of the courts in the extradition case is a separate problem. Federal judges are not supposed to be beholden to public opinion or the prevailing political tides. They are supposed to be independent, faithful only to the law, guided only by the evidence before them. Yet what is one to make of the fact that a federal judge in Los Angeles, and later a panel of appellate judges, were perfectly willing to characterize charges of ordering mass murder as a "political" crime? And when the Supreme Court, fortunately, reversed them, the two greatest libertarians of the modern judiciary, William O. Douglas and Hugo Black, dissented? This conclusion had nothing to do, at least overtly, with the fact that Yugoslavia was a Communist government; it was a shameful and unambiguous statement that shooting a single person might be murder, but ordering the deaths of thousands was a political matter.

Reasonable minds may differ over the meaning of an obscure treaty, or even whether there is sufficient evidence of mass murder in a given case. Reasonable minds should not differ over whether a man accused of genocide should go free because he ordered death for political ends. To say that murder is not murder because it occurred during a struggle between "various factions representing different theories of government" ignores the plain fact that this was not a case of politicians shooting each other. Those who died at Jasenovac or in the rocky ravines of the Croatian countryside, like those who died at Auschwitz or Treblinka, were not politicians. The Greek philosopher Bion told us that boys throw rocks at frogs in sport but the frogs die in earnest. Serbs, Jews, gypsies—and Croatians—died an earnest death, not a political one.

Is Artukovic guilty? The question must be, guilty of what? He is without question guilty of being a leader, both personally and officially, of a ruthless political movement that called itself a government while it exterminated hundreds of thousands of innocent people. He is without question guilty of putting his name to decrees that gave genocide the sanction of law. He is without question guilty of entering the United States fraudulently and illegally. Is he guilty of personally seeing to the sickening deaths of innocents, or did he, as he claimed, largely sit by while his superior and his subordinate divided that horror among themselves?

I think his guilt is beyond question. But even putting that verdict aside, what does the response of American law tell us? Two federal courts were willing to excuse the charges without bothering with the evidence. The federal agency charged with the enforcement of the deportation laws did not deport him even after a finding that he was personally guilty. Those facts should trouble us more than the question of Artukovic's personal guilt. His actions were his own, but those decisions were ours.

The controversy over Andrija Artukovic faded after a while. People stopped writing letters; newspapers stopped calling him. Throughout the sixties and seventies he lived in the same beachside home he had occupied since 1948. His children grew up and moved out; he took walks on the beach and went to church on Sundays, an aging old man no longer giving speeches to the Holy Name Society on the evils of Tito and the Communists. The Immigration and Naturalization Service stopped writing to him. The Yugoslav government did not forget him but it could do nothing more about him. Rumors reached the FBI in the mid-sixties that an Eichmann-style kidnapping was in the works, but nothing happened. After a while the rumors went away. Not until 1980, twenty-seven years after INS had lodged the file into the recesses of a cabinet, would the Artukovic case surface again.

6

JOSEP MAGYAR AND FRANK WALUS:
Ignoring the Guilty, Prosecuting the Innocent

Of all the stories that must be told about the investigation of Nazis in America, two cases stand apart from the rest—and from each other. The first is the story of the most prominent advocate of ruthless persecution in Hungary, a man whose past was thoroughly documented in the fifties by INS. But INS turned its back completely and never took the first step to deport him.

The second is the quite different story of a man who spent the war years as a scrawny farm worker in the German countryside and who found himself accused by the United States government in 1977 of Nazi persecution. Worse, he was convicted by a federal court.

Both episodes are valuable lessons on the attitudes toward Nazi war criminals in the United States. In the torpor of the fifties, prosecution of the guilty was largely ignored, even in those uncommon cases where investigators compiled all the evidence that was necessary. In the seventies, pressure to do something—anything—about Nazis increased, although the safeguard of thorough investigation had withered through disuse. In both cases, the result was injustice.

On November 29, 1956, a mysterious man with a mysterious past came into the United States from Hungary. On the surface, Count Josep Magyar* appeared to be no different from thousands of other Hun-

---

*"Josep Magyar" is a pseudonym, because the United States government never formally charged this man, now dead, in any public proceeding, and there is no reason now to subject his family to scrutiny. No other names or facts in this chapter have been changed.

garians who made it to freedom that tragic year: a political prisoner who escaped when the Hungarian freedom fighters threw open the jailhouse gates in the brief and tragic uprising soon crushed by Soviet tanks. He had eluded border guards and slipped into Austria, where he made his way to Salzburg and obtained an American visa as a Hungarian escapee. In this country, Magyar soon had an emotional reunion with his wife and children, who had entered under the DP Act in 1950, and who had despaired of ever seeing him again.

But in the crowded refugee barracks at Camp Kilmer, New Jersey, where Hungarian refugees awaited final processing, a Hungarian survivor of World War II, working on the camp staff, had recognized Magyar. The survivor reported his sighting to the Army Counter Intelligence Corps and to a Hungarian-language newspaper in New York, and the past of Josep Magyar slowly came undone. He had been no ordinary political prisoner in Budapest.

In the Final Solution, Hungary proved to be a stubborn customer at times. It joined an uneasy alliance with the Axis powers in November 1940, but throughout the war it underwent a succession of coalition governments, holding the Germans' hand with alternating degrees of enthusiasm and reluctance. Laws to restrict Jewish participation in Hungarian life and business had been enacted in 1938, but enforcement was sporadic. Hungary's fascists formed the Arrow Cross party (so called because its emblem was two crossed arrows) in the late thirties, fanning a residue of anti-Semitism in Hungary. They gained some seats in the Parliament, but that was the best they could do. Not even the pro-German coalitions could find room in their government for this fascist fringe of outcasts. The anti-Nazi premier Nicholas Kallay recalled the Arrow Cross in his memoirs: "Besides the scoundrels among the leaders, there were madmen. The retinue of those fanatics was formed mostly of broken-down failures; restless, half-educated elements; the loafers of the villages; and, principally and in vast numbers, anti-Semites." [1]

In the spring of 1944, however, angered and embarrassed by Hungary's consistent refusal to adopt the Final Solution, the Reich sent its own men to Budapest to run the government through Arrow Cross puppets under Prime Minister Dome Sztojay. Sztojay was not himself a member of Arrow Cross—he may have considered himself above such rabble—but his pro-German, anti-Semitic credentials were impeccable. For the 750,000 Jews of Hungary, fitfully oppressed but at least still alive and relatively intact, the nightmare began as parts of Europe were already being liberated. In concept, it was especially grotesque. Hungary was, in Professor Hilberg's words, "the only country in which the perpetrators knew that the war was lost when they started their operation."[2] In execution, it was swift: under the personal command of Adolf Eichmann himself, who came to Budapest, Hungary's Jews were cut down with an efficiency perfected after four years of practice in Germany, Poland, Russia, and the Baltics.

Its swiftness was awesome. In the spring of 1944, 12,000 people a day were being sent to Auschwitz; in forty-six days, more than half the 750,000 Jews in Hungary were deported and killed. By July 9, with the Americans already making their way across France and the Red Army only a few miles from the Hungarian border in the Ukraine, the vise closed around the Jews left in Budapest.

In August, however, the Jews received a miraculous reprieve—or so it seemed. The Russians broke through German lines in Romania, and Hitler cast his Hungarian concerns aside as he rushed twenty-six army divisions in an unsuccessful effort to hold the line in Romania. In the confusion, a new Hungarian government seized power and tried frantically to make peace with the Western Allies before the Russians arrived. Deportations came to a halt; even the economic sanctions against the Jews were repealed. The Germans responded by sending tanks into Budapest—not to reinforce the city against the advancing Russians but to overthrow the moderate coalition. Two days later, on October 16, 1944, the government capitulated. The swastika flew again over Budapest. The reprieve had lasted barely seven weeks.

At last the Arrow Cross had its unrestrained day. The SS installed the scruffy Ferenc Szalasi, the party's leader, as premier. "A crack-brained, miserable puppet," former premier Kallay called Szalasi. "[N]ot one man in the whole country with any claim to honesty, decency or national feeling stood behind him."[3] After six years of agitation against the Jews of Hungary, Szalasi and the Arrow Cross, under directions of the SS, were running Hungary, or at least what was left of it, as the Red Army advanced toward Budapest. Raoul Wallenberg, the heroic Swedish emissary who rescued thousands of Hungarian Jews, wrote in despair, "A number of Jewish houses were emptied of their occupants by members of the Arrow Cross. . . . Some hundreds have disappeared."

The needs of the Germans, of course, came first, and the Germans ordered Szalasi to send 50,000 Jews to the huge underground factories at Dora, in Austria, where the Nazis were desperately assembling V-2 rockets to bomb London. Four days after Szalasi took power, all Jews from sixteen to sixty who could be found in Budapest were rousted out and driven on foot—rail lines had been broken by Allied bombing—over a hundred miles in the sleet and snow to Dora. They were provided no food to sustain them on the march. The Arrow Cross gendarmes who drove them on were "absolute criminals," one survivor rescued by Wallenberg recalled. "I hate them even worse than the Germans."

Wallenberg himself, who had caught up with the wretched mass and had snatched 300 away by giving them "Swedish passports," reported, "[I]n many places the corpses of people who had died or been murdered by the Arrow Cross men covered the roadside. Nobody had thought of burying them." The Red Cross reported bluntly, "[T]he Szalasi regime simply handed over the Jews of the capital to be exterminated."[4]

The Jews who had not been herded to Dora were crammed into a makeshift ghetto to await some "ultimate disposition." They were allowed food and fuel to last fourteen days; those who survived spent three winter months there. Arrow Cross henchmen who found Jews wandering the streets dropped them from bridges into the Danube river, then shot at them for sport. Arrow Cross thugs raided an orphanage, and then a hospital, killing Jews at random. They hung Jews from lamp posts, trees, or whatever else was handy.

The streets of Budapest were strewn with the bodies of Jews killed by freezing or starvation, or by random violence of the Arrow Cross. "The only saving circumstance in those days," said Kallay, "was that the general disorganization of the Arrow Cross regime made it incapable of carrying any undertaking to its logical conclusion."[5] In February 1945 Szalasi capitulated to the Soviets. The war in Hungary was over. More than 500,000 Jews had died—almost all of them in the war's final year, and in full view of the world.

As a youth in Hungary, Count Josep Magyar had little reason to think that he would ever see such a cataclysm in Budapest, much less be caught up in it. Born at the turn of the century to a prosperous Catholic landowner in one of Hungary's most prominent families, Magyar served as a lieutenant in the Austro-Hungarian army in World War I and then got his degree from a school of agriculture.[6] His father, a prominent liberal politician and onetime minister of agriculture, following custom, gave his son the 800-acre family estate to manage. At twenty-five he married, and by 1944 he had sired eight children. Like much of the Hungarian nobility of his time, he had little to do but oversee his land holdings, but that provided his family a comfortable living. He took part in local agricultural concerns, joined up with a Catholic social action group concerned with Hungary's peasants, and in the mid-thirties drifted into right-wing politics, agitating for quotas on Jewish ownership of business and on Jewish attendance at universities. In 1939 he was elected to the Hungarian Parliament on the ticket of Ferenc Szalasi's tiny Arrow Cross party.

The Arrow Cross was not used to having counts in its ranks. Nor was the Hungarian nobility pleased to see Magyar join the fascists. He was banished from the clubs of Budapest. But Szalasi's deputy seized upon the tall, slender, somewhat pallid count and put him in charge of the party's teachings on "the Jewish question." Magyar was made the head of what he was later to admit was the "Dejewification Section" in the party apparatus. As the swastika swept east from Berlin beginning in 1939, he became the party's point man for complaints against Jewish businesses, its public spokesman for agitation in favor of restrictions on Jews, and its delegate for anti-Semitic speeches on the floor of the Parliament.

It was a responsibility he carried out with fidelity. Like other self-styled intellectual lights of Nazism, he was obsessed—and repulsed—by the very thought of sexual relations between Jews and non-Jews. On May 6, 1940, he introduced a bill that would prohibit mixed marriages and would make a Hungarian who had sexual relations with a Jew guilty of "race contamination," a crime to be punished by up to ten years in jail. Magyar was convinced that Jews hired Hungarian maids in order to deflower them, and he added a provision that would have made it a felony for any Jew to hire a Hungarian domestic younger than forty. The bill was never brought to a vote.

On February 12, 1941, he took the floor to single out by name ten Jewish businessmen who had, he said, increased both their incomes and their fortunes in recent years "when the Hungarian people became more impoverished from day to day." "The big Jews are today much stronger and powerful than ever," Magyar claimed, reciting names and incomes. And "these [figures] are only the admitted incomes, since everybody knows quite well what the teachings of the Talmud are in connection with these admissions: when a Jew has to file a tax return to the goyim, then he is not supposed to take this seriously." Magyar gathered steam: "I pose the question to the Prime Minister [at that time, the moderate Teleki], will he have the courage to use the most forceful measures against these and the other Jews too, because, if he shall not have the courage to do this then we request and demand that the regime should deliver power to the National Socialist regime, which will have the courage to solve the Jewish question radically."

Teleki ignored the question, but Magyar's bold words to the prime minister caused a furor in the chamber. In 1941, "solving the Jewish question radically" was an ominous euphemism throughout Europe. In Poland the Jewish question was about to be solved, "radically."

In July 1941 the Hungarian Parliament was debating a bill, eventually enacted, that surpassed even the notorious German law in its definition of who would be considered a Jew for purposes of legal sanctions and the prohibition on mixed marriages. But the bill did not go far enough for Magyar, who wanted criminal penalties for "Jewish race contamination." He reiterated his obsession that Jews were busily impregnating their Hungarian servant girls: "It is well known," he said, "that the Jews regard the Hungarian woman, in whichever employment relation they may be with them, as an easy prey, not only their work but their bodies too." He expounded some notions of "race-mixing" popular with Nazi theorists of the day: the children of Jewish fathers and non-Jewish mothers "have 75% of Jewish blood in their veins, because, as a rule, there is more of the father's [blood] in a newborn." "Science has proved in innumerable cases," he went on, "that Hungarian-Jewish blood-mixing . . . will result in producing freaks ill-balanced in body and soul, full of physical and mental awkwardness, but always of a Jewish appearance and with a Jewish mind." The "negro and semitic blood elements present in the Jews getting into the bloodstream of most European nations can become decidedly harmful and even fatal." When Hungarian men are away from home, Magyar proclaimed, "the enriched Jewish innkeepers, exploiting the misery of the people, freely inject their semite-negro blood" into the village girls. This "unashamed" activity is "according to the teachings of the Talmud, planned blood contamination." Magyar wound up his oration with a plea to his colleagues to punish this contamination: "[W]e cannot have a more serious and burning duty than the saving of the Hungarian blood."

Magyar's vituperation against the Jews was matched by his indignation at the perceived "persecution" of his Arrow Cross party, whose members, he claimed, were being harassed by the Hungarian government. "[P]ersecutions of the greatest proportions are going on against the believers in the National Socialist idea, today, when this idea is triumphantly sweeping all of Europe." Not that Magyar would be mistaken for a civil libertarian. In the same speech, he reminded the House, "Today when we are a warring state, we should know that the Jews together with the [moderate] Social Democratic party, which is only a cover name for the Bolshevik organization, are in the service of the enemy." "[T]herefore," he urged, "the Social Democratic Party should immediately be dissolved, the Social Democratic representatives should be expelled from Parliament and we should not stand for it that the representatives of the Jews, their defenders, could speak here again."

But Magyar's most serious step was a formal request to the minister of the interior to "have these organizations together with the Jews taken to concentration camps. The treason of these Jews," he proclaimed, to the applause of his sympathizers in the Parliament, "should be stopped."

Not even the pro-German government then in power was quite prepared to send all the Jews to concentration camps. Indeed, even in Germany, large-scale deportations were still in the secret planning stages. But only a few weeks after Magyar's speech, the Hungarians did round up some 11,000 Jews and push them over the border into the Ukraine, where they were slaughtered by German mobile killing units, dispatched to take care of the Ukrainian Jews.

In the months that followed, Magyar continued his parliamentary attacks on "the big bloodsucking Jews," calling for the resignation of the minister of the interior for his "protection" of the Jews, formally requesting the minister of education to segregate Jewish schoolchildren from Hungarians due to the "morally ravaging, and destructive influence of these Jewish schoolchildren on the Hungarians." Segregation was rather a euphemism, for Magyar proclaimed it a "pity" to "waste the knowledge and patriotic conviction of Hungarian teachers on Jewish pupils, because the Jew will never become a Hungarian."

Even after the draconian Jewish law was enacted, Magyar took the floor to rail against the high proportion of Jews in the nation's economic life: "[T]here is no such Hungarian person in the country, who has not at least once in his life been deceived, been cheated by a Jew." The "strong hand," he declared, "is missing here."

Magyar was always ready to season his invective with bizarre references to the "teachings" of the Talmud. The Talmud, he proclaimed, taught Jews to "kill the best of the goyim," and permitted "stealing, robbery and the abduction of a beautiful woman," so long as the victim was a non-Jew. His reading of the Gospel of St. John was equally perverted: "[O]ur Lord Christ, according to the Gospel, stated that [the Jews'] teachings originate from the devil."

These rantings, vile as they were, could be dismissed as the vituperation of a mean-spirited racist, except that they were being echoed all over Europe with deadly seriousness. The situation of the Jews in Hungary was precarious indeed; most of them were surviving, but they were being subjected to nakedly discriminatory laws and, like other Jews of Europe, they were finding that under Hitler's "new European order" they had few friends. Magyar's incessant carping could not have provided them any reassurance in their native land.

In June 1942, as the "emigration" and "resettlement" of Jews in Poland to the north reached full stride, Magyar became the Hungarian mouthpiece of the German Foreign Ministry. In Berlin, Foreign Minister Ribbentrop had decided the time had arrived for Hungary to begin the deportation of its Jews. Ribbentrop's protégé, Dr. Martin Luther, a convinced Nazi who was the Foreign Ministry's liaison for Jewish deportation in other countries, called in Hungary's minister in Berlin, Dome Sztojay.[7] Luther demanded that the Jews of Hungary be identified, restricted, and then "resettled" in the East. Sztojay, who prided himself on his vigorous anti-Semitism and who would later himself be installed by the Germans as prime minister, knew that Prime Minister Kallay did not share Luther's—or Sztojay's own—commitment to the Final Solution, and he apparently chose not to convey Luther's ultimatum to Kallay directly. But Count Magyar's sentiments were well known and he was, after all, privileged to speak on the floor of the Parliament.

It is not clear if Sztojay went directly to Magyar or, if he did, whether Magyar was aware that he would be addressing Prime Minister Kallay as the Hungarian mouthpiece in a process that had begun at the highest echelons of the German Foreign Ministry. But there was no mistaking the similarity between what Magyar was about to advocate and the measures that were then sending millions of German and Polish Jews to their deaths in Auschwitz and Treblinka.

As his supporters voiced their approval, Magyar began:

> My very esteemed colleague, Gyorgy Olah, proposed to the Government in one of his latest speeches to place the Jews in ghettoes. But he did not explain how the government should execute this placement. Therefore I shall submit a suggestion in this respect.
>
> Even until, in the course of the new European order the Jews are finally deported, they should partly be sent to forced labour camps and partly put into ghettoes. They should be placed into two groups. The Jews capable of working, from 18 to 60, would belong to the first group. The other Jews (Marton Bodor: Into the cemetery!—Laughter on the left)—the women, the children, the aged and the sick, approximately 62–65% of the Jewry, would be put into ghettoes. The remaining 35–38% would be placed in labour camps to be erected in every part of the country, and the labour camps would be surrounded by barbed wire.
>
> . . . This ghetto system has already very excellently worked out in Warsaw, where they had put the Jews in that part of the city in which they had already been in majority.
>
> . . . Villages and smaller cities are to be dejewified completely. To prevent the Jews from being able to leave the ghetto, is a mere question of police measures.

Prime Minister Kallay turned Count Magyar down flat. He replied that ''the incarceration of the Jews in labor camps and ghettos cannot be carried out within the existing framework of legal norms.''*[8] Magyar's pernicious mission had failed—at least for 1942.

To Ribbentrop, watching from Berlin, it was apparent that more direct measures were necessary. In 1943 he called Sztojay back into his office on the Wilhelmstrasse and demanded that Hungary get moving. Sztojay this time did not bother with Magyar. He went directly to Prime Minister Kallay and urged that the deportations begin

---

*Kallay was not a champion of the Jews, except perhaps by comparison to his counterparts in other Axis countries. During his two-year rule from March 1942 to March 1944, he stepped up the confiscation of Jewish properties and put more Jews into forced labor. But none was deported from Hungary during Kallay's regime.

quickly lest the Germans intervene directly in Budapest to do the job themselves. Kallay was growing increasingly nervous, but he held firm. He stated publicly, "Hungary will never deviate from those precepts of humanity which, in the course of its history, it has always maintained in racial and religious questions."[9]

Sztojay thus had been no more successful with Kallay directly than he had been with Magyar as his foil. But his prediction of German intervention was accurate: in March 1944 the Germans forced Kallay to flee and they moved into Budapest to run the government themselves. Their prime minister was Dome Sztojay.

In the meantime, however, Magyar came up with a new twist. In November 1942 he took the floor once again to propose an ingenious plan to take care of two of Hungary's pressing problems: the continued existence of the Jews and the country's increasing vulnerability to Allied air attacks: "A very simple method," he proclaimed, "can be employed for the purpose that Hungary should escape future air raids, which method would be worth far more than an effective air defense. One thousand Jews should be locked up in a place, they should be surrounded by machine guns, and when the first bomb would fall, these 1,000 Jews should be executed. ["Cheer and commotion on the right," notes the official transcript]. At the next occasion we should do the same, this time with 10,000 Jews, and so on. In consequence, the country would either not be bombed, or else we would rid ourselves with a very short time of the Jews."*

Sztojay lasted in power only a few months. When Szalasi took over in the final wretched days of October 1944, he gave his old colleague Magyar no government post, not that there was much of a government anyway. With the Russians only a hundred miles away, with British and American bombers pounding Budapest from the air, and with Arrow Cross thugs roaming the streets and invading orphanages, Szalasi was in control of very little. Magyar later said that he served as the Arrow Cross liaison to Szalasi, bringing him the letters and inquiries from party members, but with the disruption of rail, telephone, and mail service, this miserable office could not have amounted to much. In Hungary, as in Germany, the Third Reich was awash and sinking.

Szalasi, Magyar, and the rest of the Arrow Cross crowd managed

---

*This plan, like the others that Magyar advocated from Parliament, fortunately was never adopted.

to escape Budapest a few days before the Red Army arrived, and they made their way across the Austrian border. There, luck ran out.

The postwar coalition government in Hungary gave William (Wild Bill) Donovan, head of the OSS who was then in Salzburg, a list of 480 persons wanted for war crimes. Magyar was on the list, as were Szalasi and scores of other Arrow Cross leaders. They were soon captured in Linz, turned over to Allied authorities in the American zone of Budapest, who, as one participant later recalled, "would immediately push the prisoners across the zone boundary into the waiting arms of Hungarian Police."[10]

Magyar was tried by the Hungarian People's Court—a Communist-dominated but, at that time, an essentially independent tribunal—in Budapest, as were hundreds of his fellow Nazis, on charges of war crimes and persecution. He was sentenced to death, but this was later commuted to life imprisonment. From 1946, he faced the prospect of never leaving a jail in Budapest.

In 1950 his family came to America, convinced they would never see him again. In Budapest, Magyar passed his time teaching English, French, and German to his fellow prisoners—languages he had learned in a nobleman's education so many years earlier.

In the 1956 Hungarian uprising, the jailers—or the insurgents—opened the doors of the Budapest jail. Magyar and hundreds of other prisoners fled into the streets on October 23. But Magyar did not pause to take up arms against the Russians. He headed straight across the border to Austria and continued on to Salzburg and the American consulate. On November 13 he told the Americans he wanted to go to the United States. He filled out the papers, claiming that he was an "escapee" from Hungary, which he certainly was. He was required to list all "parties, organizations, leagues and unions" to which he had belonged. He wrote, "Arrow Cross Party, 1938–1945, member." He readily disclosed that he had been imprisoned from 1945 to 1956, as a "political prisoner." The application did not ask for further details, and he gave none.

The routine background checks apparently came back negative on Magyar. Either the Army Counter Intelligence Corps in Germany did not have the 1945 list of wanted Hungarian Nazis that had been given to Donovan of the OSS, or it was not checked. The local Austrian authorities, of course, had no record on this Hungarian. Checks with

Hungarian authorities were not part of the process in Salzburg.

The consulate was thronged with Hungarian escapees. The staff was familiar enough with the Hungarian situation in 1956, but apparently no one knew his recent history well enough to recognize the significance of Magyar's Arrow Cross membership in the 1930s and 1940s. He had been a "political prisoner." So had a lot of people in Communist Hungary. No one appears to have asked him why he was in prison. He had been released by the Freedom Fighters. He stated that he was "anti-communist." He spoke English. He was aristocratic and deferential. He had a wife and six children in America. So in ten days he had a visa; and a few days later he boarded a plane to Newark, New Jersey. His papers were thoroughly in order. Thirty-five days after being sprung from a life sentence in Hungary, Magyar was in America, with permission to stay.

The thousands of Hungarians who fled to America in 1956 were put up at Camp Kilmer, an Army base near Newark, until arrangements could be made for permanent settlement. In Magyar's case, this posed little problem. His family, who had heard of his escape shortly after it happened, was well established in Massachusetts. They had been there six years, since entering under the DP Act, and their determination and hard work had won the respect of their neighbors and fellow parishioners in the local Catholic church. Indeed, Magyar's son had joined the U.S. Army shortly after his arrival and had fought in Korea. Two other children were in college.

Although his destination and sponsorship were never in doubt, there was a lot of red tape to go through at Camp Kilmer, and Magyar was not able to join his family immediately. Had he been able to do so, he might well have stayed in the obscurity that had overtaken him as he was led off to jail in 1946.

But at Camp Kilmer, a Hungarian who had lived through the war spotted Magyar and recognized him immediately as the former head of the Dejewification Section of the Arrow Cross. He reported his information to the Army Counter Intelligence Corps at Camp Kilmer, which passed it on to the Immigration and Naturalization Service. The informant also passed the information to the editor of *Az Ember*, a Hungarian-language newspaper published in New York. In the meantime, Count Josep Magyar, perhaps unaware that he had been spotted, left Camp Kilmer for a joyful reunion with his family in Massachusetts.

On January 26, 1957, the emigré newspaper printed—in English—the following:

> Count [Josep Magyar], in charge of the department of the Hungarian Nazi Party under Szalasi to wipe out all the Jews and sentenced to life imprisonment as a war criminal, escaped from prison during the recent revolt, just reached the United States where he appeared as a Freedom Fighter. [Magyar] prepared the plans and implemented the internment of 600,000 Hungarians [and] made them "forced laborers" of Hitler later to be sacrificed to the furnace of the gas chambers.
>
> We demand an investigation of the circumstances of this man's admittance to the U.S. We call for an investigation of the documents presented by him for the right to live among a decent, God-loving peace-loving people at the expense of one who truly deserves the privilege.

But the INS was already on Magyar's case. Even before the *Az Ember* article appeared, investigators went to question the Hungarian informant—to find out who this Magyar fellow was, and indeed to find out what the "Arrow Cross" was all about.

By the end of January 1957 the probe was well underway. Led by Francis J. Lyons (now an INS judge), a team of INS investigators, working out of New York and Boston district offices, spoke to scores of Hungarian emigrés in the United States and gathered whatever documentation was available from sources outside Hungary.* They found that while many emigrés knew of Count Magyar, his vile speeches in Parliament, and his reputation as head of the Arrow Cross "Dejewification Section," few knew him directly or could testify from their own knowledge as to his activities. The State Department reported that Magyar had been "Szalasi's expert concerning anti-Jewish measures" and even "Szalasi's best friend," but it could provide little more.

This potentially serious obstacle to a strong case was dissolved, however—by Magyar himself. He agreed to be interviewed under oath by INS investigators in March 1957.

---

*The American embassy in Budapest had gone to the Hungarian government to request copies of Magyar's speeches in Parliament, but it cabled back to Washington that the prospects were "not promising." In fact, the government of Hungary appears never to have responded to the United States' request for assistance in investigating Magyar's case.

Over the course of eight hours, speaking Hungarian through an interpreter to three INS investigators (Magyar's wife and attorney were also present, but neither one interrupted the interview), Magyar told a lot of the truth and told a lot of lies. Dejected and deferential, he admitted that he had been the head of the Dejewification Section of the Arrow Cross, had spoken in Parliament for the party's goals, in which he believed, and that he had been tried and sentenced as a war criminal in Hungary after the war. But the Arrow Cross, he claimed, was not against the Jews, nor was he. He and his fellow party members simply wanted "land reform" and restrictions on the participation of Jews in public and economic life. His Dejewification Section, he explained, was simply a one-man office to hear complaints from the citizens about illegal or unscrupulous practices by Jews—a banker whose interest rates were too high, or a businessman who was not paying his employees the wages due them—and to refer such complaints to the proper local authorities to be looked into. The investigators turned to reports of his speeches, copies of which, unfortunately, had not yet been located anywhere. Asked if he had favored "removing the Jews from the social and economic life in Hungary," Magyar answered, "That was not my opinion. I only thought that all excessive incomes should be decreased." Asked if the Arrow Cross party favored, or advocated, removal of Jews from the social or economic life in Hungary, Magyar blandly replied, "I don't know anything about that." And as to reprisals against the Jews, Magyar claimed, "The [Kallay] government did even more than we wanted to"—a blatant perversion of the truth.

Magyar went on to assert that Arrow Cross members from 1939 to 1944 made no "requests . . . of the government" on "the Jewish question," thus ignoring his own repeated formal requests that the government take "the most radical measures" against the Jews, including internment and deportation. "I never attacked the Jews," Magyar lied, "only individual persons which I found guilty." He disclaimed any knowledge of any slaughter or deportations of Jews under Arrow Cross rule; "the whole deportation," he said, "was carried out by the Germans."

But Magyar's lies were almost beside the point; he had admitted that he was the Count Josep Magyar who had been the Arrow Cross's point man against the Jews and its spokesman on the Jewish question in Parliament. Lyons and his fellow investigators knew they had the right man. And a few weeks later, their big break arrived.

Copies of Magyar's speeches had been located in an archive in Vienna. When they arrived in Lyons' office, duly certified by the Austrian custodian, they proved to be pure gold: printed, word-by-word transcripts of every word spoken day to day in the Parliament—a Hungarian *Congressional Record*. Every speaker, every speech, had been faithfully recorded. When Magyar's speeches came back from the translator, the case was made. There were still loose ends to be tied up, but the speech transcripts and the interviews of scores of Hungarian witnesses who could speak firsthand of the wartime situation, particularly the role of the Arrow Cross, made the case against Magyar rock-solid. In less than four months, Lyons and his team had put together a file of material eighteen inches thick—a blueprint of Hungarian treachery.

By May 1 Lyons was ready to go to court with a warrant for Magyar's deportation. But this was not a decision that an investigator like Lyons could make on his own. In a report to their supervisors in New York, Lyons and his fellow investigator, Vincent Schiano, summarized the evidence, particularly the speeches, and concluded, in the stilted prose characteristic of investigators, "On the basis of the investigation to date, the writers are of the opinion that insofar as the charge [of persecution]* is concerned, the SUBJECT is amenable to deportation. . . . It is their opinion that the SUBJECT'S activities, including but not limited to his speeches in Parliament, are within that definition." In New York, Lyons and Schiano sat back to await the go-ahead to file the deportation case against Magyar.

The first ominous note came two weeks later. INS headquarters in Washington told the New York office not to make any decision on Magyar. "Any decision to be made in this case will be made by [INS] Commissioner [Joseph M.] Swing," New York was told.

While this was going on, INS Commissioner Swing began receiving one of the strangest batches of letters in INS history, urging mercy for Magyar. Letters seeking clemency are not unusual, but normally they come from the alien's friends. Magyar's letters came from his enemies. And they were startlingly frank.

Count Bela Teleki, an anti-Nazi Transylvanian, had been a mem-

---

*Lyons framed the charge under Section 14 of the Refugee Relief Act of 1953—the act under which Magyar's visa was issued—which prohibited entry to "any person who personally advocated or assisted in the persecution of any person or group of persons because of race, relition, or national origin."

ber of the Parliament from 1940 to 1944; he later came to New York. He told Swing that, while he opposed the Arrow Cross and all it stood for, Magyar himself was "a rather stupid, and vain man, who was flattered by the membership in Parliament. . . . Besides some reproachable stupid and aggressive speaches [sic] in Parliament, I do not think that he would personally have harmed anyone." Magyar was "a modest, good natured man, and also a very religious Catholic." Count Teleki urged mercy for "this poor, broken-hearted, elderly man." (Magyar was fifty-nine.)

A former Hungarian diplomat who said that he had been arrested by the Arrow Cross in 1944 told the INS commissioner that Magyar had never been a "harmful" member of the Arrow Cross. "I believe that he joined the movement because of his very limited knowledge of politics. I am considering him as in a certain respect a degenerated but otherwise decent man."

A fellow member of Parliament during the war years told INS, "I never failed to join those who rejected his bills," but he claimed that Magyar was "blinded by ignorance," a "good hearted man" who "lacked any common sense."

What was remarkable about these letters, apart from their bluntness, was the fact that the writers were no allies of Magyar. There is no indication that the letters were orchestrated by Magyar, or indeed by anyone.

There were other factors that put Magyar—and Magyar's family—in a sympathetic light. He had several children, including a U.S. Army veteran, from whom he had been separated for ten years. He apparently had had no direct responsibility for the persecution he had repeatedly advocated on the floor of the Parliament. And he had served ten years in jail for his collaborationist activities.

Meanwhile, months passed; what should have been routine approval for a clear-cut deportation case was not forthcoming. Lyons' and Schiano's May 1 report went nowhere.

By August the New York office advised that it was still awaiting word from Washington. More months went by. In April 1958 the Southeast Regional Office forwarded a list of names of Hungarian witnesses to New York and asked that they be checked out. Lyons replied, somewhat testily, that the names had been checked out long ago: all the evidence was in.

Finally, on July 1, 1958—fourteen months after the investigation had been completed—the commissioner's office made its decision. Magyar, it said, should be "placed in non-priority category"—in effect, the case was killed. The reason? "[T]he several equities involved." No explanation was given.

It was as simple as that. The case was discontinued. There was no further investigation, and no charges were ever filed against Count Josep Magyar.

Magyar, scion of Hungarian nobility, the spokesman for Nazism in Hungary, took a job as a janitor in a museum. Twelve years later, in 1970, at age seventy-two, he died of a heart attack in a New England city.

Was justice done in this case? Apparently INS thought so. Though it never said why, "the equities" that led INS to decline deportation appear to have been three. First, he was a middle-aged man—sixty when the decision was made—with a large family. Second, he had served ten years in jail. And third, he was the beneficiary of the pity of his enemies—and perhaps INS itself.

But how valid were these considerations? As to his family situation, there is a provision in the law of deportation that the judge—after hearing the case and finding the alien deportable—can grant clemency if deportation would cause hardship to the family. But that was not the procedure the INS followed for Magyar. The full evidence, on both sides, was never presented to a judge.

As to Magyar's imprisonment, there is little to be said for the argument that he had "suffered enough." The INS's role was not to decide whether Magyar was guilty of a crime or had served an adequate sentence. It was to determine if he should be allowed to remain in the United States. The decision to deport has nothing to do with whether the alien might also be a criminal. To put it differently, Magyar's ten years in prison should not have been a free pass to allow him to come to the United States.

Even if Magyar had been deported, he would not necessarily have gone back to Hungary. He had entered the United States from Austria, and Austria was required to take him back if he was deported. For that matter, he could have gone to almost any country willing to take him. Perhaps he should have gone back to Hungary to serve out his life sentence. But even if that would have been unfair or unjust, he still could have been deported from this country.

That brings us to the third—and on its surface the most appeal-ing—of the "equities": Magyar's alleged role as a simpleminded dupe of the Hungarian Nazis. But does this pathetic portrait justify INS's hands-off attitude? It does not, for several reasons.

To explain away Magyar's role as simply that of a rather dim-witted mouthpiece for someone else's propaganda is too facile, and almost certainly wrong. In the first place, it is inconceivable that any-one, no matter what his intelligence, could mouth the words that Mag-yar spoke without realizing that he was trafficking in the vilest sort of racist filth. There was no subtlety or ambiguity in Magyar's speeches; they were blatant appeals, in the crudest of terms, to man's darkest prejudices. No decent person could repeat these words today, much less in a public assembly, without gagging on them. Magyar spoke them with enthusiasm on the floor of the Parliament in Budapest. The call for internment of Jews may have originated in Berlin, to be sure, and probably the grotesque idea to machine-gun 10,000 Jews in re-sponse to Allied air raids was someone else's idea as well, but no sane person could speak like this without realizing the barbarity of his words. As for his more routine carping on the "bloodsuckers" and "race contamination" and the "treachery" of the Jews as supposedly taught by the Talmud—does it matter that such words may have been written, if indeed they were, by some other Arrow Cross stalwart? Magyar cannot be excused on the ground that the ideas, or the words, did not spring full-blown and unassisted from his intellect.

Moreover, Magyar never claimed—never even hinted—over the course of an exhaustive eight-hour interview with INS investigators that he was simply reciting what he had been given to recite. Had he said, "Gentlemen, my actions were not fully my own; I was pre-vailed upon by others to do what I did," then his defenders' letters would have to be considered more closely. But he took quite the op-posite position. He said that he had spoken what he believed, but that his requests and his rhetoric really were quite modest—an assertion flatly contradicted by the official records. It is beside the point whether in 1957 he truly believed that his speeches had been limited to "land reform" and rather moderate sanctions against the Jews, or whether, on the other hand, he hoped that INS would never get its hands on the real thing. If he himself did not suggest that he had been used as a pawn by others, how much credence should INS have given, or can we give, to that view put forth by the anti-Nazi emigrés, who wrote on his behalf?

It is, of course, possible to be manipulated without realizing it. But that happens when one acts as one thinks best for himself, without realizing that he is serving, at the manipulator's behest, the quite distinct interests of the manipulator. In Magyar's case, he was serving the anti-Semitic interests of the Arrow Cross party. If his own interests actually lay elsewhere, such as with "land reform," he would have realized that he was being manipulated by racists. Even had he consented to that manipulation, he would surely have pleaded it to INS. But he did no such thing. He repeatedly affirmed that he meant just what he said in Parliament.

Finally, if Magyar had been as gullible and simpleminded as his reluctant defenders suggested, one would expect to find symptoms of gullibility and simplemindedness in the course of a searching, day-long interrogation into his past. There is nothing of the sort. He was skillful at evading questions that he did not wish to answer. Though fluent in English, he spoke through an interpreter.* He was adept at describing the activities of his "Dejewification Section" in the most innocuous of terms. He declined to characterize the vicious anti-Semitism of the Arrow Cross as anything other than well-intentioned patriotism. He was careful to portray Communism as the great enemy of the Hungarian people. He professed no knowledge of events that were common knowledge. When he had to, he could backpedal to wipe out an apparently significant admission. He consistently minimized his own complicity in persecution and repeatedly shifted the focus of the questions to other politicians.

That these defensive ploys were doomed to failure in the light of all the other evidence INS was then gathering is not to say they were simpleminded. Magyar did not know what other evidence INS had, except that it was pretty clear that they did not have the smoking gun— copies of his speeches. So he did what any reasonably intelligent criminal trying to save his skin would do: he presented a coherent, cohesive version of the known facts in such a way as to dissipate, or at least minimize, his own involvement with the crime. His day-long interrogation, had it been introduced in court, would not have amounted

---

*This is a great benefit to someone who understands English. When the interrogator puts the question, the witness can deliberate his answer while the interpreter is translating. After giving his answer, the witness can monitor the interpreter's choice of words. If the witness realizes he has said something he ought not, he can "continue" his answer (in his native tongue) to modify it, or at least thoroughly confuse it. This manipulation is almost always impossible to prevent (and usually even difficult to detect).

to a confession of persecution. Prisons are full of convicts who wish they could have done as well at the hands of their interrogators.

INS interviewed only one of the letter-writers, so perhaps the pleas for mercy did not play much of a role in the INS decision. We do not know what did, except that, in 1958, INS had lost whatever enthusiasm it might have had for the prosecution of Nazis. It almost certainly saw no reason to deport an anti-Communist (even if he was also viciously anti-Semitic) back to Hungary (even if he could have gone to Austria), particularly when it meant separating him from his family in the United States. A large, religious family of Army veterans and college students is not entirely irrelevant, perhaps; the point is that the law gives the judge, not the commissioner of the INS, the power to determine just what significance that has, and then only after all the evidence has been heard. No judge ever heard this case. And so the man who called for internment, deportation, and machine-gunning of Jews in Hungary, and who hailed Nazism's "triumphant sweep" of Europe, lived out his days in the United States, pushing a broom in a quiet museum.

Josep Magyar was the persecutor unprosecuted. For Frank Walus, the government was not so reluctant. His is the story of a dangerous combination: an ignorant and bullheaded prosecution and a federal judge who cared little about the rights of a defendant.

The case against Walus, a fifty-four-year-old factory worker who lived on the southwest side of Chicago, should never have been filed. It began in 1973 when Walus, a Polish-born immigrant who had come to the United States in 1959, evicted a boarder named Michael Alper after an argument.[11] That apparently led to bad blood between them; Walus and Alper exchanged threatening words when they met in the street, and Walus grumbled to his neighbors about Alper's integrity.

In 1974, a year after his eviction and in the middle of this apparent feud, Alper told a Chicago Jewish agency that several months before the eviction his former landlord had bragged about having been a Nazi in the Polish cities of Kielce and Czestochowa, where the large Jewish populations had been brutally persecuted by the Nazis.

This allegation, born in suspicious circumstances, made its way to the Chicago office of the Immigration and Naturalization Service and to Simon Wiesenthal in Vienna. By 1976 the INS was under pressure to do something about Nazis, and they sent Walus' name and a rather grainy, washed-out enlargement of his 1959 visa photograph to Israel to see if the Israeli police had any information.

Somewhere along the way—precisely where is not clear—the accusation against Walus came to include the charge that Walus had been not only a Nazi but a member of the Gestapo. The Israeli police placed an advertisement in local newspapers seeking survivors of Kielce and Czestochowa; the advertisement mentioned that the name of the suspect under investigation was Frank Walus.

When survivors came forward, they were shown the INS photograph and were asked if they could identify the man. Several survivors did, telling the police that Walus had been a Gestapo officer who had beaten and killed Jews in those two cities.

The Israeli police reported their results back to Chicago, and the United States Attorney filed suit in federal court on January 26, 1977, charging Walus with atrocities as a member of the Gestapo and seeking to revoke his naturalization.

In the fourteen months before trial, there were several developments that should have given the prosecutors pause. The most obvious would have struck them immediately if they had had a better grasp on history: The Gestapo was a branch of the SS, the elite corps of the master race; no Poles were allowed.

More ominous for the prosecution's case, Walus' lawyer had obtained from German archives the records of the Allgemeine Ortskrankenkasse (AOK), the German health insurance program. According to these records, Walus had been sent from Poland to Ulm, Germany, south of Stuttgart and hundreds of miles from Kielce and Czestochowa, in 1940 as an eighteen-year-old. The records indicated that he was a forced laborer—millions of Poles were—and had spent the entire war years working on various farms. German farmers had made the required payments to the AOK, which had posted them in its ledgers. The entries demonstrated unbroken service. Walus gave his attorney the names of the four or five farm wives he had worked for; they all remembered him and gave statements to that effect. But the government did not back away from its case.

When the trial began in March 1978, the prosecution presented several survivors of the ghettos of Kielce and Czestochowa. They testified of the atrocities they had seen with their eyes—one witness described how a Gestapo officer had shot a Jewish woman, in front of her two children, and then had shot the children too. Another told of

watching the officer herd a group of children into a building; shots
were heard, then silence. A third witness said the man had beaten a
Jew to death with an iron pipe.

The witnesses did seem to have the same man in mind, but there
was some question as to whether it was Frank Walus. Walus was, at
five feet four inches, a short man, yet the witnesses who were themselves five-four or so described the Gestapo man as a little taller than
they were. Witnesses who could estimate the man's age placed him
at about twenty-five or twenty-six; Walus would have been eighteen
in 1940, when some of the events took place, or twenty in 1942, when
other atrocities were committed. The witnesses were not manifestly
wrong—recollections of height after thirty-five years can be hazy, and
there was unanimous agreement that the Gestapo man was not particularly tall—but the identifications were virtually the government's entire case, and cross-examination by Walus' attorney would obviously
be crucial.

But, to Walus' great misfortune, the presiding judge was the late
Julius Hoffman, the aged curmudgeon best known for his intemperate
conduct during the famous "Chicago 7" case of the late sixties.
Hoffman had a well-earned reputation as a sarcastic, injudicious cynic
who injected himself into the thick of any case heard before him. When
Walus' lawyer, Robert Korenkiewicz, attempted to cross-examine
witnesses on the accuracy of their identifications, he ran into a judicial buzz saw. He asked one witness, "Can you be more specific and
tell us approximately how much taller [the Gestapo man] was than
you?" Unwisely, the government prosecutor objected; Hoffman told
Korenkiewicz, "That is an absurd question. I sustain the objection
to it."

Korenkiewicz asked another witness to describe the voice of the
Gestapo man—a perfectly good question where identification is in
dispute. But Hoffman disallowed it: "I think that exceeds the limits
of fair cross-examination," he ruled.

At times Hoffman's conduct bordered on the farcical. One witness identified Walus in the courtroom as the man who had beaten
his victim to death with an iron bar in Czestochowa. But Walus had
been seated in the courtroom—thus obscuring his height—and Korenkiewicz asked, "So when you made that identification this morning,
the only view you had of [Walus] was from his stomach upward, isn't
that a fact?"

The witness agreed that this was true.

Judge Hoffman interrupted: "Are you suggesting that this witness could see his stomach?"

Korenkiewicz didn't get the joke. "I asked if he could only see the man from his stomach up."

Hoffman delivered the punch line: "How can a man's stomach be seen, either standing or sitting, without an X-ray or some other instrument?"

On another occasion, Hoffman forbade Korenkiewicz to use the word "Gestapo," because it was "not an English word. We conduct trials in the United States courts in English." (Hoffman later relented from this frolic and allowed Korenkiewicz to use the forbidden word.)

At the end of the prosecution's case, Korenkiewicz made a routine motion to dismiss the charges on grounds that the evidence against Walus was insufficient. Hoffman rejected the motion, but his explanation was revealing: "The [prosecution], the court now holds, has at this time established evidence as required by law which is clear, convincing and unequivocal and does not leave any of the issues in doubt in the opinion of the court that the defendant did commit war atrocities . . . and that he concealed the facts when he obtained his certificate of naturalization."

It was a nicely worded verdict, but it was announced a little too soon. Walus had not yet put on his defense.

The prosecution had suggested, without any evidence to support it, that the AOK records establishing that Walus had been a farm laborer throughout the war were forgeries prepared by the Gestapo, or perhaps by Walus himself, to shield him from being found out. The documents were obviously the strongest point in the defense case, and Korenkiewicz somehow managed to find the German clerk who had prepared them in Berlin, years ago, and he summoned her to Chicago. She testified that she recognized her handwriting, and that the records had not been altered. The defense also called the farmers' wives who remembered Frank Walus working on their farms during the time the prosecution placed him in Poland.

That evidence was not enough to cast any doubt on the verdict Judge Hoffman had already reached. In May 1978 he handed down his decision revoking Walus' citizenship. He found the testimony of the survivors "consistent" and "powerful" and generally ignored the defense evidence except to note that the farmers' wives had been married to members of the Nazi party and thus had a motivation to protect a former Gestapo member. A few months later, Korenkiewicz produced additional evidence—five Polish forced laborers who were ready to testify that they had known Walus in Ulm during the war, and some old German residency papers showing that Walus had been in Germany in 1940. Korenkiewicz asked Hoffman to order a new trial in light of this evidence. Hoffman refused.

Korenkiewicz appealed the verdict to the court of appeals, which heard oral argument in 1979. While the court was considering its decision, the Office of Special Investigations was established, and several weeks after I came aboard, the court of appeals handed down its decision.

It did not reverse Judge Hoffman outright, but it did vacate the verdict and order that a new trial be held at which Korenkiewicz' newly discovered evidence could be considered. It had sharp words for Judge Hoffman's handling of the trial, particularly his "most disturbing" tendency to cut off "crucial" cross-examination on the identity question, and it ordered that the new trial be held before a different judge.

As I read the court of appeals' decision—my first real introduction to the Walus case—I too was disturbed. The German health insurance records were unquestionably significant, and I had a hard time believing, as the prosecution had contended at trial, that in 1978 a group of farmers' wives would come to Chicago to testify falsely in favor of a former Gestapo officer otherwise unknown to them, just because their husbands had been party members during the war.

With the creation of OSI, responsibility for the investigation and prosecution of Nazi war criminals had passed from the United States Attorneys and the INS to our office, and I had no doubt about what to do in the Walus case. The court of appeals had ordered a new trial, but if Walus was guilty of Nazi crimes, we obviously needed more convincing evidence than the prosecution had presented in Chicago, and if he was not guilty—a very distinct possibility—we had no business putting him through a trial again. Either way, we had to reinvestigate the case from the ground up.

I called in OSI's chief investigator and told him that the Walus case would be the top priority in the Office. I told him to go to Ulm personally, first to interview the farmers' wives and then to knock on every door in town if that's what it took to find every person who had lived there during the war, and to see if anyone remembered Walus from those years. I told him to take photospreads containing Walus' photograph—a 1940 photograph, not the 1959 one that was used with the Israeli witnesses. I sent a researcher to Poland to examine the records of the Polish war crimes commission, to see if there was anything relating to Walus. I sent another investigator to New York with orders to interview every known survivor of Kielce and Czestochowa living there with a similar photospread.

I retained an independent document analyst in Germany to conduct thorough tests on the AOK records to determine whether they had been forged or altered in any way. I told an OSI attorney headed to Israel on another case to reinterview the witnesses and report to me his conclusions as to their credibility and the strength of their testimony. Finally, I assigned an OSI historian to visit the National Archives and all known repositories of records dealing with the Nazis in Poland to see if there was any evidence linking Walus to atrocities there.

My aim was to follow two distinct lines of investigation: first, to reexamine the existing evidence, both prosecution and defense; second, to search for any new evidence that would shed light on the truth.

The investigation took nearly nine months to complete, but when it was over the answer was clear. In Ulm, several persons previously unknown to either the prosecution or the defense readily identified Walus' picture as that of the frail farm worker who had spent the entire war there. One, in fact, was a retired priest who recalled that Walus had attended Mass every Sunday, year in and year out. The document analyst reported that the AOK cards were perfectly in order. Not one survivor of Kielce or Czestochowa identified Walus' photo. There was no trace of Walus in any records, here or in Poland, dealing with Nazi activities in that country.

I believed that the Israeli witnesses who testified against Walus did so honestly and sincerely. Their testimony was consistent, and I was sure that the atrocities they recounted actually took place. Their physical descriptions of the person who had done it were not totally at odds with the way Walus might have appeared, but those descriptions could have fit any number of other people. And they had seen a poor-quality photo taken seventeen years after the events. Under the circumstances, I could not base a prosecution on their uncorroborated testimony.

I called Tom Sullivan, the United States Attorney in Chicago (whose predecessor had filed the original case), and reviewed the findings with him. He agreed with me that the case had to be withdrawn. On November 26, 1980, I issued a statement disclosing the results of the new investigation, which concluded:

> [T]he striking absence of corroborating evidence despite a lengthy and exhaustive investigation—and indeed the undeniable weight of evidence tending to indicate that Walus spent the war years as a farm worker in Germany—compels the conclusion that we could not responsibly go forward with a new trial. Nearly forty years ago, the Supreme Court of the United States held that the precious right of American citizenship could not be revoked unless the evidence justifying revocation was clear and convincing. In this case, the evidence plainly falls short of that standard. Under the circumstances, the choice is clear. The prosecution is over.*

We learned a number of lessons from the Walus experience. The Israeli witnesses from Kielce and Czestochowa had been shown a poorly defined photograph and had been told that the suspect's name was Frank Walus. Assuming that there was some resemblance to the actual Gestapo criminal in those ghettos, the witnesses would be naturally reluctant to admit to any doubts when facing Frank Walus at trial. So, with the ready cooperation of the Israeli police, we reformed the photo ID procedures so that all spreads were prepared in our office using contemporaneous photographs of good quality arranged in a permanent spread. When we placed advertisements in Jewish newspapers looking for survivors of a certain place, we never disclosed the name of the suspect. The Israeli authorities agreed to follow the same procedure when working on our behalf.

Because the Polish war crimes commission had told Walus' lawyer that it could not release information to individuals (thus preventing the trial court from learning that the Poles had no information on Walus, an exculpatory fact), we notified defense attorneys that they

---

*The government reimbursed Walus to the extent authorized by law for the costs he had incurred in the case. This did not include attorneys' fees, which were substantial; reimbursement of attorneys' fees by the government is generally prohibited by law.

A Chicago lawyers' newspaper, which had criticized the Walus prosecution when it was taking place, charged that I had delayed announcing my decision until after the 1980 elections to avoid an adverse reaction against President Carter from Jewish voters. Baloney.

could send any search request to OSI for forwarding as an official U.S. government request. Every suspect was interviewed and given a chance to tell us his story before a case was filed.

We also learned to be wary of any case where there were no documents and no good reason why not. And the entire process reinforced my instinctive belief that when the United States government charges a person with having been a Nazi war criminal, it had better be right, because if it is wrong the consequences are disastrous.

But the most enduring lesson to come out of the Walus case is that an office like OSI was needed not only to prosecute the guilty but to protect the innocent. Had the original accusations against Walus been made at a time when OSI existed, they never would have seen a courtroom. More accurate photographs would have been used with the Israeli witnesses. Polish archives would have been searched as part of the investigation. The German records would have been located. Our staff learned where to find evidence if it existed, and to recognize when it did not.

My determination to prosecute guilty Nazi criminals was unshakable, and it was shared by every member of OSI's staff. We spent enormous amounts of time, and necessarily a lot of money, on many investigations that only slowly yielded up the evidence of guilt that we needed. No case was abandoned because it was too hard. Once filed, no case was thrown out of court; no conviction was reversed. But if the evidence was not there, it was my obligation to close the file, and I did.

7

VIOREL TRIFA AND OTTO VON BOLSCHWING:
Pursuing the Guilty

The prosecution of Frank Walus and the refusal to prosecute Josep Magyar are examples of government ineptitude that verges on corruption—not the monetary sort, but corruption of a public responsibility. The case of Viorel Trifa, a Romanian fascist who attained prominence as a clergyman and church leader in this country, threatened to take the same path.* As with Magyar, the United States government ignored charges of persecution for years; when the case was finally filed in court in 1975 it immediately stalled in a paralyzing seizure of official neglect.

But Trifa's story has an ending quite different from Magyar's. In fact, it has a double-barreled ending, because OSI's successful pursuit of Trifa not only brought him face to face with deportation but led us to the startling discovery of his SS benefactor.

The strands of this story became woven together in Bucharest, the capital of Romania, in 1941 when a strange and sinister partnership was struck between two unlikely conspirators. One was Trifa, a young Romanian propagandist and demagogue, a member of the inner circle of the Iron Guard, the viciously anti-Semitic Romanian fascist movement. The other was Otto von Bolschwing, the chief of the SS Security Service—the *Sicherheitsdienst,* or SD—in Bucharest. Unlike Trifa, Bolschwing was a descendant of nobility, a man whose suave

---

*Trifa changed his name from ''Viorel'' to ''Valerian'' when he became a bishop.

manner and wordly outlook marked him as a rising star in the ranks of the SS.

As their paths crossed in Bucharest in 1941, the demagogue and the aristocrat were firmly convinced that Hitler's New Order would change the world, and each was dedicated to bringing that about and reaping the rewards of power that it would surely bring. Living a life of prosperity in America was the last thing on their minds.

Otto Albrecht Alfred von Bolschwing was born in the right place at the right time—Prussia, in 1909, the scion of generations of land-holders.[1] At seventeen he went to London as a trainee for an import-export firm, returning to Berlin in 1930 where he was, according to his SS application, "a consultant to English financial institutions engaged in industrial financing."

In 1932, as Hitler was rising to power, the young Bolschwing joined the Nazi party. Fluent in English and French, he struck off to Palestine in 1933, where he set up a building supply firm. Palestine, governed by the British, was a crossroads of intrigue and strange liaisons in the thirties. Bolschwing thrived on contacts with Arabs, Jews, and Germans, and he soon came under the wing of Leopold von Mildenstein, the SD officer in Palestine.

The SD was the espionage and intelligence arm of the SS, responsible for finding out and reporting on sensitive political developments and anti-Nazi tendencies, not to the German government but to SS leaders. Throughout the 1930s the SS, technically only a Nazi party organization, grew in power and influence until it rivaled the organs of the state itself. It meddled in foreign affairs, and it deployed armed military units side by side with the Wehrmacht, the German army. As the "intelligence" branch, the SD was the nerve center of the complex SS organization, staffed by persons of birth, education, and training. Headed by the infamous and shrewd Reinhold Heydrich, who answered to no one but Reichsführer-SS Himmler (who in turn answered to no one but the Führer), the SD was the place to be for bright young Nazis on the make.

Palestine was one of the most active places for the SD in the mid-1930s. Its agent there, a Dr. Reichert, the correspondent of the German News Agency, had sources on both sides of the Arab-Jewish conflict.[2] It was Reichert who had introduced Bolschwing to the SD.

Bolschwing, who could see where opportunity lay as well as the next man in Germany, took to the SD like a magnet. He funneled a constant stream of reports to Mildenstein, who approvingly passed them on to Berlin, where some of them came to the attention of the head of the SS, Himmler himself.

Unfortunately for Bolschwing, however, his reports were being regularly intercepted by the British, who administered Palestine under the Balfour Mandate of 1923, and in 1936 the British decided that they could do without Bolschwing in their midst. They refused to renew his residence permit, and he reluctantly prepared to leave Palestine. He told Mildenstein, who meanwhile had returned to Berlin to head up Section II 112 (Jewish Desk) in the SD, that he was looking about to start a new business elsewhere, and would be willing to place his entire organization, whatever it might be, "completely at the disposal of" the SD.

Mildenstein decided to bring the bright and eager Bolschwing back to Berlin to work on the SD Jewish desk. Bolschwing eagerly accepted, and came back to Germany in late 1936 to help the SS solve the "Jewish problem."

The "Jewish problem" was at a critical stage for the Nazis in 1937. Only one thing was clear: there was to be no room for Jewish influence in the affairs of the Thousand-Year Reich, and even that point was far more obvious to the Nazis than to the Jews themselves. Measures against the Jews had begun shortly after Hitler became chancellor in 1933: laws were issued to define who was a Jew; Jews were forced out of the German civil service; businesses owned by Jews were boycotted; anti-Jewish propaganda increased; police officers looked the other way as Jewish property, and Jews themselves, were attacked by street toughs.

But in late 1936 these measures, ominous as they were, hardly amounted to a comprehensive solution to any Jewish problem; what that solution should be was a controversial subject in SS circles. Forced deportation, let alone mass death, had not yet occurred to the Nazis, much less the Jews. Many Jewish businesses continued to operate; Jews were not forced to leave Germany (although some foresighted ones did); many Jews, accustomed to varying degrees of oppression, believed that this latest wave of unpleasantness would pass soon enough if they were patient.

The SS was facing a perplexing problem. On the one hand, they wanted to eliminate Jewish influence in business, education, the professions, and so forth—to get the Jews out of German life; on the other they were unwilling to disrupt the German economy to achieve this goal. The SS was at first happy to see Jews depart, but then became unhappy at the thought that they were taking assets and capital with them. And when they decreed that the property of any departing Jew would be forfeited to the state, emigration slowed at once. The SS didn't know whether it should deter emigration or take advantage of it.

As Mildenstein brought Bolschwing back from Palestine and put him to work on the question, he also spotted another likely recruit—an obsequious junior officer named Adolf Eichmann, who was whiling away his time to no discernible end on the SD's Freemasonry desk.

Eichmann, in the words of one historian, "caught the eye by the ludicrously subservient manner in which he greeted any senior officer; his rule was to regard any SS commander as a superior being, and whenever an officer passed through the hall (and a good many did), he sprang to attention and clicked his heels."[3] Eichmann at that time was not known for anti-Semitism; he was, according to a colleague, "a most colorless creature—the typical subordinate, pedantic, punctilious . . . devoid of any thorough knowledge. . . . "[4]

Eichmann was to become the architect of the Final Solution, although there was no hint of the fearsome heights that career would reach when he began it in 1937. But Bolschwing was there. Interrogated by the Israelis prior to his trial in 1962, Eichmann recalled, "The first time ever that I was occupied with Jewish matters was when Mildenstein visited me at my workplace [the Freemasonry desk] at the Main Office of Reich Security together with Bolschwing—never before that."[5] It is probably a true statement.

With his two protégés, Mildenstein set about to come up with measures to deal with Germany's Jews. On January 12 1937, Bolschwing submitted his agenda, entitled "Zum Judenproblem." It was a seventeen-page prospectus for forcing Jews out of Germany, which Bolschwing summarized in his introduction: "The Jews in the entire world represent a nation which is not bound by a country or by a people but by money. Therefore, they are and must always be an eternal enemy of National Socialism. . . . Jews are among the most dangerous enemies—because they are never entirely apprehensible."

Bolschwing went on: "The leading thought of the following explanations is to 'purge Germany of the Jews.' This can only be carried out when the basis of livelihood, i.e., the possibility of economic activity, is taken away from the Jews of Germany. The promotion of emigration to territories where the Jews cannot harm the Reich is an absolute necessity especially with respect to the younger generation.''

Bolschwing had a three-point plan for carrying out this ''emigration.'' First, the Nazi state would require the licensing of all businesses in those areas that Bolschwing thought were controlled by Jews: clothing and textiles, banking and finance, real estate, tax consulting, and so forth. This, argued Bolschwing, ''makes it possible to apply [licensing] exclusively to Jews and gives the possibility of excluding Jews from the economy and thus from Germany by means of an increased or decreased withdrawal (or renewing) of licenses.''

The second plank in this plan was an ''increase in political pressure.'' Bolschwing noted that ''If the economic pressure is intended to get the Jews closer to the idea of emigration, the political pressure will promote this movement to a greater degree.'' This political pressure would be comprised of a number of initiatives: propaganda (which Bolschwing termed ''clarification and objectivity'') because ''The [German] people must recognize that the Jew can never be bound to a nation, that he is and will always remain the international 'agitator' and thus is an enemy of Germany all over the world.'' Propaganda would in turn be bolstered by ''intimidation''—''excesses in order to take away the sense of security from the Jews.'' In a word, terrorism. ''Even though this is an illegal method,'' Bolschwing noted calmly, ''it has a long-lasting effect . . .''

With propaganda and terrorism as the official state policy, Germany would be ready for Bolschwing's third and final plank: ''the promotion of emigration.'' ''Special attention must be paid to the fact that the Jewish emigration is effected in a *concentrated* manner, i.e., only to certain countries in order to avoid creating a hostile group in a number of countries which constantly agitates in the respective countries against Germany.'' Bolschwing nominated the South American countries of Ecuador, Colombia, and Venezuela as suitable, in addition to Palestine, because they were ''politically of no importance'' and would ''not represent a political danger to Germany even with strong agitation.''

''The Jew has not yet come to terms with the fact that Germany will be closed to him forever,'' Bolschwing concluded. Implementation of his plan ''would make it clear to the Jews in Germany what the policy is.'' He added a cautionary note, lest the point be missed: ''As experience has taught us, half measures are particularly detrimental and insufficient . . .''

Bolschwing's superiors in the SD noted that his general ideas were not very original—''repression of the Jewish influence in Germany (eliminating the possibility of livelihood) [and] promotion of emigration are not new and have repeatedly been the object of comprehensive discussions,'' noted one. But they were impressed with Bolschwing and ''his practical experience covering many years,'' and they wanted him to draft something ''in a more exactly defined form'' to be submitted to Himmler ''who, in his turn, can then submit them to the Führer or to the Reich cabinet for its assessment and decision making.''

Over the next few months, Bolschwing set to work to develop the specifics. Whether these ever reached Himmler is not clear; what is clear is that in 1938, as the economic vise tightened around the Jews, a series of Aryanization laws revoked the licenses of Jewish doctors and lawyers and forced the liquidation of Jewish enterprises in real estate, finance, and similar matters.[6] If Bolschwing was not the genesis of these laws, he was at least close to them. He saw the world as a good SS officer should.

By 1938 Bolschwing and Eichmann were working with representatives of the Reichsbank on a scheme whereby foreign currency payments from Jewish organizations abroad to help Austrian Jews flee that country should go—not to the Austrian Jewish organizations—but to the SD. The SD would then arrange the deportations at a much lower cost than the foreign organizations believed, and keep for itself the profits. Interrogated in Israel in 1962, Eichmann readily recalled the negotiations, although he said he had left the technical details to Bolschwing to work out.[7]

But the most startling aspect of Bolschwing's work for the Jewish affairs section was to arrange a rendezvous between Eichmann and a most unlikely partner—the Zionist movement. The SS wanted the Jews out of Germany; the Zionists wanted Jews in Palestine. In Berlin, the possibilities of this improbable alliance did not escape the SD, and Herbert Hagen, who had succeeded Mildenstein as head of the SD's Jewish affairs section, asked Bolschwing, with his Palestinian connections, if he could set up liaisons so that the idea could be explored.

Bolschwing, happy to oblige, got in touch with his erstwhile sponsor in Palestine, Dr. Reichert of the German News Agency, who went to the Haganah, the Palestinian Jews' military and intelligence organization. As Eichmann recalled it later, he received a call from his colleague, "the only man who, from his own personal knowledge, could tell me all about the country that I was interested in most in my official position": Otto von Bolschwing. "Mr. von Bolschwing told me that a gentleman from Haganah is in Berlin and brought me together with him."[8]

The "gentleman from Haganah" was Commander Feivel Polkes, a Polish-born accountant, who explained to Eichmann over lunch in Berlin that he would "give powerful support to German foreign policy interests in the Middle East" in return for Germany's allowing Jews to emigrate to Palestine without penalty. Eichmann and Hagen, intrigued by the idea of such a trade-off, procured Heydrich's permission to travel to Palestine to pursue it further with the Haganah.[9]

Polkes was ready to deal, and perhaps the course of history would have been far different had a deal been made. But the idea of an independent Jewish state, or even a strong Jewish presence in Palestine, sent shivers through Hitler's policy makers, who put an end to German support of such heresy no matter how neatly it might accommodate SS thinking on ridding Germany of Jews.

Historian Heinz Höhne provided the epitaph to the broken engagement between the Zionists and the SS: "The SD intellectuals of the Herbert Hagen type had at least attempted to see the Jewish question other than in black and white, to move towards a solution which, while conforming to National-Socialist dogma, bore some relation to reality." When these plans failed, and as jurisdiction over the Jewish question passed to the Gestapo in 1939, the fate of the Jews became incomparably darker. For the Gestapo, says Höhne, "the Jewish question was simply an aspect of State security; the political leadership would decide how far they should or should not go."[10]

But the meetings that Bolschwing had arranged had lasting consequence. When Himmler and Heydrich, the head of the SD, were looking for someone to take charge of the Jewish problem in the reorganization of the SS in 1939, they chose the man who had demonstrated such resourcefulness in 1937 by going to Palestine: the dutiful Adolph Eichmann. He was promoted to SS Sturmbannführer (major) and was placed in charge of the Gestapo's section dealing with the evacuation of Jews. It was from this platform that he was to oversee the murders of six million Jews in the next six years.

Suppose, for a moment, that Eichmann had been found wanting, or had uncharacteristically declined an invitation from his superiors to take on a new assignment. Whom might Himmler and Heydrich have chosen? Perhaps someone who, like Eichmann, had displayed unstinting loyalty to the SD; who, like Eichmann, had experience as a middle-level bureaucrat in Section II 112; perhaps someone who had written a well-received report laying out the options to the Jewish problem; someone who had far better connections than Eichmann had. Otto von Bolschwing might have been an ideal candidate.

But by the end of 1939 the SD had other plans for Otto von Bolschwing. In his days as an international businessman, before Palestine, he had spent some time in the Balkans, and as war broke out across Europe, the Balkans were to prove a very sensitive area. Heydrich sent Bolschwing to Bucharest, Romania, as head of the SD there. Once again, Bolschwing was to find himself on a fault line of history.

As the chief of the SD—the espionage and dirty tricks arm of the SS—in Bucharest, Bolschwing was responsible for gathering intelligence on all political movements in the country for SD head Reinhard Heydrich in Berlin, and for planning secret operations to advance the goals of the SS. It was a sensitive post in a sensitive country, for Romanian oil fields were vitally important to the German war effort and Hitler could not long tolerate any instability or uncertainty there.

The SD at this time also found itself—or put itself—in the middle of a growing bureaucratic hostility between the SS and the German Foreign Ministry. For years, Himmler's SS, officially only a party organization, had been feuding with the Foreign Ministry over the increasingly powerful voice of the SS in shaping German actions abroad. The SS, after all, was responsible for the solution of the Jewish question. And as SS officers worked hand in hand with home-grown fascists to carry out terror campaigns against the local Jews, the Foreign Ministry was becoming ever more jealous of SS inroads. Foreign Minister Joachim von Ribbentrop was as ardently Nazi and as devoted to Hitler as the SS, and was wasting no tears over Jews. But foreign ministers always get nervous when foreign policy is shaped out of their sight, and Ribbentrop was no exception. In Berlin,

Himmler and Ribbentrop warily circled each other, preparing for the showdown. It came in Romania.

Since the early 1930s, the fascist and anti-Semitic Iron Guard organization had been growing in power as it railed against the "Jewish influence" in Romania. The Guard was as nationalist as it was fascist, and was tinged with a fanatic mysticism inspired by its leader, the charismatic Corneliu Codreanu. Their platform, such as it was, had been published by a young editor and ardent Guardist named Viorel Trifa in his newspaper *Libertate*: "to absolve this nation of its sins, to awaken it, to help it get rid of the kike and the domination by politicians, and to create a better future."[11]

The "kike," in fact, was the object of *Libertate*'s—and the Iron Guard's—fulminating hatred: by history a thief, an exploiter, a traitor, a corrupter. No excess was too great for *Libertate*. "Fat and opulent, [the Jew] stands in front of his store with his kike-women and kike-children," Trifa wrote, "while the Romanian passes by in the street, bowing to the earth."[12] The crudest and most revolting cartoons accompanied this analysis of Romanian affairs. The chief of the American legation in Budapest explained the Iron Guard to Washington: "bereft of leadership, . . . the organization [is] undisciplined and uninspired and [has] accumulated a following of irresponsible riffraff . . ."[13]

Riffraff they may have been to American eyes, but the Guard's simplistic appeals to nationalism and anti-Semitism found vociferous support among Romanian workers and peasants, and caught the eye of the SS—no amateurs themselves when it came to nationalism and Jew-baiting. When Codreanu was murdered by anti-Guard forces in 1938, the movement lost its inspirational leader; control passed to a cabal of loud-mouthed toughs headed by Codreanu's former adjutant Horia Sima, *Libertate* editor Trifa, and a handful of others.

In September 1940 General Ion Antonescu, a firm ally of Hitler, became dictator of Romania. Antonescu was not an Iron Guardist himself, but he made concessions to the strength of the movement when he installed the Guard's nominal head, Horia Sima, as his deputy. Other Iron Guardists were chosen to head the foreign, interior, and labor ministries.

This was not enough for the Iron Guard. They wanted the entire government; at the least, they wanted to make Antonescu bend to their will. When the Guardists sought out German support for their plans, they found it in the person of the SD chief in Bucharest, Otto von Bolschwing.

Bolschwing secretly pledged SD support to the Iron Guard as they plotted an insurrection against General Antonescu. It was a doomed endeavor. The strong-willed Antonescu proposed to be nobody's puppet, least of all the puppet of this undisciplined band of rabble-rousers. And, although neither Bolschwing nor the Iron Guard knew it, Hitler had already decided to back Antonescu, not the Guardists, in any Romanian power struggle. He was convinced, correctly, that Antonescu, backed by the army, was the stronger force in Romania; the demagogues and mystics of the Iron Guard were volatile and emotional, bent on disruption and civil war. Romanian oil supply lines would not be secure under their headstrong rule.[14]

Although the full details will probably never be known, it is almost certain that, in the first weeks of January 1941, Bolschwing met with Iron Guard leaders, including Horia Sima and Viorel Trifa, at the SD house on the German embassy grounds in Bucharest. That Sima and Trifa and company were plotting an actual coup d'etat against Antonescu is not entirely certain; such a move required planning, and clear thinking was not their strongest suit. They may have simply decided to stir up the natives with some nationalist flag-waving, get them running through the streets, and see what might happen. Perhaps Antonescu would be forced to listen more closely to them. Bolschwing certainly did nothing to discourage their efforts; he led them to believe that the SD stood behind them.

Early in January 1941 Bolschwing returned to Berlin, very possibly for consultations with his SS superiors to plan the imminent hullabaloo. He returned to Bucharest January 13.

By January 19, 1941, the situation in Bucharest was unstable to the point of volatility. Antonescu, faced with escalating Iron Guard bombast, was edgy; the Guard members were restive and unrestrained. As tension between the Guard and the Antonescu regime increased, Trifa clambered onto a podium in Bucharest to address an unruly rally on Sunday afternoon, January 19, 1941. He engaged in the usual semicoherent invocations against Judaism ("the service of Adolf Hitler," he proclaimed, "is to have ripped aside the mask from the visage of Jewish Freemasonry and to lead today's struggle to eliminate its domination"), but Trifa added a new twist: a tirade against democracy. The war in Europe, he declared, was "a struggle be-

tween two eras and two philosophies.'' One era was that of the French
Revolution: ''Liberty, Equality, Fraternity.'' But, said Trifa, ''Egal-
itarian ideas have been useful to a single class of people—they have
been useful to the kikes.'' The era of democracy, he shouted, ''must
be annihilated, . . . and a new order must be enthroned.'' For Trifa,
England was a particularly evil force; what others saw to be the spread
of democracy Trifa now revealed to be a cunning device for the Jew
to ''spread his meshes over the entire world.''*[15]

Trifa's shrill speech set off a series of demonstrations that, in the
next few days, fed upon themselves in the intrigue-thickened air of
the Romanian capital and drew the Iron Guard into full armed confrontation with Antonescu's forces. Mobs ran in the streets of Bucharest; Iron Guard sympathizers seized the radio station; Guardists who
were shot down by army troops became instant martyrs. Antonescu
at first held his troops largely in check, but as disorder spread from
day to day, he grew increasingly besieged.

Finally, on January 23, he sought help from the German embassy;
Foreign Minister Ribbentrop, watching the situation closely from Berlin,
sent a cable assuring Antonescu that he had the full support of Hitler,
who wished the general to put down the disorder as decisively as possible, using whatever means were available. Antonescu struck out at
the Iron Guard with his forces, aided by a German military contin-
gent stationed in Bucharest, and after a few hours the abortive uprising collapsed.

Those who ventured out into the streets of Bucharest as quiet returned found a sickening sight. Spurred by the speeches of Trifa and
other Iron Guard demagogues, the mob had surged through the Jewish quarter of Bucharest, seizing Jews, or suspected Jews. The American ambassador reported that, at the slaughterhouse, there were ''sixty
Jewish corpses on the hooks used for carcasses, all skinned. The
quantity of blood about [seemed to indicate] that they had been skinned
alive.''[16] Their throats had been cut in a horrifying parody of the ko-
sher tradition. Some had been beheaded.

Synagogues had been burned to the ground; sacred vestments and
Torah scrolls had been defiled or burned; frightened Jews seeking
sanctuary in the temples had been stoned or beaten to death. Muti-

---

*Rabble-rousers have excoriated Jews for devising many evils; Trifa may have been the first to
accuse the Jews of unleashing democracy on an unsuspecting world.

lated corpses of Jews unfortunate enough to have been in the streets when the mob arrived were found lying in the gutter. Ninety-two bodies were found in the forest outside the city. The total number of Jewish dead was probably 200 to 500. The Iron Guard had seen to it that all of them had died terrified.

The instigators of this insurrection and frenzied killing managed to survive, through the intervention of their patron, SD chief Otto von Bolschwing. No doubt unaware of the Führer's proclaimed support for Antonescu, Bolschwing had spirited Trifa and the other rebels off to sanctuary in the SD house on the grounds of the German legation, which had immunity from the incursion of Romanian authorities.

Bolschwing was in an exceedingly dangerous position, sheltering the faction that had tried to depose a general supported by the Führer. But Bolschwing, ever sensitive to who held the power, was able to shield his role in the plotting and convince the Foreign Ministry's man in Bucharest, Hermann Neubacher, that he, Bolschwing, should now act as a go-between to arrange a surrender of the Guardists in return for safe passage out of Romania.[17]

Neubacher sent a cable to Foreign Minister Ribbentrop on February 6:

> Bolschwing has supported my efforts [to end the confrontation between the Guard and Antonescu] in a deserving manner. After the street fighting ended, Bolschwing found himself in a highly difficult situation since the leaders of the Guard . . . had been declared rebels. Bolschwing could not simply surrender to the rabble and expose to immediate arrest the men gathered under his protection. I am of the opinion that he had only in mind the honor of the [SD] when he continued to take care of the men who had unexpectedly run into danger. It was a mistake that he did not immediately inform the [German Ambassador] whom he did not want to burden with the responsibility. Out of my own experience, I feel obligated to intercede in favor of Bolschwing's way of acting and would ask the Imperial Minister of Foreign Affairs [Ribbentrop] to apprise the competent authorities of my judgment.[18]

Ribbentrop, however, was in no mood to heap praise on the SS cap of Bolschwing. When he learned of Bolschwing's role in sheltering the Iron Guardists, he saw the opportunity he needed to drive a wedge between Hitler and the SS. Ribbentrop gave Hitler all the juicy details of how the SS in Romania was working to depose Hitler's friend and ally Antonescu. The Führer was not at all pleased. He sent Manfred von Killinger—a Foreign Ministry official who had served as German consul general in San Francisco—to Bucharest to submit a full report on what Bolschwing had done.

Killinger quickly discovered that Bolschwing had had more to do with the uprising than simply sheltering a few of its leaders afterward—he had been closely involved in plotting it. "The fact that [Trifa and other Iron Guard leaders] were hidden in this extraterritorial house [i.e., the SD house on embassy grounds] proves how closely the SD group was connected with the leadership of the [Iron Guard] which led the rebellion," Killinger reported. When "Bolschwing had to confess this to me, he gave the impression of being absolutely prostrate and had tears in his eyes, although he is otherwise a brave man. I could not avoid the impression that he was deeply shaken like someone who has suffered a great disappointment and defeat and considers the fight to be lost."[19]

Indeed, for Bolschwing at that point the fight was lost. Killinger concluded that "The SD ought to have put a stop to the [Iron Guard's] efforts to overthrow Antonescu. This was not done. The [Iron Guard] was certainly encouraged by the attitude of the SD."[20]

Bolschwing was recalled to Berlin and tossed into the cellar of the Gestapo headquarters, where he spent several months. Very probably he would have been executed had it not been for the personal intervention of Himmler.[21]

Bolschwing was later to claim that his time in jail was for anti-Nazi activities, for opposing the Führer. This is, at best, a highly misleading half-truth. Bolschwing would never have dreamed of opposing the Führer. Faced with two pro-Nazi, anti-Semitic factions struggling for control of Romania, he picked the wrong side and got found out.

But Bolschwing's misstep had greater consequences. "Such inroads had been made into the SD's prestige" as a result of his actions, wrote one historian, "that Ribbentrop finally plucked up his courage to bring the sinister [SS] attachés to heel. . . . Himmler gave way. On August 9, 1941, he concluded a new agreement with Ribbentrop" severely curtailing the powers of the SD abroad and providing that all their correspondence with SD headquarters (RSHA) in Berlin would pass through the Foreign Ministry.[22] Ribbentrop was able to consolidate his influence throughout Southeastern Europe—Croatia, Hungary, Romania, Czechoslovakia, and Bulgaria. Bolschwing's adventurism had given the SS a setback in its competition with the Nazi diplomats.

In Bucharest, meanwhile, the Iron Guard uprising played itself out in a most curious fashion. One would have expected that the failed rebels, sheltered by the disgraced SD leader, would have been promptly delivered up to the victorious Antonescu for swift and fatal justice. But in the world of the SS, let alone Romania, nothing was simple.

Antonescu was reluctant simply to shoot the rebels lest he touch off a popular uprising among the population that might weaken his still tenuous control over the country. He had been forced to call on Hitler once to aid him; a second such episode would have been embarrassing. Antonescu was not unsympathetic to the nationalist anti-Semitic dogma of the Iron Guard; he just wanted its leaders out of his hair. He worked out a deal with the Germans: the Iron Guard leaders would be confined in Germany.

That suited Ribbentrop. The Foreign Ministry, now firmly in control of the situation, was primarily interested in stabilizing Antonescu. If packing the leaders off to Germany would return Romania and its oil fields to normalcy, the Foreign Ministry would oblige, no matter how indisposed it was to the Guard itself. Ribbentrop warned the Guardists that any political agitation from the sidelines would result in immediate extradition to Romania. And, he might have added, trial by firing squad.

Antonescu was happy to have the Guardists serve five-year terms in work camps in Germany: all except Trifa. "One of the most guilty authors of the uprising," Antonescu told the Germans. "It is absolutely necessary that Trifa be punished with the greatest severity since the serious nature of his guilt and the danger to the security of the state which he represents is quite extraordinary."[23]

The Germans ignored Antonescu's request, as he probably suspected they would. The Foreign Ministry was not interested in indulging Antonescu's pique at Trifa at the risk of continuing the inflammation of domestic politics in Bucharest. On March 4, 1941, Trifa and the other Iron Guard leaders, clad in German military uniforms, were driven to a deserted railroad junction outside of Bucharest and ignominiously trundled into a few third-class rail cars hitched onto a freight train bound for Vienna. There, SS officials put them on a train for Berlin.

If Antonescu thought the plotters would be doing hard time in Germany (and he did), he was mistaken. The "prisoners" were remanded to the custody of the SS—the very organization that had supported the Iron Guard insurrection in the first place. Trifa and his colleagues visited the coffeehouses of Berlin; some engaged in periodic discussion to plan a victorious return to Romania, but these sporadic plots went nowhere. Complaining of stomach troubles, Trifa discovered that he could recuperate at SS health spas, and for two years he made the rounds from baths to Berlin to baths again. In January 1942 he wrote his colleagues from Bad Kissingen with an account of his day:

> Wake up at 7:00 am; from 7:30 to 9:00 take the waters at the spring; 9:00 to 9:00 to 9:30 breakfast; 3 times a week from 9:30 to 10:30 salt baths; 10:00 to 11:00 reading; 2 hours sleep; 3:00 to 5:00 reading again; 5:00 to 6:00 taking the waters; 6:00 to 7:00 going for a walk; 7:00 dinner, and then 7:30–10:45 reading or the movies. At 11:00 pm, I am in bed.[24]

It was, considering the alternatives, a lovely way to spend the war. On February 6, 1942, Trifa sent a postcard back to Berlin: "The weather continues to be splendid." He thought he might stay a few more weeks.

The Iron Guard, like most revolutionary movements, had always been an amalgam of theorists and demagogues. Trifa was among the latter. Other exiled leaders might sit in their quarters in Berlin and spin conceptual webs of political philosophy for the day they would return to Bucharest. Trifa was not interested. Separated from the mobs, unable to find an audience in Germany, he was perfectly happy to take the baths and go to the movies, grumbling occasionally that he was not being treated like the important political refugee he considered himself to be.

This idyllic life came to an end early in 1943, however, when Horia Sima, still the nominal head of the Iron Guard in exile, booked a train seat in Berlin and traveled to Rome to seek support for his sputtering movement. The "escape" sorely embarrassed the Germans in the eyes of Antonescu, for the Guardists were supposed to have been in confinement. As a result, Trifa and his colleagues (including the inept Sima, who was quickly picked up by German agents in Italy) were clapped into the concentration camp at Dachau.

Dachau was no Bad Kissingen, but for Trifa and his mates it was certainly not the Dachau reserved for Jews and political prisoners. The exiles, through no skill of their own, had the Germans over a bit of a barrel. The SS feared that Antonescu's commitment to the Führer was wavering in the face of Soviet advances on the Eastern Front, and they could not afford to alienate the Guardists, who might have to ride to the rescue some day in Bucharest if Antonescu fell—or was pushed—from power. At Dachau, the SS set aside a corner of the camp for the Guardists and gave the men separate rooms, a lounge area with a radio, and a monthly stipend of fifty reichsmarks for spending money. Sima was given a manservant. Camp authorities were instructed that the Guard leaders were to be "treated well and in a humane fashion," and they were.[25] In fact, Sima protested vigorously when Himmler suggested after a while that he might like a transfer to another camp. Trifa, deprived of his baths and cinemas, busied himself by writing a few chapters for a history of the Iron Guard the exiles were putting together.

As time passed, it should have become evident that, as a political force, the Iron Guard had been neutered. Antonescu abandoned the Axis in the face of the Soviet invasion in 1944, and German forces retreated, but Himmler, whose touch with reality was slipping, prodded Sima into establishing a "national government" of Romania. Sima could not get into Romania, so he pitched camp in Vienna; he and Himmler exchanged regular cables about the imminent return to power of the New Order. But these geldings had grown too swaybacked in exile to be put back in harness again. The Romanian people, enticed by Soviet promises of territorial gains, ignored them, and when the Germans capitulated in May 1945 the Iron Guard had gotten no closer to Bucharest than Vienna.

Trifa was not deluded by Sima's calls for a return to power; the days of glory were over and he knew it. While Sima set up shop in Vienna, Trifa walked out of Dachau and headed by himself to Rome, arriving there shortly before the end of the war. He spent several years teaching at a Catholic missionary college.

In 1948, after Congress passed the Displaced Persons Act, Trifa left the Catholics and applied for admission to the United States. He proudly displayed to American officials his anti-Nazi credentials: he had been a journalist for a "religious newspaper" until he was "arrested by the Gestapo" in 1941 and "interned" at Dachau for four years until his "escape." It was a story any fortunate Jew or anti-Nazi might have told, and many did. The difference was that their stories were true.

Trifa did not enlighten American officials on his 1941 speechifying calling for an annihilation of democracy; he did not describe his role as a catalyst for the riots that left Jews hanging on meathooks; he did not explain that his "arrest" by the Gestapo was a sweetheart deal that took him to the spas of Bad Kissingen, or that his "internment" had been in private quarters at an SS guest house at its facility in Dachau. He denied that he had been a member of the Iron Guard.

DP authorities in Italy were no experts on Romanian politics; Trifa got his visa in good time and came to New York on July 17, 1950.

And what of Otto von Bolschwing, former businessman in Palestine, former expert on the Jewish problem, former SD chief in Bucharest? After February 1941 he and Trifa were both, in their ways, "prisoners of the Gestapo," but Bolschwing's career was about to take a very different path. He likewise would come to the United States, but not through a displaced persons camp.

Bolschwing was later to claim that he worked for the "Gehlen Organization" from the end of the war through 1949. General Reinhard Gehlen had been the chief German military intelligence expert on Soviet forces during the war and had compiled a reputation for unprecedented accuracy on Soviet arms and strategy. After the war he turned himself and his organization over to the Americans, and became a subsidiary of American intelligence. He and his network of spies and informers were our only real source of intelligence on Soviet troop strength, weaponry, and military plans in Eastern Europe after the war. Gehlen's organization later became the Bundesnachrichtendienst, the West German Intelligence Service, with Gehlen at its head until 1968.

Precisely what Bolschwing did for the Gehlen organization is not clear, but the most likely hypothesis is that he gathered information rather than analyzed it. Bolschwing had no particular expertise on the Soviet Union and had never had any exposure at all to its military.

But he had proven himself an adroit opportunist and he could certainly have been useful in running a network of agents in both the American and Soviet zones of occupied Germany.

In 1949 Bolschwing left Gehlen and went to work for a United States government intelligence operation until 1954, when he came to the United States. He is reported to have been a spotter—recruiting others to carry out the actual operations of gathering information in Soviet-controlled areas. But regardless of his actual tasks, his four years of service for Gehlen would have certainly qualified him for the intelligence business.

What did the United States government know about Bolschwing when it recruited him? Did it know—should it have known—about his career from 1937 to 1941 in the service of the SD? Did it know that he had written a solution to the Jewish problem? Did it know that he had been involved in plotting the Iron Guard insurrection in Bucharest?

Bolschwing gave American officials a "life history" in 1949 that was a clever perversion of the truth. According to Bolschwing's account, he was a dedicated anti-Nazi from 1932 until the end of the war and managed to stay one step ahead of party officials trying to nail him for his anti-Nazi activities. He admitted that in Bucharest he had assisted the Iron Guard, but he explained that he did so only to counter Hitler's ally, General Antonescu, and that by supporting the Guard he was able to insulate it from direct Nazi influence.

As to Eichmann, Bolschwing's only mention was that Eichmann had approached him in prison in 1942 and asked him to join Eichmann's office to work on the Final Solution. Bolschwing said that, upright man that he was, he had declined Eichmann's invitation. Bolschwing even claimed that he had contacts to the July 20, 1944, plot to kill Hitler.

Could the truth have been learned from other sources? Certainly it was possible. The files of the German Foreign Ministry were available to the Americans—a thorough check of these files would have laid out his role in Bucharest in detail. But this would not necessarily have conflicted with Bolschwing's own tale that he was working against Antonescu and hence Hitler.

There is another point that meshes with Bolschwing's account of himself. He had been tossed into a Gestapo jail and this fact was an excellent buttress to his false story of resistance. And the story found support from an unlikely source—Dieter Wisliceny, a former SS man and deportation expert for Adolph Eichmann in Czechoslovakia and Hungary.

Allied authorities hunting for Eichmann found Wisliceny, who provided them a full statement of what he knew about Eichmann and his operations. (Wisliceny was executed in Czechoslovakia in 1948.) Wisliceny had known Bolschwing somewhat in the old II 112 days in Berlin in 1937–38; the two had gone their separate ways when von Bolschwing went to Bucharest in 1940. But Wisliceny told American authorities only that Bolschwing had been an "SD collaborator" in 1937–39. He did not mention Section II 112. Wisliceny also said that, according to what he knew, Bolschwing had been "arrested and placed in a concentration camp [sic] on Himmler's orders" and was there "for two years." This was only partly true; Bolschwing was confined in Gestapo headquarters, and only for several months, although Wisliceny probably did not know that. But his account gave credibility to Bolschwing's story that he had been an anti-Nazi. Why else would Himmler have arrested him?

Bolschwing's SS file at the Berlin Document Center contained another curious reference that supported his story. In January 1945 he was given a humiliating demotion to private and drummed out of the SS. The reason for this action is not given in the file and it remains obscure today; it may have to do with his 1944 marriage to a woman who was allegedly of Jewish descent—a sure ticket out of the SS. But whatever the actual reason, it would have dovetailed, in a rough sort of way, with his story of anti-Nazi activities and Wisliceny's report of his jailing by the Gestapo.

There is another point to be kept in mind. Bolschwing's life history given to American officials was a pack of lies. Intelligence organizations don't like to hire people who lie to them, because they might lie again, or they might be hiding something. If U.S. officials knew that Bolschwing was lying to them, it does not seem likely that they would have hired him. At the least, they would have confronted him with the evidence of his lies. There is no indication that this happened, which means either that the Americans did not know the truth or they knew it but did not confront him with it; the latter course would make little sense.

We do not know whether the government knew the full story of Bolschwing's background. But if it did not, it was hoodwinked into hiring someone that it ought to have known more about.

U.S. intelligence officials were later to contend that they did not know the details of Bolschwing's turn on the Jewish desk of the SD until Eichmann was captured and interrogated in 1960—by which time Bolschwing had been a U.S. resident for six years and a citizen for almost two.*

In 1961, long after Bolschwing had come to America, he applied for a job with the International Cooperation Agency (ICA). The ICA routinely checked within the government for information on him. Bolschwing's former superiors, knowing then of Eichmann's disclosures, told Bolschwing to withdraw his application from ICA. One can argue that, had the Americans known this information in 1949, they would not have hired Bolschwing, but one must also recognize that standards in 1961 were different from 1949. The possibility remains open that our government knew Bolschwing's background in 1949 and hired him anyway. Based on the information now available, we do not know.

What we do know is that, in 1953, Bolschwing decided he wanted to come to the United States. When he applied for a visa, he wrote on his State Department application that he had been a member of the Nazi party in 1932 and had been in the Waffen SS—the military branch of the SS, which he was not—from 1939 to 1941. His erstwhile intelligence superiors told State that Bolschwing had worked for them and that he had a "complete clearance."

By 1953 the Displaced Persons Act had expired and neither Nazi party membership nor service in the SS armed forces necessarily disqualified an applicant for entry to the United States. The consul general in Munich would have been concerned only if he thought that Bolschwing might be a "subversive." † The official reassurance no doubt set at ease whatever qualms the consul might otherwise have had on this former Nazi party member, and so State issued Bolsch-

---

*Bolschwing severed his intelligence connection following his immigration to the United States in 1954.

†The Immigration Act of 1952 excluded insane persons, drug addicts, alcoholics, lepers, paupers, beggars, vagrants, criminals, polygamists, prostitutes, pimps, sexual deviants, public charges, former deportees, stowaways, undocumented travelers, draft dodgers, drug traffickers, "anarchists, Communists, or other political subversives," those seeking to overthrow the government, and persons who had abetted illegal immigration in the past.

It did not exclude Nazis or those who had assisted in the persecution of innocent people. This loophole was closed only in 1979, when a bill sponsored by Congresswoman Elizabeth Holtzman added Nazi persecutors to the list of those excluded from immigration.

wing, his wife, and his fourteen-year-old son routine immigration visas under the regular German quota.

Bolschwing's former superiors also gave him a letter, addressed
to the Commissioner of INS, stating that Bolschwing had been employed by the United States government and that a "full investigation" had yielded "no reason to believe" that Bolschwing was
inadmissible to the United States or posed a security threat. Technically, these statements were correct; Bolschwing's loyalty to the United
States—after the war—was well established. He was not inadmissible
under the law. The letter did not discuss Bolschwing's wartime activities.

Bolschwing arrived in New York on February 2, 1954—in style,
aboard the Italian luxury liner *Andrea Doria*. With his visa in hand
and his character reference from U.S. officials, he had no problem
getting in.

Let us look at a number of questions. First, did Bolschwing take
part in the persecution of Jews or other innocent people? I believe he
did. Not in the sense of an Ivan Demjanjuk, for Bolschwing probably
never laid a hand on anyone. Not even in the sense of an Andrija
Artukovic, for Bolschwing never directly ordered the killing of anyone, nor did he preside over a force of killers. But Bolschwing's proposals on solving the "Jewish problem" in 1937 laid out a scheme
of overt discrimination, propaganda, and terrorism against the Jews
of Germany. Proposals very similar to his were all adopted, and the
Jews of Germany suffered grievously as a result. It was a process that
led, without interruption, to the death camps of Auschwitz and Treblinka. It cannot be proven that the proposals that were adopted were
precisely Bolschwing's, or that they were adopted because he advocated them. God knows he was not the only one pushing this program
of persecution.

But those who advocate persecution cannot later claim innocence
because the persecution was actually implemented by others, and
Bolschwing cannot escape a moral liability for the consequences of
the acts he himself was urging. His may have been only one voice in
the mob, but he bears responsibility for the actions of the mob.

Similarly, we cannot show a direct causal connection between
Bolschwing's covert support for the Iron Guard in Bucharest and the
Jews who were hung on meathooks when the Guard's supporters
rampaged through the streets. Bolschwing did not create the Iron Guard,

and there is no evidence that he encouraged the consequences that followed the crackbrained harangues of Viorel Trifa and his fellow bigots in 1941. But again, one cannot support the forces of violence and disorder and then claim innocence when those forces erupt. It is entirely likely that, were it not for the quiet support of the SD, the Iron Guardists would have kept closer rein on their raging hormones, at least in early 1941, and the victims of the uprising might have survived a while longer.

So if Otto von Bolschwing does not stand in exactly the same shoes as Demjanjuk or. Artukovic, he does stand in the same dock, accused of complicity in the same crimes. His role was not to wield the iron pipe, or sign the death warrants, but to stand on the sidelines, warily encouraging those who did. The law distinguishes between the criminal and those who aid and abet him, but it makes them equally guilty, and subject to the same punishment. Had Bolschwing ever stood trial for his role in Section II 112, or in the Iron Guard uprising in 1941, he would have had to face his punishment.

Once in this country, Trifa and Bolschwing followed separate paths; as far as I know, they never renewed their bloody acquaintanceship. But each was atypical of the Nazi influx to America, because each attained some prominence.

Trifa chose a church. He became head of the Romanian Orthodox Episcopate in the United States, a congregation of Romanian exiles and their families. Operating from the Vatra, the palatial church headquarters in Grass Lake, Michigan, he was surrounded by seminarians and sycophants. He was named to the governing board of the National Council of Churches. In 1955, less than four years after his arrival, he gave the opening prayer before one of the United States Senate's daily sessions. Like the spas of wartime, it was a good life.

But Trifa had a nemesis. His name was Charles Kremer, a dentist in New York, who had come to this country from Romania long before the war. When Dr. Kremer learned of Trifa's presence in America, he waged a one-man letter-writing campaign to the Immigration and Naturalization Service, urging them to investigate the background of this man and the murder of Jews in Romania in January 1941.

Charlie Kremer is a person one can get tired of very quickly. He is crotchety and self-centered, with a talent for annoying, and usually alienating, those whose help he needs most. He never takes no for an answer. As a result, he has few allies, which is probably just as well, since Kremer is not a man who works well with others. But he is very, very persistent.

When Charlie Kremer started writing letters to the INS in the early fifties, INS ignored him. In 1957 Trifa was naturalized as an American citizen.

Kremer did not go away. He kept up a steady stream of letters to INS, demanding that they "do something" about Valerian Trifa. Trifa ignored him, and so did INS. But Kremer found one ally in Ralph Blumenthal of *The New York Times*, who wrote a story in 1975 about Trifa's background. The United States Attorney in Detroit had to do something. He filed a denaturalization suit against Trifa, but very little happened after that. The case sat in court files, unpursued.

When the INS "special litigation unit" was formed in 1977, the Trifa case was assigned to attorney Eugene Thirolf, and he brought it with him when OSI was created in 1979. It was not considered a plum. Romanian politics were complex and obscure, the case had been languishing for years in federal court, the Romanian government was less than cooperative in providing historical documents from its archives, and whoever handled the case had to deal with Charlie Kremer. But Gene Thirolf was a very determined man and a very good lawyer. He plowed into the Trifa case, working on nothing else.

When Romania continued to balk at providing documents, Elizabeth Holtzman testified before the House Ways and Means Committee that most-favored-nation trade benefits should be withheld from Romania until that country provided greater assistance to the Justice Department. Romania got the point. It provided OSI with a raft of documentary material from the Iron Guard files.

Working with OSI attorney Kathleen Coleman and Washington lawyer Nathan Lewin, who had volunteered his time and considerable trial expertise to assist us, Thirolf assembled the evidence on Trifa—document piled on document, all of which were made available to Trifa's lawyers. Finally, Judge Cornelia Kennedy in Detroit set the case for trial on October 14, 1980.

On August 25 the last thing in the world we expected happened in Detroit. Trifa walked into the office of the United States Attorney and surrendered his certificate of naturalization. He and his lawyers issued a book-length sob story of this Romanian nationalist and theologian, persecuted no end by the United States government.

We could scarcely believe our ears when the United States Attorney called. There had been no hint that Trifa was considering such a move. We knew our evidence was strong, but there was obviously no guarantee that we would win the case. Now, to our amazaement, Trifa had surrendered without a fight.

We could not figure out why. He had an obvious motivation to keep the voluminous evidence from becoming public, but his surrender of citizenship simply advanced the deportation stage of the proceedings at which the evidence would come out anyway. But before we filed papers seeking his deportation, I insisted on a full hearing in federal court to formalize his surrender of citizenship. At that hearing, Trifa's lawyer insisted over and again that the surrender was voluntary, that there were no conditions, that the denaturalization case was over. The judge issued a formal order revoking Trifa's citizenship.

A few weeks later, Trifa's perfidy became clear. As soon as we filed deportation papers, Trifa appealed the voluntary surrender of his certificate. It was a sneaky and unprincipled move, designed to buy time without any legal basis whatever. But Trifa, or his lawyers, took advantage of one fact: no matter how flimsy the case, it takes time to get it thrown out of the judicial system. OSI spent one full year waiting for the court of appeals to dismiss the appeal, which it did as soon as the case was argued before it. But in the meantime the deportation proceedings were stayed, because the INS judge did not want to go forward with deportation while the issue of citizenship was still tied up in the federal courts. For Trifa, a patent abuse of the American courts was a good price to pay for an additional year of life in America.

The deportation hearing was eventually set for October 4, 1982. We were fully prepared to go, and on the first day of trial Judge Bellino D'Ambrosio heard the testimony of events in Bucharest, and the background of the Iron Guard, delivered by Professor Béla Vago of the University of Haifa, the free world's leading expert on modern Romanian history.

After court had recessed for the day, Trifa's lawyers approached me in the halls. Trifa wanted to make a deal, they said. He would admit to a technical count of illegal entry, and concede his deportability, if we would drop the remaining charges.

I turned them down flat. We had come too far in this case to let Trifa escape by pleading to a technicality, even if it meant victory for us in the end. Spurning a certain victory was probably a reckless move on my part, but I had no stomach for any more of his machinations, and I felt strongly that Trifa had made a second career of portraying himself as a martyr at the hands of the federal government. Accepting his offer would have enabled him to continue this charade. I was certain that he would weep and moan in the press that he was an innocent Romanian patriot, unable to fight the United States government forever, forced to agree to deportation on a technicality only to save his church the expense of defending him. No deal, I said.

The hearing continued. More evidence of Trifa's bilious anti-Semitic propaganda in *Libertate* came out on the public record on the second day. That night, his lawyers approached me again. Okay, they said, what kind of deal do we have to make to stop this hearing?

I told them that any guilty plea would have to include an admission that he had been a leader of the Iron Guard movement and had intentionally perjured himself to come to America. I wanted the record to be clear that Trifa was not only an anti-Semitic fascist but a liar as well, whose life and career in America had been possible only through his determined falsehoods to gain entry. And Trifa would have to stand up in open court and admit those facts personally. He could not hide behind his lawyers on this one. Finally, there would have to be an ironclad guarantee that he would not later appeal or attack the deportation order in an appellate court.

The lawyers agreed to put the proposal to Trifa. "I presume," said one of them, "that you would insist that his admissions be under oath?"

"I won't give him that dignity," I said. "He's shown what his oath is worth."

On October 7 Trifa stood before Judge D'Ambrosio in Detroit and admitted that he had been an Iron Guard leader, that he had been ineligible to come here under the DP Act, that he had known that, and that he had perjured himself to obtain a fraudulent visa. He conceded that he was deportable from the United States and that he would leave within sixty days after arrangements were made with another country to take him in.

I watched him as he stood at the lectern in the middle of the courtroom. In other cases I often had great difficulty imagining what the elderly man in the courtroom must have looked like in his younger days as an SS officer, an auxiliary storm trooper, or whatever. With

Trifa, I had no such trouble. At sixty-eight, he was sleek and well-groomed. If the proceedings were taking any toll on him, it did not show. In the high-ceilinged courtroom, he had instinctively put on the practiced aspect of ceremonial solemnity that so suits bishops and generals. It was not at all difficult to see him as the demagogue, the smooth-talking instigator of disorder that left blood on everyone's hands but his own, the ambitious editor of bigotry and cunning. It was, in fact, a lot easier to envision his past than to accept his present as a bishop tending to the spiritual values of his flock.

For Otto von Bolschwing, there was no Charlie Kremer to point a finger. We discovered Bolschwing through our own kind of pursuit—the dogged examination of old files.

As Gene Thirolf, working the Trifa file, trudged through the German Foreign Ministry's 1941 memos on the Iron Guard rebellion, he accumulated a list of people who had been involved—people who, if they were still alive, might shed light on the Iron Guard and strengthen our case against Trifa. Thirolf sent a cable to see if the German government might know the whereabouts of some former SS officers, including one known to us from the old files only as "von Bolschwing." The unexpected reply came back: "von Bolschwing" was Otto von Bolschwing, the head of the SD in Bucharest—and he had emigrated to the United States in 1954.

Thirolf requisitioned Bolschwing's immigration file from INS and quickly tracked him down to Sacramento, California. Bolschwing had passed an eventful career in the United States. From 1955 to 1963, according to his papers, he had been employed by the Warner-Lambert Pharmaceutical Company, and then he had been a self-employed business and trade consultant until 1970, except for two years with the German subsidiary of the Cabot Corporation of Boston. He described himself as the Vice President for Business Affairs of the Transcontinental Computer Investment Corporation in Sacramento. Neighbors described him as a "perfect continental gentleman."

In the press of preparing the Trifa case, however, Thirolf had little time to devote to Bolschwing. That task fell to Jeffrey Mausner when OSI was created in 1979. Mausner put together the dossier on Bolschwing, and, as was our custom, we interviewed the subject before we filed a case.

Bolschwing was, by this time, an elderly man, and not in good health. His son, an attorney, proposed a deal: Bolschwing would give up his citizenship if we would agree not to deport him.

It was a deal I was often offered at OSI, and I rejected it every time. My logic was simple: the United States government could not be in the position of offering a Nazi persecutor a guarantee against deportation, no matter what he offered in return. It would have defeated our whole purpose.

Bolschwing was lucid, but given his obvious poor health, it was not clear to us that he would be able to undergo the strenuous process of preparing his legal defense to deportation charges. I offered a proposal in return: if he surrendered his citizenship, we would refrain from filing a deportation case *if* a doctor appointed by the court certified that Bolschwing was so ill that he could not assist his attorney in preparing a defense. He would be required to undergo periodic medical examinations. If his health improved to the point where he could devote himself to his defense, we would file the deportation case.

In offering this proposal, I felt we were giving up nothing. Federal courts have held that, in criminal cases, a defendant cannot be prosecuted if he is incompetent, but deportation regulations do not contain a similar provision. Yet I could not in good conscience put a man on trial if he was too ill to work with his attorney to prepare his defense. I felt that deportation was at least as severe a result as a prison sentence, and that the Justice Department should not expel someone from the country if he could not defend himself. To do so would have been, in my opinion, contrary to basic concepts of due process. Even Nazi war criminals were entitled to their defense.

Bolschwing and his son agreed to the proposal, and his citizenship was revoked by consent decree. Three months later, Bolschwing died in California.

Trifa still lives in the Vatra, in Grass Lake, Michigan. To date, no country has agreed to take him in, and so he has not yet been deported. OSI is working with the State Department, contacting foreign governments in an effort to find one that will accept him. Trifa himself is shopping for a home too. Sitting on his estate in January 1984, he mused to a reporter, "I'm not looking for any place too hot. Or too cold. I'm looking for a place with a high standard of living, with culture."

He remains today, like all Nazi criminals in America, thoroughly, almost defiantly, unrepentant. He denies the fact that 270,000 Jews were murdered in Romania. "Not a single Jew was killed in Romania. At least not because he was Jewish." Asked about the vicious "kike" articles he published in his newspaper forty years ago, he is unashamed: "They were anti-Jewish," he says, his voice rising. "And they were true." And what of the six million Jews killed throughout Europe in the Holocaust? "I don't know if they were killed or not," says Trifa. "I didn't see any bodies."

But of one thing he is sure. Like Romania then, he is today the victim of a Jewish conspiracy. "The Jews . . . controlled so much of economic life in Romania," he said. "They have enough power [in the United States] to throw me out. Why should I be in the position I'm in without Jewish pressure?

"I am a man," he explains, "who happened to get put in a moment in history when some people wanted to make a point. The point was to revive the Holocaust. But all this talk by the Jews about the Holocaust is going to backfire. Against the Jews." Pressed to explain what he has in mind, Trifa's voice rises again. "Something will be done. The interest in the Holocaust will backfire."[26]

Trifa has changed not at all in forty years. He is today the same bigoted fascist he was as a young man in Bucharest. For him, America is not a place where people of various religions and nationalities seek to live in peace with each other. It has been little more than a place of sanctuary, comfort, and prosperity. Because he has never understood America, he seems to have little understanding that, at long last, America has rejected him.

8

FINDING NAZIS:
How OSI Worked

Shortly after I came to the Office of Special Investigations in January 1980, a reporter asked me how long I thought the office would exist. I thought a moment about the backlog of files we had inherited from INS and said, "Four or five years, maybe."

Three and a half years later, as I was clearing out my desk, I was interviewed by another reporter. How much longer for OSI? he asked. "Four or five years," I told him.

When I had answered the first reporter, I was thinking very much in the conventional frame of mind of the prosecutor. You investigate a murder when you come across a body; you don't walk the streets looking for one. And you prosecute Nazis by checking out leads when Nazis are reported to you.

But I soon came to believe that our responsibility was greater than that. The mandate of the Office of Special Investigations was to investigate and prosecute Nazi war criminals in the United States. We could not simply react to other people's allegations. We ourselves had to find out who the Nazis in America were. How we found them, and what we did with them, would determine the success or failure of OSI. By the end of 1983, our efforts had uncovered enough suspects to keep us prosecuting at least through the middle of the decade.

In 1980, however, the first problem was to define whom we were looking for. Although the term "Nazi war criminal" is generally used, it implies that the murders of millions of innocent people had something to do with war. They did not.

The experts on the "Jewish problem," the staffs of the death camps and concentration camps, the auxiliary storm troopers and "police," the racist demagogues and propagandists, all the contemptible people who created the Holocaust, were not fighting a war. They were implementing a hideous social policy far behind the front lines. The war was a separate event, and far away. No one was shooting at them. They lived in comfortable quarters with three meals a day and all the fringe benefits. While the infantry and the panzers and the navy and the Luftwaffe were engaged in combat against the Allies to secure new territory for the Reich, the makers of the Holocaust were working to make sure that the Reich would be Judenfrei. There were no soldiers in the Gestapo, or the death camps or the Jewish Affairs Section of the SS, and the crimes committed there were not "war crimes."*

My working definition of the Nazi criminals we were after was taken from the 1978 Holtzman amendment to the Immigration Act[1]— the first provision since the expiration of the Displaced Persons Act in 1952 that made Nazis inadmissible to America, and deportable from America. That amendment covered every alien who "ordered, incited, assisted, or otherwise participated in the persecution of any person because of race, religion, national origin, or political opinion" in conjunction with the Nazi regimes of Europe. (In 1980 the Immigration Act was amended to extend this definition to all persons who had taken part in persecution, whether under the Nazis or anyone else, anywhere in the world.)

The definition under the Holtzman amendment does not limit the victims to Jews, nor should it, of course. The essence of persecution is that the victim suffers not for what he has done, but for who he is, and so we investigated and prosecuted cases where the victims were gypsies, minority nationalities, Jehovah's Witnesses, or other disfavored groups.†

---

*Having said that, I admit that the phrase is so common, and so convenient, that I usually use it myself, and I do here.

†There is a vigorous debate among scholars whether the term "Holocaust" should be applied to the deaths of eleven million innocent people at the hands of the Nazis, or whether it should denote only the Final Solution to the Jewish Problem and the six million Jews who died as a result. Those who believe it must be reserved for the deaths of Jews emphasize that, while the deaths of all eleven million were equally tragic and equally to be condemned, the Jews were the only group that was singled out for extinction. To say that every innocent victim of Nazism died in the "Holocaust," they argue, diffuses the unique evil of Nazism and implies that it lashed out indiscriminately at eleven million people. In the words of Elie Wiesel, not every victim was a Jew, but every Jew was a victim.

This is a compelling argument, and anyone who seeks to understand Nazi persecution cannot forget that the Nazis sought the extinction of all Jews and of Judaism itself; no other religion or political belief or category of people was so marked. Once that is fixed in mind, the question of what the term "Holocaust" should comprehend becomes academic.

Persecution included killing, torture, and brutality; it included economic reprisals such as the confiscation of property; it included the enforcement of discriminatory laws. And it included propaganda or incitement that advocated these actions.

I had one rule that was followed in every case: No action would be filed in court unless we could prove that the defendant himself personally took part in, or incited, the persecution of which he stood accused. No one was prosecuted for belonging to the Nazi party or its fascist counterparts throughout Europe if there was no evidence, beyond that, of culpability. I realize that an argument can be made that anyone who was a member of the Nazi party or the SS, or supported their policies, "assisted" in persecution by creating an environment where it could be carried out with impunity. But I was a prosecutor, and my definition had to be more strict than that.

In the case of guards at death camps, we believed—and proved in court—that every guard necessarily took part in persecution, and thus it was not necessary to prove individual acts of persecution, although we usually did so. In fact, I dislike the term "guard" in this context; it implies someone akin to a conventional prison guard, who maintains order among inmates. The Jews at death camps were not "inmates," the guards did not maintain order, and no one was "concentrated" in the camps. The guards at Nazi death camps had one function only, which was to increase the speed and efficiency of death. Contrary to what many people might assume, and what many guards contended at trial, guards at death camps were volunteers. Anyone who felt he was not cut out for that gruesome work could be reassigned without penalty or fear for his safety.

We also had to prove, of course, that the defendant entered the United States illegally, because the whole point of the prosecution was to revoke his citizenship and ultimately to deport him. This was seldom a difficult matter, because anyone who had assisted the Nazis was barred by the Displaced Persons Act.* And because no one could

---

*Some people came in under the Refugee Relief Act, which was in effect from 1952 to 1956, but that act likewise contained a prohibition on former Nazi persecutors.

Where entry took place under the normal procedures of the Immigration Act of 1952, which did not bar Nazis until the Holtzman amendment of 1978, our task was slightly more complex. In those cases, we produced the State Department officials who had issued the visas; they testified that they had the discretion to deny a visa to anyone who, in their opinion, would not have been a desirable immigrant, and that this certainly included Nazi war criminals.

become a naturalized citizen unless he had entered legally and lived here for five years, whenever we proved illegal entry we showed the basis for revoking citizenship.

This latter principle—that illegal entry precluded lawful naturalization and thus we did not have to show illegality in the naturalization process itself—was a crucial point, because the naturalization application was quite superficial. As a general matter, it sought information on the applicant only for the years since his entry, and thus many Nazi criminals (and other illegal aliens) could fill it out in perfect truthfulness. When the Supreme Court agreed to hear Fedorenko's appeal, Attorney General Benjamin Civiletti emphasized that point to the court, and the court upheld it.[2]

Our necessary emphasis on misrepresentation and concealment in the immigration process created some concern among former DPs, particularly Ukrainians and Balts, who had shaved years off their true age in order to present what they thought would be a more attractive face on their applications. I met with representatives of these groups and assured them that I had no interest at all in prosecuting anyone who had done nothing worse than lie about his age.

My insistence on evidence of persecution stemmed from two somewhat related concerns. First, I wanted no witch-hunts, prosecuting people whose actual guilt was uncertain. And second, I believed that no judge in America would deport a middle-aged or elderly man (or woman) who had lived in the United States for thirty years for no reason other than that he had once been a fascist and had lied on some application forms. It was hard enough investigating true criminals; I had no desire to bog ourselves down in prosecuting people who had simply joined the Nazi party.

To carry out this work, OSI had a first-rate staff of people: twenty lawyers, seven historians, four investigators, and a phalanx of researchers, analysts, paralegals, and secretaries, fifty people in all. None of the lawyers or investigators had any detailed knowledge of Nazi war crimes before we came to OSI; the historians, on the other hand, were experts. But the lawyers, thrust into complex investigations and trials, came to have a very respectable knowledge of the Nazi period after a very short time. And we made generous use of experts from academia in the United States and Europe.

We were a diverse group of people, but we worked closely and soon came to fit together well. One reporter noted, "The atmosphere in [the] busy office is distinctly bullish, and there is a strong sense of camaraderie'' as we went about our work.[3]

Some of our people were Jewish, some were not; it made no difference to me in hiring and I never bothered to count. I received many résumés from lawyers whose families had been directly affected by the Holocaust; they were survivors, or they had lost close relatives, or both. Some of these applicants emphasized to me that they felt a deep and burning commitment to track down the perpetrators of the Holocaust.

Such entreaties made me uneasy, and while I could sympathize with their commitment, I turned down several applicants whose zeal struck me as excessive for a prosecutor. I needed lawyers who could be objective in appraising evidence, and in presenting cases in court. We were federal prosecutors, not personal representatives of those murdered by the Nazis; I could not afford the risk that a staff member's moral commitment might be so consuming as to subconsciously affect his objectivity. If the evidence in a prospective case was weak, we had to know it, and to know where and why it was weak, so that we could strengthen it, and if we could not strengthen it, close it. A prosecution, like a seawall, is only as strong as its weakest point; all the evidence in the world of Nazi persecution means nothing if our evidence against the prospective defendant himself is uncertain.

Before I approved the prosecution of any case, therefore, I required a detailed memo setting forth the basis for the charge, the expected testimony of the witnesses (and assessments of their credibility), the documentary evidence, the anticipated defenses, and our responses to those defenses. I could not personally interview the witnesses in every case before it was filed; I had to rely on the objectivity and honesty of the attorneys, historians, and investigators who did and who gave me the prosecution memo for decision. I soon recognized those attorneys who were objective and those who took liberties with the evidence, those who dealt honestly with weaknesses in cases and those who tried to conceal them. The good ones stayed.

At OSI we were certainly not immune to the emotional responses that the evidence could evoke—the photographs of the death camps, the cold-blooded body counts in official documents, the anguish of a survivor recalling events of forty years ago that still filled him with terror. But that made objectivity more important, not less.

At times this evidence led me to feel that we were prosecutors like no others, that we had been given a serious and historic responsibility transcending the dimensions of any single case. The verdicts in our cases went beyond the guilt or innocence of a particular defendant; each one helped to complete the historical record on what America had done in response to the Holocaust.

Yet at these times particularly we had to remember that we were prosecutors first, last, and always, and the same rules applied to us as to any prosecutor who sought indictment and conviction of a common criminal. We could not use a trial as a platform to air social or philosophical issues, no matter how important those issues might be or how useful the trial might be in illuminating them. We could not take shortcuts with the evidence, or cut corners with the law, or try cases in the press, acting on some belief that the enormity of the crimes or the importance of bringing the guilty to justice could somehow excuse such things. No witness took the stand to emphasize the importance of deporting Nazis; no OSI attorney argued to the judge that the delay of decades now justified special measures in determining guilt. Like the prosecution of a common murderer, there was no place in our case for anything that did not lead directly to probative evidence on the issues the judge had to decide in determining the fate of the single defendant before him.

Forty years ago the Supreme Court held that trials to revoke citizenship were different from ordinary civil trials; the government had to prove illegality by "clear and convincing" evidence, not simply the "preponderance" of the evidence that determines other civil cases. This standard of proof made our work far more exacting—as a practical matter, we had the same burden as the prosecution in criminal cases—but we never argued to any judge that the standard should be relaxed. On the contrary, we began each case by reaffirming that standard and acknowledging to the judge that we had to meet it to succeed. American citizenship should not be revoked on evidence that is doubtful.

I was certainly not insensitive to the greater issues that each trial involved. On the contrary, because I was aware of the unique and historic dimensions of our task I was determined that we take scrupulous care not to turn our trials into public debates on the evils of the Holocaust or the American record in investigating its perpetrators. Trials are intended to elicit facts so that judgments—sometimes profound judgments, as in these cases—can be rendered. Only if the trials

have integrity as trials can they serve any purpose afterward in illuminating the social or historical issues that give rise to them.

The business of putting together a nearly worldwide effort to investigate Nazis in America did not take place in the courtroom, however. OSI depended heavily on the cooperation and goodwill of other
governments, and I found that I could best secure this cooperation by
sitting down with those who could give it and speaking to them directly. And time after time I saw how great was the distance from the
federal courts of America to the capitals of the rest of the world.

After negotiating the arrangements for witnesses and documents
in Moscow in January 1980, I followed up with visits to other East-
ern-bloc capitals, particularly East Berlin, Warsaw, and Prague, to
strike similar agreements. In East Berlin I found prosecutors very interested in the details of the Moscow agreement, and I sensed that
they were being careful to follow that lead. In Warsaw, on the other
hand, I made the mistake of emphasizing at the outset the details of
Soviet cooperation. "This is Poland," one official interrupted. "We
will do things here the Polish way." The Soviets were not mentioned
again, and the Polish government agreed not only to allow depositions but to give us unrestricted access to Polish archives, a conces-
sion I was never able to win from the Soviets.

In the beautiful city of Prague in 1982, prior to my first meeting
with Czech officials, I got a gloomy forecast from the U.S. ambassador. "I will do whatever I can to help you," he said, "but our
relations with the Czech government these days are cool. Don't be
optimistic." At our conference a few hours later, I opened by expressing my admiration for the great beauty of the city—surely one
of the loveliest in Europe—and I mentioned that my wife's grandparents had emigrated to America from Prague early in the century.

Oh, said one foreign ministry official, and what were their names?
Poljacik, I replied, fervently hoping that no present-day dissident bore
that name. Apparently not; there were smiles and nods all around the
table. I mentioned that my mother-in-law was fluent in Czech and I
hoped to buy some books that she could read to our children. Ah yes,
said one official, let me tell you the best shop to visit. . . .

The Czechs promised full cooperation, which no doubt they would
have done anyway, but the meeting, begun on that homey note, progressed perhaps more warmly than it otherwise might have, a re-

minder that personal touches can sometimes accomplish what official relations might not.

That night, in fact, my deputy Neal Sher and I were guests of the Czech Foreign Ministry for dinner in a Prague restaurant. As we entered and crossed the main floor to our private room, I could have sworn the pianist was playing "Home on the Range." I listened; he was. He followed with "The Tennessee Waltz" and after that "Blowin' in the Wind." Then "Home on the Range" again, and the whole medley was repeated. One of our hosts turned to me. "We asked him to play American music," he said, "in honor of your visit." Cowboys, Patti Page, and Bob Dylan, the American repertoire of a Czech pianist. Wonderful.

Traveling in Europe, I always tried to take night trains between cities, partly because I like trains and partly because it saved hours: I could sleep and move at the same time. Usually these were pleasant experiences; the Red Arrow Express, for example, that leaves Leningrad at midnight and arrives in Moscow eight hours later, is a marvel. Russian trains are wider than their European counterparts and the toasty berths are almost as large as Soviet hotel rooms. Grandmotherly attendants ply the travelers with steaming coffee in glasses with silver filigreed holders as the wide-track express whooshes smoothly through the night. Or the West German train from Munich to Vienna on a Sunday afternoon offered a lush panorama of the Black Forest, the Blue Danube, and the Vienna Woods.

Other times, however, train travel could be unsettling. Neal Sher and I once arrived in Warsaw for an overnight visit, with a plane ticket on the only flight to East Berlin the following day. An alert Polish woman at the American embassy thought to confirm the reservation, only to be told that Interflug, the airline of the German Democratic Republic, had decided to cancel the flight. We quickly booked berths on an overnight train to Berlin, but when we arrived at the station at 11:30 p.m. we found that our berths were already occupied, there was no space in the car, and the conductor, a German, was supremely uninterested in our tickets, our passports, or our predicament.

Poland was under martial law, and it was not a happy time. Armed squads were patrolling the station, ready to enforce the midnight curfew. The conductor swung aboard, ready to depart. Our Polish escort, a woman of education and charm, was decidedly anxious. She had to be off the streets in thirty minutes, but she could not very well leave us stranded in the station. She ran up to the next car and spoke with great animation to its conductor, this one a Pole. There was no charm involved. As nearly as I could determine, her message was short and to the point: these are American diplomats, she warned, they have tickets on this train, and if they do not get on, right now, heads will roll in the Rail Ministry. The conductor shrugged and disappeared into his car. A few minutes later he returned, took our tickets, and showed us to top and bottom berths, slightly rumpled but very welcome. Gratefully, I pressed a couple of dollar bills in his palm as the train pulled out. The next morning, as we approached East Berlin, I noticed a young man with a backpack stretched out in the train's narrow corridor, glaring at us. I understood why our beds had been a bit wrinkled. As we debarked, he was demanding a refund from the conductor, who did not speak German and who was supremely uninterested in his predicament.

After my first trip to Israel in 1980, I promised Nancy that if I ever returned, I would take her with me. In June 1981 I was invited to the World Gathering of Jewish Holocaust Survivors, and we went together to one of the truly historic events of our time. From all over the world, 10,000 survivors, the Jews the Nazis could not kill, gathered in Jerusalem. My purpose in being there was to contact survivors' organizations and elicit their support in our never-ending search for witnesses. But the most stirring moments were the opening ceremonies at Yad Vashem, the Israeli Holocaust memorial, and the closing ceremonies a few days later at the Western (Wailing) Wall in the old city.

The gathering was a memorial to those who had perished but, in the Jewish tradition, it was also a reaffirmation of life, a victorious return of those who had gone through hell. At the opening ceremonies, held under the stars on an unusually cool night, a children's choir sang on the steps of Yad Vashem. Behind them, on a large raised screen, captured German films from Poland showed the Jewish children of the Holocaust generation being herded into railroad cars. The contrast was heartbreaking. Here, as so often for Nancy and me, the unspeakable tragedy of the Holocaust came home in thinking of the children. Then on the screen came films of Israeli children today— laughing, playing, frolicking at the beach, studying in school. Incredibly, a program that had begun with such pathos ended in a soaring spirit of hope and promise. ''To life'' is the Jewish benediction.

For three days the pilgrims met, talked, cried. The bulletin boards were covered with messages: "Did anyone know Jakob Kalman of Lodz? I am his daughter," and a hotel phone number. While we were there, Israeli television carried a heart-stopping story. A woman from America who as a young girl in Poland had escaped from the ghetto when her entire family was killed sat down with an Israeli student at a computer listing the names of all Israeli citizens. Like many other survivors at the gathering, she was seeking details of her family; perhaps a cousin from another town had survived and might be in Israel. The student entered the information on the computer, punched a few buttons. She waited, then looked up from the keyboard. Tell me your father's date of birth, she said quietly. The woman did. The girl looked at her. Your father survived, she said. He is alive, on a kibbutz here. Forty years after she had mourned his death, the woman was reunited with her father.

At the conclusion of the gathering, there was another ceremony, at the Western Wall: six young men and women, born to survivors after the Holocaust, stood with their parents and on behalf of Jewish youth everywhere pledged to pass the story of the Holocaust to their children, and to commit them to pass it to theirs, a sacred commitment never to forget. Six candles were lit, one for each million lives lost. High on the wall, six rabbis in colorful robes blew the shofar, the ancient ram's horn trumpet. Around us, thousands of men and women fell silent. Beside us, an old woman fingered the blue numbers that an SS man had tattooed in her arm forty years before. Tonight that arm hugged her grandchild. To life, to life.

How did we find Nazi war criminals in America? Some might conjure up images of stealth and surveillance, clandestine meetings in shadows with secretive informants reporting miraculous chance confrontations in city streets between a death camp survivor and his former warder. But this is not how Nazis were investigated in America.

When OSI came into being in the summer of 1979, the grab bag of some 350 files that we inherited from INS contained many anonymous letters with vague claims against various people. Such letters continued to come in every week at OSI, and all of them were read, but I soon dubbed them "my-neighbor-is-a-Nazi" letters. My landlord has a German shepherd and a crew cut, more than one reported, he must be a Nazi. My building super is a snoop and speaks with an accent; please investigate him.

Sometimes an over-the-transom allegation contained enough specific information that we could carry out a serious investigation, but I don't recall that any of them ever yielded enough evidence to prosecute. In fact, many of the "suspects" turned out to have been born after the war, or to have come to America long before it. We soon culled this junk out of the files and focused on more serious matters.

Most of our cases were made by the tedious method of examining old documents. Our biggest trove was the list of 50,000 SS officers and concentration camp guards compiled by the SS and captured by the Allies after the war. We obtained a copy from the Berlin Document Center and began the slow process of going through the names one by one, comparing them to INS immigration files. We got several hits, including that of Conrad Schellong, about whom more in a moment.

We used similar methods with lists of lesser bulk. For example, at one point we were investigating the possibility that a Lithuanian immigrant had been a member of a punitive detachment that the Nazis had sent to Minsk in Byelorussia to kill Jews there. We asked the Soviets for any membership rosters or payroll records from that detachment. We received a full roster, a copy of the original German document, with scores of names, ranks, and birthdates on it. We promptly ran all the names through INS immigration records—and found that a dozen or more of them had come to the United States.

Sometimes searching such lists produced very little. We had reams of names of members of the Iron Guard, many of whom are in the United States. Like members of the Nazi party, they belonged to a fascist and anti-Semitic organization and I have not the slightest sympathy for any of them. But we could tie very few of them to instances of persecution.

None of the people we were looking at in these preliminary stages were ever aware they were under investigation by the Department of Justice. Only when an investigation had progressed to the point of substantial evidence of persecution did we inform the subject of our interest, and then we gave him the opportunity to meet with our investigators and provide whatever information or explanation he wished.

The interview opportunity served two purposes: First, as a matter of basic fairness, it ensured that we did not go off to court with formal charges that could be refuted by some evidence known only to the subject (although, in fact, subjects seldom were able to exculpate themselves). The other purpose was to give the suspect a chance to incriminate himself further. I was amazed by the number of people who agreed to talk to us and ended up by giving us damning admissions that we could never have obtained anywhere else. Everyone was told that he was not obligated to talk to us and that anything he said could be used against him in court. Still they talked—not to unburden their consciences, but because they thought they could explain away the incriminating evidence and have us leave them alone.

A typical example went like this: Captured German documents showed that a man living in the United States had been a member of the local auxiliaries in his village; other documents contained his signature reporting the details of actions against Jews. At the interview, the subject readily identified his signature (score one for the prosecution), admitted that he had been in the auxiliary unit (two), but told us that he signed the document only on orders and hadn't had anything to do with the killing of the Jews. What they did not realize was that every piece in the puzzle is important; by providing details of their actions and denying only the obviously damning, they had given us the best evidence of guilt—their own admissions.

Joe Lynch, a retired New York City cop and a former chief of the Brooklyn organized-crime strike force, had no peer in these interviews. I never heard him raise his voice in three years, but in half a dozen cases he came back to Washington with the words of the suspect verifying the details of his own complicity.

We worked closely with Simon Wiesenthal on a number of cases. Wiesenthal, who was instrumental in gathering evidence on Hermine Braunsteiner that ultimately led to her denaturalization and extradition in the seventies (see chapter 3), operates from a small office in Vienna, but his contacts extend throughout the world. For nearly forty years he has gathered information which he then passes on to prosecutors so that legal action can be taken against Nazi criminals. Whenever he came across information that someone might be in America, he conveyed it to me, and we pursued it from there. He is a true ''Nazi hunter''; we were prosecutors—two quite different roles. But we worked well together. I found him to be a man of utmost integrity, with a deep commitment to the due process of law.

Many people, particularly Eastern European emigrés, demanded to know why OSI was not investigating Communist persecution. The Soviets, they reminded us, were as capable of atrocities as the Na-

zis—deporting innocent people to Siberia, liquidating political enemies, and all the rest. Why should the government go only after Nazis?

My answer was simple. Communist criminals do not come to
America when their crimes are complete, and I can't prosecute someone who is not here. But my answer always included a promise: If
anyone could give me information on any person within the reach of
our law today who had taken part in the persecution of innocent people, for any reason under any regime, I would personally see that a
full investigation was carried out.

How successful were we in finding and prosecuting Nazi war
criminals in America? It is almost impossible to answer the first part—
finding them—because we do not know how many came here, much
less how many are still alive today. In the three and a half years of
my tenure as Director of the Office of Special Investigations, no
promising lead was ignored, no avenue of investigation was ne-
glected. And certainly no individual against whom we compiled sufficient evidence of persecution went unprosecuted. I am sure that
continues to be true today, because my successor as Director of the
Office was Neal Sher, who was my deputy throughout my tenure.

Yet I think it would be irresponsible of me to suggest that OSI
found, or is now finding, every single Nazi war criminal in the United
States. Given the large number of those who came here, I can only
say that we prosecuted every one we could find. But there are no doubt
a number, still alive, who have not been found. I doubt that they are
much different from those we have prosecuted, but they might be
luckier: evidence of their crimes may have been destroyed; witnesses
may be impossible to locate; their deception may have been cleverer.
We can only do our best: to follow every avenue. Our success is not
entirely within our control.

As to our success in prosecution, however, the record is clear.
From OSI's creation in the summer of 1979 through July 1, 1984, we
filed forty-eight cases, including the handful we inherited from Sam
Zutty's INS task force. Thirty of these were denaturalization cases;
eighteen of them were deportation cases, including six where citizenship had previously been revoked after a denaturalization trial.*

---

*It was and remains OSI policy to file deportation proceedings against every competent de-
fendant whose citizenship is revoked. The fact that only four deportation cases have thus far
been filed against ex-citizens is due to one of two factors: either the appeals in the citizenship
cases are not final, or the defendant died during the appeal process.

We went to trial on sixteen of the denaturalization cases; we won fourteen of them, and every one that was appealed by the defendant was upheld.* Of the remaining fourteen denaturalization cases, seven were awaiting trial on July 1, 1984; four defendants died prior to trial (including two suicides); three were withdrawn by OSI (two of which had been filed by INS on what we later determined to be insufficient evidence).

Of the eighteen deportation cases we handled, two had been lost by INS and we were not able to reverse those judgments on appeal. We obtained final orders of deportation as to two others; one was deported and one is awaiting deportation. In five cases we won deportation orders and in one case we lost; all six are on appeal. Trials or verdicts are pending in the other eight cases.

Our record to date, therefore, has been an exceedingly strong one: there has been a total of twenty-four verdicts handed down in cases tried by OSI, twenty-one of which have been in our favor.

The process, one must understand, is an exceptionally slow one due to the structure of citizenship and deportation laws. A denaturalization case is tried in federal court, whose verdict may be appealed to the U.S. court of appeals and then to the Supreme Court, which may or may not decide to hear the case. A deportation case is tried before an administrative judge, whose verdict may be appealed first to the Board of Immigration Appeals, then to the U.S. court of appeals, then to the Supreme Court. The two proceedings cannot be combined under present law. Thus, a naturalized citizen determined to exhaust all his appeals can go before seven separate forums before he can actually be deported.

This lugubrious process would take several years even if there were no delays in handing down decisions; unfortunately there are very often severe delays. In one case in federal court in Philadelphia, the trial ended in December 1981; the verdict was handed down in July 1983, more than eighteen months later. In one deportation case, the judge gave his decision more than a year after the trial had ended; in another case, the delay was nineteen months. Nor were delays confined to the trial level. In one deportation case, the Board of Immigration Appeals issued its decision more than fourteen months after it heard arguments.

---

*Four of the fourteen are pending on appeal as of July 1, 1984.

In denaturalization cases, we waited an average of five months after the trial ended to hear the verdict; in deportation cases, the average wait was twice as long. This does not include the time between filing the case and going to trial, which commonly consumed a year or more.

Some delay is inevitable and necessary. After a suit is filed, the defendant needs time to prepare his case; after it is tried, the judge needs time to consider the evidence, make up his mind, and write his decision and the reasons for it. Still, the process moves so slowly that sometimes I am amazed that anyone is deported from the United States for any reason. Some days I felt like Hamlet, who in his melancholy list of the whips and scorns of time gave prominent place to "the law's delay."

Many of the Eastern European emigré groups who bombarded me with criticism over OSI's efforts demanded to know why jury trials were not provided to the defendant. My answer was that I had no objection to jury trials, but no control over the matter either; Congress has not included denaturalization in that category of civil cases where jury trials were allowed. Go to Congress, I told them; if Congress changes the law, we'll have jury trials. Many days I wished them Godspeed in that effort. Juries, at least, are locked up until they decide the case.

Beyond all the courthouse delay, however, is a problem that is just now beginning to loom. An order of deportation, no matter how final or how long it took to win, is a useless piece of paper unless the United States can find a country willing to take the deportee in. Archbishop Trifa, eighteen months after the final order of deportation, sits in Michigan because to date no other country has agreed to receive him. We cannot take a deportee three miles to sea in a dory and cut the line, and so until we locate a place for him to go he stays in the United States. And since he has committed no crime here, he is a free man.

In only one case has a deportation been effected: Hans Lipschis, a Lithuanian Volksdeutsche and a guard at Auschwitz, who came to Chicago in 1956 and worked as a janitor in a suburban elementary school. He never applied for American citizenship; he kept the German citizenship that he proudly received in 1943. In 1982 he agreed to be deported rather than contest OSI's charges against him. West Germany had to take him back, and it did in April 1983.[4]

But most of OSI's defendants did not retain their former citizenship, and so no country is obligated to take them in. And few are willing. As one foreign official told me candidly, "Who wants to import America's war criminals?" These men are old, or soon will be; they have no particular skills or assets that make them attractive to other nations, and no country, apparently, wants to put itself in the awkward position of taking a Nazi war criminal back. A country that did so could, of course, put the man on trial for his crimes (and West Germany requested and received our file on Lipschis), but it is not obligated to, and most countries today show little enthusiasm for the task. The West German government has made it clear that it will not accept anyone who is not a German citizen. Israel has requested the extradition of Demjanjuk, but there is a strong split in that country between those who believe that it is Israel's historic obligation to place Nazi criminals on trial and those who believe that Israel should not be a dumping ground for aged Nazis. To date, Adolf Eichmann has been the only foreigner tried on war crimes charges in Israel, and I am sure that many Israelis feel that trial is a tough act to follow.

I believe that the objective of the United States government should be to remove these people from the country; where they go is secondary. Had Australia or Zambia or anyplace in between volunteered to take these people, I would have gladly sent every one there. Ideally, I would like to see each of them stand trial on charges of war crimes, to be judged fairly and to be sentenced appropriately. If countries of the world were competing against each other for the privilege of receiving Nazi criminals, I would have chosen a country that was prepared to hold a trial. Our challenge now is not to pick among contestants, but to find a country willing to take these criminals off our hands.

Despite the delays and frustrations of seeing these cases through, there have been satisfying victories along the way. Of the eighteen cases that OSI tried in its first three years, some stand out more clearly than others, because they remind us that justice, however delayed, can still be done. One of these was the case of Bohdan Koziy.

Koziy is a fifty-eight-year-old* motel owner in Fort Lauderdale, Florida, who from 1941 to 1944 had been a Ukrainian auxiliary under

---

*All ages are given as of the time of trial.

the Nazi occupation. He came to the United States in December 1949 under the Displaced Persons Act by claiming that he had spent the war as a "tailor's apprentice and farmer's helper." He became an American citizen in 1956 in Utica, New York, where he worked in a gas station. Later he bought a motel in Clinton, New York, and in 1972 he and his wife moved to Fort Lauderdale where they owned and operated the Flying Cloud Motel near the white Florida beaches.

Our case against Koziy was similar in some respects to the case against Wolodymir Osidach (see Chapter 1). Koziy, we contended, had joined the Ukrainian police in the Stanislau region in 1941 when the Germans moved in, and had taken part in the murders of the Jews of his area. We had several witnesses from the Soviet Union and Poland who testified, on videotape, that they had known Koziy, and they described his role in the killing of Stanislau's Jews.*

Our case was strong—we had two German insurance documents listing Koziy as a member of the local auxiliaries—but it was particularly poignant because several of the witnesses clearly recalled that Koziy had made Jewish children his special victims. Maria Ilikovska, a sixty-eight-year-old Ukrainian housewife, saw Koziy kill a twelve-year-old boy who had been caught hiding in the town after the rest of the Jews had been deported. "I watched the scene, how Koziy took out his gun and shot the boy at the back of his head," she testified. Pressed on her identification, she grew indignant. "I am absolutely certain," she said. "I am an old woman and I am telling the truth."

Not all witnesses knew Koziy by name; they testified that the man they had seen, whatever his name, was the man who had married the burgermeister's daughter. We checked the marriage records from 1943. Koziy's wife was the daughter of the mayor.

Four witnesses told of watching in fear as Koziy snatched three-year-old Monica Singer, daughter of the Jewish town doctor, from her home and dragged her to the police station. The child understood, too early, what was to happen. She cried out to her mother, who had followed, pleading for her release. "Mother, he's going to shoot me," the girl cried. "And I want to live!" Koziy took out his pistol and her mother turned away, unable to watch.

---

*As in every case, we notified Koziy's attorneys of the depositions and offered to pay all expenses so that they could cross-examine the witnesses. They refused to go, and then tried to throw the depositions out of court on grounds they had not cross-examined. The judge was not impressed, and, after viewing the testimony on videotape, allowed it to stand.

Anton Vatseb, his eyes fixed in horror on the unfolding scene, told what happened next. Koziy stood the child against a wall. "Then he stepped back around ten steps and then he shot." Vatseb paused. "As far as I remember, he shot twice."

Vatseb recalled another murder—a teen-age Jewish girl hiding in a barn on the outskirts of the village. "Koziy walked right to the barn. We heard two shots and some time passed and Koziy walked out of the barn. There was a smirk on his face and he said, 'Now I'll have a pleasant dinner.' " Vatseb paused again. "He had a great passion," he said. "A passion for killing people."

Koziy's defense was to admit nothing, to deny everything, to impugn the government, and to portray himself as a victim of "Soviet fabrication." He was not a Ukrainian policeman, he said; he was a "resistance fighter," operating against the Nazis. Yet he had somehow omitted to mention his resistance activities when he applied for a visa, despite the fact that resistance fighters received favored consideration under the DP Act. And at trial he grudgingly conceded, after the witnesses had been heard, that he had worn the uniform of a Ukrainian policeman, but he contended that this was just a cover for his underground activities. He brought his wife and her father to the stand to testify he had never done anything wrong. He even produced a witness, a Ukrainian living in Canada, to testify that she had seen him in a hospital bed at the time of the murders of the children.

OSI attorney Jovi Tenev took care of her on cross-examination. Her story was false. She admitted that Koziy, an old friend, had called her to say "the Jewish put him in this trouble" and that she agreed to testify "because I know you from my country and what can I say bad [sic] for you?"

Koziy's defense that the two German insurance documents were Soviet forgeries fell apart in a particularly embarrassing fashion. He claimed that certain pinholes in the documents were the traces left by a Soviet forger. Koziy held the documents up in court, pointing to the tiny telltale holes. "We did a better [forgery] job in [the] underground, without modern machinery," he testified smugly.

When our document expert took the stand, he had another explanation for the little holes. He had made them a few months earlier, he testified, when he took microscopic ink and paper samples to test the documents for authenticity. And the documents were entirely authentic.

Federal Judge James Paine handed down his decision on March 29, 1982. He ruled that Koziy had taken part in the persecution of innocent people and had concealed his activities when he came to the United States. Koziy's citizenship was revoked.

The opinion was straightforward, without evident emotion, which is as it should be. But there was one sentence that gave us particular satisfaction. Referring to the testimony of the events outside the police station, Judge Paine concluded, "The defendant personally and single-handedly murdered the female child of Dr. Singer."[5]

Thirty-nine years after the child's death, her killer had been brought to justice in Florida.

Not every case that we prosecuted involved a former displaced person. Conrad Schellong, for example, had to wait until the time was right to come to America.

The Displaced Persons Act, as we have seen, forbade the immigration of Nazi war criminals, but this restriction was very easy to evade for those Eastern Europeans willing to lie, because there was no effective enforcement scheme. The Berlin Document Center (BDC) did not have records of the local Nazi organizations in Eastern Europe, much less of the personnel rolls of the auxiliary police, storm troopers, and so forth. But the BDC did have the SS records of Germans and Austrians, so former Nazis from those countries were far less successful in avoiding detection, and many were deterred from trying.

The picture changed with the expiration of the Displaced Persons Act in 1952. The Immigration Act passed in that year contained no prohibition on former Nazis. As a result, the German and Austrian Nazis who were bottlenecked through 1952 found it a much easier go afterward. This is not to say that Nazi service was totally irrelevant, or that State or INS authorities were powerless to prohibit the entry of former Nazis. Granting of visas was, and is, a very discretionary matter; a consul who decides that the applicant is not a desirable immigrant can deny a visa for that reason alone.

But the demise of the DP Act brought the disassembly of Nazi-checking procedures, and for German Nazis who wanted to take a try at immigration, their chances improved dramatically. One who did was Schellong, a former SS officer who came to the United States in 1957.

Schellong was an early and convinced Nazi. As a twenty-four-year-old he joined the SS and served at Dachau, the Third Reich's first concentration camp, which opened in 1934 to confine political prisoners and other enemies of the state. Dachau, just outside Munich in Bavaria, was the West Point of Nazi concentration camps. Its junior officers in the thirties rose to positions of command at the major death camps in the forties.

Schellong quickly rose to the rank of SS-Hauptsturmführer (captain) and was given command of the training detachment—teaching new SS recruits how to handle the victims. He later became commander of the guard company, known as the "SS Death's Head Unit," supervising the SS storm troopers who herded the prisoners and saw that everything ran in clockwork fashion.

In 1939, with the invasion of Poland, Schellong transferred to the Waffen SS, the military arm, and served through the war; by 1945 he was a lieutenant colonel.

In 1956 Schellong applied for a visa to come to America. In filling out his biography, he omitted any reference to his concentration camp background. Instead, he claimed that he had joined the Waffen SS in 1934 and had served in military roles until the end of the war. For the visa examiner, this did not appear to be a particular obstacle. Schellong had been a soldier.

There was one problem that the visa examiner did not realize. The Waffen SS was not formed until 1939, and so Schellong could not have joined it in 1934. But this discrepancy went unnoticed, and Schellong came to the United states, settling in Chicago.

In 1962 he applied for naturalization. When the naturalization examiner saw that Schellong had been a member of the SS as early as 1934, his eyebrows went up. He asked Schellong directly: Did you ever have anything to do with concentration camps? Oh, no, said Schellong, I was just a soldier.

Fine, said the examiner, let's just put that under oath, and in writing. Schellong wrote on his naturalization application: "The Waffen SS was part of the German Army. I like to be soldier and I signed in 1934. . . . I had never to do any service in a concentration camp and never arrest one man in this matter. I was only a soldier."

He became a citizen on July 17, 1962.

As we went through the list of 50,000 SS officers and concentration camp guards, one of the first names to hit was Conrad Heinrich

Schellong. We pulled his immigration file and saw what he had written on his visa and naturalization applications. The discrepancy struck us immediately. According to the SS list, Schellong had joined that organization in 1934, but his story of being a soldier was a fabrication.

Working with German records and survivors of Dachau, we put together the picture of Schellong. He had been a disciplined and dedicated overseer in one of the biggest concentration camps in Germany.

The trial was as close as we ever got to an open-and-shut case. It took place in 1982, despite the request of Schellong's attorney that it be postponed until 1999 to give him time to prepare, and OSI attorneys Joe Lynch and Janet DeCosta put on a solid case. Schellong's defense, if it can be called that, was that his service at Dachau was indeed not "in" a concentration camp, so that his 1962 statement was correct; he served only "at" Dachau, and was stationed beyond the camp's perimeter as a guard against enemies.

It was a ridiculous defense. In 1934 Munich was under no threat of military attack and needed no guards beyond its perimeters. And no one believed his semantic distinction. The judge ruled that, had Schellong told the truth, his petition for naturalization would have been denied for "lack of good moral character," as the law provides. The court of appeals affirmed the decision in August 1983, and deportation proceedings are now under way.[6]

We also filed a deportation case against Edgars Laipenieks, a sixty-eight-year-old Latvian who had fled after the war to Chile, where he became a citizen. Laipenieks came to the United States in 1960 as a permanent resident alien, and found employment at a number of schools and colleges, principally in California, as a track coach. Laipenieks had been a well-known athlete in Latvia prior to the war, and had participated in the 1936 Berlin Olympics. When the Germans entered Latvia in 1941, Laipenieks had joined the Latvian Political Police—the Nazi-controlled force of indigenous henchmen—and had spent most of the war years as an enforcer at the Riga Central Prison, the Nazis' holding tank for Jews and political enemies.

After he entered the United States in 1960, Laipenieks volunteered his services to the CIA, offering to ferret out information on Eastern European nationals who visited the United States. The CIA accepted his offer. Like most informants, he provided information on a piecework basis as he came across it. When INS began an investigation of him in 1976, Laipenieks brandished his "CIA connection" and wrote to the agency asking for assistance in getting INS to go away.

Laipenieks, in fact, was not deportable at all in 1976, because he had entered the United States under the Immigration Act of 1952, which contained no prohibition on Nazis until the Holtzman amendment of 1978 inserted one. In 1976 INS informed the CIA that Laipenieks was "not amenable to deportation under existing laws," and the CIA passed this information along to Laipenieks.

On January 13, 1980, about a week after I had joined OSI, ABC-TV broadcast a special on Nazi war criminals, and prominent on their roster was Edgars Laipenieks who, according to the broadcast, was not being prosecuted by the United States government because of his CIA connection.

When I went into the office the next day, I asked for a full briefing on the Laipenieks case. We pulled the file and found that INS had closed the investigation because there was no law under which he could be deported. But the Holtzman Amendment had since solved that problem. I assigned the case for immediate investigation. I told the CIA that if the evidence of persecution satisfied me, I would file for his deportation.

The case was filed and it came up for trial in February 1982. The trial judge initially ruled against us, but this verdict was overturned on appeal and Laipenieks was ordered deported. His appeal to the federal courts is now pending.

In this case or any other case, I would have entertained no objection from the CIA or anyone else unless it could have been shown that prosecution would have jeopardized a legitimate national security interest of the United States. And if that showing could be made, I would have referred the matter to the assistant attorney general, or the attorney general himself if necessary, for a decision. I was not insensitive to the needs of national security, but I felt strongly that I had an obligation to prosecute where the evidence justified it. If national security was more important, a decision not to file would have to come from my superiors in the Justice Department.

It turned out to be an academic question. No federal agency, including the CIA, ever objected to any prosecution or tried to call us off any investigation.

Not every case ended with a verdict. Some ended with a suicide.

On June 29, 1983, the Office of Special Investigations filed suit in federal court in Boston charging that Michael Popczuk, a sixty-three-year-old carpenter living in nearby Lynn, had been a Ukrainian auxiliary in the Antoniny region who had harnessed Jews to wooden carts and forced them to pull cargo between villages, beating them as he would a horse. We also charged that Popczuk had participated in a roundup of 600 Jewish men, women, and children in the village of Manivtsy. Eyewitnesses from the Soviet Union were ready to testify.[7]

We did not need them. Eight days after the case was filed, Popczuk put a shotgun to his head and pulled the trigger.

In Chicago, Albert Deutscher, a sixty-one-year-old railway worker who came to the United States in 1952 as a Ukrainian Volksdeutsche, was charged in December 1981 with having concealed his role in the slaughter of Jews near his home in Odessa. According to our complaint, Deutscher had been one of a band of paramilitaries who regularly met trains crammed with Jewish victims and shot them as they were driven out.[8]

The day after the complaint was filed, Deutscher jumped in front of a speeding freight train in Chicago. He was killed instantly. The coroner ruled the death a suicide.

Is there a "typical" Nazi war criminal who came to the United States? They came from many different countries; their roles in persecution varied from the one-on-one brutality of John Demjanjuk and Wolodymir Osidach and Bohdan Koziy to the executive terrorism of Andrija Artukovic and the sidelines manipulation of Viorel Trifa and Otto von Bolschwing. But when they looked to America, their behavior assumed a definite pattern.

Most of them in this country took jobs in the middle of the middle class: motel owner, butcher, bookkeeper, factory worker, school janitor, tailor, loading dock supervisor, draftsman, railwayman, and so on. There were a few exceptions—Bolschwing was a business executive, Trifa a church official—but the exceptions are vivid against the pallid background of more ordinary lives.

The one thing that nearly all of them shared was that, once in America, they became model citizens and quiet neighbors. Only one of them, to my knowledge, ever had a police record, and that was for a drunk and disorderly charge. None of them was associated with the American Nazi fringe, anti-Semitic movements, extremist political organizations, or any other echoes of Nazism. In fact, none of them was active in mainstream political movements, or in local politics beyond the PTA. A few of them claimed membership in ostensibly anti-Communist organizations, but my impression is that these were primarily ethnic social clubs which included a few anti-Soviet speeches at their annual picnics. Certainly none of the defendants could be genuinely characterized as a political activist. Their one abiding trait seems to have been a determination to stay anonymous and to cultivate the good will of their neighbors.

Most succeeded very nicely in this. In the early days, whenever we filed a case against a defendant the local papers paid a call on the neighbors to see what it was like living next door to an accused Nazi war criminal. The universal reaction was one of puzzled disbelief. This fellow a Nazi? No. He and his wife are nice folks. They keep their lawn mowed, and they always smile, and they put out jack-o'-lanterns on Halloween, just like us. No, they would say, shaking their heads; those guys in Washington must have the wrong man.

But another thread ran repeatedly through these reactions. Few neighbors really knew the man.

"All I know is that he is a nice man and a good neighbor," said a woman who lived near Karl Linnas in Greenlawn, Long Island.[9] Linnas was later stripped of his citizenship when a federal court found he had abused and executed innocent men, women, and children in Estonia.

"They are good people, from what I can see," said a neighbor of Sergei Kowalchuk in Philadelphia.[10] Kowalchuk was proven to have persecuted the Jews of Lubomyl in the Ukraine while a member of the Ukrainian auxiliary police.

Of Albert Deutscher, who jumped in front of a train, a neighbor in Brookfield, Illinois, said, "When he walks by, he always said 'Hi.' He's a very quiet man."[11]

A reporter who spent the day interviewing neighbors of Arnolds Trucis in Philadelphia concluded that Trucis was "a man whom everyone recognized on sight but no one knew." One housewife who had lived next door to Trucis for years said, "Everybody [is] asking, 'Who is he?'"[12]

Trucis was, according to the charges filed against him, a member

of the Latvian Auxiliary Security Police from the first days of the
German invasion in July 1941 until November 1943, a man who had
assaulted and abused innocent people, mainly Jews. Shortly after his
attorney returned from depositions in Latvia, where several witnesses
recounted their experiences at Trucis' hands, he met with his client.
A few days later, Trucis died of a heart attack.

Hans Lipschis, the Auschwitz guard, likewise left behind some
surprised neighbors when he agreed to be deported back to Germany.
"That sweet man? I can't believe it," said one woman. "They keep
up their property," said another neighbor. "They are very quiet." [13]

These were ordinary people. They drew no attention to themselves, asked no special favors, raised no voices. They spoke to their
neighbors on the sidewalks but seldom took them into their homes.
They wanted to be left alone, but not so obviously that people might
begin to wonder why. So they did not run, and they did not hide.
They took on a protective coloration. They did whatever their neighbors did. They became citizens; they flew the flag. They did not talk
about the war, or about the Jews, ever. And in cities throughout the
country, their neighbors never suspected a thing. After years of living
next door, their neighbors could still ask themselves, "Who is he?"

The Displaced Persons Commission, in its final report, concluded, "[T]he displaced persons are almost indistinguishable from
the rest of the people in the communities that welcomed them." [14] In
the thirty-two years since that was written, the protective coloration
has become permanent.

And what of Andrija Artukovic, the most prominent Nazi of all in
the United States, the one whose protective coloration washed away
in four years, who was ordered deported in 1952?

By 1960 (see Chapter 5) his deportation to Yugoslavia had been
stayed on grounds that he might suffer persecution there, and he was
living quietly in Southern California in a home owned by his brother
on the beach. The Immigration and Naturalization Service was telling
correspondents that efforts were being made to secure his deportation
to some other country, but in fact it was doing nothing at all.

In 1978 a little-noticed provision was added to the Holtzman
amendment; no person guilty of persecution himself, it read, would
be eligible for a stay of deportation based on his fear of persecution
elsewhere. Among congressional insiders, it was known as the "Artukovic clause."

At OSI, we took the Artukovic clause and ran with it. We filed a motion with the Board of Immigration Appeals asking that the stay be lifted—indeed, we pointed out, the stay was now in violation of the law. OSI attorney Rod Smith argued the case before the board in July 1980, and one full year later BIA handed down its decision: the stay was rescinded and the original order of deportation was reinstated. At long last, thirty-three years after he had sneaked into America, Artukovic had to go.

Artukovic appealed the decision—there is always an appeal—to the federal court of appeals in California, the same one that had blocked his extradition in 1957 by ruling that the murder of hundreds of thousands of Serbs and Jews was a "political" crime. This time, the court heard the latest arguments and, like the Board of Immigration Appeals, it too waited a year to announce its decision.

Artukovic's deportation hearing had been held a very long time ago, the court said—almost thirty years, to be exact. The law making people like him ineligible for stays of deportation had been passed much more recently. The court ruled that Artukovic was entitled to a brand-new hearing before he could actually be deported.[15]

The decision was a swift kick in the gut. In 1952 Artukovic had been found guilty of massive persecution in Croatia from 1941 to 1945. Not even Artukovic's attorney had claimed that there were any new witnesses, any new evidence, that might exonerate his client at this late date. And as we had pointed out to the court of appeals, the facts on which the revocation of the stay was based—Artukovic's complicity in persecution—had been the subject of a full hearing in 1952, and Artukovic had lost. How could anything that had happened since 1952 make him any the less guilty? What would be the point of proving things that had already been proved, especially when the government would be at an enormous disadvantage with the passage of thirty years?

The court of appeals ruled against us, and refused to entertain our petition for reconsideration. What it had done, literally, was to put the case against Artukovic all the way back to square one. We would have to prove guilt as if Artukovic had just been discovered in California for the first time in 1982—as if the events of the past thirty years simply had not happened.

This was the greatest injustice of all. One of Europe's major war criminals, a man who had come to America under a false name on a sixty-day visa and refused to leave, a man who was ordered deported after a full hearing, now had his slate wiped entirely clean. The government would have to find witnesses and documents last seen thirty years ago and prove again what he had done in Croatia. And then, assuming this could be proven anew, Artukovic could appeal to the BIA—and then to this same federal court of appeals.

The decision had been handed down two days after Artukovic's eighty-third birthday.

9

KLAUS BARBIE:
"We Have Delayed Justice in Lyon"

The case of Klaus Barbie was surely among the most unusual investigations the Department of Justice has ever conducted. It began with the abrupt expulsion from Bolivia of one of the most wanted Nazis in the world, and it ended with an unprecedented diplomatic apology from the United States to France. Between these two headline events was a six-month investigation that almost ended before it began, and that, once begun, assembled a startling story: how American intelligence used the "Butcher of Lyon" to spy on the Communists, lied to the State Department about it, and then secretly turned Barbie over to a sinister Croatian priest in Rome for delivery to South America.

I conducted that investigation, and the pieces of a fascinating and repugnant puzzle came together. This small, slightly paunchy man with piercing blue eyes had flourished in treachery, from the shadows of occupied France to the thin sunshine of Bolivia. He could be as shrewd and dispassionate as the gray cat he sometimes held on his lap at Gestapo headquarters in Lyon, or as affable as any other businessman sipping coffee in an outdoor café on a sunny La Paz boulevard. He could order the deaths of dozens of French orphans for the Nazi SS, and he could sort out the tangled factions of the German Communist party for the United States Army.

In German-occupied France, the city of Lyon, France's second largest, was the home of the Maquis—the French Resistance. When the SS moved into Lyon in 1942, it made neutralization of the Resistance one of its top priorities. The security police and intelligence arms of

the SS were consolidated under Hauptsturmführer (SS captain) Heinz
Hollert. Hollert's deputy was a highly regarded Obersturmführer (SS
first lieutenant) named Klaus Barbie.

Barbie seemed ideally suited for the assignment. Born twenty-nine
years earlier in a small village on the banks of the Rhine, he had joined
the SS in 1935 at age twenty-two. Barbie's early assignments as an
SS intelligence officer in Germany and occupied Holland had marked
him as bright, capable, and loyal. His commanders had rated him
"especially hardworking and responsible," dedicated "completely and
intensively" to Nazi ideology, an officer whose "SS bearing on duty
and off was irreproachable." When he arrived in Lyon in November
1942 as second-in-command of the SS network there, he was given
the responsibility of going after the leaders of the Resistance.

It was a wise choice by the SS. Skillfully manipulating a network
of French informants, Barbie captured General Delestraint, the commander of the military arm of the Resistance, and a short time later
captured the leader of the Resistance, Jean Moulin. It is not clear even
today if Barbie knew that the man in his grip was Moulin, the grand
prize. But for Moulin, it made little difference. Barbie battered him
savagely and turned him over to SS headquarters in Paris. "Only his
eyes seemed to be alive," said a Frenchman who saw him there.[1]
Moulin died in Paris, without breaking. It was a devastating blow to
the Free French.

Moulin and the other Maquis leaders who were captured had been
brought to Lyon's Montluc prison for interrogation by Barbie and his
men. "He was a monster," one Resistance fighter recalled. "He struck
with no hesitation. He stopped when we fainted. Then he made us
come to by kicking us in the stomach, in the kidneys and abdomen.
If that was not enough they dropped you in a tub full of ice water.
After the tub, the blackjack, which puffs up the skin, and the acid
injected into the bladder. . . ."[2]

Another Frenchman had a slightly different experience at Barbie's
hands. "He did not touch me; he only looked on." But as he looked
on, his henchmen burned the feet of their victim with a hot iron.[3]

At St. Genis-Laval, an ancient French fortress, 110 prisoners suspected of Resistance activities were handcuffed and mowed down by
machine-gun fire on August 20, 1944. Their bodies were burned, and
the house in which they died was dynamited.

But combating the Resistance was not the only assignment of the

SS in Lyon. There were Jews there. Under the French collaboration-ist government at Vichy, they had been relatively safe. Under the SS, they were not. The Gestapo moved in.

Klaus Barbie was named chief of the Gestapo in Lyon. It was an assignment he took on with the same dedication and proficiency he had shown throughout his carer. By November 1944 some 14,000 Jews were arrested. More than half of those were deported to the death camp at Auschwitz; more than half the remainder were killed in Lyon.

In February 1943 Barbie took a platoon of Gestapo men to the Lyon headquarters of the Union General of Jews in France. He walked in and closed the doors behind him. He rounded up whoever was there, and whoever came through the doors that day, eighty-six in all. They were sent to Auschwitz.

On April 6, 1944, at four in the morning, the Gestapo raided the orphanage at Isieux, north of Lyon. Fifty-two children were dragged from their beds and loaded onto trucks. They were transferred to trains and sent to Auschwitz.

On August 11, when the Allies were fighting across France and Paris was only two weeks from liberation, a rail convoy left Lyon bound, like the others, for Auschwitz. Six hundred fifty people were crammed inside.

A week later, with rail service to Auschwitz no longer reliable, seventy Jews were simply shot.

For Barbie, moral issues were for others to worry about. "There are no war crimes," he said later. "There are only acts of war."[4]

By November of 1944 the Germans were forced out of Lyon by Allied armies. The carnage was over. In May 1945 the Germans sur-rendered. But Klaus Barbie was still at large.

La Paz, Bolivia, is the highest city in the world, and one of the least accessible. Nearly two and a half miles above sea level—and domi-nated by the magnificent Illimani mountain, which rises almost two miles above that—La Paz's brilliant blue sky and thin air sear the vis-itor's eyes and lungs. On its streets, sturdy, barrel-chested, copper-skinned women in bowler hats mix with the taller, fair-skinned de-scendants of Spaniards. La Paz is the capital of the poorest country in South America, isolated and provincial. Except for an occasional sidewalk café, it has nothing whatever in common with Lyon, half a world away.

By 1982 it was no secret that "Klaus Altmann," a sixty-eight-year-old German emigré and businessman fond of passing the mornings in one of those cafés, was actually Klaus Barbie. Ten years before, Beate Klarsfeld, a French woman investigating the escape of Nazis after the war, had exposed the soft-spoken "Don Klaus" of La Paz as the man who had once been the Lyon chief of the Gestapo, the Butcher of Lyon.

Altmann immediately denied that he was Barbie, but France filed a formal extradition request with the government of Bolivia, charging Barbie with war crimes. Barbie stayed out of sight, confident that Bolivian justice would never send him back to France.

His confidence was no accident. Bolivia's president was General Hugo Banzer, a right-wing dictator who ruled the country with the aid of a dreaded secret police that specialized in torture and repression. One of Banzer's closest advisers was the dapper, urbane Klaus Altmann.

France's extradition case slowly worked its way through the Bolivian courts, and in December 1974 the Supreme Court of Bolivia ruled that, as a Bolivian citizen, "Altmann" could not be extradited to France. As far as Bolivia was concerned, the case was closed.

As years passed, Altmann/Barbie became a symbol of the world's indifference to former Nazis. He lived openly, passing hours each day in a La Paz café, tending to business and meeting with a wide variety of friends and contacts. His children were grown; he lived with his wife. "A nice, quiet couple," said a neighbor.[5] He had, it seemed, little to fear. He stayed close to the power, and especially close to the various military juntas that had run Bolivia for years.

But political power changes hands sooner or later, especially in Bolivia, where seventy presidents and eleven constitutions have come and gone in the last century and a half. Banzer was deposed in 1977, setting off a series of coups, countercoups, and disputed elections until July 1980, when General Luis García Meza, the new head of Bolivia's armed forces, muscled in. García Meza's regime was widely believed, both inside and outside the country, to be up to its epaulets in the lucrative and burgeoning cocaine trade that begins with the harvest of the coca plant in the fertile mountain plains of Bolivia.

Barbie may not have been directly involved in the cocaine trade, but he was instrumental in training and supporting the paramilitary forces that allowed it to prosper. García Meza provided just the sort of "government" that allowed Barbie to thrive, but unfortunately for Barbie, García Meza's hold on political control was no more secure than that of the others who had succeeded Banzer. With the Bolivian economy in chaos, García Meza's regime finally proved to be too much even for the chronically set-upon Bolivians. In October 1982 García Meza and his military cronies beat a retreat to Argentina, leaving the country to a civilian government.

It was, for a while, a discouraging sign for Klaus Barbie. With his friends gone, Barbie lost his connections and became a conspicuous target for civilian president Hernan Siles, who desperately needed to restore Bolivia's credibility in the eyes of countries that could help its battered economy. And earlier in the year, the West German government had requested Barbie's extradition. While no action had yet been taken on it, there was no telling what the new government would do.

Still, Bolivia had no extradition treaty with West Germany, and the Supreme Court had rejected France's request on that very point a decade earlier. And whether Barbie knew it or not, the West German embassy in La Paz was treating the matter rather casually. It did not bring its request officially to the attention of the new government, explaining privately that, with all the turmoil, it would wait a while and take up the extradition request all in good time. Barbie's citizenship papers had somehow disappeared after the unsuccessful French extradition request in 1972, and the German embassy was aware that a favorable decision without those papers was unlikely. The German government had been under some public pressure back home to do something about Barbie, and it had done something: it had filed an extradition request. Whether that request was ever granted was not a matter of great concern to the German government.

Barbie, meanwhile, had apparently concluded that the prevailing winds in La Paz were favorable again. After disappearing from public view in the summer of 1982 with the departure of his sponsors, he resumed his accustomed place at the Club La Paz café, relaxed and smiling, as 1983 began. A one-way ticket to Bonn in the New Year did not seem very likely. Still, Barbie had a favorite spot in the café: he was in a corner, his back to the wall.

Yet if the courts were slow to act on the extradition request, the civilian government had other means of ending the embarrassment of this notorious Nazi strolling the boulevards of La Paz. On January

25, 1983, Barbie was arrested and jailed by the comptroller general of Bolivia on charges that he had defaulted on a contract with the state-owned mining corporation and owed the government the equivalent of ten thousand dollars. The interior minister telephoned the German embassy the morning after Barbie's arrest and announced that he was prepared to put Barbie on the following day's Lufthansa flight from La Paz to Frankfurt. It was to be an expulsion, pure and simple: Barbie would simply be thrown out of Bolivia and into the arms of the West Germans.

The Germans were astounded, and quickly protested that they could not accept Barbie under those circumstances. It was too short notice, they said. It would circumvent the extradition case. Besides, Barbie might escape when the flight touched down en route to Frankfurt. Filing an extradition case to placate critics at home was one thing; actually getting Barbie was quite another, and the Germans wanted no part of it. The German embassy told the interior minister that it would not cooperate in any attempt to expel Barbie to Germany.[6]

The German refusal put the Bolivians in a tight spot. Barbie's lawyers had quickly paid the debt for which he had ostensibly been arrested, but if Barbie was released from his prison cell he would surely get out of La Paz and take to the lush green fields of Bolivia, a legal no-man's-land controlled by his old friends, the paramilitaries. Barbie was one of the few bargaining chits that the Siles government could use in its bid to regain respectability for Bolivia; it could not easily afford to let him out of its custody, particularly in light of the worldwide publicity that the arrest had generated. Releasing him now would be worse than never having arrested him—Barbie would be gone, and the government could be accused of setting up a sham arrest to precipitate his disappearance.

The French ambassador, meanwhile, had gotten wind of the Interior Ministry's offer to the Germans and he hastily cabled Paris to prepare a new extradition request that he could lodge with the Bolivian courts. Yet, the Interior Ministry's offer to expel Barbie to the Germans could not easily be repeated to the French, for Barbie had never been a citizen of France. Much as the civilian government wanted to get rid of Barbie, it was now walking an exceedingly thin line: expulsion to Germany could be characterized as simply returning a former German citizen to his homeland, but expelling him to France risked the appearance of naked lawlessness, a position that might backfire on the Bolivians, anxious for respectability in the eyes of the world. By going through a new attempt at extradition, both France and Bolivia could preserve the legal norms, but there was scant hope that the courts would grant such a request, and it would take considerable time in any event. And, with the debt to the mining company paid off, Barbie's lawyers were besieging the courts with petitions for his release.

Finally, the Bolivians took the chance. They hustled Barbie onto a Bolivian military jet and flew him to French Guiana, just north of Brazil. There, at dawn on February 5, he was transferred under tight security to a French military jet headed to the country Barbie once knew as the Frankreich.

The gamble worked. The French, showing none of the hypocrisy that had characterized the German ploy, were relieved and gratified to have their hands on Barbie, and let it be known that the Bolivians' action would have a salutary effect on relations between the two countries. Within Bolivia, there was some grumbling from rightist opponents to Siles's government, but as a practical matter there was nothing they could do. Barbie was gone. And the overwhelming reaction from the rest of the world was that the Bolivians had acted honorably; it was now up to France to place the Butcher of Lyon before the courts for an accounting of his actions.

As for Barbie, headed to France in the military jet, the issues were no more complex now than they had been forty years before. "I did my duty," he said. "I have forgotten. If they have not forgotten, that is their business." [7]

The French had not forgotten. When Barbie landed in France, he was placed in a closed van and delivered to Montluc prison, the former Gestapo interrogation headquarters. He was charged with eight counts of crimes against humanity: the liquidation of the Union General of Jews in France; the deportation of 650 French men, women, and children on the last convoy to Auschwitz; the arrest and torture and execution of scores of Lyon's Jews; the deportation of fifty-two orphaned children from Isieux.

In March President Siles visited Paris and was warmly greeted by President François Mitterrand. Siles brought a wreath to lay at the grave of Jean Moulin; he also brought a request for agricultural and energy assistance. President Mitterrand toasted him as a symbol of "the courageous struggle of the Bolivian people" and promised "as much [aid] as [our] means will allow." [8]

But in the intense publicity that surrounded the expulsion of Barbie from a jail in La Paz to the old military prison in Lyon, new and startling accusations came from both sides of the Atlantic. In Paris, Serge Klarsfeld, a lawyer whose parents had been killed by the Nazis, and whose wife had been instrumental in tracking Barbie down to Bolivia a decade earlier, charged that Barbie had been employed by American intelligence after the war and that the Americans had assisted his escape to South America to prevent his trial by the French.

At about the same time, a former counterintelligence agent for the United States Army called NBC News to say that he had worked with Barbie in Germany after the war and had paid him to provide information on Soviet activities in Europe. NBC put him on the "Today Show" to repeat his allegations; ABC interviewed the Klarsfelds on "Nightline" that night, and *The New York Times* ran a front-page story the following day, February 8, that raised questions of how Barbie had escaped Allied authorities after the war, how he had got to South America, and whether American officials had blocked French attempts to put him on trial.

All of a sudden Barbie's alleged "American connection" was hot news. The State Department, the CIA, and the Pentagon were all refusing to comment. As the government's Nazi expert in residence, I started getting calls from all over the country: What did I know about Barbie's past?

I didn't know a damn thing, and I said so. OSI had been investigating Nazis in America for three years, but Nazis in Bolivia—or in France, for that matter—were out of our jurisdiction. I had, of course, been following the reports of Barbie's arrest and expulsion with great interest like everyone else, but the allegations that he had worked for American intelligence caught me by surprise.

I did not know, but I wanted to find out. Any allegations that Americans had conspired with former Nazis could not be ignored. I was proud of OSI's hard-earned reputation for thoroughness. I did not want to be learning about American involvement with Nazi war criminals from *The New York Times*, and I did not want the Justice Department to sit on the sidelines while someone else dug up the facts.

I also wanted some authorization from the front office to pursue the matter, since it did fall outside OSI's mandate. On February 9 I sent a memo to D. Lowell Jensen, the assistant attorney general in charge of the Criminal Division, requesting permission to conduct a preliminary inquiry into the allegations to see if there was any evidence to support them, and to determine what the Department of Justice should do if there was. "This matter cannot be ignored or expected to go away," I noted.

Jensen gave me the go-ahead on Friday, February 11, and I called the Pentagon to see the Director of Army Counter Intelligence about the case. When I arrived in his office I saw a single file, almost three inches thick, with a red cover sheet marked "Secret." He pushed it toward me. "That's the Barbie file," he said.

I leafed through the dossier. The pages were not all in order, and many of the copies were fuzzy, but there was no mistaking its significance. It was thick with postwar memos from one officer to another, discussing Klaus Barbie: his recruitment, his activities for the Army, the allegations by the French that he was a war criminal, discussions of what to do. At the top of the file, the most recent document was dated March 27, 1951. It was a page and a half, signed by two Army intelligence agents, describing how they had escorted Barbie to Genoa, Italy, with false papers under the name "Altmann" and had arranged his departure to Bolivia. Under "Remarks" the memo concluded, "Complete operation was without incident."

So the charges were true. Barbie had been an Army intelligence operative after the war, and the Army had sent him to South America. Did they know he had been the head of the Gestapo in Lyon? Did they know he was wanted by the French? Who authorized his escape? Did he work for the CIA too? What had he done for us in the years since 1951?

I spent the rest of the week, and the long weekend that followed, going through the Army's file, trying to make sense of it. Slowly I assembled a chronology of events on 3×5 cards, and a list of names and titles of Army officers who had been involved. I called the CIA and the State Department and told them I wanted to see everything they had on Barbie.

I also sent a memo to the Immigration and Naturalization Service, asking them to produce any records they might have of any entries by Barbie (or "Altmann") to the United States. It was a bit of a long shot, especially since INS records are often filed helter-skelter, but within a few days I received clear copies of entry cards filled out in the name of Klaus Altmann. The birthdates matched those on the phony passport he had received in Genoa in 1951. He had come to the United

States twice in 1969 and 1970. The list of questions was getting longer: Why did he come here? What did he do here? Who arranged it?

During these few weeks of the "preliminary inquiry" the television networks and the major newspapers were calling me almost daily with bits and pieces of information they had tracked down: Colonel X says he remembers Barbie; Captain Y says Agent Z handled him; Agent Z remembers nothing. Did I know where Mr. A could be found? Here's Mr. B's phone number; we're going on tonight with an interview of Colonel X; and on and on.

I was in a tough spot. I could not give out any information, because it was classified and because I did not want to reveal anything until the attorney general decided whether to conduct a full investigation. At the same time, I was eager to have all the information I could get. It was a one-way street, and that was the way it had to be.

Finally, two weeks after I had received the file from the Army, I sent a memo to Assistant Attorney General Jensen. I laid out what we knew—that Barbie had been recruited, used, and dispatched to Bolivia by the Army, and that he had come to the United States twice, for reasons we knew not—and I listed the options that were available. I concluded that, since the events took place so long ago and prosecution for any crimes would probably be barred by the statute of limitations, the Department of Justice would be technically correct to decline further action. But I recommended that we go forward anyway with a full investigation. The evidence of American complicity with Barbie was unmistakable, and if we did not put together the story, every network, newspaper, and self-styled Nazi hunter would do it for us. There was no telling what patchwork version of history would come out of that.

I felt strongly that the relationship between Klaus Barbie and the United States government was an important and sensitive episode that raised serious questions about our role in the postwar world and the accountability of our institutions. Was there some circumstance that could justify the Army or other agencies employing a former Gestapo leader? Had we knowingly recruited and used a wanted war criminal? How had it been decided to relocate him with a new identity in South America, and why? Had there been a cover-up of illegal acts?

In the end, my argument for a full-blown investigation came down to a simple point. Whatever the Barbie story might be, it had to be ascertained, completely and accurately, and disclosed to the public, honestly and without equivocation. I could think of no one better able to do that than the Department of Justice.

Assistant Attorney General Jensen quickly agreed with my recommendation, and two days later we called in representatives of the Army, the Defense Department, the State Department, and the CIA to tell them that we would be going ahead with a full-scale investigation as soon as the attorney general approved it, and that we expected their full cooperation from start to finish. There was no disagreement from any of them. They, like us, were being besieged from the press and Congress with demands that the entire matter be investigated, and they were not at all reluctant to toss the whole case into our lap to get it out of their own. As I sat at the conference table in Jensen's office, watching head after head nodding in assent to our proposal, I made a mental note: if we screw this one up, we can never claim we didn't know what we were getting into.

I was ready. A few weeks before Barbie's arrest I had told Jensen's deputy, Mark Richard, that I would be submitting my resignation from OSI soon. I had been on the job three years, and it was time to move on. As Jensen left the meeting to see the attorney general, however, I had a renewed sense of excitement and anticipation. Wherever it was going to lead, this would be one hell of an investigation.

That evening, back in my own office, the expected call from Jensen came. But he had unexpected news. Attorney General William French Smith had decided that there would be no investigation of Klaus Barbie.

I was stunned. The thought that Smith would not go along with the recommendation, particularly after it had been fully endorsed by the man Smith had chosen to run the Criminal Division, had never even occurred to me. But Smith did not think the case was important. If Congress or the press wanted an investigation, they could do it themselves.

Fortunately, someone prevailed upon Smith not to announce his decision, at least for the time being. And until something was officially released, I could truthfully tell the press and congressional staff, now calling daily for news of whether an investigation would take place, that the attorney general had not announced his decision. I did not tell them that in fact he had decided against it. Until he announced it, there was always hope that it could be reversed.

In fact, I was sure that if Smith did announce a refusal to look into the Barbie matter, the outcry from Congress would be so swift and critical that the White House would force him to recant. As days went by and pressure mounted, I became convinced that one way or another, the investigation would go forward. Smith would either have to announce it forthrightly, or else announce there would be no investigation and then, I was sure, reverse himself a day or two later under inevitable administration and congressional pressure. As the investigator-in-waiting, I glumly contemplated the difficulties I would face if the investigation got off to such a clumsy start.

As if to prove me right, *The New York Times* weighed in with a scornful editorial. "Is it really too much to ask the United States to admit or deny having shielded one of Germany's most notorious war criminals from postwar justice in France?" it began. "[T]he State Department refuses comment and the Central Intelligence Agency refers inquiries to the Pentagon. . . . [T]he Army suggests consulting the Justice Department, whose officials say they don't know a thing. . . . Is it shame that ties our Government's tongue? The days of stonewalling have turned to weeks. Does anyone in authority think that after so many years of dogged pursuit, this matter will be forgotten?"[9]

I doubted the editorial would solve anything. It was widely believed in the Justice Department that Smith read the *Times* editorials daily and then did precisely what they did not want. I was sure that would be especially true when the *Times* was baiting him.

But demands for an investigation continued to build from quarters that Smith could not so easily ignore. The White House staff, noting the lack of action, began to make inquiries. A draft letter to the president, urging a full investigation, started making the rounds on Capitol Hill, picking up new signatures each day. Chairman Peter Rodino of the House Judiciary Committee wrote directly to Smith. "I believe it is imperative that a thorough investigation of the Barbie matter be undertaken," he told the attorney general. "[T]he case of Klaus Barbie is potentially too important a part of the historical record to be left unattended."[10]

I could see the Department of Justice setting a course for disaster. I had done little else for two weeks other than take telephone calls from House staff, Senate staff, the State Department, the Pentagon, and the press, all with the same question: When is the attorney general going to announce the investigation? I stayed noncommittal through long days of increasing frustration.

But those on deck sometimes see things that those in the wheelhouse cannot, or do not want to, see. The attorney general showed no interest at all in learning what was happening. Finally, on March 10, I wrote a blunt memo to Jensen. "In the last 7 days," I said, "it is becoming increasingly clear to me that if the Attorney General announces a decision not to investigate the Barbie controversy, the reaction against the Department will be immediate, widespread, and adverse." I reviewed the building impatience. "We must realize the advantage of quick, decisive action in undertaking this matter. I therefore urge that an investigation be announced forthwith and that we begin it without delay. The price of not doing so will be unacceptably high."

Still nothing came from Smith's office. Finally, on March 14, nearly two weeks after the meeting in Jensen's office and Smith's initial turndown, I was preparing to leave the office after another day of silence from above when I got a call from a network correspondent who had been following the story since the beginning. He told me he would go on the air in an hour with an update on questions raised by the Barbie case, including the question of why the attorney general refused to take any action on it. The clear implication was that something was being covered up.

I called the attorney general's press secretary to alert him to the upcoming story. Scarcely half an hour later he called me back. Smith had decided to authorize the investigation.

I was jubilant, but the first thing I did was call back the correspondent. Sorry, I was told, he can't come to the phone; he's taping a story for broadcast. Get him, I said, he'll want to talk to me. He did. I told him of Smith's decision, and he re-taped the story five minutes before air time. An embarrassing jab at the attorney general—and, more importantly, the Department of Justice—was averted at the last possible moment, and all it cost was a decision that should have been made two weeks before. Thus are wise decisions reached in the executive branch of government.

We were at last under way, and I wanted to plan exactly how we would go about the investigation. Jensen and I had agreed that I would turn over OSI to my deputy, Neal Sher, so that I could devote full time to investigating Barbie. I chose four people from OSI to assist me: Richard Sullivan, a skilled cross-examiner whose instincts and judgment I respected; David Marwell, an experienced and careful historian who could find documents in archives when no one else could; and two investigators, Edward Bourguignon, who had just joined OSI's staff after ten years in military counterintelligence, and Bert Falbaum, who could always find a way, somehow, to get anything done. I backed them up with Diane Kelly, OSI's administrative assistant, who would be responsible for cataloguing the voluminous documents that would soon be coming in, and OSI's chief historian, George Garand, who had been working with military records since the end of World War II.

At our first planning session, I laid out the subject areas we would have to explore: What Barbie did during the war; how he came to be recruited by the Army; how he operated and what he produced for us; what the Army and the State Department had told the French government (and what they knew when they did); how Barbie's escape to Bolivia had been arranged; whether Barbie had worked for the CIA, the Army, or anyone else in his Bolivian years.

Marwell would help State Department archivists go through their dusty files to locate whatever they could, and analyze it. Bourguignon and Falbaum would compile a roster of the names that appeared in Army files, and then track them down to see if they were dead or alive. Sullivan and I would go through CIA records and begin interviewing the most important witnesses.

First, however, I flew to Paris to brief our ambassador, Evan Galbraith, on the investigation and to enlist his support in approaching the French Justice Ministry with my request that we be allowed to interview Barbie in his Lyon prison cell. I knew the chances would be no better than fifty-fifty. The French had enough problems in preparing the case against Barbie, which was then scheduled for trial in the fall of 1983, and there was little benefit to them in allowing an American investigator to talk to their defendant. But the attempt had to be made.

Back in Washington, I arranged with the Bolivian ambassador for Sullivan and I to go to La Paz the following week to find out what we could there. The ambassador was gracious and helpful and promised to do whatever he could to assist us. The real help, however, was to come from the American embassy in La Paz, whose political officer, Dan Strasser, put me in touch with Bolivians of every background.

Before departing on the all-night flight to Bolivia, I made sure those staying in Washington knew the standards that were to be followed. First, every clue and every lead that might illuminate the relationship between Klaus Barbie and the United States government over a period of nearly four decades would be pursued, wherever it might lead. Second, the investigation would be objective and scrupulously fair. No conclusions would be drawn until all the evidence was in. Third, meticulous records would be kept—of every interview, every request to another agency fo information or assistance, every inquiry we received or sent out. Fourth, I expected immediate and complete compliance from every government office for every request we made for information or access. Nothing would be off limits; nothing would be held back. Any foot-dragging was to be reported to me at once. Fifth, there would be no leaks to the press, on or off the record, of what we were finding. The press had its job to do; we had ours. And finally, the report submitted to the attorney general would be the complete story, top to bottom, as exhaustive as I could make it. No relevant facts would be omitted.

In setting those standards, I was acutely aware that my report, which was finally issued in August of 1983, would be intensely scrutinized by the press and by Congress, and that I would very likely be called to testify on it. I wanted the report complete to a fault, and our records in order.

When we had completed our investigation, my report had grown to almost two hundred pages. It began with events immediately after the war, when the United States and its allies divided the defeated Germany into zones of occupation, and when Klaus Barbie had been unknown to American forces except as the name of the leader of the Gestapo in Lyon. Here, adapted and condensed from my report to the attorney general, is what we found about Klaus Barbie and the United States government:

BARBIE'S RECRUITMENT AND
USE BY THE U.S. ARMY
1947–1949

Following its defeat in May 1945, Germany was divided into four zones occupied by the United States, Great Britain, the

Soviet Union, and France. Within each zone, the occupying power was responsible for all military and civil affairs. In the U.S. zone, which included southern and eastern Germany to the Czech and Austrian borders, the military authority was the multi-service European Command (EUCOM).

One of EUCOM's components was the 66th Counter Intelligence Corps (CIC) detachment, which had as its basic mission the protection of the U.S. zone against espionage, sabotage, and subversion. As a practical matter, in those pre-CIA days, the Counter Intelligence Corps was the U.S. eyes and ears in Germany, relying on its own military and civilian agents, and German informants, to gather information on political developments in that turbulent arena. The 66th CIC headquarters staff (stationed in Frankfurt until September 1949, when it moved to Stuttgart) supervised field operations primarily through a dozen regions, each with a regional headquarters and several field offices.

Beginning in late 1945 or early 1946, a group of former SS officers still at large formed a clandestine "resistance" organization in occupied Germany. The leaders of this organization planned to approach occupation authorities with a strange proposal: that they be given the responsibility of German administration in the British and American zones, thus ensuring a strong, experienced corps of postwar leaders loyal to Germany and opposed to Communism. CIC learned of this organization in May 1946 and infiltrated a CIC agent, posing as a Swiss Nazi, to report on the organization's activities.

As more information came to CIC, it became apparent that one of the leading figures in this organization was a man living in Marburg who called himself "Becker" but who was in fact Klaus Barbie. In January 1947 CIC Headquarters sent its Region III office, which covered the Marburg area, a copy of its "Central Personalities Index Card" identifying Barbie as the former head of the Gestapo in Lyon. Barbie was described as "[l]ong a member of the SD . . . [a] dangerous conspirator."

CIC assembled a profile of the organization, its several dozen members and three or four leaders, including Barbie, whose group was believed responsible for "the procurement of supplies for the organization and the establishment of an intelligence network throughout the British and American zones."

CIC, working closely with British intelligence, decided that the time had come to wipe out the SS organization, and on February 23, 1947, it staged Operation Selection Board, a search and arrest sweep throughout the American zone. Some 70 persons, including several thought to have been in Barbie's group, were arrested and detained for interrogation. But Barbie himself was not found. (He later claimed he had jumped out a bathroom window and escaped when CIC agents broke down the front door of the house in which he was staying.)

CIC remained hopeful, however, that Barbie would be found, and its agents in Region III kept the Marburg house under surveillance to arrest him should he ever return there. But Barbie did not go back to Marburg. By April 1947 he had made his way to Memmingen, a small city in CIC's Region IV, some 65 miles west of Munich. At least for the time being, he had eluded the Selection Board dragnet.

While Region III pressed the search for Barbie in Marburg, CIC agent Robert S. Taylor, stationed in Memmingen, located Barbie through a far different procedure. Since April 1946 one of agent Taylor's carded informants (paid sources) in Memmingen had been Kurt Merk, a former Abwehr (military intelligence) specialist who had served in France during the war. On April 10, 1947, Merk told Taylor he had "met, quite by accident, an old friend of his from France" by the name of Barbie, who had "excellent connections to sources of CIC information." Taylor recognized Barbie's name immediately as one of the chief targets of Operation Selection Board.

But Taylor did not notify Headquarters of his find. He checked with his superior, Lieutenant Colonel Dale Garvey, Commanding Officer of Region IV, and they decided that Barbie could be better used as an informant for CIC.

Barbie impressed Taylor at that time as "an honest man, both intellectually and personally, absolutely without nerves or fear. He is strongly anti-Communist and a Nazi idealist who believes that he and his beliefs were betrayed by the Nazis in power." Only in June, some two months after Barbie had been put to work, did Region IV report his use to CIC Headquarters in Frankfurt. Taylor requested that Barbie "be allowed to retain his freedom for as long as he works for this Agent. It is felt that his value as an informant infinitely outweighs any use he may have in prison." Region IV endorsed Taylor's re-

quest. "It is emphasized," said the Region's operations officer to CIC Headquarters, "that Subject's value as an informant
cannot be overlooked."

When no response came from Headquarters, Taylor placed
increasing reliance on both Merk and Barbie in the summer
of 1947. Merk had developed a net of 48 to 52 informants
throughout Germany and, indeed, much of Eastern Europe.
Barbie was Merk's chief assistant, taking on, as Region IV
later reported, "the important position of establishing a long
range penetration of French intelligence installations in the
French Zone," which by the fall of 1947 was "beginning to
show consistently excellent results."

On October 29, 1947, however, Major Earl Browning, the
S-3 (Operations Officer) at CIC Headquarters, directed Region IV to arrest Barbie and send him to the European Command Intelligence Center at Oberursel, near Frankfurt, for
"detailed interrogation." But Browning was not interested in
Barbie's wartime activities with the SS; he wanted to know
what Barbie knew about the present whereabouts of SS officers still at large. When the commanding officer of Region IV
protested that Barbie's arrest would disrupt the Region's "exceedingly successful" work in gathering information on French
intelligence activities, Browning wrote back a reassuring note.
Barbie's "subversive activity" was "not of the nature to demand his imprisonment" and he would be returned to Region
IV when the interrogation about other SS officers was completed.

Region IV obediently placed Barbie under a friendly arrest
on December 11, and he was sent to Oberursel for interrogation there.

In reviewing the events surrounding Barbie's arrest in 1947,
it is apparent that there was no concern over Barbie's Gestapo
background or any of his wartime activities. Barbie's background was distinctly subordinate to Region IV's interest in
using him to penetrate French intelligence—and, increasingly, Soviet intelligence in the U.S. zone—and Headquarters' interest in extracting from him information about other
SS officers involved in postwar "subversive activities."

In Oberursel, Barbie provided his interrogators with a rather
benign portrait of his activities during the war, acknowledging that he had been a member of the SD and its foreign in-

telligence branch, but making no mention of his Gestapo service. He gave them information on other SS officers, although whether that information was accurate is difficult to determine.

By the spring of 1948 his examination was over, and the officer who had interrogated him noted, "Barbie is ready to return to Memmingen to continue with his work." And it was clear why he was. "Although Barbie claims to be anti-Communist, it is felt that the main reason for his great efforts and endeavors to work for the Western Allies is based on a desire to obtain his personal freedom. . . . His present employment [with CIC] offers him personal freedom, the liberty to be with his family, a decent wage, an apartment, and security."

But there was another reason—the Army's own interest—for keeping Barbie on the payroll. The officer who had interrogated Barbie concluded, "Because of Barbie's activities with CIC Region IV during 1947, it is not deemed advisable to intern him. . . . His knowledge as to the mission of CIC, its agents, subagents, funds, etc. is too great." If he were jailed, Barbie might escape and turn to French or British intelligence with his extensive knowledge of CIC operations.

Thus, it was clear by the spring of 1948 that Barbie's eight months of service to Region IV from April to December 1947 had already placed him in an unusually advantageous position. Not only did Region IV want him back; any attempt to jail him at that point would have risked the prospect that, if he escaped, he would go to the French or the British—and carry all his CIC secrets with him. As one CIC agent recalled in 1950, "At that time the revelation of [Barbie's] connection to CIC as an informant would have been a serious blow to CIC's prestige in the eyes of the British. His continued employment then with CIC was based on his utility and the desire to CIC to obviate an embarrassing situation."

On May 10, 1948, its task complete, ECIC returned Barbie to CIC Headquarters for further assignment.

While Barbie was being questioned at ECIC from December 1947 to May 1948, Merk's net had been undergoing some turmoil. His superiors in Region IV were growing increasingly dissatisfied with his performance, and the net had been drastically pared from 50 informants to about 12. In fact, CIC Headquarters was dubious about whether it should be continued at all, and Major Browning directed Region IV to submit a detailed "plan for approval by this headquarters" on how Merk and Barbie would be used in the future, including the scope of their activity, their targets, the CIC agents to whom they would be responsible, and so forth. Browning noted that Headquarters approval would be required for "any future employment of [Barbie and Merk] and their net."

Region IV responded by moving the net in the summer of 1948 from Memmingen to Augsburg, operating from a municipal swimming pool where Americans and Germans could come and go without arousing suspicion. For the next nine months, Merk and Barbie and their handful of colleagues infiltrated Soviet attempts to gather information from the U.S. zone of occupied Germany, and penetrated French intelligence agencies—widely believed to be Communist-dominated—in both the U.S. and French zones. They not only tried to elicit information from German members and employees, but to turn Soviet or French agents to the American side. One of their techniques was to seek out as many former Gestapo and SS informants as possible, especially those who had infiltrated the German Communist party for the Nazis. Their American supervisors reported that Merk and Barbie had "slowly but satisfactorily" progressed in this endeavor, penetrating the Communist party and its agents and gathering "not . . . sensational, but very informative intelligence."

But Headquarters was concerned that the net was too large to be run securely, and after months of discussion, it ordered Region IV to disband the net in April 1949. Merk was to be dropped from CIC's rolls, but Headquarters ordered that Barbie remain employed "primarily for the purpose of recruiting informants."

This marked the end of Merk's active service to CIC, and it marked the end of a network of informants that at its peak had extended throughout Germany and much of Eastern Europe, at least as far as any American could figure it out. But it was not, nor was it intended to be, the end of Barbie's services as a full-time employee of the Army. He stayed in Augsburg with his family—his wife, a daughter born just after the war started, and a son born just after it ended—and concentrated on gathering information on Communist party activities for Region IV. He completed his second full year on the Army payroll.

Meanwhile, in 1948 the French had entered the picture. In Paris, the French government was preparing a treason prosecution against René Hardy, a French Resistance leader who was accused of betraying his organization to Barbie and the Gestapo. In May 1948, and again in July, with the cooperation of U.S. military authorities, agents of the Sûreté interrogated Barbie face to face in Frankfurt and Munich. The transcripts of these sessions make clear, however, that the French officials questioned Barbie only on the subject of his actions involving Hardy and the French Resistance; they did not question Barbie on his own involvement in war crimes.

Later, the French requested that Barbie be sent to Paris to testify in person against Hardy. But CIC was most reluctant to release Barbie to the French. They were concerned that Barbie would be interrogated "in the usual French manner" and forced to reveal information pertaining not only to Hardy but also to Barbie's own activities with CIC and his penetration of French intelligence.

So a deal was struck with the French. Barbie would not go to Paris; French officials would return to the U.S. zone and take Barbie's testimony there. Three times in early 1949, they questioned Barbie about René Hardy, and nothing else. A CIC officer noted that the French representatives procured "sufficient information to satisfy their needs." Later, two CIC officers were to recall that, during these repeated sessions, "no mention was ever made by [French officials] that Barbie was wanted as a war criminal," and indeed there was no indication "that [Barbie] was involved in war crimes" at all.

In retrospect, it is clear that by allowing French officials to have access to Barbie, CIC was taking a very great risk that its employment of Barbie would sooner or later become public, or at least widely known in the French government. But this risk did not appear to concern anyone; CIC's apprehension was only that Barbie's use might become known to the British, and embarrass CIC in British eyes, because Barbie had been recruited from the wanted list of the U.S.-British dragnet in 1947.

The most reasonable conclusion to be drawn is that the French had indeed given CIC no indication that Barbie himself was wanted, and thus there was no reason to hide him from French eyes. The conclusion that CIC had no indication at this point that Barbie was a suspected war criminal is sup-

ported by CIC's response to the events that were to follow—
when the consequences of CIC's risk became very public indeed.

On May 14, 1949—the date on which CIC officials were
later to maintain they had their first inkling that Barbie may
have been a war criminal—a news item appeared in a Paris
newspaper headlined "Arrest Barbie Our Torturer!" Date-
lined Dijon, in the Jura region of France, it reported:

> The Resistance personnel of Jura are scandalized. Klaus
> Barbie, who in 1944 was a commissioner with the German SD
> of Long-le-Saunier, is free. During the occupation he burned
> his victims with an acetylene torch to make them confess dur-
> ing interrogations which lasted more than 48 hours. He is re-
> sponsible for the tragic days of Easter 1944, when the region
> of Saint Claude was literally terrorized. His activity extended
> also to the area of Franche-Compte where deaths totalled more
> than 5,000.
>
> Klaus Barbie is a peaceable businessman in Munich, U.S.
> zone. . . .

The newspaper clipping made its way to CIC Headquarters,
which a few days later directed Region IV to interrogate Barbie "to determine the truth of the allegations." Headquarters
told Region IV: "Although it was known to this headquarters
that during the German occupation of France subject had per-
formed several successful missions and had been responsible
for the arrest of a number of French Resistance personnel . . .
[i]t was not, however, known that such barbaric methods had
been employed by subject to obtain confessions from his victims." And Headquarters directed that Barbie "be dropped
administratively as an informant but that relations with same
be maintained as in the past until necessary action is dictated
by the State Department and/or the Department of the Army."

In Augsburg, the new Region XII (formerly part of Region
IV) was not happy with HQ's position, and its reply—delivered two months after HQ's order—makes clear that the allegations of torture did not bring an immediate end to Barbie's
services. Captain Eugene Kolb, Region XII's operations officer, replied:

> . . . In compliance with the directions contained in [the HQ

order], this office has no course but to administratively drop subject as an informant.

. . . Subject is now considered to be the most reliable informant [Region XII] has. Subject has in the past two (2) months been used mainly to effect penetration and to "turn" certain targets. He has been quite successful in the accomplishment of most of these missions.

. . . [I]t is the belief of [Region XII's agents] that subject is intelligent and skillful enough to accomplish a successful interrogation by use of his head and consequently did not require the use of his hands. This office consequently feels that while the charges against subject may possibly be true they are probably not true.

As the foregoing correspondence indicates, CIC HQ directed that Barbie be dropped as an informant but that Region XII should keep itself informed of Barbie's whereabouts so that he could be arrested and turned over to the French for trial if so directed by higher United States authorities. And Region XII answered, although with palpable reluctance, that Barbie had been, or would be, dropped.

In fact there is no indication that anyone in CIC notified either the State Department or the Department of the Army of Barbie's situation. And it is quite clear that Barbie was not dropped as an informant, despite HQ's order and Region XII's promise. Region XII continued to use Barbie throughout 1949 and 1950.

After six months of silence following this exchange of messages, Region XII sent a request to HQ that it be "advised as to the proper method and scope of maintaining contact" with Barbie. Region XII added a rather telling postscript, however: "Subject is still under the impression that he is viewed by this office as a source, and is not aware of the fact that this office is only maintaining contact with him to keep track of him, in the event French authorities desire to try him as a war criminal."

This statement plainly suggested to Headquarters that, despite its orders to the contrary, Barbie was still being used, for if he was "under the impression" that he was still being used as a source, he must have been providing information, as a source would. And Headquarters would hardly have believed that Region XII was studiously ignoring the information that their best source had been providing for the previous eight months.

Two weeks later, HQ advised Region XII to maintain contact with Barbie as originally ordered and to continue to pay him so that he could be apprehended if the French requested his extradition. But there was another reason—and perhaps a more compelling one: "Since subject's sole income is derived from CIC, it is felt that to discontinue paying him would not only make him aware of his changed status but would also force him to seek employment elsewhere in the only trade which he knows, Intelligence. The latter possibility will be avoided, lest this organization be further embarrassed by subject." But HQ added, "It is . . . desired that subject not be made aware that his status with this organization has been altered."

In short, Headquarters was telling Region XII, to prevent Barbie from discovering that he is no longer being used, you may continue to use him.

In fact, Region XII did continue to use him. Thus, the correspondence between Headquarters and Region XII in the eight months after the charges of torture was little more than an exercise that, even on paper, could hardly mask what the agents in Augsburg and the headquarters staff in Stuttgart both recognized: despite the accusations of the Resistance fighters in France, Barbie was too valuable, and too sensitive, to let go. The price of letting him go would have been considerable embarrassment to CIC, the loss of an important assistant in Augsburg, and the possible disclosure to another government of CIC's operations and procedures. Headquarters apparently—and the field personnel in Augsburg certainly—considered that price too high to pay.

Headquarters' studied neglect was very likely reinforced by the fact that the outcry from the Jurassian Resistance had failed to bring forth any noticeable response from higher Army levels or from the civilian U.S. occupation authorities in Germany. As time went by, therefore, the allegations reported in the French press in May 1949 seemed to fade away. By April 1950 Barbie completed his third year as a full-time employee of the Counter Intelligence Corps.

Although there is no evidence that CIC was aware of it, the charges that Barbie was living as a free man in the U.S. zone did not fade away in 1949. They precipitated an escalating series of exchanges between French and American diplomatic officials over the whereabouts of Klaus Barbie. These exchanges involved, on the one hand, the French Ambassador to the United States and French diplomatic representatives in occupied Germany and, on the other hand, the U.S. State Department in Washington and the offices of the U.S. High Commission for Germany (HICOG), located in Frankfurt. U.S. military authorities, including CIC and EUCOM, its parent organization, were not drawn into the picture until a year after the exchanges began.

Apparently prodded by the efforts of the former Resistance fighters in the Jura protesting the fact that Barbie was "a peaceable businessman" living in the U.S. zone, French authorities in Germany wrote to HICOG's predecessor in June 1949 to ask if "an investigation could be initiated in order to find out if a certain Barbie, Klaus, who is wanted by the French Authorities for war crimes, is residing in Munich." This inquiry made no mention of any connection between Barbie and the Army or any other American authorities, and there is no evidence at all to suggest that the American diplomatic authorities to whom the inquiry was addressed would have reason to know of such a connection.

U.S. officials made routine inquiries of the German police, and passed on to the French the police reply that no "Klaus Barbie" was registered as living or working in Munich, but that, in response to the inquiry, his name had been placed on a "wanted" list should he turn up anywhere.

The French escalated the inquiry. On November 7, 1949, the French Embassy in Washington delivered a formal note to the State Department demanding Barbie's surrender, and notifying the State Department that Barbie had been interviewed by the Sûreté "in the official premises of American occupation authorities."

The State Department, which knew nothing about Barbie, checked with HICOG, which likewise knew nothing except that the French had made an inquiry earlier that year. HICOG told State to tell the French that, since HICOG was responsible for extradition matters in the U.S. zone, the French government could file any extradition request directly with HICOG.

The French did just that. Henri Lebegue, Counselor for Judicial Affairs in the French High Commissioner's Office in Baden-Baden, French Zone, sent a letter on March 2, 1950, to Robert Bowie, General Counsel of HICOG, detailing the war crimes charges against Barbie in France and referring to the earlier interrogation of Barbie by the Sûreté in connection with the Hardy trial. Lebegue assumed, without saying so, that HICOG authorities must have been aware of Barbie's presence in the U.S. zone of Germany.

In fact, however, no one in HICOG knew anything about Barbie. When the General Counsel's office asked the Public Safety Branch (which had handled the initial French inquiries a year earlier), its chief replied, "The inference of the several communications from the French authorities that Barbie is being granted refuge in the U.S. zone is unjustified and unwarranted."

This was, of course, a considerable overstatement. Although the Public Safety Branch was merely a liaison to local German police agencies and would not have (and in fact did not have) any knowledge of military intelligence activities, neither were any inquiries made of the Army to determine if they knew of Klaus Barbie.

Nonetheless, the HICOG General Counsel's office drew upon this letter and replied to Lebegue that HICOG's "efforts" to locate Barbie had been "unsuccessful" and that more information on "his alleged place of refuge in the United States Zone" would be necessary if HICOG was to make any headway on the French request for information.

As this letter made its way to Lebegue in late April 1950, however, events in Paris were about to alter the entire matter very sharply.

In Paris, the trial of René Hardy was under way, and on April 28, 1950, the prosecution read into evidence the deposition taken from Barbie by French authorities a year earlier. The Barbie depositions made public for the first time the fact that Barbie had not only been free in the U.S. zone when the depositions were taken but had been protected by U.S. authorities. Hardy's lawyer emphasized the point, claiming that it was "scandalous" for American authorities to protect Barbie "for security reasons." The presiding judge, although he allowed Barbie's evidence to be read, called Barbie "a sinister torturer and a war criminal."

The French press immediately went to the Public Information Division of EUCOM for confirmation of the charges that the Army was employing and protecting Barbie. On May 3, CIC Technical Specialist Joseph Vidal, who had supervised the disassembly of the Barbie-Merk net in 1948–49 and who knew its history better than anyone else, gave CIC's commanding officer, Colonel David Erskine, a lengthy memorandum on Barbie. The past concern for embarrassment to CIC now apparently swept aside by the publicity, Vidal told Colonel Erskine that "[b]y virtue of the fact that this headquarters has had time to liquidate the net operating in the French zone, CIC sees no reason for denying the French the extradition of Barbie" should such a request be made.*

Vidal's recommendation that CIC should give Barbie up was not to prevail, however. On the following day, May 4, 1950, a meeting was convened at CIC headquarters. Present were Colonel Erskine, the 66th CIC commanding officer; his deputy; his operations officer and assistant operations officer; and Vidal. A crucial step was taken. It was decided at this meeting, according to Vidal's contemporaneous note, "that Barbie should not be placed in [the] hands of [the] French . . ."

The charges by Hardy's lawyer that Barbie was being protected by U.S. authorities caused as immediate an impact at HICOG as they did at CIC. The U.S. Embassy in Paris, on April 28, the day the charges were made, sent an urgent cable to HICOG asking what it knew about Barbie. HICOG sent back a cable stating that the charges of U.S. protection were "unjustified and unwarranted," but a few days later, on May 3, it sent a follow-up cable: "[I]nformation received today indicates our statement regarding presence in the U.S. Zone may possibly be inaccurate or incomplete."

It was on May 3 that EUCOM had learned from CIC that Barbie had once been employed by CIC. But CIC had also told EUCOM—falsely—that Barbie's employment had ended a year earlier, in May 1949, the date of the published charges in the French newspaper. EUCOM presumably passed this information along to HICOG, notifying it for the first time that Barbie indeed had been employed by the Army. HICOG's ca-

---

*As noted earlier, CIC and EUCOM were unaware of Lebegue's March 2 letter to HICOG requesting Barbie's delivery.

ble to Paris, therefore, that its previous denial of charges of protection were "inaccurate or incomplete" presumably reflected this new information.

But an important question is presented here. Did the "new information" that EUCOM had passed to HICOG include the fact that Barbie was still—on May 3—in CIC's custody, or did it simply confirm that Barbie had once been in CIC custody but had since been let go?

The question of whether HICOG knew on May 3 that Barbie was still in U.S. Army hands is crucial because HICOG's subsequent communications with the French, without exception, were based on the premise that HICOG did not know where Barbie was. If in fact HICOG knew that CIC was still in touch with Barbie, those statements would be a misrepresentation of what HICOG knew.

The evidence compels the conclusion that HICOG did not know on May 3, and in fact never knew, that Barbie's relationship with CIC was a continuing one. This conclusion is based on the following facts. First, there is no indication in any of HICOG's internal memoranda of any awareness that Barbie was still in CIC's custody. In fact, several internal memos and letters indicate a contrary belief. HICOG and State Department personnel would have had no reason to carry on such a charade in dealing among themselves, and it is almost inconceivable that they could have done so perfectly.

Second, on June 16, CIC and EUCOM officials met with HICOG's Director of Intelligence (see below) and told him that Barbie had disappeared earlier in 1950; presumably they would not have done so had EUCOM already told HICOG on May 3 that Barbie was still in CIC's hands. Moreover, no one HICOG expressed any incredulity on June 16, as presumably they would have if contrary information had come their way on May 3.

Thus, on May 3, HICOG did not know of Barbie's continuing employment by CIC; it knew only that Barbie had once been in CIC's control.

Throughout May and June of 1950, the French pressed their request for Barbie's surrender. Lebegue of the French Mission in Germany continued to provide HICOG with information (as HICOG had requested he do), including photographs of Barbie and affidavits from his victims. And in Paris, the

U.S. Embassy, which knew no more of the Barbie story than HICOG, was facing a constant and embarrassing barrage from French Resistance leaders, politicians, newspapers, and residents of Lyon.

On June 2 a political officer from the Embassy wrote to E. Allan Lightner, the Deputy Political Adviser at HICOG: "We should very much like to have some word of advice from you as to how to handle this kind of protest, for it seems obvious that the matter is not dying down . . ." Lightner replied: "While Barbier [sic] is known to have been residing in the U.S. zone and in fact was interviewed there by French officials on several occasions in 1948 and early 1949, the fact that American authorities have been unable to locate him during the course of their recent investigations is hardly extraordinary in view of the wide publicity that has been given to the French extradition demands. This publicity undoubtedly was known to Barbier himself, since he has disappeared from the place where he had been residing."

Although Lightner did not know it, Barbie had not "disappeared from the place he had been residing" at all. But CIC, which knew exactly where he was, had not been asked about him. The "recent investigations" which Lightner mentioned were those being carried out by the Public Safety Branch of HICOG and the German police—both of which were totally in the dark where Klaus Barbie was concerned. They could not find him because the Army was hiding him.

HICOG, of course, had no vested interest in protecting Barbie and every incentive to turn him over to the French to defuse a growing diplomatic controversy and to take the Embassy in Paris out of the uncomfortable position it found itself in. Had HICOG known of CIC's continuing involvement with Barbie, it certainly would not have bothered with the German police; it would have gone straight to EUCOM and CIC.

Finally, John J. McCloy, the U.S. High Commissioner and the head of HICOG, did just that. He decided, in Lightner's words at the time, to "smoke out EUCOM on the matter to see how far they would go in helping to find this character" that they had once employed.

On June 16, therefore, Benjamin Shute, Director of the Office of Intelligence at HICOG, met at EUCOM HQ in Heidelberg with Brigadier General Robert Taylor, Director of

Intelligence at EUCOM, and Major Wilson, Operations Officer of CIC. Shute's memorandum of this meeting states that
General Taylor and Major Wilson told him that "[o]n May
24, 1949, [Barbie's] employment by CIC was discontinued,
following publication in France of charges that Barbie was a
war criminal. He has not been employed by them since that
time, although they did keep in contact with him until late
April 1950." Shute stated, "CIC has not been in touch with
him since late April 1950 and does not know his present
whereabouts."

These representations by CIC and EUCOM were false.
Barbie's employment was not discontinued in 1949, nor did
CIC lose touch with him in late April 1950. CIC was continuing to use Barbie in Augsburg. In fact, from April 1947, when
Barbie was first recruited by CIC, until March 1951, when he
departed for South America, CIC knew where Barbie was at
all times. CIC employed him and paid him throughout that
period.

Shute took the Taylor-Wilson statements at face value (and
there appears to be no reason that he should not have) and
reported back to HICOG: "[T]he policy question is presented
of whether U.S.-French relations would be more damaged by
delivery of Barbie, assuming we could find him, than by non-
delivery. We are in a position to make a statement to the French
about our termination of his employment and about our loss
of contact with him . . ."*

In fact, under Shute's prodding, the State Department cabled HICOG on July 1 that, whatever embarrassment the Army
might suffer from having one of its former informants (and
his secrets) turned over to the French, it would be better to
extradite Barbie and restore good relations with the French than
to refuse extradition, if and when he was ever found.

---

*Some recent critics, in light of my report, have insisted that Shute ought to have pursued the
matter further. These critics, of course, have the advantage of knowing what Shute did not—
that the Army was hiding Barbie—and so it is easy for them to point to this June 16 meeting
and proclaim that had Shute only pressed harder, the plot would have come undone.

None of the critics, however, offers any convincing evidence of why Shute should have
disbelieved the Army's statements. He was, after all, dealing with the head of Army counterintelligence in Europe, and I am aware of no evidence that ought to have suggested to Shute
that General Taylor and Major Wilson were not being truthful. Had Shute in fact probed more
deeply, he might have discovered the truth, and then again he might not have. But I cannot
fault Shute for relying on the word of General Taylor.

That was the go-ahead that HICOG needed to get the extradition paperwork moving. It sent arrest warrants to its attorneys throughout Germany and, as a formality, sent a routine "extradition clearance" form to EUCOM, requesting its non-objection to the extradition of Barbie. On September 9 EUCOM's intelligence division told CIC, "It is proposed that this Division notify HICOG that it has no objection to the extradition of Barbie. Further propose that HICOG be notified informally that Barbie is no longer under the control" of EUCOM or CIC. Five days later, CIC notified EUCOM that it could proceed.

There is no evidence whatever that, in September, Barbie was "no longer under the control" of the Army, and the only feasible explanation appears to be that those statements are false. This deception would be consistent with CIC's and EUCOM's false statements on June 16 to Shute; indeed, it brings those statements up to date. Having misrepresented Barbie's status once to HICOG, CIC and EUCOM appear to have found it expedient to do so again. The May 4 decision not to place Barbie in the hands of the French was being strictly adhered to.

At HICOG, therefore, the Barbie affair was dying a quiet death, because the decision to approve the extradition of Barbie and actually finding Barbie were two quite different things. On January 31, 1951, HICOG informed the French authorities in Germany that "continuous efforts to locate Barbie are being made." That was an exaggeration, since in fact neither HICOG nor the German police had any idea of where Barbie might be found, and as a result they were doing nothing more than keeping his name on the "wanted" list should he ever wander into their nets for some other reason. But it made little difference whether HICOG was exaggerating or not. By January 1951 the Army was preparing Barbie for his final voyage out of Europe.

Throughout the summer of 1950, while HICOG and the State Department were approving Barbie's extradition if he were ever found, Barbie remained at Augsburg in a CIC safe house with his family, interrogating CIC targets and turning foreign agents to work for CIC. But now there were risks in this situation. If he were to be picked up for any minor event, or if he were betrayed, he would come to the attention of HICOG and his extradition to France would soon follow. Barbie himself was, according to information forwarded to CIC HQ by Region XII, "living in constant fear of being apprehended by the French."

In December 1950 a way out of this tense situation arose when the 66th CIC detachment learned of a clandestine operation being used by its sister organization, the 430th CIC detachment in Austria.

Unbeknown to the 66th, the 430th had for several years been involved in a means of evacuation, or escape, for defectors or informants who had come to Austria from the Soviet zone or Soviet bloc countries. This mechanism was a sort of underground railroad, dubbed a "rat line," and it ran from Austria to Italy, where it relied on a Croatian priest, Father Krunoslav Dragonovic, who was attached to a seminary in Rome where Croatian youths studied for the priesthood.

Dragonovic used this base to operate an escape service for Croatian nationalists fleeing from Yugoslav authorities, obtaining passports from the Red Cross and visas from various South American countries.*

When the 430th CIC learned of this operation, they saw a convenient and ready-made pipeline out of Austria and Europe that, for a price, Dragonovic was willing to share with CIC. Under the modus operandi devised by Dragonovic and the 430th, defectors from the East were escorted by the CIC to Italy and turned over to Dragonovic.

The 430th was under no illusions as to Dragonovic; he was "known and recorded as a Fascist, war criminal, etc.," according to documents of the 430th CIC, "and his contacts with South American diplomats of a similar class are not generally approved by US State Department officials . . ." The 430th saw some advantage, however, in cloaking its "visitors" with displaced-persons status and in dealing with someone who had ties to the Catholic Church: "[W]e may be able to state, if forced, that the turning over of a DP [Displaced Person] to a Welfare Organization falls in line with our democratic way of thinking and that we are not engaged in illegal disposition of war criminals, defectees and the like."

---

*It is very likely that Dragonovic arranged the escape of Andrija Artukovic's patron Ante Pavelic, the head of the "Independent State of Croatia." See Chapter 5.

The 430th paid Dragonovic $1,000 to $1,400 per defector—a considerable sum of money in postwar Europe, and there was little doubt in the minds of Army agents who dealt with Dragonovic that much of that money was going into his own pocket.

In December 1950 the 66th CIC headquarters learned about the rat line operation. Lieutenant John Hobbins, who was in the Technical Specialist section, traveled to Salzburg and met on December 11 with officers of the 430th and its parent organization, the G-2 (Intelligence Branch) of United States Forces Austria (USFA). He filed a report that began as follows:

> a. The 430th CIC Detachment has been operating what they term a "Ratline" evacuation system to Central and South America without serious repercussions during the past three (3) years. At the cost of approximately $1,000 each adult (US legal tender) 430th CIC is transferring evacuees to Italy where they are provided with legal documentation obtained through devious means there. . . .
>
> b. Representatives of the 430th CIC state that, if necessary, they are prepared to undertake the following action upon request. If an informant will agree to emigrate to any available South or Central American country, [an agent from the 430th CIC] will visit this headquarters to be briefed on the individual case and interview the emigrant. Upon being provided with the necessary funds, the 430th will assume responsibility for transferring the individual to Italy and arranging his emigration. The estimated time requirement for completion of a case is six (6) to sixteen (16) weeks.

It must have been clear to anyone reading Hobbins' memo that the rat line was operating, if not outside the law, at least at the very edges of it. For example, if normal travel documents from Germany to Italy could not be obtained from the Combined Travel Board, which authorized military travel in Europe, an alternate method was available: an Allied forces "way bill." But the 430th considered this alternative a "very sensitive" method which "under no circumstances [was to] become known to HICOG or any agency controlling travel." Hobbins noted his impression that, with this method, further documents would have to be "surreptitiously obtained" in Vienna.

In addition, payment was to be made in U.S. currency—an
unusual procedure in occupied Europe and one that was con-
ducive to black market operations. The normal price was
$1,000, but "VIP treatment" was available for $1,400. Furthermore, money was not to be transferred through "normal
command channels" but directly from 66th personnel to 430th
personnel. Hobbins reported: "The problem of taking the
money across the Austrian border may be circumvented by
means of transferring it by courier as a secret document properly sealed and stamped."

But, however dubious the rat line may have appeared to be,
Hobbins' memo came at the right time for the 66th CIC. It
offered a fast, proven, and above all secret escape route for
the 66th's most important, and most sensitive, informant.

In January 1951 the decision was made to put Barbie in the
rat line.* The 66th CIC forwarded its recommendation to
EUCOM; by February 12 the name "Klaus Altmann" first
appears in a cable from 66th CIC headquarters, thus suggesting that, by that date, EUCOM had approved the request and
had notified 430th CIC authorities in Austria, who had in turn
notified Dragonovic and had received from Dragonovic the
pseudonym of "Altmann" to be used on travel documents.

The Combined Travel Board issued "Altmann" a "temporary travel document" No. 0121454 on February 21, 1951,
valid for travel as far as Italy. A second travel document was
issued for "Altmann's" wife and two children.

Arrangements for Barbie and his family to leave Augsburg
were now in place. Two CIC agents from Austria went to
Augsburg and, on March 9, accompanied "Altmann," his wife
and family by train to Salzburg. Two days later, Altmann and
his family continued the journey to Genoa, arriving the following day, March 12. They were housed in a Genoa hotel
and were taken over by Father Dragonovic. Dragonovic obtained for Altmann and his family two very important documents: an immigrant visa to Bolivia (see Appendix, page 348)
and a substitute passport from the International Committee of
the Red Cross (ICRC).

---

*The events surrounding the decision are not entirely clear because there are missing from Bar-
bie's dossier some thirteen documents covering the period of his escape. The events are recon-
structed here based on existing documents, the dossier's index, and to a certain extent the
recollection of witnesses.

A few days later, passage was booked for the family on an Italian ship. All was ready. On March 23 Klaus Barbie, his wife and family, under the name of Altmann, left Genoa bound for Buenos Aires.

The report filed by the CIC agents who accompanied the family noted that the "[c]omplete operation was without incident." (See photograph).

On April 3 66th CIC HQ commended everyone involved for the "extremely efficient manner" in which "the final disposal of an extremely sensitive individual" was handled. It concluded: "This case is considered closed by Intelligence Division, European Command, and this detachment."

Barbie and his family were apparently the only persons whom the 66th CIC detachment placed in Dragonovic's rat line out of Europe. On January 22, 1952, nearly a year afterward, the 66th CIC reported to EUCOM on its "resettlement activities" for refugees. It noted that there was "one instance wherein the 430th CIC's aid was solicited [which] involved a highly complicated disposal problem [in] which the 430th CIC Detachment accommodated this Detachment on a courtesy basis."

Aside from CIC, did the CIA* or any other U.S. intelligence agency have any involvement with Barbie prior to his departure for South America?

There is no evidence on which one could reasonably conclude that Barbie had a relationship with any other U.S. government agency during this time. The basis for this conclusion is as follows:

1. There is no evidence in Barbie's CIC dossier that he worked at any time for any agency other than CIC. This investigation has established that, had the situation been otherwise, the CIC dossier would have reflected it.

2. There is no evidence in CIA files that the CIA had any relationship with Barbie prior to 1951 (or, as explained in the following section, thereafter).

3. It was the overwhelming consensus of former CIC agents interviewed in this investigation that CIC did not conduct joint operations with CIA or, except in very rare circumstances,

---

*The CIA was established in 1948.

maintain joint control over informants. Interviews of CIC personnel familiar with Barbie's use during the years 1947–1951 establish that there was no involvement with any other agency in his case.

Klaus Barbie and his family took up residence in Bolivia in 1951, and he lived there, with perhaps some interruptions, until he was expelled to France in 1983.*

One of the primary objectives of the investigation was to determine whether Barbie had any relationship with the CIA or any other U.S. intelligence agency from the time of his arrival in Bolivia in 1951 until the present time.

The conclusion that follows is necessarily based on the representation of CIA personnel that all material in the custody of CIA relating to Barbie and other subjects requested in the course of the investigation was produced for our inspection. I believe that to be the case, based on my examination of the materials and my discussions with CIA staff.

It is my conclusion that at no time from the end of World War II to the present has the Central Intelligence Agency had any relationship with Klaus Barbie. I base this conclusion on the following facts.

1. Nothing in the CIA's files demonstrates, or can be taken as evidence of, a relationship between the CIA and Barbie. There is no indication that Barbie ever reported to the CIA, was employed or paid by that agency, or was notified, directly or indirectly, of matters that the CIA wished to gather information on. Interviews of CIA officials were consistent with this fact.

2. A 1965 internal memorandum based on a review of the files conducted by CIA personnel states that Barbie was used by the Army until 1951 and that there is "no current operational interest in subject."

3. A cable in March 1967 states that there are no "traces" on Altmann.

4. A cable in 1972 states "There has been no rpt [repeat] no [CIA] contact or connection of any kind with subject."

---

* Barbie's son Klaus-Georg was killed in a hang gliding accident in 1980, at age 33. Barbie's wife died in 1982. His daughter lives in Europe.

Records of the Immigration and Naturalization Service establish that Altmann came to the United States twice—once in July 1969 for eight days and once in January 1970 for twelve days.

On both occasions when Barbie entered, he had an A-2 visa granted by the United States Embassy in La Paz. A-2 visas were routinely granted by the Embassy to holders of Bolivian diplomatic passports, which Barbie had as manager of Transmaritima Boliviana (TMB), the state-owned Bolivian shipping company. At the time, the name Klaus Altmann was not entered in the State Department visa lookout books, and so there was no reason for the Embassy not to issue the visa. The Embassy had no reason to associate Klaus Altmann with the name Klaus Barbie; in any event, the name of Barbie was not entered on the visa lookout either.

In 1969 Altmann and several TMB officers came to the United States and met with the shipping agent for TMB, an American firm in New Orleans. The head of this firm recalls that he discussed shipping business with the TMB delegation, and in particular the prospects of obtaining cargoes for TMB to ship to Bolivia. The agent did in fact arrange two cargoes of flour for TMB.

There is no evidence that Barbie/Altmann or TMB was engaged in anything illegal or improper during this visit, and the agent's activities appear to have been entirely legitimate efforts made in the normal course of business on behalf of his client.

It would be impossible to state that at no time during either of his visits to the United States did Barbie engage in any illegal or improper activities. However, there is no evidence of impropriety; in any event, it is reasonably certain that his visits were not connected to any agency or activity of the U.S. government.

By mid-July 1983, some four months after the investigation had officially begun, I had assembled the foregoing picture of Klaus Barbie and the United States government. Sullivan, Marwell, Bourguignon, Falbaum, and I had talked to nearly fifty witnesses and scores of other people as we sought information and assembled it into a cohesive picture. We had reviewed tens of thousands of pages of documents from the Army, the State Department, the Central Intelligence Agency, the Berlin Document Center, and the French Ministries of Justice and Foreign Affairs. Many documents had been on microfilm, but many more had been originals, growing brittle with the passage of forty years.

But, as in any investigation, the information had not marched neatly into place. There were false leads and discordant memories, dead ends that had to be battered down so we could push on. We never knew which trails would lead us through the thicket and which would get us nowhere. The Bolivian phase of the investigation, for example, had some of each.

The Bolivians were friendly and cooperative, and as I made the rounds of the various ministries with Dan Strasser from the American embassy, who seemed to know everyone in the government, I became convinced that they were genuinely interested in helping me. After all, they had thrown Barbie out of Bolivia in the first place. But they could provide little specific information. They were not close to the factions that Barbie had been close to, and records were virtually nonexistent. In the last few years, with Bolivian governments sweeping in and out like the tides, records relating to Klaus Barbie had been washed away, probably stolen. When I asked one undersecretary if his office could provide records on Barbie, he frowned. "Mr. Ryan, you must understand," he said, thoughtfully pursing his lips, "the records of the Bolivian government are not, let us say, meticulously organized."

Indeed they were not. I had a hint of that just before leaving Washington for La Paz, when Strasser had called from La Paz to say that a Bolivian citizen had offered to sell the embassy the travel documents that Barbie/Altmann had used to make his way from Europe to Bolivia—the travel permits, the Red Cross passport, the visas. How much? I wanted to know. We don't know, said Strasser. Maybe a few thousand dollars, maybe less.

I met with Assistant Attorney General Lowell Jensen and requested authority to buy the documents with Justice Department funds. He was reluctant, and as we talked it over, I couldn't disagree with him. We both had visions of me meeting a shadowy figure in a dark alley and handing over greenbacks for official Bolivian files. It could easily have been a setup for an arrest, or an ambush.

In La Paz, however, I met with the salesman—fortunately, he

agreed to come to the well-lighted offices of the American embassy. He was a slightly built Bolivian man, no older than twenty-five, perhaps a student. He did not tell me his name, and I dubbed him Luis. He showed me the documents, and I quickly saw that they were originals, extremely important to the case, and obtainable nowhere else. (These are the documents relating to Barbie in the Appendix of this book, pages 348–52.) He said he had paid $3,000 for them in 1973, and now only wished to get his $3,000 out of it. It was a palpably false story—three thousand American dollars is a fortune in La Paz— but since I had nothing to spend, it hardly mattered. I asked if we could make photographs of the documents in the embassy, for free.

Luis said he would "think about it," but we both knew he was not going to do it. If I made photos, he no longer had a market for his most valuable possession. But before he left, I told him to call me at my hotel that night, whatever his decision.

After he left, I called a journalist who, I knew, would be very interested in the documents. I did not want to act as a broker, but I told him he might get a call from a fellow with something to sell, and that if he did he should definitely take a look at the product. That night, when Luis called, I gave him the journalist's phone number.

The next day the journalist showed me his newly acquired papers, and let me borrow them long enough to put them under a high-resolution camera at the embassy. As I returned them, I asked how much he had paid.

"I offered two hundred dollars," he told me, "and Luis said he wanted three thousand. We compromised. I gave him three hundred." Luis drove a hard bargain, I noted dryly.

Some of the information I uncovered in Bolivia was tantalizing, even if not directly germane to the United States. Acting on a tip, I set up a meeting with a man who had known Barbie. Although it was a brilliantly sunny day, the small room in his threadbare hotel was dark. The shade in the lone window kept out the light, but not the sounds of La Paz's busiest street a few stories below.

This man, well-dressed and sophisticated, told a story that I was later able to confirm, at least in its most important parts. Some years earlier, Altmann had approached him with a most unusual list of names—a compendium of Soviet agents operating in the "Southern Cone" of South America. Where had Barbie obtained the names? I asked.

The man looked at me in surprise. "From ODESSA, of course."

ODESSA? I said. Tell me, what exactly do you mean by that?

He must have thought I was the most naive investigator in the Americas. "ODESSA," he said. "The network of former SS agents who work for the security police forces in South America."

And had ODESSA penetrated the KGB? I asked.

He shrugged. "Who knows? But he had the list."

And was the list accurate?

He looked at me directly. "Si, señor. The list was right."

That story, strange as it was, was topped by another one that I could not confirm. I met with a Bolivian who appeared to be honest and straightforward. He told me that in the sixties, before Transmaritima had been formed, Barbie and other members of ODESSA in other countries had formed a shipping company, registered in Europe, that dealt in arms—buying in Europe, selling throughout the world. According to this officer, the company had purchased a large quantity of artillery from a European maker shortly after the French had announced an embargo on arms sales to Israel in the wake of the 1967 war. The artillery was ostensibly headed to Bolivia, but on the high seas the cargo freighter pulled alongside another freighter—from Israel. The artillery was transferred to the Israeli freighter, and ODESSA made a nice profit on the deal.

A network of former Nazi officers selling weapons to Israel? It sounded too fantastic to be true, but the officer assured me that he had read an internal Bolivian report that documented the entire transaction. The report was kept in a highly secure vault in the Defense Ministry, and he was not at all sure he could get to it. If he could, he said, he would see if a copy could be made.

I never heard from him again, and, despite his apparent credibility, I have no knowledge that such a report actually exists, or that such a transaction ever took place. But as I left our meeting place on a quiet street of attractive homes in a La Paz neighborhood, I began to wonder if the thin air was affecting my brain. If the Butcher of Lyon was selling arms to Israelis, who was on the side of whom?

Despite my improbable meetings with Bolivians drawing lines connecting ODESSA, the KGB, and the Israelis, my week in La Paz produced little tangible evidence beyond the travel documents that Luis had sold to the journalist. I interviewed several former employees of

Transmaritima and satisfied myself that, at least as far as they knew, Barbie's visits to the United States had been strictly business. And I spoke to several Americans familiar with espionage activities who told a convincing story that they had never sought out Barbie, nor he them. That much, at least, I was able to confirm elsewhere.

The signals coming from France during this time were decidedly mixed. I wanted to review the internal French correspondence on Barbie to see if that could shed any light on what the American files had revealed. Although I thought it unlikely, it was always possible that a French diplomatic cable or a confidential memo might have said, "HICOG tells us that the Army has Barbie, but they cannot officially acknowledge it to us." That would have thrown the whole investigation off into a new direction, recasting HICOG and the State Department from victims of Army deception to participants in it. More importantly, it would have established that HICOG's representations to the French were false. (There proved to be no such cable, or anything like it.)

I also wanted to interrogate Klaus Barbie in Lyon. The embassy in Paris had cabled me that the French were not likely to grant an interview of Barbie, and would rely on the "judicial assistance" treaty between France and the United States. That treaty provided for such official interviews, but only if there was a pending court proceeding in the requesting country. The United States had nothing in court, of course, and we very likely never would. I read the embassy's rather complex analysis of the judicial assistance agreement with concern; if the French insisted on adhering to it, I would not be talking to Barbie.

I wired the embassy with an unorthodox proposal. Forget the treaty, I told them. This is not a question of "judicial assistance" after all, precisely *because* we have no "judicial" proceeding. It is simply a matter of a United States official named Ryan who wishes to talk to a person in France named Barbie. So Barbie happens to be in a French prison. Well, what of it; if the French are willing to allow an interview, they can do it on this basis.

It was rather a slick idea, I realized, but it had an appealing logic to it. If the French were willing to go along with an interview— and that was a very big "if"—they could agree with me that the treaty simply did not apply, and that we could do whatever we might agree to.

The embassy took a dim view of this approach, but I pressed them to present it to the French Ministry of Justice, and they finally agreed to do it.

Meanwhile, David Marwell and I flew to Paris and spent several days trudging through the Foreign Ministry's thick but rather haphazardly organized file of diplomatic correspondence with HICOG. Like many aspects of the investigation, it was worthwhile not because we found any smoking guns, but because we did not find any. The French were indeed mystified by HICOG's lack of knowledge, but nothing in the file suggested that HICOG was not acting in good faith. Ironically, we discovered that the French Foreign Ministry was not aware until fairly late in the negotiations that the French police had interviewed Barbie in the American zone. This unawareness by the right hand of what the left was doing was a Gallic reflection of the same unawareness by HICOG of what the Army was doing.

While I was in Paris, the embassy arranged a meeting for me in the French Ministry of Justice, so I could meet face to face with Barbie's custodians and explain my proposal directly. But after half an hour in the office of the deputy chief of staff—an ornate chamber that would have fit nicely into the palace at Versailles—it was becoming clear that all my logic and whatever charm I could muster was having little effect. My host was a man of graciousness and courtesy who listened carefully and who understood, I believe, exactly what I was proposing. But he kept returning, ever so politely, to the matter of the treaty, and what could the French government do if the Americans had no proceeding in court, so that the treaty could be invoked? "Yes but," I kept saying, and "yes but" he kept saying, and I came to understand that I was not going to get any closer to Barbie than that room. Some words are avoided in the diplomatic lexicon, and an outright "no" is often one of them. The Barbie case was a very sensitive one in France, and I believe the French government, knowing that my report would become public, had no desire to give Klaus Barbie access, even indirectly, to the outside world.

I was disappointed that I would not be talking to Barbie, of course. But as I flew back to Washington, I had to recognize the real reason for my disappointment. It was not so much the investigation, which would proceed with or without an interview. I wanted to confront Barbie personally. I wanted to deal face to face with this man of many faces—the personification of the SS officer, the match of the French

Resistance, the Butcher of Lyon, the resourceful intelligence operative, the brains of the Bolivian secret police, the genial "Don Klaus"
of the sidewalk café, the broken prisoner of French justice. I wanted
to interrogate the interrogator, to look him in the eye, to get some
clue of this complex and evil and shrewd and manipulative man who
could serve Nazis and Americans and Bolivians in war or peace.

Damn, I thought, at 35,000 feet. I wish I were in Lyon right now.

Yet most of my time was spent not in Paris or La Paz, but in
Washington going through files, or on airplanes going to interview
witnesses. At times I felt as if I were in a presidential campaign—
breakfast in Chicago, lunch in Colorado Springs, dinner in Savan-
nah—and at other times I felt as if I were organizing a reunion of the
66th Counter Intelligence Corps. Between us, we interviewed former
Army, State, and CIA officials in twenty-five states.

All of the witnesses were cooperative; only once did I have to
suggest, to a retired spy, that a subpoena might refresh his memory.
(Actually, just the mention of a subpoena refreshed his memory.) But
the information they provided was, with a few exceptions, not terribly helpful in putting the story together. All memories fade after thirty
years or more, of course; more importantly, the documents that we
had analyzed before setting out to talk to the witnesses provided a
wealth of detail that no memory, however sharp, could match. And
no witness had the big picture. Each had played a role, usually a fairly
narrow role, in the recruitment, deployment, and escape of Klaus
Barbie.

Still, the interviews were helpful in giving us an idea of the conditions the Army and the State Department were working under in the
postwar years, and what they did to function under those conditions.
Some retired soldiers were sensitive to the moral issues posed by the
employment of a former SS officer; others were oblivious to it, or
pretended to be. Almost without exception, the former Army officers
emphasized the enormously high priority imposed at the time on
gathering information on Communist activities in occupied Germany.

"You can't imagine," said a former CIC captain, "how desperate we were for information. No one knew what the Russians were
planning, and no one was there to find out except the Counter Intelligence Corps of the United States Army." When the Central Intelligence Agency was created in 1948, a somewhat suspicious rivalry
quickly arose between the two organizations. "We tolerated them,"

one Army officer after another told us, "but we hardly ever worked with them. And they had a lot more money than we did." (Former CIA agents told us the same thing, except that they said the Army had all the money.)

As I talked to these men, usually in the privacy of their homes, a pattern began to emerge. They were bona fide spies, or had been, but they did not fit any popular image of secret agents. Most of them could as easily have been supply officers or personnel administrators. They had been patriotic without thinking much about it, diligent in carrying out their duties, often overwhelmed by the magnitude of their mission, and too involved in the gathering of information to plan much in the way of dirty tricks. In a tough situation, they had been doing the best they could. They clung to Barbie, whatever misgivings they may have had about him personally, because he made their jobs easier: he produced large amounts of reliable information from his informants, and reliable information was the CIC's whole reason for being.

By mid-July, as I realized that the investigation was just about completed, I had a growing feeling that I could not simply submit a strictly factual, chronological account. The events had to be put in perspective; some mortar was needed to hold the bricks together. And it was becoming increasingly clear that my report would be addressed to the attorney general only as a formality; the real audience would be the public. I knew the public would draw its own conclusions, but I felt now a growing need to tell mine as well.

Two things in particular needed to be addressed. The decision to recruit and use Barbie in 1947 had seemed to me at the outset of the investigation to have been a cynical and terribly insensitive action, made with what must have been a coarse disregard for everything we had fought the war for. Now, after having plunged back into those turbulent postwar years, I saw that it was not that simple.

I also felt strongly that the Army's action in lying to HICOG and later arranging Barbie's escape from Bolivia had to be seen for what it was under the law: an obstruction of justice. I pulled out my copy of the federal criminal code. Title 18, Section 1505: "Whoever corruptly . . . obstructs or impedes . . . the due and proper administration of the law under which a proceeding is being had before [a] department or agency of the United States" commits an obstruction of justice. HICOG had a responsibility under American law to decide whether to grant the French request for extradition and to deliver Bar-

bie once the decision had been made in France's favor. The Army
had obstructed HICOG in carrying out that responsibility.

With the facts assembled in their final form, ready to go to the
attorney general, I stayed home for a few days and organized my
thoughts, my impressions, my discussions with those who had known
Barbie and decided his future. I wanted to convey both the ambigui-
ties and the constants—that things may not have been as simple as
they seemed, and that actions taken in 1947 had to be considered in
light of 1947 realities, but that certain standards of law and integrity
must be honored, whatever the pressures that those realities imposed.
I had to be judgmental without being self-righteous, to be fair to those
who had made difficult decisions but objective enough to demonstrate
where, and why, those decisions went wrong.

These were my conclusions as I presented them in my report to
the attorney general:

> . . . I cannot conclude that those who made the decision to em-
> ploy and rely on Klaus Barbie ought now to be vilified for the
> decision. Any one of us, had we been there, might have made
> the opposite decision. But one must recognize that those who did
> in fact have to make a decision made a defensible one, even if
> it was not the only defensible one. The decision to enlist Bar-
> bie's assistance was neither cynical nor corrupt.
>
> My conclusion that the decision to employ Klaus Barbie—and
> in fact it was a continuing series of decisions throughout 1947,
> 1948, and 1949—was a defensible one depends upon the fact that
> the persons who made those decisions cannot be charged with
> knowledge that Barbie committed, or likely committed, or was
> wanted for, war crimes or crimes against humanity. Whether he
> did in fact commit such crimes is an issue now to be decided in
> a French court. But the decision to use a former Nazi, even a
> former Gestapo officer, is one thing; the decision to use a person
> wanted for war crimes is another. The argument advanced above
> that the United States could legitimately justify the use of a for-
> mer Gestapo officer cannot be extended to include the use of a
> person guilty of war crimes: first, there are limits to what may
> be done in the name of intelligence gathering, however neces-
> sary that task may be; second, use of a known or suspected war
> criminal would amount to a protection of that person from the
> judicial process.
>
> But I am persuaded as a result of this investigation that CIC

personnel had no reliable indication until at least May 1949, some two years after Barbie was first employed, that he was suspected of war crimes or crimes against humanity. . . .

For these reasons, therefore, I conclude that CIC's actions through May of 1949 in recruiting and using Barbie, though subject to valid criticism by those who find use of a Gestapo official under any circumstances reprehensible, did not amount to the knowing use of a war criminal. The decision to use Barbie was a defensible one, made in good faith by those who believed that they were advancing legitimate and important national security interests. . . .

On the other hand, the evidence yielded in this investigation and discussed in the body of the report justifies the conclusion that, by its decision on May 4, 1950, not to cooperate with efforts to obtain Barbie's surrender, and by its false statements to HICOG on June 16, 1950, that Barbie's whereabouts were unknown, responsible officials of the Army interfered with the lawful and proper administration of justice. They knowingly obstructed the bona fide efforts of the office of the United States High Commission for Germany to carry out its lawful obligation to effect the extradition of war criminals. . . .

As to Dragonovic's rat line, the evidence establishes that the 430th CIC in Austria had been using it for several years as a means of providing defectors and informants with a safe and secret passage out of Europe. This investigation yielded no evidence that the 430th CIC had used the rat line as a means of escape for suspected Nazi war criminals.

The use of the rat line for informants and defectors raises troubling questions of ethical and legal conduct. The United States Army certainly had an obligation to protect from harm those informants who had assisted the Army at substantial risk, as well as defectors whose discovery in the American zone would have jeopardized their lives and safety. Furthermore, there was nothing inherently wrong in evacuating such persons from Europe to places of sanctuary in South America. But to carry out this obligation by relying on the intercession of a foreign national whose own background and interests were suspect, by concealing information from United States agencies, and by possibly violating lawful regulations on travel, currency, and documentation, the Army did not act responsibly.

The proper course, when faced with the necessity of bringing such people to safety, would have been to arrange, with due authority, an approved and lawful mechanism for their safe passage. This mechanism could have been arranged to operate covertly; there is no inherent contradiction between lawful action and covert action. But there is an important distinction between lawfully establishing a covert escape route and covertly taking advantage of a secretive and unauthorized scheme.

In addition, the rat line procedure took unnecessary and ill-advised security risks by placing sensitive informants and defectors in the unsupervised control of a foreign agent. One cannot exclude the possibility that United States intelligence methods or information were compromised when defectors and informants were turned over to Dragonovic. It is abundantly clear that Dragonovic was not loyal to the United States; he simply accommodated United States requests to the extent they were consistent with, or could advance, his own objectives in assisting his compatriots.

But, questionable as these actions may have been from a legal or security standpoint, they do not appear to have risen to the level of an obstruction of justice other than in the Barbie case. This investigation examined all materials known to exist on the operation of the rat line and interviewed all persons now alive known to have been involved with it. No other case was found where a suspected Nazi war criminal was placed in the rat line, or where the rat line was used to evacuate a person wanted by either the United States government or any of its postwar allies.

The decision to invoke the rat line to arrange Barbie's escape from Europe, under the circumstances, amounted to a further and final step in the 66th CIC's obstruction of HICOG's attempts to carry out its lawful obligation to decide the extradition of Klaus Barbie. By arranging his escape to South America, the responsible officials of the 66th CIC insured that Barbie would not be brought to justice in France.

RECOMMENDATIONS

Although it is my belief, based on the available evidence, that officers of the CIC engaged in an obstruction of justice by concealing Barbie from HICOG, the question of criminal prosecution is moot because the statute of limitations requires that any indictment be brought within five years after commission of the offense.

It should be clear enough that the Barbie episode cannot be condoned and should not be repeated. But I find no solutions in legislative or regulatory proposals.

The most regrettable act was the concealment of Barbie from

HICOG. But obstruction of justice was then and is now pro-
scribed by criminal statute.

The use of Barbie is a difficult question. But there can be, in
my opinion, no meaningful or enforceable regulation to define
whom intelligence agencies may and may not use as informants.
The very nature of intelligence gathering abroad requires the use
of informants, and it would be grossly unrealistic to require that
they be subject to the same standards of character, uprightness,
and conduct that are required for, say, civil or military service
with the United States government.

This is not to suggest that any person, regardless of background or status, may properly be used or that the sole consideration is the value of his information. Clearly, no informant
should be used or protected under circumstances that would con-
stitute an obstruction of justice, as happened here, or where some
other statute would be violated.

But given the almost infinite variety of circumstances that an
intelligence agency encounters in the course of its operations, it
would be exceedingly difficult to define a class of eligible informants based on their background or status. And any such line-
drawing would require the comparison of the two fundamentally
dissimilar considerations discussed at the beginning of this section: the need for information of strategic importance versus the
repugnance of dealing with criminals, or former enemies, or brutal thugs, or officials of evil institutions. Even if there were a
consensus on whom we ought not to deal with, any workable
definition would be so broad as to be useless to those who must
apply it, or so narrow that it would be of little practical significance.

In the past thirty years, and particularly in the last decade, this
nation has recognized that, however necessary and valuable intelligence services may be, they cannot be allowed to operate in
darkness or to be wholly shielded from the democratic processes
of accountability that we apply to the rest of our government.
There have been profound changes in the way that intelligence
agencies operate and, as importantly, in the way that they are
accountable for those operations.

It would be naive to think that this greater accountability will,
by itself, prevent another Barbie episode. But it is not naive to
believe that we have seen the end of the attitude that anything is
permissible, including the obstruction of justice, if it falls under
the cloak of intelligence. In the files of the Barbie case, and in
interviews conducted in the course of this investigation, there

seems to have been no awareness on anyone's part that United States officers and employees were obstructing justice. The only evident concerns were operational ones. If the reforms of the past decade lead an intelligence officer faced with a similar choice in the future to realize that these cannot be the exclusive concerns, and that he is accountable under the law for the choice he must make, then we will have accomplished something worthwhile.

There the report, for the moment, ended. But I was left with an uneasy sense that something was missing. The report itself was complete, but it was a chronicle of dishonor, and circumstances had given me the responsibility of writing the final chapter. A full investigation and a full disclosure would, in some sense, do credit to the United States, but it seemed a rather passive act. Now that we had revealed what had happened, what were we going to do about it?

I had concluded that conventional steps—prosecution, a change in the law—were not available or feasible. Yet officers of the United States had been responsible, in the end, for more than just obstructing HICOG and breaking an American statute. By snatching Barbie from the French judicial process and spiriting him halfway around the world, they had violated the fabric of justice under law that holds together all democratic societies. I felt strongly that we had to do more than simply describe that act. We had to acknowledge the wound it had inflicted on the commitment to the rule of law, a commitment that America shares with all civilized nations.

I therefore concluded my report with an appeal to the attorney general:

As the investigation of Klaus Barbie has shown, officers of the United States government were directly responsible for protecting a person wanted by the government of France on criminal charges and in arranging his escape from the law. As a direct result of that action, Klaus Barbie did not stand trial in France in 1950; he spent 33 years as a free man and a fugitive from justice, and the fact that he is awaiting trial today in France is due entirely to the persistence of the government of France and the cooperation of the present government of Bolivia.

It is true that the obstruction of efforts to apprehend and extradite Barbie were not condoned in any official sense by the United States government. But neither can this episode be considered as merely the unfortunate action of renegade officers. They were acting within the scope of their official duties. Their actions were taken not for personal gain, or to shield them personally from liability or discipline, but to protect what they believed to be the interests of the United States Army and the United States government. Under these circumstances, whatever may be their personal culpability, the United States government cannot disclaim responsibility for their actions.

Whether Barbie is guilty or innocent of the crimes with which he is charged will be decided by a French court. But whatever the verdict, his appointment with justice is long overdue. It is a principle of democracy and the rule of law that justice delayed is justice denied. If we are to be faithful to that principle—and we should be faithful to it—we cannot pretend that it applies only within our borders and nowhere else. We have delayed justice in Lyon.

I therefore believe it appropriate, and I so recommend, that the United States government express to the government of France its regret for its responsibility in delaying the due process of law in the case of Klaus Barbie.

This is a matter of decency, and of honorable conduct. It should be, I believe, the final chapter by the United States in this case.

On August 12, 1983, the chargé d'affaires of the French embassy in Washington was called to the State Department. He was given a copy of my report, together with a formal diplomatic note signed by George P. Shultz, the secretary of state, expressing, on behalf of the United States, "deep regrets to the Government of France" for delaying justice in Lyon.

When the report was released publicly three days later, it made headlines throughout the United States and Europe. Editorial reaction, both here and abroad, was highly favorable toward the report, if not to the events described in it.

"How rare it is for a proud and powerful nation to admit shabby behavior," proclaimed *The New York Times*. "That's just what the United States has done in the Klaus Barbie case. Shameful as the episode was, the admission of blame the United States made Tuesday, first to itself and then to France, goes far to redeem national honor. . . . The salvaged honor comes from a comprehensive Justice Department report that serves history and invites us to learn from it. . . . Mr. Ryan argues eloquently that expediency is not the only guidepost [and the] report summons the courage needed to say that the United States is sorry." [11]

In Germany, the *Stuttgarter Zeitung* wrote, "The way the U.S. government handled the Barbie affair showed a powerful and impressive capacity for democratic self-purging." [12]

But the response that gave me the greatest satisfaction was simply stated by the minister of justice of France, Robert Badinter, in a short note to the attorney general a few weeks after the report was released. "This particularly rigorous work," he wrote, "reveals a concern for the investigation of the truth that honors your country."

NAZIS AND AMERICA:
The Verdict

The work of OSI continues today, but it is not too early, I think, to draw some conclusions about this recent effort against Nazi war criminals: why we did not do it earlier, why we finally did it at all, what it has meant. Few people can be satisfied with the way things developed. For some, it is a national scandal that we did not deport Nazi criminals thirty-five years ago; for others, it is a waste of money that we should be doing so in 1984. Many people have asked a question that reveals their own uncertainty: Nazis never should have been allowed in, but now, thirty-five years later, have they not somehow earned a right to stay?

Before considering such questions, we need to put events in some perspective to see how we came to be where we are today. As I stated at the outset, this is less a story of Nazis than it is of America. The Nazis' aim was simple: to get in and keep quiet. The response of Americans was considerably more complex, and in the turbulence of the postwar years, we had a very difficult time deciding what our attitudes should be. Opposition to Nazism as such was the easy part; we all agreed on that. But when Nazis became Americans, what then?

My conclusion is that we have never known how to deal with Nazi war criminals in this country, and so our actions have been marked by ambivalence and equivocation. We have said one thing and let another happen. Our opposition to the immigration of Nazi war criminals after the war was genuine only in the sense that we believed that we did not want them in America. But this was little more than a wish that they would stay away, because the barriers we erected were ineffective. And the quarter century after the wave of migration ended was marked by an utter absence of any policy designed to recognize, let alone deal with, the festering problem of Nazis in America. Only in recent years, in the course of reexamining our entire response to the Holocaust, has the indecision ended, at least officially, and our commitment to legal action emerged.

American ambivalence over the issue of Nazi criminals took shape early, in the immediate postwar period when it became evident that the hordes of European refugees were not just Europe's problem but our own. When we enacted the Displaced Persons Act of 1948, we in effect guaranteed that Nazi war criminals would enter the United States. That act made a show of barring such people, but this pronouncement was neutralized even as it was being written, by stronger and more explicit preferences that were flatly inconsistent with it— the 40 percent preference for Baltic refugees, the 30 percent preference for farmers, and the bizarre allocation of 50,000 visas for Volksdeutsche.

By reserving four of every ten visas for Balts, we were overcome by an anti-Communism that virtually presumed that anyone fleeing the "forcibly incorporated" Baltic countries was a devoted anti-Communist and therefore a desirable immigrant—even though journalists, military authorities and visiting Congressmen were reporting that Balt camps were thick with collaborators who had retreated to Germany in the closing days of the war.

At a time when America's economy was losing its ability to support the agricultural work force we had at home, we demanded more farm workers from Europe and thus placed a heavy burden on the Displaced Persons Commission to come up with rural Eastern Europeans; some were farmers and some were not, but the pressure to put them on boats for America was far stronger than the incentive—and, in most cases, even the ability—to check their backgrounds closely.

The DP and State Department authorities in Europe immediately understood that if Balts and farmers did not get visas, virtually no one else could. The camp authorities were not blind to what was happening, but a consensus seemed to develop that the greatest benefit to the greatest number of worthy refugees lay in passing as many bodies as possible through the pipeline. "Hydraulic pressures," they cited later, to keep up "production."

And, finally, the allotment of 50,000 reserved seats for Volksdeutsche gathered up members of what was probably the largest single pro-German community outside the boundaries of the Third Reich itself, a community whose collaboration was so notorious that the IRO excluded them *en masse* from its resettlement efforts.

I have talked to many DP and consular officials, and I am convinced that few if any of them intentionally passed known collaborators through. Indeed, nearly all of them recall—and OSI has documented—case after case where visas were refused to those whose collaboration was evident. But these rejects were the unlucky ones. It was easy to lie. The background and investigative checks were haphazard affairs, and the criminals they screened out were vastly outnumbered by the many they did not.

When the DP officials left Europe after four years, nearly 400,000 refugees had come in. No doubt the majority of them were worthy and good. But the collaborators among them were not the inevitable, inconsequential by-product of a massive rescue. We were handing out visas too freely to allow any excuse that the collaborators were merely gate-crashers who slipped through a guarded door.

Hovering above all the preferences imbedded in the DP Act was the fact that the quickest way to be turned down for a visa, excluding perhaps black-marketeering activities, was to be suspected of Communist sympathies. And refugees soon learned that, whether they were in a preferred group or not, their chances of winning a visa could be augmented by professing a heartfelt opposition to Communism. This became a readily available camouflage to anyone who fled Eastern Europe to save his own skin, and it required no proof beyond the applicant's own statements and his freedom from Communist elements, real or imagined, in the DP camps. Woe to the refugee who flirted with Communism in the camps, or who associated with those who did, or who was accused of associating with those who did. Army investigators landed on these cases with both feet, and many were turned away. But for those who opposed Communism, the path to America was open, and it required only moderate skill to negotiate the barriers.

No truly effective barrier to Nazi war criminals could coexist with the overriding preferences for Balts, Volksdeutsche, and farmers of all nationalities. This is not only because there was substantial collaboration among Balts and Volksdeutsche, but because the DP Act adopted as its most important criterion, in most cases, not what the applicant had done during the war, but who he was: by nationality, ancestry, professed occupation. Applicants who were neither Balts nor Volksdeutsche could still call themselves farmers and get favored consideration—a tactic that death camp guards, in particular, seemed to favor, perhaps because so many of them came from rural backgrounds in the Ukraine.

This structural defect in the act was aggravated by the inability of investigators and consular officials in Europe to conduct any meaningful background check on individual applicants due to the unavailability of SS records for Eastern Europeans. This problem surely would have existed, to some extent, whether the act had different preferences or no preferences at all. But the preferences Congress did impose forced the screening officials to deal with a rich mix of war criminals, and thus made the inability to screen them effectively all the more serious.

This is how Nazi war criminals came to America: a flawed piece of legislation, aggravated by enormous pressure to produce immigrants and a lack of information that made lying easy and detection extremely difficult. And when the Displaced Persons Act expired in 1952, the Immigration and Nationality Act of that year abandoned even the legal exclusion on former Nazis—not to mention the rudimentary record checks of the Berlin Document Center—and so the gates were opened to a new category of war criminals: the Germans themselves, typified by Conrad Schellong.*

In the introduction, I expressed skepticism that any involvement of United States intelligence agencies in "smuggling" war criminals into the U.S. could have been a major factor in the presence of Nazis here. It should now be clear why. Nazis who wanted to come to America did not need government sponsors.

I am aware of only a handful of cases where one could conclude that U.S. officials assisted or sponsored the entry of Nazi war criminals into the United States, and even in some of those cases, such as Bolschwing, questions remain whether the officials knew the incriminating background of the individuals involved. Perhaps there are ad-

---

*In addition to the Immigration and Nationality Act, the Refugee Relief Act of 1952—which was designed to benefit the continuing flow of refugees from Eastern to Western Europe—contained no effective enforcement mechanism against the Nazi war criminals it ostensibly barred until it expired in 1956. There were even cases where applicants who had been refused visas under the Displaced Persons Act because of their Nazi backgrounds applied again under the Refugee Relief Act—and were accepted, by officials who used Communism as the litmus test of eligibility and spent little time checking DP records or interrogating applicants on what they had done during the long-ago war.

ditional cases of which I am unaware, but I gravely doubt that there was ever any organized or widespread conspiracy to bring known Nazi war criminals to this country, for any purpose.*

Indeed, to anyone who takes a few minutes to think about it, such asserted "conspiracies" to import Nazis would never make much sense anyway. In the first place, any services these Nazis might have been able to perform for us could have been executed far better in Europe than in the United States. The value of ex-Nazis was not that we had a need for genocidists; we wanted experienced anti-Communist operatives, and we wanted them in Europe, particularly in occupied Germany and in Soviet-bloc nations. We did not need them in New York or Washington or Chicago. Second, Nazi criminals by definition were subject to trial and punishment by the Allies after the war and so they were in no position to bargain for generous rewards such as entry to the United States. People like Barbie were willing to work for cigarettes and living quarters—and, of course, immunity from prosecution.

Third, immigration of Nazis into America was, after all, illegal after the war and thus would have required elaborate techniques of planning and concealment—not only in arranging travel, but in arranging the lives of the criminals in this country. To what end? If sanctuary was deemed necessary, collaborators could be resettled in Europe, or even hustled to South America, far more easily than they could be protected in the United States, and with far smaller chance of discovery or embarrassment afterwards. When the Army decided to evacuate Barbie, it handed him over to a Croatian in Rome and that was the end of it. It wasn't legal, but at least it was simple. Sending Barbie to America was never even considered, for what should be obvious reasons: he would have been a time bomb with a lifetime fuse. Who needed that in our own back yard? We could buy sanctuary far less expensively.

In matters like this, it is of course impossible to prove a negative, so I cannot responsibly say that there was never anywhere at any time

---

*Talk is often loose in this area. I am regularly cited the case of General Reinhard Gehlen (see Chapter 7)—who came to Washington to plan his postwar intelligence activities for us—as an example of the United States government bringing a Nazi war criminal to America. But Gehlen was a military intelligence specialist and an expert on Soviet strategy for the Nazi high command during the war. He never had anything to do with persecution. Perhaps the United States should not have relied on him after the war as heavily as it did for Soviet intelligence, but that is a question quite separate from the use of a Nazi war criminal.

any government-sponsored plan to bring Nazi criminals to the United States. But the manifest improbability of the whole idea, combined with the utter lack of reputable evidence to date that any such plan ever actually existed, certainly puts the burden of proving its existence on those who would have us believe it, and no conspiracy theorist I am acquainted with (and I'm probably acquainted with the lot of them) has even come close to demonstrating that it ever happened. So we may properly be skeptical. Instances where known Nazi criminals came to the United States through official sponsorship were few and isolated; though numbers are elusive, I doubt it would have exceeded a small roomful of people at the very most.

It should be clearly understood that such actions, to the extent they occurred, are indefensible. After two hundred thousand American families lost fathers, sons and husbands to the Nazis, no United States government official had any justification, ever, for allowing a Nazi criminal to live in America. But given these minute numbers, what do we then say of the boatload after boatload of Nazi persecutors who came in amongst the 400,000 displaced persons from 1948 to 1952, carrying visas authorized by a public law?

If we seek to assess the blame for the infiltration of Nazi criminals into America, we ought not kid ourselves. They came in not because unaccountable officials ran amok, but because we enacted laws that made entry so easy. If we now summon forth the scapegoats of unlikely conspiracies to bear the responsibility for us, and still more if we prefer these fuzzy allegations to the undeniable evidence that stares us in the face, then we have learned nothing from our failures of the postwar years.

Our indecision on Nazi war criminals continued in this country, with our failure to deport them or even to investigate them. At least for the DP authorities in Europe, there had been excuses of sorts: they ran the risk of admitting Nazis so that they would be sure of admitting the worthy refugees. But not even that rationale can be extended to the Immigration and Naturalization Service at home. Enforcement of the law against Nazis would not have jeopardized the security of those refugees who had a right to be here.

The decision not to pursue Nazis, like the decision to leave the doors open to begin with, was never articulated. I doubt that it was even decided, in any real sense. To mount a campaign against Nazi criminals would have required action: planning, organization, resources. No one at INS took the initiative, and no one from the president to the Congress to the people thought to ask why. Tolerance of Nazis thus became not so much a policy as the inevitable result of an absence of policy.

Given the absence of any affirmative policy to investigate and deport illegal Nazi aliens, even the pursuit of individual cases was doomed to failure. No channels of communication were opened to Eastern European countries, no funds were set aside, no caseloads were adjusted to accommodate a time-consuming case, no assistance or centralized supervision came from Washington. Dossiers that could have formed the basis of solid cases gathered dust until eventually they were forgotten. Veterans of this process had little enthusiasm for pursuing other Nazi cases. Promotions and advancement came to those who produced. There was no publicity, no public debate, no congressional hearing on INS enforcement policy. But the enforcement arm of INS got the message, which was that the Nazi cases led only to dead ends.

By the mid-fifties, therefore, faced with a general lack of public interest, the absence of any clearly defined priorities that included Nazis, and only so many hours in the workweek, the pursuit of Nazi war criminals went from sporadic to virtually nonexistent. Some people have charged that INS was actually corrupt, but I doubt, at least as to Nazis, that any favors were traded. INS's investigators were unsupported, its supervisors were indifferent, and its judges, with rare exceptions, were insensitive. That was all that was necessary to accomplish nothing.

And yet to make the INS the scapegoat is shortsighted, and leads us away from the true answer as to who was responsible. INS failed because we as a nation failed. Then as now, the INS, like every other bureaucracy, had as its priorities the ones that we gave it—not much more and not much less. By our inaction, we in effect told INS not to be concerned with Nazi war criminals. There was no direction from the executive, the Congress, or the public, and so there was no incentive to spend great amounts of time on cases that were difficult to understand and almost impossible to prove.

Had INS announced in 1951, say, that it was mounting a major effort against illegal Nazi aliens, setting aside $2.3 million annually and assigning the cases to an office of special investigations for vigorous action, I doubt that a single voice would have been raised in protest. Indeed, given assurances of fair, nonpolitical enforcement against true persecutors, most Americans would have considered such action a moral obligation on our part. We were no more pro-Nazi in 1951 than we had been in 1948 or 1941.

But bureaucracies, especially weak bureaucracies like INS, are not very good at discovering moral priorities in their work; they respond to priorities articulated for them by Congress, the executive, or the people. They are uneasy trying to fight the good fight unless they hear demands from their constituencies in Congress or the electorate. By our inaction we let INS believe that the good fight against Nazis had ended in 1945. We did not demand that it pursue Nazis, and it did not.

If INS failed because we failed, what was the reason for our failure? In one sense, there was no general public knowledge of Nazi war criminals at large in the United States, but that ignorance was self-imposed. What we knew of European refugees when we passed the DP Act, and what we put in that act, ought to have alerted us to the situation that would face us when 400,000 people came in under the priorities of that act.

We did not know, I think, because we did not want to know. We did not want to know about Nazi war criminals nor about the Holocaust in general. The prominence we gave to the specter of Communism contributed to this—Communism was perceived as a domestic threat, Nazism was not—but there were more complex forces at work. A curtain of silence had fallen over the Holocaust, in this country and in much of the world. With rare exceptions, it was not studied or discussed or analyzed in public. It was as if the world wanted to put the Holocaust behind it, to close the books, to treat it as an inexplicable aberration that had burned across Europe.

America was not unique in its silence, but it was, certainly, silent. The Holocaust was not taught in history classes in our schools; there were few if any discussions of it in public forums; books and firsthand accounts were few.* The celebrated trial of Adolph Eich-

---

*There were exceptions to this pattern. *The Diary of Anne Frank* was a best seller in 1952, and Elie Wiesel published *Night*, his powerful story of a Jewish boy in Hungary, in 1958. Raul Hilberg's *The Destruction of the European Jews,* still the definitive account of how the Holocaust was engineered, appeared in 1960. But none of these events produced real change in American attitudes, at least not such that our actions were affected. In contrast to Hilberg's scholarly work, William Shirer's *The Rise and Fall of the Third Reich* was a great popular success in 1960, but that book concentrated largely on the political and military aspects of Germany and the war. Fewer than fifty of its 1,200 pages dealt with the Holocaust.

mann in Jerusalem in 1962 had little impact on our own attitudes toward Nazis in hiding.

In 1962, six months after Eichmann was executed, Charles Allen,
an independent journalist in New York, wrote to the Justice Department with information on sixteen alleged Nazi war criminals in the
United States. His questions were simple but pointed: Is the Justice
Department aware of these allegations? Are they true? What is being
done to investigate them? INS responded several weeks later, listing
the status of each of the sixteen: "Viorel Trifa: His petition for naturalization was granted . . . Karl Linnas: His petition for naturalization was granted . . . Mecius Paskevicius: His petition for
naturalization was granted . . ." and so forth. They are citizens, and
that, INS implied, is the end of the matter.

Allen wrote back repeating his question: What is being done to
investigate the allegations of Nazi crimes against these people? His
answer from an assistant in the Justice Department: "I cannot see what
further information this Department is able to supply to you." [1] Nothing was being done, and nobody was interested.

The discovery of Hermine Braunsteiner in New York in 1964
confirmed our hibernation but did not change it. A few newspaper
articles, a few hate letters to her, and the case was forgotten. The
protracted negotiations leading to Braunsteiner's noncommital surrender of citizenship in 1971 excited little interest.

The Jewish community was not immune to this torpor, nor was
Europe. In 1971 the Union of American Hebrew Congregations
(UAHC) found a pervasive lack of interest in the Holocaust among
Jewish youth. They see the Holocaust as "ancient history," said one
rabbi, disturbed at the conclusion. Said another: Youths ask "why
they should become so excited about the murder of Jews a generation
ago when the Vietnamese, Bengalese and many other peoples are being
brutally killed" today. [2]

In Germany, forty-eight cases were pending against accused Nazi
criminals in the mid-seventies. Yet they were being ignored by the
German press, and Craig Whitney of *The New York Times* reported
that "the prosecutors say no one is interested in their work any more."
Whitney concluded, "Increasingly, West Germany has turned away
from the Nazi past as something long ago paid for and long since
overcome." [3] An estimated three thousand Nazi criminals who had
not been brought to trial would escape prosecution when the statute
of limitations on Nazi crimes expired in 1979.

Yet in 1976, only five years after the UAHC rabbis found no interest in the Holocaust among Jewish youth, Terrence Des Pres, a professor of English at Colgate University reported, "In the classroom, a generation of young adults has arrived, Jewish and non-Jewish alike, who are now prepared to face the worst. . . . [T]his spring there are 141 students in 'Literature of the Holocaust' at Colgate. The room is filled with an intensity of concern I am tempted to describe as religious." *[4]

In 1978 NBC broadcast four nights of "Holocaust," a dramatized, and dramatic, account of the destruction of the Jews. Nearly half of all American homes—120 million people—were absorbed in it. The series was later syndicated in Europe, where it reached similarly large audiences.

A few months afterward, the Anti-Defamation League announced that high school pilot programs on the study of the Holocaust had begun in fifty school districts across the country, from New York to Los Angeles, from Decatur, Georgia, to Great Barrington, Massachusetts.[5]

And by 1979, only a few years after Craig Whitney's pessimistic prognosis in Germany, a worldwide protest over the expiration of the statute of limitations persuaded West Germany to extend it indefinitely.

Clearly something had happened in the seventies, here and abroad, among Jew and non-Jew. There was a reawakening of interest—some would call it a reawakening of conscience—in the Holocaust. A quarter century after the war ended, the curtain of silence lifted, not least in America. No single event was responsible. It was the coming of age of a new generation, a generation that had not lived through the war and had pressing questions for those who had. The older generation of veterans and survivors, facing these questions for the first time in a quarter century, had questions of its own. At long last, both the young and the old could look at the Holocaust. Indeed, they found they could not look away.

It was just as this tide began to run that, in 1972, INS began the deportation hearings against Hermine Braunsteiner—the first public proceedings in the case and the first testimony on Nazi war crimes in this country in nearly fifteen years. For many Americans these were

---

*In that year, Des Pres published *The Survivor*, a powerful and seminal treatise on life in the death camps, although Des Pres was born in Illinois in 1939.

the first voices they had ever heard from the Holocaust. Germany requested extradition, and Braunsteiner departed in 1973. Dr. Karbach of the World Jewish Congress sent his homemade list of Nazi criminals to INS. Congress took notice.

Both Joshua Eilberg and Elizabeth Holtzman prodded INS to do something, and kept up a steady stream of criticism and publicity as INS foundered through its various attempts—the project control office of the mid-1970s and the special litigation unit of the late 1970s. OSI's birth, induced by Congress in 1979, was the direct result of this seven-year gestation period.

The most striking aspect of this history is that we were prodded at the beginning of each postwar decade by the question of Nazis in America; we simply did not respond until the seventies. In the early fifties, the publicity surrounding Artukovic's discovery in Los Angeles ("Accused Wartime 'Butcher' in L.A.," blared the banner headline of the Los Angeles *Daily News*) brought no calls from Congress for INS to account for its efforts against Nazis. Indeed, the only congressional response was a series of private bills to legalize Artukovic's presence. Ten years later, neither the Eichmann trial nor the discovery of Hermine Braunsteiner brought forth any stir; Charles Allen was told to go away, and he found no one in Congress willing to help him.

Holtzman and Eilberg deserve full credit for their persistence, but I think they harnessed, rather than created, the crucial factor in our awakening. That factor was the passage of time, the coming to maturity of a new generation, the replacement of wounds by scar tissue in the generation that fought and suffered, and to some extent the cyclical reexamination of history that each generation must initiate. It was a realization by the survivors that they were aging, and that much was yet untold, and the realization by their children—and all children born after the war—that there was much they did not know about events that had profoundly influenced their world.

The concern over the presence of Nazi criminals in America, therefore, was one aspect of a broad reawakening to the Holocaust, a realization that the Holocaust is still unfinished business forty years later. But unlike study, and memorials, and resolutions—all of which have their place—the prosecution of Nazi criminals in America was one of the few things the government could still *do* after forty years. The U.S. government has made a week in April official Days of Remembrance; it has commissioned a Holocaust memorial and museum to be built in Washington; it has sponsored seminars on the study of American actions. These steps are beneficial, but they are retrospective in nature. There is nothing retrospective or abstract about OSI's work: real people are investigated, placed on trial, stripped of their citizenship, deported. It is the invocation of official action that makes this initiative unique.

I am, in fact, uncomfortable at any suggestion that the prosecution of Nazi criminals is one aspect of the government's greater efforts to see that the Holocaust is not forgotten. We are not placing people on trial as a symbolic gesture, or to serve some larger purpose of conscience. We are putting them on trial because they broke the law. That is the only reason people should be put on trial. Demjanjuk, Osidach, Schellong, and the rest are not put in the public eye, and placed in jeopardy of their right to live in America, to answer for the guilt of the Nazi regime or to remind Americans that these crimes took place. They are on trial to answer specific and detailed charges of their own conduct during the Holocaust and immediately after it.

While I believe that this effort was born of a reawakened concern with the Holocaust, it stands quite apart from nearly every other manifestation of that concern, because it calls individual people to account for their individual acts, and it imposes legal sanctions on those acts. At OSI, we were prosecutors doing the public's work of enforcing the law. If that work also serves to bring home to the public the crimes of the Nazis, then by all means let us learn from it, but that lesson must be a by-product of the work and not the purpose of it. What we are doing today is no more, and certainly no less, than should have been done years ago.

And that raises the inevitable question: why now? Why, thirty-four years after the end of the war, should we have begun proceedings against those whom we resolutely ignored for so many years?

To many Americans, the necessity and justice of bringing accused Nazi criminals before the law, even at this late date, are self-evident. Many Americans believe, as I do, that thirty-four years of inaction by our government is no justification for continued inaction. And yet others whose good faith and commitment to the law cannot be doubted have asked, "Why now?" Why, after all these years, is it necessary to reopen the scars of a generation ago and disrupt the lives of people who have lived among us for more than three decades? Why must the

United States investigate a group of men who are now in their sixties or seventies, who pose no present danger to anyone, and who have lived unremarkable and generally productive lives in this country? Why now, when many Nazis have already died, do we spend $2.5 million a year on prosecuting those who are still alive? Should we not be spending this money to prosecute gangsters, drug dealers, terrorists— people who pose a present threat?

I could answer by saying that we are really, after all, spending relatively little—the budget of OSI amounts to one-tenth of one percent of the budget for the Department of Justice. But to say that 99.9 percent of the funds are spent elsewhere does not answer the underlying question, which is not primarily a financial one.

What has happened in the past thirty years that should give rise to the feeling on the part of some that we ought to let it be, to turn to problems more immediate than Nazis? Certainly our attitudes toward the crimes themselves have not softened with the passage of time. Civilized persons of all ages, all faiths, all nationalities are unanimous in their revulsion at the Holocaust, and in their condemnation of those who carried it out.

Many people assume that those who perpetrated the Holocaust have lived for forty years with grief and contrition in their hearts. They have paid the price, or so it is believed—why hound them to their graves? My answer is that such an assumption, so far as I can tell, is simply wrong. I see no evidence whatever that any of these men have been even slightly discomforted, let alone tormented, by their actions in the past. To the contrary, when faced with overwhelming evidence of their complicity, they blandly deny they were even present at the scene, or if they admit that they were there, they minimize the significance of their actions and then rationalize even that. Death camp guards, for example, explain that they chose the death camps because it was an easier life than being a POW or serving on the front. They say this not by way of contrition, but by way of justification, as if to say, what else could you have expected me to do? I am aware of no Nazi criminal who has come forward, even after being formally accused in legal proceedings, to say, "At last you have found me out. Let me unburden my conscience, let me atone for the past." It does not happen. Conscience has nothing to do with it, and so those who counsel us to refrain out of a humane consideration for the sufferings of the guilty are, to my mind, misinformed.

This brings us to the strongest argument against a search for Nazi war criminals today. These people, so the argument goes, have lived thirty-five peaceful and productive years in the United States. They have raised families here, they have held jobs and paid taxes, they have sent their children to school, they have retired, they are drawing their pensions and cultivating their gardens. They have harmed no one here, they have not agitated for a Fourth Reich or anything else, they have not even been outspokenly anti-Semitic or anti-anything else. Americans have, after all, taken justifiable pride in being a land of refugees, where the descendants of long-ago debtors, outcasts, and thieves are among our leading citizens. Therefore, they say, there should be a statute of limitations in spirit if there isn't one in law. Without condoning the crimes, there comes a time, they say, when we should just let the criminals be.

No. However magnanimous such generosity of spirit may appear to be, however much we may be attracted by its well-intentioned appeal to our instincts for compassion and forgiveness, we must decline its invitation. The generation that witnessed the Holocaust, and its children, have an utterly unavoidable responsibility to act on what we have seen. Much of the record of our actions has already been written, and that record is in large part one of silence, in which we can find little reason for pride. But if it is true, as I believe it might be, that our silence immediately after the Holocaust was not due entirely to apathy but, at least in part, to the inability to respond intelligently to such a massive wound to the human race, then the record is not beyond salvage. But no longer can we claim the inability to respond. The post-traumatic shock, if that is indeed what it was, is over, and some of the assailants still survive to be confronted with the evidence of their acts. If we turn away from our responsibility to act, we will have set the example for future generations. Indeed, it may be our actions today that will reveal to those generations whether our silence after the event was a genuine reaction to the trauma or simply a failure of concern.

If we believe, as we must believe, that no one anywhere shall be allowed to perpetrate another Holocaust, we cannot content ourselves with promises that we will take stern action the next time, whilst we turn our backs on the criminals who are demonstrably guilty. We cannot say that we will pursue the criminals of the future as we grant an amnesty to the original criminals because they have succeeded for so long in concealing their crimes. We cannot condemn genocide, past or future, and excuse the genocidists who live among us because they have lived among us for so long already. Future generations will not believe pious statements of condemnation and resolve that are unsupported by action, nor should they.

But we need not look only to future centuries to find the obligation to act in the last decades of this one. The pattern of persecution in Nazi Europe had an unprecedented end, but not an unprecedented beginning. The Holocaust did not begin with gas chambers. The first steps took place in the mid-1930s, when the civil rights of Jews were gradually but inexorably restricted, and when persons of all religions or no religion were imprisoned because they were deemed politically dangerous to the Third Reich. Later in the thirties, expropriation acts forced Jews to surrender, as the price of escape, their property, their savings, their personal possessions.

Still later, looting and burning and theft of property owned by Jews went unpunished and, indeed, were implicitly condoned and encouraged. Then came the Final Solution—the "resettlement in the East" that led directly to places whose very names have become synonomous with unmeasurable horror: Treblinka, Maidanek, Auschwitz. When repression and discrimination began in the thirties, there was no master blueprint that contemplated gas chambers and furnaces a decade later. Mass murder was conceived only in 1941 as the most logical and efficient culmination of the entire process of vengeance. Had the people of Germany not turned their backs on their fellow human beings in the thirties, there may have been no death camps in the forties.

Political repression, racial and religious persecution, and cruel discrimination did not begin in Germany of the thirties, but more to the point, neither did they end there. It is the sad truth of the postwar world, a truth with which we all are familiar, that repression and discrimination have been too much with us, throughout the world.

I do not suggest that discrimination and intolerance lead inevitably to the mass persecution, let alone mass murder, that took place in Europe forty years ago. But we can no longer say that it never can happen. It has happened, once. Who among us would dare say that it could never happen again, somewhere in the world? And if there is anyone so bold as to say that, can he look to Cambodia, or Biafra of a decade ago, or Uganda, and still say that mass death is never an extension of political persecution?

Look to the next century, or look to our own. The lesson is the same. The Holocaust was mass murder as political policy, and civilized people must reject it in every form, at every opportunity. Of the hundreds of thousands who carried out this campaign in Germany and Europe forty years ago, those who remain in the United States today are only the aging remnants. Yet we know they are here and we know that they broke the law to get here and stay here and live here in peace. To say that they pose no danger to anyone because they are old people misses the point entirely. We are proceeding against them under the law not because of what they might do in the future but because to look the other way would be necessarily to forgive what they did in the past.

We give them law. How much law did they give their victims? How much due process was there at Treblinka, or in the villages of the Ukraine? When the Jews of Bucharest were hung on meathooks, where were hearings, or appeals or rules of evidence or defense lawyers? By what conceivable right are these men who let loose havoc and terror entitled to the protection of the laws of a country they are not even entitled to be in? Rage, not reason, is the heart's response to see the law protect these men in ways it never protected those they murdered, or those whose lives they mutilated.

But recognize why we give them benefit of law. It is not for their sake but for ours. The repulsive bullies who destroyed millions of families and then ran to America are entitled to nothing from our hearts but contempt. Yet they are entitled to law, not because they have earned it but because we cannot afford to sacrifice it. A civilized society that resorts to barbarism to deal with barbarians begins to let go of its civilization. It is our adherence to the law that separates us from them.

What we are doing today should have been done thirty-five years ago. But to grant these people repose from the law in 1984 would mean that their thirty-five years of silence and our thirty-five years of inaction somehow atone for their awful crimes, and that justice is the result. We should not accept that insidious logic, nor can we accept it merely because the criminals are fewer and older today.

And so, to those who ask "Why now?" I say "If not now, when?" Shall we do nothing now and await instead, God forbid, some new Holocaust that will give us a new generation of Nazis, a younger, longer list of defendants? However late the date, it is still within the power of our nation, still within the reach of the law, to call to ac-

count those criminals who still live among us. It can yet be done.
That is why it must be done.

Does our endeavor fail because the number of people actually deported will be small? I believe not, so long as our resolve is demonstrated by action. The small number of actual deportees reflects a
number of quite disparate factors: the difficulty in gathering evidence
after so many years; the determination not to prosecute unless the evidence is strong; the right of the accused to a full defense in the judicial process; the legal requirement that citizenship, and even alien
residence, not be revoked except on "clear and convincing" evidence; the judicial delay, in some cases, in handing down verdicts;
the seemingly endless ladder of hearings and appeals; the reluctance
of other nations to effectuate our legal orders by allowing the deportees in.

Some of these factors—the difficulty of compiling evidence, the
reluctance of other nations—are beyond our control. Some represent
deeply held convictions of due process of law that we will not sacrifice regardless of the crime. Some factors can and should be cor-
rected: the protracted appeals and the delay in arriving at verdicts.
But while the foreshortening of the judicial mechanics might speed
the deportations of individual criminals, a consummation devoutly to
be wished, it would not bring cardinal changes to the numbers deported. Considering that the criminals once numbered in the thousands, whether we deport five or fifty will not, by itself, significantly
affect the historical record.

The true significance of bringing Nazi persecutors to account for
their crimes in American courts lies not in the number of actual deportees, but in their expulsion from the body of citizens. By revoking
citizenship, the polity—the American people joined together in a society and a government—takes the most solemn and drastic step
available to it: the civil equivalent of excommunication. Citizenship
is the most fundamental right accorded to any member of the polity;
its revocation is a highly unusual and difficult procedure, and it represents the judgment of the polity that the individual does not share
its commitment to the basic values on which the society is founded.

Citizenship is the most fundamental right of association in a free
society—the right to have all other rights, as Chief Justice Earl Warren called it. Citizenship entitles the bearer to a full voice, equal to

any other, in the conduct of the nation's affairs. From the days of Rome when, as President Kennedy reminded us at the Berlin Wall, "the proudest boast was 'Civis Romanus sum,' " citizenship has been the guarantee of rights at home and protection abroad.[6] But beyond the specific rights that citizenship confers, it serves a highly important role as the most intimate badge of association that a people can bestow on an individual. Whatever our background, ability, political belief, age, religion, or other attributes, citizenship is the one bond we share with other citizens. It is our one credential of entry into the political process.

It may seem anomalous, then, that citizenship in the United States is the easiest right to obtain and the most difficult to lose. The Fourteenth Amendment to the Constitution is explicit: "All persons born or naturalized in the United States . . . are citizens of the United States . . ." This covenant is absolute; a child born in this country to parents who are here briefly and even illegally is a citizen forever. And an alien admitted for permanent residence need only live here for five years and be "a person of good moral character, attached to the principles of the Constitution." Citizenship is then his for the asking. There are no quotas or waiting lists.

Citizenship cannot be lost except in two ways: voluntary surrender or denaturalization by a federal court. Even denaturalization can be precipitated only by fraud or illegality in the naturalization process itself, and then only if the fraud or illegality can be proven virtually beyond a reasonable doubt. For this reason, denaturalization trials are exceedingly rare.*

But the ease of obtaining citizenship and the difficulty of losing it are not at all inconsistent with the high value we place on it. In a pluralist society such as ours, the broad availability of citizenship represents our belief that the political process ought to include, not exclude, as many persons as possible, so that democratic institutions can operate for the greatest good. A totalitarian society has no real use for a broad base of citizenship, because participation in the political process is severely limited; a truly democratic society, on the other hand, cannot function without it. Citizenship becomes the lowest common denominator, because we believe that all people ought to have

---

* Aside from the cases brought by OSI, there are virtually no other denaturalization cases in the courts today.

a voice in how they are governed. To make citizenship difficult to attain for those who live here, or to subject it to easy rescission once attained, would compromise our commitment to democratic values.

It is precisely because the loss of citizenship is so very difficult, rare, and solemn that its revocation from Nazi criminals is such a significant step. A verdict of denaturalization is a formal decree of expulsion from our political body, a judgment that the individual is not fit to share the single common bond that unites the rest of us: the bond of citizenship. To date, eleven Nazi criminals have been denaturalized. By any statistical measure, the number is insignificant, but we have firmly established the principle that such persons are not entitled to be citizens of the United States. The results of future cases will depend only on the evidence, not on the principle itself. The Supreme Court made that clear when it upheld the denaturalization of Feodor Fedorenko, the guard at Treblinka. That is why it was so important at OSI that we prove the individual defendant's participation in persecution. There must be no doubt that these people lost their citizenship not because they were immigration chiselers but because they abused and persecuted innocent people in the greatest wave of terrorism and death the world can remember.

The significance of losing citizenship is highly symbolic, of course: for the ex-citizen, daily life changes little. He is entitled to welfare benefits, including Social Security,* he loses no home, or income, or police protection, or freedom in any tangible sense. He loses his vote in presidential elections, and his right to a passport. Yet, however symbolic, the loss is not to be denigrated; to be evicted from the polity may not affect the reject's daily life but it is a highly momentous and resolute step by the polity. In this sense, the ex-citizen is grievously stigmatized; as pervasive as our commitment to democratic ideals may be, we tell him, it cannot tolerate you.

The ex-citizen, the expelled citizen, becomes stigmatized far more than his new status as an alien might suggest. A legal alien, in fact, has no stigma at all. Though he is not yet a member of the polity, he has been admitted to residence and placed on a probation period, after which citizenship is available to him. Even an illegal alien has no particular social stigma: we refuse to admit him because he has not

---

*Social Security benefits are revoked only on actual deportation from the United States.

complied with our minimal procedures. We remove him if he is detected. But he is a trespasser. The ex-citizen is an outcast.

The denaturalized man or woman may not be sensitive to the shame of expulsion. More than a year after his denaturalization and the order for his deportation, Trifa blamed his misfortune on "Jewish pressure" and his own asserted lack of financial means to continue his fight. But it is not the ex-citizen's sensitivity that is important to us; it is our integrity as a polity. Whether he feels the stigma of expulsion or not is irrelevant; what is important is that we have righted the balance of citizenship by withdrawing it from him. We have, in a small measure, restored its integrity for the rest of us.

Once citizenship has been stripped, the ex-citizen is subject to deportation (although he must be accorded a hearing on this question as well). An order of deportation is less momentous, from the polity's point of view, than an order of denaturalization; it is merely a judgment that the individual's presence in this country is illegal. In this sense, an order of deportation against a Nazi war criminal is no different than an order of deportation against a student who has overstayed his visa, and so deportation proceedings are far more common than denaturalization trials. And as the judgmental consequences recede, the practical consequences increase: the deportee is physically removed from the country and must take up life elsewhere.

In most deportation cases, effectuation of the decision is easy, even routine. Nearly all aliens are citizens of another country, and under international law that country has no choice but to take them back. But for the ex-citizen, this is not so. Under the laws of most nations, taking citizenship in a foreign country—the United States, for example—amounts to a surrender of the original citizenship. Revocation of American citizenship does not restore the previous status; it creates a man without a country. No nation is required to take him. Deportation thus requires the consent of another country—the original homeland or some other—to take him in, and of course this consent may be granted or withheld.

Bishop Trifa, in his shortsighted way, may feel he has beaten the system because we have not yet effectuated his deportation, and so in a shortsighted way he has. But he sits in his Michigan estate for one reason only: no nation in the world, including this one, wants him or deems him fit to live among them.

As a matter of international law, we could banish him to one or another deserted island we own in the Pacific Ocean, to let him live out his days as the legal outcast he is. Had we such laws among ourselves as would allow that sort of thing, I would have invoked them. But we do not, and it is probably best that we do not, for banishment laws have never suited a free people under law. Yet there should be no doubt in our own mind that Trifa, and any other Nazi criminal whose deportation we have ordered but cannot effect because his odious character is known to all, remains a reject of a free society.

If our resolve to rid ourselves of Nazi criminals is genuine, we must pursue every possibility of deportation, knocking on every foreign door in a good-faith attempt to carry out the deportation, and this indeed has been and continues to be the recent American policy regarding Nazi criminals. But because the result of that effort is determined by a factor we cannot directly control—the sovereign decision of a foreign nation—the success or failure of the effort is irrelevant to the judgment of whether we have acted with resolve.

The question that we must ask ourselves, and that future generations must ask, is not how large was the quantity of Nazi criminals we shipped out, but rather: how seriously did we attempt to prevent their entry to begin with, and how genuine was our determination to expel them from our polity afterwards?

The first question has been answered, and not to our credit, for the record is clear that preventing the entry of Nazi criminals to the United States was not a high priority, and was not taken seriously. And the answer to the second question is indelibly marred by our equivocation and inaction throughout the quarter century following the postwar immigration of the late forties and early fifties. We will always be answerable for the fact that we waited so long, and we should be answerable for it.

But the resolve we have marshaled in the past several years shows that our record in dealing with Nazi criminals is not entirely beyond salvage. Our equivocation and indecision on how to deal with Nazi criminals appears now to have been resolved, in the only way that befits a people who truly believe in the injustice of persecution and the integrity of the law.

APPENDIX

Росіи

Grösse: 175 cm
лицо овальное
Gesichtsform: oval
волосы темнорусые
Haarfarbe: dklblond
глаза серые
Augenfarbe: grau
Особые приметы -
Besondere Merkmale:
шрам на спине
Narbe auf dem
Rücken
ДЕМЬЯНЮК
Familienname: Demjanjuk
Иван Николаевич
Vor- und Vatersname: Iwan/Nikolai
род
geboren am: 3.4.20
в Дубой Махарцувци запорожской обл.
geboren in: Duboimachariwzi/Saporosche
украинец
Nationalität: Ukrainer   в немцы Окуов
Abkommandiert am 22.9.42 zu Л.Г.Окгоу
                                    в собибор
Abkommandiert am 27.3.73 zu Sobibor
Abkommandiert am _____ zu ___
Abkommandiert am _____ zu ___
Abkommandiert am _____ zu ___

Empfangene Ausrüstungsgegenständ

Mütze:	1	Koppel:		
Mantel:	1	Seitengewehrtasche:		
Bluse:	1	Handschuhe:		
Hose:	1	Unterhemd:		
Stiefel:		Unterhosen:		
Schnurschuhe:	1	Wollweste:		
Socken:	1	Badehose		
Fusslappen:			1	
Essgeschirr:				
Brotbeutel:				
Trinkbecher:				
Feldflasche:				
Wolldecken:	1			
Gewehr Nr.:				
Seitengewehr Nr.:				

Ausgegeben: Richtig empfan

1   2   3   4   5

OPPOSITE PAGE AND ABOVE: A key piece of evidence in the Demjanjuk trial: his ID card and photo from the Trawniki training camp for SS guards, just before he was stationed at Treblinka. The handwritten notations are a Russian translation made in 1948.

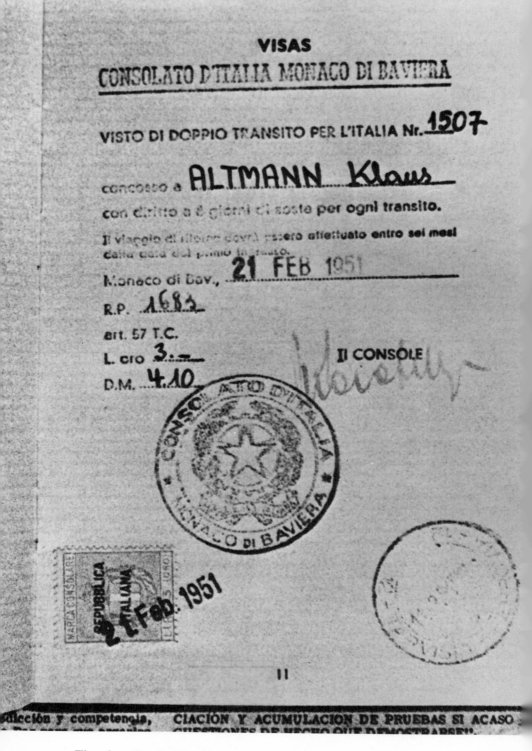

VISAS

CONSOLATO D'ITALIA MONACO DI BAVIERA

VISTO DI DOPPIO TRANSITO PER L'ITALIA Nr. 1507

concesso a **ALTMANN Klaus**

con diritto a 6 giorni di sosta per ogni transito.

Il viaggio di ritorno dovrà essere effettuato entro sei mesi dalla data del primo ingresso.

Monaco di Bav., **21 FEB 1951**

R.P. 1683

art. 57 T.C.

L. oro 3.—

D.M. 4.10

II CONSOLE

REPUBBLICA ITALIANA 2. Feb. 1951

II

llección y competencia, CIACIÓN Y ACUMULACIÓN DE PRUEBAS SI ACASO

The visa allowing Barbie to enter Italy en route to Bolivia.

Photograph — Photographie — Lichtbild

Holder — Detenteur — Inhaber

Wife — Epouse — Gattin

4

This document, if properly visaed, is valid for travel t

Ce document, muni des visas appropries, est valide po
se rendre en :

Mit vorschriftsmäßiger Einreisegenehmigung ist dies
Pass gültig für :

The following areas ONLY:
Austria, Belgium, Denmark, France, Greece, Italy, Liechtenstein,
Luxembourg, Netherlands, Norway, Saar, Sweden, Switzerland, and
United Kingdom of Great Britain specifically endorsed otherwise on page

Valable seulement pour:
L'Autriche, le Belgique, le Danemark, la France, le Grèce, l'Italie,
Liechtenstein, Luxembourg, la Hollande, la Norvège, la Sarre, la
Suisse, le Suède, la Grande Bretagne SAUF mention spéciale
page No.

Nur für die folgenden Gebiete:
Österreich, Belgien, Dänemark, Frankreich, Griechenland, Italien,
Liechtenstein, Luxemburg, Holland, Norwegen, Saar, Schweden, Schweiz
und Großbritannien, wenn nicht besonders vermerkt auf Seite

Valid to :
Valable jusqu'au : 21 FEB 1953
Gültig bis zum :

Issued at : MUNICH
Délivré à :
Ausgestellt in :

On :
Le : 21 FEB 1951
Am :

By :
Par : COMBINED TRAVEL BOARD
Von :

J. J. URMAN

The travel document, issued by the Allied Combined Travel Board,
enabling "Klaus Altmann" to travel to Italy, whence he departed for
Bolivia, 1951.

27 March

MEMORANDUM FOR THE RECORD

SUBJECT: Disposal of Dropped Intelligence Informant

    Reference letter Hq ZUCOM, ID 350.09 (GID/OPS), dated 28 February 1961, re ALTMANN, Klaus, and family.

    1. Pursuant to instructions received from Lt. Col. J. W. Dobson, Chief of Operations, G2, USFA, these Agents undertook the mission of disposal through Operation RAT LINE of Subject and family.

    2. On or about 9 March 1951 the following persons were transferred from AUGSBURG, Germany, to SALZBURG, Austria:

        a. ALTMANN, Klaus, born 25 October 1915 in KRONSTADT, Rumania

        b. ALTMANN, Regina, born 7 December 1915 in KRONSTADT, Rumania

        c. ALTMANN, Ute, born 30 June 1941 in KRONSTADT, Rumania —

        d. ALTMANN, Klaus-Joerg, born 11 December 1946 in KASSEL, Germany

    3. On or about 11 March 1951 the above-mentioned persons travelled from SALZBURG, Austria, to GENOA, Italy, by train using Combined Travel Board documents issued by CTB, MUNICH, bearing Austrian transit visa, Italian transit visa, and a TRIESTE Military Entry Permit.

    4. The family arrived in GENOA on 12 March 1951 and was housed at the Hotel NAZIONALE, at which time the family was taken over by the Italian representative of Operation RAT LINE.

    5. On 16 March 1951 the above-mentioned representative obtained the following necessary documents and visas for travel of family to its destination:

        a. ALTMANN, Klaus, International Red Cross Passport #18.573 issued in GENOA, Italy, on 16 March 1951, bearing Bolivian visa #144 issued by the Bolivian Consul at GENOA, Italy, on 16 March 1951, having Argentinian transit visa #17.487 issued by the Argentinian Consul in GENOA on 19 March 51.

        b. ALTMANN, Regina, International Red Cross Passport #18.574 issued in GENOA, Italy, on 16 March 1961, bearing Bolivian visa #145 issued by the Bolivian Consul at GENOA, Italy, on 16 March 1951, having Argentinian transit visa #17.488 issued by the Argentinian Consul in GENOA on 19 March 51.

        c. ALTMANN, Ute, and ALTMANN, Klaus-Joerg, listed on each of the above-mentioned passports.

Page No. 1 of 2 Pages.

Copy No 1 of 2 Copies

G-2 TS Reg. No. 282

subject: "Disposal of Dropped Intelligence Informant" dtd 27 March 51

6. The above-mentioned family departed from GENOA on the "CORINTHIA" on 23 March 1951. The estimated time of arrival in Argentina is 20 April 51.

REMARKS: Complete operation was without incident.

2 Incls.
Incl 1 - 5 photos
Incl 2 - Cy receipt dtd 9 Mar 51
    for $3200 (Original
    signed by NEAGOY)

GEORGE NEAGOY
S/A   CIC

JACK R. GAY
S/A   CIC

No. 2 of 2 Pages.
No. 1 of 2 Copies

OPPOSITE PAGE AND ABOVE: Proof that the U.S. Army evacuated Barbie to Bolivia—a March 27, 1951, report on the "Disposal of Dropped Intelligence Informant" in which Army agents report that "Altmann" and his family were escorted to Genoa for the voyage to Bolivia. The agents noted that "Complete operation was without incident."

TOP: "Altmann's" application for a Bolivian visa, listing Father Drago-novic as a reference. BOTTOM: The visa authorizing "Klaus Altmann" and his family to travel to Bolivia.

CASES FILED BY THE OFFICE OF SPECIAL INVESTIGATIONS
THROUGH JULY 1, 1984*

Basil Artishenko, West Brunswick, New Jersey.

Born Byelorussia, 1923. Entered U.S. 1949. Naturalized 1954.

Summary of allegation: During the Nazi occupation of Byelorussia, Artishenko was a member of his local police force and participated in the persecution and execution of unarmed gypsies and other civilians, including women and children.

Legal history: Denaturalization action filed November 12, 1982. Awaiting trial.

Andrija Artukovic, Orange County, California.

Born Klobuk, Herzegovina (now Yugoslavia), 1899. Entered U.S. 1948. Never naturalized.

Summary of allegation: As Minister of the Interior of the Independent State of Croatia, Artukovic was responsible for the massacres of hundreds of thousands of Serbs and Jews.

Legal history: Ordered deported 1952. Deportation stayed 1959. Deportation order reinstated 1981 but reversed by U.S. Court of Appeals for the Ninth Circuit 1982. Motion to reopen proceedings filed by OSI February 1984.

Henrikas Benkunskas, Chicago, Illinois.

Born Kaunas, Lithuania, 1920. Entered U.S. 1949. Never naturalized.

Summary of allegation: While a member of the Lithuanian auxiliaries, Benkunskas took part in a massacre of Jews and other civilians in the Minsk-Slutsk area on October 6, 1941.

Legal history: Deportation charges filed March 25, 1984. Awaiting trial.

Antanas Bernotas, Hartford, Connecticut.

Born Siauliai, Lithuania, 1908. Entered U.S. 1948. Never naturalized.

Summary of allegation: Bernotas was an officer of the Lithuanian Security Police and participated in the persecution of Jews and suspected anti-Nazi political activists.

Legal history: Deportation charges filed 1983. Awaiting trial.

Otto von Bolschwing, Sacramento, California.

Born Schoenbruck, Germany, 1909. Entered U.S. 1954. Naturalized 1959.

Summary of allegation: von Bolschwing served in the SS and the "Jew-

---

*Including, where noted, cases filed prior to the establishment of OSI by the Immigration and Naturalization Service and/or United States Attorneys.

ish Affairs'' office of the SD, where he worked on proposals to persecute German Jews. He was later head of the SD in Bucharest, Romania.

Legal history: Denaturalization action filed 1981 and von Bolschwing consented to a surrender of his citizenship later that year. He died shortly afterwards.

John Demjanjuk, Cleveland, Ohio.

Born Dub Macharenzi, Ukraine, 1920. Entered U.S. 1952. Naturalized 1958.

Summary of allegation: Demjanjuk operated the gas chamber at Treblinka and abused and persecuted Jewish prisoners.

Legal history: Citizenship revoked following trial in 1981; affirmed by U.S. Court of Appeals 1982; review by Supreme Court denied 1982. Deportation charges filed 1982. Trial held 1983. Ordered deported June 1984. On appeal to Board of Immigration Appeals.

Michael Dercacz, Brooklyn, New York.

Born Zheldec, Ukraine, 1909. Entered U.S. 1949. Naturalized 1954.

Summary of allegation: Dercacz was a member of the Ukrainian police in Lvov and participated in the execution of Jews in that area.

Legal history: Denaturalization action filed 1980 and citizenship revoked by summary judgment 1982. Deportation charges filed 1982. Dercacz died in New York August 1983, one week before trial was to begin.

Karlis Detlavs, Baltimore, Maryland.

Born 1911, Latvia. Entered U.S. 1950. Never naturalized.

Summary of allegation: Detlavs allegedly took part in persecution of Jews as a member of the Latvian Auxiliary Security Police.

Legal history: INS filed deportation charges in 1978 and trial was held in 1979, prior to creation of OSI. Charges dismissed for insufficient evidence 1980. Affirmed by the Board of Immigration Appeals 1981. Detlavs died in Baltimore in 1983.

Albert Deutscher, Chicago, Illinois.

Born Odessa, Ukraine, 1920. Entered U.S. 1952. Naturalized 1957.

Summary of allegation: Deutscher was a member of a Nazi paramilitary organization and participated in the mass executions of Jews near Worms.

Legal history: Denaturalization action filed December 1981. Deutscher committed suicide the following day.

Feodor Fedorenko, Waterbury, Connecticut.

Born Sivasch, Ukraine, 1907. Entered U.S. 1949. Naturalized 1970.

Summary of allegation: Fedorenko was a guard at Treblinka and took part in the persecution of Jewish prisoners there.

Legal history: INS filed denaturalization proceedings 1977. Charges dismissed after trial 1978. Reversed by U.S. Court of Appeals and citizenship revoked 1979. Reviewed by the Supreme Court and upheld 1981.

Deportation charges filed 1981. Ordered deported 1983. Upheld by Board of Immigration Appeals, April 17, 1984. On appeal to U.S. Court of Appeals.

Vytautas Gudauskas, Gilbertville, Massachusetts.

Born Lithuania, 1918. Entered U.S. 1951. Naturalized 1975.

Summary of allegation: During the Nazi occupation of Lithuania, Gudauskas was a member of the auxiliaries and murdered Jews and other civilians.

Legal history: Denaturalization action filed June 4, 1984. Awaiting trial.

Vilis Hazners, Albany, New York.

Born Latvia, 1905. Entered U.S. 1956. Never naturalized.

Summary of allegation: Hazners is alleged to have participated in persecution as a member of the Latvian *schutzmannschaft* (a police organization).

Legal history: INS filed deportation charges 1977. Charges dismissed for insufficient evidence 1980. Affirmed by Board of Immigration Appeals 1981.

Anatoly Hrusitzky, Orlando, Florida.

Born Sevastopol, Russia, 1917. Entered U.S. 1959. Naturalized 1975.

Summary of allegation: Hrusitzky served as a member of the Ukrainian police in his village and participated in the persecution and murder of unarmed civilian Jewish men, women and children.

Legal history: Denaturalization action filed August 9, 1983. Awaiting trial.

Jurgis Juodis, St. Petersburg, Florida.

Born Kaunas District, Lithuania, 1911. Entered U.S. 1949. Naturalized 1955.

Summary of allegation: Juodis served in an SS-controlled Lithuanian police battalion as a commissioned officer, and commanded actions involving the assault, arrest, detention and murder of unarmed Jews and other civilians in Lithuania and Byelorussia.

Legal history: Denaturalization action filed October 26, 1981. Awaiting trial.

Liudas Kairys, Chicago, Illinois.

Born Lithuania, 1920. Entered U.S. 1949. Naturalized 1957.

Summary of allegation: Kairys served with the SS auxiliary guard units at Treblinka and personally assisted in the persecution of unarmed Jewish civilians there and in Lublin, Poland.

Legal history: Denaturalization action filed August 13, 1980, and tried in June 1982. Awaiting a verdict.

Bronius Kaminskas, Hartford, Connecticut.
Born Kraziai, Lithuania, 1903. Entered U.S. 1947. Never naturalized.
Summary of allegation: Kaminskas participated in the shooting of approximately 200 Jews in Lithuania in August 1941.
Legal history: Deportation charges filed by INS 1976. Kaminskas has been certified by a court-appointed doctor as incompetent to stand trial.

Talivaldis Karklins, Los Angeles, California.
Born Madona, Latvia, 1914. Entered U.S. 1956. Naturalized 1963.
Summary of allegation: Karklins was a member of the Latvian police and took part in the persecution of Jews; he was later the commandant of the Madona concentration camp.
Legal history: Denaturalization action filed 1981. Karklins died in Monterey Park, California, in February 1983, one month before trial was to begin.

Juozas Kisielaitis, Boston, Massachusetts.
Born Lithuania, 1920. Entered U.S. 1963. Never naturalized.
Summary of allegation: While a member of the Lithuanian auxiliaries, Kisielaitis took part in a massacre of Jews and other civilians in the Minsk-Slutsk area in 1941.
Legal history: Deportation charges filed May 19, 1984. Awaiting trial.

Jonas Klimavicius, Kennebunkport, Maine.
Born Lithuania, 1907. Entered U.S. 1949. Naturalized 1954.
Summary of allegation: During the Nazi occupation of Lithuania, Klimavicius was a member of the auxiliaries and murdered Jews and other civilians.
Legal history: Denaturalization action filed May 30, 1984. Awaiting trial.

Sergei Kowalchuk, Philadelphia, Pa.
Born Kremianec, Poland, 1920. Entered U.S. 1950. Naturalized 1960.
Summary of allegation: Kowalchuk was a member of the Nazi-controlled Ukrainian police in Luboml, Poland, and participated in the persecution of Jewish civilians.
Legal history: Denaturalization case filed January 1977 and tried in October 1981. Citizenship was revoked by the court's decision on July 1, 1983. Kowalchuk's appeal is pending.

Bohdan Koziy, Ft. Lauderdale, Florida.
Born Pukasiwici, Poland, 1923. Entered U.S. 1949. Naturalized 1956.

Summary of allegation: Koziy served as a member of the Ukrainian police in Lysiec, Ukraine, and participated in the murder of unarmed civilians.
Legal history: Denaturalization case filed October 20, 1979. Tried September 1981. Citizenship was revoked by the court's decision on March 29, 1982. Court of appeals affirmed verdict February 27, 1984.

Reinhold Kulle, Chicago, Illinois.
Born Silesia, Germany (now Poland), 1921. Entered U.S. 1957. Never naturalized.
Summary of allegation: Kulle served as a guard leader and SS instructor with the SS Death's Head battalion at Gross-Rosen concentration camp and participated in the persecution of prisoners there. His duties included the armed supervision of slave labor squads.
Legal history: Deportation charges filed 1982 and tried 1983. A verdict is pending.

Juozas Kungys, Clifton, New Jersey.
Born Reistru, Lithuania, 1915. Entered U.S. 1948. Naturalized 1954.
Summary of allegation: Kungys was alleged to have participated in the killing of innocent people in Lithuania and the confiscation of property from Jews in the ghetto of Kedainiai.
Legal history: Denaturalization action filed July 1981 and tried in April 1983. The district court handed down its verdict in favor of Kungys on September 28, 1983. The appeal of the Justice Department is pending.

Edgars Laipenieks, San Diego, California.
Born Rucava, Latvia, 1913. Entered U.S. (from Chile) 1960. Never naturalized.
Summary of allegation: Laipenieks was a member of the Latvian Security Police at the Riga Central Prison and took part in the beating and killing of unarmed prisoners, primarily Jews.
Legal history: Deportation charges filed 1981 and tried 1982. Laipenieks was ruled not deportable, but this verdict was reversed by the Board of Immigration Appeals in 1983 and he was ordered deported. His appeal to the U. S. Court of Appeals is pending.

Alexander Lehmann, Cleveland, Ohio.
Born Zaporozhe, Ukraine, 1919. Entered U.S. 1957. Never naturalized.
Summary of allegation: Lehmann served as deputy chief of the Ukrainian police at Zaporozhe and ordered and assisted in the persecution and killing of unarmed Jews, including a mass murder of 300 Jews in 1942.
Legal history: Deportation charges filed 1981. Trial held in 1983. On February 27, 1984, Lehmann was ordered deported to West Germany.

Karl Linnas, Greenlawn, Long Island, New York.

Born Tartu, Estonia, 1919. Entered U.S. 1951. Naturalized 1960.

Summary of allegation: Linnas was a supervisor at a concentration camp near Tartu, where he took part in the abuse and execution of civilian prisoners.

Legal history: Denaturalization charges filed 1979. Trial held 1981 and citizenship revoked. Affirmed by the U. S. Court of Appeals and review denied by the Supreme Court 1982. Deportation charges filed 1982 and tried 1983. Ordered deported 1983. Linnas' appeal now pending before the Board of Immigration Appeals.

Hans Lipschis, Chicago, Illinois.

Born Kretinga, Lithuania, 1919. Entered U.S. 1956. Never naturalized.

Summary of allegation: Lipschis was a member of the SS Death's Head battalion at Auschwitz and took part in the persecution of Jews there.

Legal history: Deportation charges were filed June 1982, and Lipschis consented to deportation rather than face trial. He was deported to the Federal Republic of Germany in 1983.

Boleslavs Maikovskis, New York, New York.

Born 1904, Rezekne, Latvia. Entered U.S. 1951. Never naturalized.

Summary of allegation: Maikovskis allegedly persecuted Jews and other innocent people as chief of police in Rezekne, Latvia.

Legal history: INS filed charges in 1976 and went to trial in 1977 but discontinued the prosecution in 1978. OSI resumed the prosecution in 1981 but Maikovskis was ruled not deportable in 1983. OSI's appeal to the Board of Immigration Appeals is now pending.

Wolodymir Osidach, Philadelphia, Pennsylvania.

Born Galicia, Poland (Ukraine), 1904. Entered U.S. 1949. Naturalized 1963.

Summary of allegation: Osidach was commandant of the Ukrainian police at Rawa-Ruska, Ukraine, and took part in the roundup and extermination of Jews of that town.

Legal history: Denaturalization action filed 1979 and citizenship revoked after trial 1981. Osidach died while his case was on appeal.

Kazys Palciauskas, St. Petersburg, Florida.

Born Siauliai, Lithuania, 1907. Entered U.S. 1949. Naturalized 1954.

Summary of allegation: From June 1941, when the Nazis occupied Lithuania, until May 1942, Palciauskas was the mayor of Kaunas, the capital of Lithuania. In this capacity, he ordered the internment of the 20,000 Jews of

Kaunas in the ghetto and promulgated orders confiscating their property and requiring them to wear the Star of David.

Legal history: Denaturalization action filed June 1981 and tried December 1982. The court revoked Palciauskas' citizenship in March 1983. Court of appeals affirmed verdict June 18, 1984.

Mecis Paskevicius, Miami, Florida.

Born Ukmerge, Lithuania, 1901. Entered U.S. 1950. Naturalized 1962.

Summary of allegation: Paskevicius served in the Lithuanian Security Police and took part in the beating and murder of Jews and others.

Legal history: Citizenship revoked by consent decree 1979. Deportation charges filed 1980. Paskevicius has been certified by a court-appointed doctor as incompetent to stand trial.

Michael Popczuk, Lynn, Massachusetts.

Born Antoniny, Ukraine, 1919. Entered U.S. 1954. Naturalized 1961.

Summary of allegation: Popczuk was a member of the Ukrainian police and took part in the roundup and beatings of Jews.

Legal history: Denaturalization action filed 1983. Popczuk committed suicide eight days later.

Conrad Schellong, Chicago, Illinois.

Born Dresden, Germany, 1910. Entered U.S. 1957. Naturalized 1962.

Summary of allegation: Schellong was an SS *Hauptsturmführer* (captain) at Dachau where he trained new recruits for concentration camp duty and supervised the guard details of the camp.

Legal history: Denaturalization charges filed 1981 and citizenship revoked after trial 1982. Affirmed by the U.S. Court of Appeals 1983 and review denied by the Supreme Court 1984. Deportation charges filed 1983 and trial held 1984. Verdict is pending.

Mykola Schuk, Allentown, Pennsylvania.

Born Stolin, Poland, 1909. Entered U.S. 1947. Naturalized 1951.

Summary of allegation: As a member of the Nazi-affiliated Ukrainian police in the Gorodische district, Schuk participated in the beating and killing of unarmed Jews and other civilians.

Legal history: Denaturalization action filed February 1983. Awaiting trial.

Vladimir Sokolov, New Haven, Connecticut.

Born Orel, Russia, 1913. Entered U.S. 1951. Naturalized 1957.

Summary of allegation: Sokolov was employed by a Nazi propaganda unit as a writer and editor of a Russian-language newspaper in Orel. He urged that Jews be persecuted and annihilated and that Nazi rule be extended to the United States and throughout the world.

Legal history: Denaturalization action filed January 1982. Awaiting trial.

Elmars Sprogis, Long Island, New York.

Born Jaunjelgava, Latvia, 1914. Entered U.S. 1950. Naturalized 1962.

Summary of allegation: Sprogis served as assistant police chief of the Gulbene police in Latvia and assisted the Nazis in murdering Jews and confiscating their property. He was later the police chief of Madona, Latvia, and participated in a punitive expedition in Byelorussia in which villages were burned and innocent villagers arrested or shot.

Legal history: Denaturalization action filed June 1982 and tried in October 1983. District court handed down verdict in favor of Sprogis May 21, 1984. Justice Department appeal is pending.

George Theodorovich, Albany, New York.

Born Szuparka, Poland, 1922. Entered U.S. 1948. Naturalized 1960.

Summary of allegation: Theodorovich was a member of the Ukrainian police in Lvov and participated in the persecution and murder of unarmed Jewish civilians in Lvov.

Legal history: Denaturalization action filed August 1983. Citizenship revoked by order of the court in January 1984.

Valerian (Viorel) Trifa, Grass Lake, Michigan.

Born Transylvania, Romania, 1914. Entered U.S. 1950. Naturalized 1957.

Summary of allegation: Trifa was a leader of the fascist Iron Guard in Romania and a newspaper editor; in each capacity he advocated the persecution of Jews.

Legal history: Defendant consented to the surrender of his citizenship in 1980 rather than face trial. He then appealed the order to which he had consented; it was upheld by the U.S. Court of Appeals in 1981, and he sought review by the Supreme Court, which was denied in 1982. Defendant then consented to deportation rather than face trial in 1982. He waived all appeals and is now under a final order of deportation. No country has yet agreed to accept him.

Arnolds Trucis, Philadelphia, Pennsylvania.

Born Valka, Latvia, 1909. Entered U.S. 1951. Naturalized 1956.

Summary of allegation: Trucis was a member of the Latvian Auxiliary Security Police and took part in the beating and abuse of Jews.

Legal history: Denaturalization action filed 1980. Trucis died in 1981 before the case came to trial.

Antanas Virkutis, Chicago, Illinois.

Born Uzliekne, Lithuania, 1913. Entered U.S. 1949. Naturalized 1954.

Summary of allegation: Virkutis was warden of the Siauliai Prison in Lithuania and assisted in the incarceration and persecution of Jews and other innocent civilians, including prisoners of war who died from starvation and exposure.

Legal history: Denaturalization action filed March 1983. Awaiting trial.

NOTES

INTRODUCTION

For sources of material regarding Demjanjuk and Artukovic, see the chapters dealing with those subjects.

1. F.B. Czarnomski, ed., *The Eloquence of Winston Churchill* (New York: Signet Key ed., 1957), p. 65.

2. Roger W. Shugg and H.A. DeWeerd, *World War II* (Washington: Infantry Journal Press, 1946), p. 5.

3. Jackson quote: International Military Tribunal, *Trial of the Major War Criminals*, v. 19, p. 397.

CHAPTER I

1. Osidach's personal data, and the testimony of the witnesses quoted later in the chapter, are taken from the exhibits and record in *United States v. Wolodymir Osidach*, CA No. 79-4212, U.S.D.C., E.D. Pa.

2. Leonard Dinnerstein, *America and the Survivors of the Holocaust* (New York: Columbia University Press, 1982), p. 276. Professor Dinnerstein's excellent work is the only recent book of which I am aware dealing with the DP Act. See Malcolm Proudfoot, *European Refugees: 1939–1952* (London: Faber & Faber, 1952); Jacques Vernant, *The Refugee in the Post-War World* (New Haven: Yale University Press, 1953).

3. Raul Hilberg, *The Destruction of the European Jews* (New York: Harper Colophon ed., 1979), p. 196.

4. Hilberg, op. cit., pp. 187–90.

5. Document 3257-PS, IMT, December 2, 1941, inserted in *Congressional Record*, August 2, 1948, p. A4891.

6. Document NO-3149, IMT, September 19, 1941; see Hilberg, op. cit., p. 205.

7. Document NO-4997, IMT; see Hilberg, op. cit., p. 206.

8. Document 3943-PS, IMT, June 17, 1942.

9. Hilberg, op. cit., p. 205.

10. Document 3876-PS, IMT, January 1–31, 1942.

11. Document 3943-PS, IMT, June 17, 1942.

12. Heinz Höhne, *The Order of the Death's Head* (London: Pan Books ed., 1972), p. 333.

13. Höhne, op. cit., p. 335.

14. Hilberg, op. cit., p. 767.

15. Dinnerstein, op. cit., p. 17.

16. Ira Hirschmann, *The Embers Still Burn* (New York: Simon and Schuster, 1949), p. 235.

17. Hilberg, op. cit., p. 633.

18. Report of Earl G. Harrison (emissary of President Truman), September 30, 1945, reprinted in Dinnerstein, op. cit., pp. 292–93.

19. Harrison, op. cit., pp. 293, 300–301.

20. Quoted in Dinnerstein, op. cit., p. 21.

21. Ibid.

22. Hirschmann, op. cit., pp. 122–23.

23. Maurice Rosen, special assistant to the Camps Administrator, to S.M. Keeney, chief of the Italian UNRRA Mission, quoted in Hirschmann, op. cit., p. 227.

24. *New York Times*, October 19, 1945.

25. Quoted in *Washington Post*, December 31, 1945, p. 3.

26. Kathryn C. Hulme (UNRRA worker in the DP camps), *The Wild Place* (Boston: Little Brown, 1953), p. 9.

27. Statement of Secretary of State George Marshall, July 16, 1947, reprinted in *The Displaced Persons Problem*, Department of State Publication 2899 (GPO 1947), p. 4.

28. Dinnerstein, op. cit., p. 113.

29. Dinnerstein, op. cit., p. 112.

30. Vol. 7 Foreign Relations of the United States 645, 703 (1946).

31. Cited in Dinnerstein, op. cit., p. 115.

32. Dinnerstein, op. cit., p. 140.

33. 62 Statutes at Large 1009 (1948).

34. Hulme, op. cit., p. 225.

35. Dinnerstein, op. cit., pp. 156, 166–67.

36. Dinnerstein, op. cit., p. 167.

37. Earl G. Harrison, supra, quoted in Dinnerstein, op. cit., p. 172.

38. *The DP Story: The Final Report of the United States Displaced Persons Commission*, Table 2 (1952), p. 366.

39. Quoted in Hilberg, op. cit., p. 732.

40. Dinnerstein, op. cit., p. 169.

41. Ibid., p. 139–40.

42. Ibid., pp. 171, 237.

43. Ibid., p. 123.

44. Quoted ibid., p. 124.

45. *The DP Story*, op. cit., p. 28.

46. Abraham Duker, "Admitting Pogromists and Excluding Their Victims," *The Reconstructionist* v. 14 (October 1, 1948), pp. 21, 23.

47. Ibid.

48. *Congressional Record* op. cit., A4891–A4892.

49. Duker, op. cit., pp. 22, 25, 27.

50. *New York Post*, November 21, 1948.

51. *New York Times*, August 30, 1948.

52. IRO Constitution: 62 Statutes at Large 3037, TIAS 1846.

53. Edward M. Glazek, Hearings before the Subcommittee on Amendments to the Displaced Persons Act, Committee on the Judiciary, United States Senate, 81st Cong., 1st and 2d Sess. ("McCarran hearings") (February 3, 1950), p. 493.

54. Section 13, Displaced Persons Act, 62 Stat. 1014.

55. McCarran hearings, op. cit. (February 6, 1950), p. 871.

56. *The DP Story*, op. cit., p. 144.

57. Dinnerstein, op. cit., p. 193.

58. Ibid., p. 194.

59. Ibid., p. 193.

60. McCarran hearings, op. cit., p. 493.

61. Quoted in Dinnerstein, op. cit., p. 197.

62. *The DP Story*, op. cit., p. 79.

63. Ibid., pp. 79–81.

64. McCarran hearings, op. cit., p. 498; Dinnerstein, op. cit., pp. 195–196.

65. McCarran hearings, op. cit., p. 493.

66. "We apply for farmers": *The DP story*, op. cit., p. 226–7.

67. Ibid., p. 244, Table 16.

68. McCarran hearings, op. cit., p. 495.

69. *The DP Story*, op. cit., p. 140.

70. Ibid., p. 79.

71. 64 Statutes at Large 219 et. seq. (June 16, 1950).

72. *The DP Story*, op. cit., Table 2 and p. 349.

73. Ibid., p. 349.

74. Ibid., p. 84, Table 3.

75. Ibid., p. 292.

CHAPTER II

1. Message of President Truman to Congress, March 12, 1947, in Ruhl J. Bartlett, ed., *The Record of American Diplomacy* (New York: Alfred A. Knopf, 1948), pp. 727, 728.

2. Reported in Joseph C. Goulden, *The Best Years* (New York: Atheneum, 1976), p. 249.

3. Ibid., pp. 307, 318, 314.

4. Quoted in William Manchester, *The Glory and the Dream* (Boston: Little, Brown, 1973), p. 610.

5. Goulden, *op. cit.*, p. 304.

6. Ibid., p. 340.

7. Richard H. Rovere, *Senator Joe McCarthy* (Cleveland: World Meridian ed., 1960), p. 3.

8. Goulden, op. cit., p. 308.

9. Hearings before the Subcommittee on Immigration, Citizenship and International Law, Committee on the Judiciary, House of Representatives, 95th Cong., 2d Sess. ("July 1978 hearings") (July 19–21, 1978), p. 128.

10. Raul Hilberg, *The Destruction of the European Jews* (New York: Harper Colophon ed., 1979), p. 767.

11. Ibid., p. 343.

12. Ibid., p. 337.

13. Ibid., p. 342.

14. Heinrich Friedmann: INS File A7405009.

15. Jakob Tencer: INS File A7403127.

16. Jonas Lewy: INS File A7407454.

17. INS File A6421949; *United States ex. rel. Malaxa* v. *Savoretti,* 139 F. Supp. 143 (U.S.D.C., S.D. Fla. 1956).

18. Antanas Spokevicius: INS File A7488222.

19. Felix Krasnauskas: INS File A7922501.

20. Laszlo Agh: INS File A6801064.

21. Kornel Lang: INS File A8225123.

22. "proper inspiration": July 1978 hearings, op. cit., p. 146.

23. "Widespread Conspiracy to Obstruct Probes of Alleged Nazi War Criminals Not Supported by Available Evidence—Controversy May Continue," GGD 78–73 (May 15, 1978), reprinted in Hearing before the Subcommittee on Immigration, Citizenship and International Law of the Committee on the Judiciary, House of Representatives, 95th Cong., 1st Sess. (August 3, 1977), pp. 159–233.

24. *New York Times,* July 14, 1964.

25. *United States* v. *Hermine Braunsteiner Ryan,* CA No. 68-C-848 (U.S.D.C., E.D. N.Y.).

26. *New York Times*, July 14, 1964.

27. *United States* v. *Hermine Braunsteiner Ryan*, CA No. 68-C-848.

28. pp. 159–160. Braunsteiner testimony: INS File A11592337.

29. *New York Times*, September 23, 1972, p. 36.

30. CA No. 73-C-391 (U.S.D.C., E.D. N.Y.)

31. *New York Times*, August 8, 1973, p. 1.

32. *New York Times*, November 27, 1975, p. 3.

33. July 1978 hearings, op. cit., p. 125.

34. Press release, Office of Rep. Elizabeth Holtzman, April 3, 1974.

35. *New York Times*, June 6, 1974.

36. Eilberg to Henry A. Kissinger, June 26, 1974, reprinted in Hearing before the Subcommittee on Immigration, Citizenship and International Law, Committee on the Judiciary, House of Representatives, 95th Cong., 1st Sess. ("August 1977 hearing"), p. 69.

37. Linwood Holton to Eilberg, July 5, 1974, reprinted ibid., p. 70.

38. Eilberg to Kissinger, July 9, 1974, reprinted ibid., pp. 70–71.

39. Holton to Eilberg, August 1, 1974, reprinted ibid., p. 71.

40. Eilberg to the President, August 22, 1974, reprinted ibid., p. 71.

41. Max L. Friedersdorf to Eilberg, November 21, 1974, reprinted ibid., pp. 72–73.

42. Robert J. McCloskey to Eilberg, July 29, 1975, reprinted ibid., pp. 75–76.

43. Leonard F. Walentynowicz to Eilberg, October 31, 1975, reprinted ibid., pp. 76–77.

44. Walentynowicz to Eilberg, January 12, 1976, reprinted ibid., p. 78.

45. Holtzman to Kissinger, May 20, 1975, released by Holtzman August 25, 1975.

46. State Department memorandum, January 7, 1976, copy in author's files.

47. Exhibit in *United States* v. *Wolodymir Osidach*, CA No. 79-4212, U.S.D.C., E.D. Pa.

48. Eilberg to Edward H. Levi, June 25, 1976, reprinted in August 1977 hearing, pp. 79–80.

49. INS press release, August 12, 1976, reprinted ibid., pp. 81–82.

50. August 1977 hearing, op. cit., pp. 26–27, July 1978 hearings, op. cit., p. 124.

51. August 1977 hearing, op. cit., pp. 24–30; Hearings before the Subcommittee on Immigration, Refugees, and International Law of the Committee on the Judiciary, House of Representatives, 96th Cong., 1st Sess. ("March 1979 hearings"), pp. 122–30.

52. March 1979 hearings, op. cit., p. 100.

53. Boleslavs Maikovskis: INS File A8194566.

54. Vilis Hazners: INS File A10305336.

55. Karlis Detlavs: INS File A7925159.

56. *United States* v. *Fedorenko*, CA No. 77-2668-Civ-NCR, U.S.D.C., S.D. Fla.

57. *United States* v. *Walus*, 453 F. Supp. 699 (N.D. Ill. 1978), *vacated*, 616 F.2d 283 (7th Cir. 1980).

58. March 1979 hearings, op. cit., p. 101.

59. *United States* v. *Osidach*, 513 F. Supp. 51 (E.D. Pa. 1981).

CHAPTER III

The account of the Moscow negotiations is taken from my contemporaneous notes; the practices followed in the depositions are based on my personal experience and those of my colleagues at OSI.

1. David Shipler, *Russia: Broken Idols, Solemn Dreams* (New York: Times Books, 1983), pp. 279–80.

CHAPTER IV

The descriptions of Treblinka are compiled from an amalgam of sources, principally the following: Gitta Sereny, *Into That Darkness* (Vintage ed., 1983); American Jewish Committee, *The Black Book* (1946); Samuel Rajzman, "Uprising in Treblinka," reprinted in Hearings before the Committee on Foreign Affairs, House of Representatives, 79th Cong., 1st Sess. (1945), pp. 120–25; Konnilyn Feig, *Hitler's Death Camps* (London: Holmes & Meier, 1979); Alexander Donat, ed., *The Death Camp Treblinka: A Documentary* (New York: Holocaust Library, New York, 1979). This material has been augmented by witness statements and testimony of Treblinka survivors, principally in the cases of Demjanjuk and Fedorenko. As one might expect, not all of the details or recollections are precisely consistent. And because few people were at Treblinka throughout its fourteen-month existence, even accurate memories may recall installations and practices differently, depending on what weeks or months they were there. But these discrepancies do not seriously detract from their accounts.

In addition to the above material, Jean-François Steiner's *Treblinka* (NAL ed., 1979) is widely available in the United States. This is a dramatic and powerful book but, as Simone de Beauvoir notes in her preface, Steiner "has not denied himself a certain directorial freedom." Because a number of Treblinka survivors to whom I have spoken dispute vigorously the accuracy of Steiner's account, I have not relied on it here in my description of Treblinka. In its overall descriptions of what Treblinka was like, however, I believe it to be accurate enough for the lay reader, and it is certainly a gripping work.

Gitta Sereny's *Into That Darkness* is also widely available in the United States in its paperback edition. This book is based on Sereny's extensive interviews with the commandant of Treblinka, Franz Stangl, and her own considerable research. Its historical accuracy is above dispute, and it is particularly fascinating because it affords an intimate glimpse of the man in charge of that place.

1. Raul Hilberg, *The Destruction of the European Jews* (New York: Harper Colophon ed., 1979), p. 320.

2. Jankel Wiernik, "One Year in Treblinka" (1944), in Donat, op. cit., pp. 157–59.

3. Sereny, op. cit., p. 157.

4. Feig, op. cit., p. 296; Black Book, op. cit., p. 399; Donat, op. cit., p. 14; Sereny, op. cit., p. 250.

5. Sereny, op. cit., pp. 17, 250.

6. Ibid., p. 100; Hilberg, op. cit., p. 572.

7. Sereny, op. cit., p. 100; Terrence Des Pres, Introduction to Steiner, op. cit., p. xiv.

8. Hilberg, op. cit., p. 565.

9. Donat, op. cit., p. 94.

10. Sereny, op. cit., p. 155.

11. Wiernik in Donat, op. cit., p. 168.

12. Sereny, op. cit., p. 149.

13. Testimony of Rajchman at trial of Demjanjuk, pp. 495–96.

14. Donat, op. cit., p. 311.

15. Immigration and Naturalization Service, "Activity Relative to Alleged Nazi War Criminals" (March 1977).

16. The quotes are from their testimony at the trial of Demjanjuk.

17. *Cleveland Plain Dealer*, February 9, 1981, p. 6-A.

18. All testimony in this chapter is taken from the trial transcript. *United States* v. *John Demjanjuk*, CA No. C77-923, U.S.D.C., N.D. Ohio.

19. *Cleveland Press*, February 18, 1981, p. A-5.

20. *Schneiderman* v. *United States*, 320 U.S. 118 (1943).

21. *United States* v. *Demjanjuk*, No. C77-923, June 23, 1981, affirmed, No. 81-3415 (6th Cir. 1982), cert. denied, No. 82-414, November 29, 1982.

CHAPTER V

Unless otherwise specified, references in the text to the proceedings, testimony, and correspondence are from INS file A7095961, Andrija Artukovic.

1. William L. Shirer, *The Rise and Fall of the Third Reich* (New York: Simon and Schuster, 1960), p. 828.

2. See generally Ivan Avakumovic, "Yugoslavia's Fascist Movements," and Dimitrije Djordevic, "Fascism in Yugoslavia 1918–1941," in Peter Sugar ed., *Native Fascism in the Successor States 1918–1944* (Santa Barbara: ABC Clio, 1971); Wilhelm Hoettl, *The Secret Front* 148–174 (London: Weidenfeld & Nicolson, 1953); Dusko Doder, *The Yugoslavs* (New York: Vintage ed., 1979), pp. 18–22.

3. Fred Singleton, *Twentieth Century Yugoslavia* (New York: Columbia University Press, 1976), p. 88.

4. Singleton, op. cit., p. 196.

5. Raphael Lemkin, *Axis Rule in Occupied Europe* (Washington: Carnegie Endowment, 1944), pp. 252–60, 606–26; Vladimir Dedijer, et al., *History of Yugoslavia* (New York: McGraw Hill, 1974), p. 582. Additional material is taken from the authenticated exhibits to the deportation hearing. See INS file.

6. Singleton, op. cit., p. 89.

7. R.H. Bailey, *Partisans and Guerillas* (New York: Time-Life Books, 1974), p. 87.

8. Bailey, op. cit., p. 87. Photograph of sawing: author's possession.

9. Hoettl, op. cit., pp. 167–68; Singleton, op. cit., p. 89.

10. Doder, op. cit., p. 26.

11. Fitzroy Maclean, *The Heretic* (New York: Harper & Brothers, 1957), pp. 124–25.

12. Hoettl, op. cit., p. 168.

13. Maclean, op. cit., pp. 125–28.

14. Dedijer et al., op. cit., p. 582 (200,000 to 600,000 killed); Singleton, op. cit., p. 88 (350,000 killed); Alex Dragnich, *Tito's Promised Land* (New Brunswick: Rutgers University Press, 1954) (over 500,000 killed), p. 19.

15. Raul Hilberg, *The Destruction of the European Jews* (New York: Harper Colophon ed., 1979), pp. 454, 455–57 (to be reissued in a revised edition, Fall 1984, by Holmes & Meier, New York); Lemkin, op. cit., pp. 625–26.

16. Hilberg, op. cit., p. 353.

17. INS file.

18. Lemkin, op. cit., 613–26.

19. Singleton, op. cit., p. 197; Nora Levin, *The Holocaust* (New York: Thomas Y. Crowell, 1968), p. 514.

20. OSI file 146-2-47-424.

21. Lemkin, op. cit., pp. 615–16.

22. Dragnich, op. cit., pp. 21, 30–31; Maclean, op. cit., pp. 131, 251.

23. Maclean, op. cit., p. 257; Hoettl, op. cit., pp. 323–25; Hilberg, op. cit., p. 711.

24. *Los Angeles Times*, August 30, 1951.
25. *Artukovic* v. *Boyle*, 107 F. Supp. 11 (U.S.D.C., S.D. Calif. 1952).
26. *Woodby* v. *INS*, 385 U.S. 276 (1966).
27. *Artukovic* v. *Boyle*, op. cit.
28. *In re Andrija Artukovic*, A-7095961 (4/3/53).
29. *Ivancevic* v. *Artukovic*, 211 F.2d 565 (9th Cir. 1954).
30. Singleton, op. cit., p. 66.
31. *Artukovic* v. *Ivancevic*, 348 U.S. 818 (1954).
32. *Artukovic* v. *Boyle*, 140 F. Supp. 245 (U.S.D.C., S.D. Calif. 1956).
33. *In re John Martinovich*, A-2990330 (October 31, 1956).
34. *Karadzole* v. *Artukovic*, 247 F.2nd 198 (9th Cir. 1957).
35. *Karadzole* v. *Artukovic*, 355 U.S. 393 (1958).
36. *United States ex rel. Karadzole* v. *Artukovic*, 170 F. Supp. 383 (U.S.D.C., S.D. Calif. 1959).
37. *Long Beach Press Telegram*, May 20, 1961, p. A-3.

CHAPTER VI

The account of events in Hungary is drawn principally from the following sources: Raul Hilberg, *Destruction of the European Jews* (New York: Harper Colophon ed., 1979), pp. 509–54; John Bierman, *Righteous Gentile* (New York: Viking Press, 1981); Nicholas Kallay, *Hungarian Premier* (New York: Columbia University Press, 1954); Nicholas Horthy, *Memoirs* (New York: Robt. Speller & Sons, 1956).

1. Kallay, op. cit., p. 224.
2. Hilberg, op. cit., p. 510.
3. Kallay, op. cit., p. 471–72.
4. In Bierman, op. cit., p. 76, 81, 84, 85.
5. Kallay, op. cit., p. 473.
6. The material dealing with the man identified here as Magyar (including certified translations of the Hungarian parliamentary debates) is from the numbered INS file.
7. Hilberg, op. cit., pp. 350–53, 521–23.
8. Hilberg, op. cit., p. 523.
9. Ibid., p. 526.
10. Interview of M. Himler in INS file.
11. The genesis of the case is from Flora Johnson, "The Persecution of Frank Walus," Reader (Chicago), v. 10, No. 16 (January 23, 1981). For the judicial proceedings, see *United States* v. *Walus*, 453 F. Supp. 699 (N.D. Ill. 1978) (Judge Hoffman) and 616 F.2d 283 (7th Cir. 1980) (court of appeals).

CHAPTER VII

1. Bolschwing: OSI File 146-2-47-265.

2. Heinz Höhne, *The Order of the Death's Head* (London: Pan Books ed., 1972), p. 209.

3. Ibid., p. 307.

4. Dieter Wisliceny to CIC, October 27, 1946, OSI file.

5. Eichmann interrogation (transcript), OSI file, p. 1,034.

6. Hilberg, op. cit., p. 85ff.

7. Eichmann interrogation (transcript), OSI file, pp. 311–14.

8. Ibid., p. 69.

9. Höhne, op. cit., p. 309.

10. Ibid., p. 321.

11. Dr. Peter Black, *Viorel Trifa and the Iron Guard* (unpublished MS, 1982, copy in OSI files), pp. 8–38.

12. Ibid., pp. 8–40.

13. Report of Gunther, February 5, 1941, p. 3, quoted in ibid., pp. 9-5.

14. Wilhelm Hoettl, *The Secret Front* (Weidenfeld & Nicholson, London, 1953), pp. 174–75, 179.

15. Quoted in Black, op. cit., pp. 9-21 to 9-23.

16. Gunther to State, January 30, 1941, quoted in Black, op. cit., p. 9-109.

17. Hoettl, op. cit., pp. 180–81.

18. Neubacher (Killinger) to Ribbentrop, February 8, 1941. U.S. National Archives, Documents of the German Foreign Ministry, No. 478092.

19. Killinger to Ribbentrop, February 26, 1941. U.S. National Archives, Documents of the German Foreign Ministry, v. 12, No. 94.

20. Ibid.

21. Hoettl, op. cit., pp. 181–82.

22. Höhne, op. cit., p. 267. See Hoettl, op. cit., p. 268.

23. Black, op. cit., pp. 10–12.

24. Ibid., pp. 10–35.

25. Ibid., pp. 10–74..

26. *New York Times*, February 2, 1984.

CHAPTER VIII

1. P. L. 95-549, 92 Stat. 2065 (October 30, 1978).

2. *Fedorenko* v. *United States*, 449 U.S. 490 (1981).

3. *Philadelphia Inquirer*, July 14, 1980, p. 3-C.

4. Hans Lipschis: INS file A10682861.

5. *United States* v. *Koziy*, No. 79-6640-Civ (U.S.D.C., S.D. Fla.) (March 29, 1982).

6. *United States* v. *Schellong*, 457 F. Supp. 569 (N.D. Ill. 1982), aff'd. No. 82-2948 (7th Cir. August 24, 1983).

7. *United States* v. *Popczuk*, No. 83-1886-K U.S.D.C., D. Mass., 6/28/83.

8. *United States* v. *Deutscher*, No. 81C-7043, U.S.D.C., N.D. Ill., 12/17/81.

9. *New York Times*, October 18, 1976, p. 16.

10. Ibid.

11. *Chicago Tribune*, December 19, 1981, p. 4.

12. *Philadelphia Inquirer*, July 14, 1980, p. 1-C.

13. *Chicago Tribune*, June 10, 1982.

14. *The DP Story: The Final Report of the United States Displaced Persons Commission* (1952), p. 349.

15. *United States* v. *Artukovic*, No. 81-7415 (9th Cir., December 1, 1982).

CHAPTER IX

Unless otherwise indicated below, all factual statements of the activities of Klaus Barbie and various officers of the United States government are taken from the report that I wrote for the Department of Justice: *Klaus Barbie and the United States Government: A Report to the Attorney General* (August 1983). This report, 218 pages in length, relies in turn on several hundred documents which were simultaneously released in a separate volume, "Exhibits to the Report."

The abridged version of the report in chapter 9 is less than half the length of the report itself. This version contains sufficient detail so that the reader may understand my conclusions and recommendations, and may intelligently draw his own conclusions. But necessarily much of the evidence leading to factual findings is omitted here. The evidence may be found in the report itself, and the reader is referred to the report and the separate volume of exhibits, which are available through the Government Printing Office at a nominal charge.

1. Henri Nogueres, quoted in *Le Point*, No. 543, February 14, 1983, p. 51. (*"seuls les yeux paraissaient vivre en lui."*)

2. Maurice Boudet, quoted in *Paris Match*, February 1983, p. 42.

3. André Devigny, quoted ibid, p. 43.

4. Quoted by Eugène Mannoni, a French journalist who interviewed Barbie in 1973, in *Le Point*, No. 543, February 14, 1983, p. 54 (*"Il n'y a pas de crimes de guerre. Il n'existe que des actes de guerre."*).

5. Quoted in *New York Times*, October 17, 1982, p. 22.

6. Based on interviews and memoranda of sources that must remain confidential.

7. *New York Times*, February 14, 1983, p. 5.

8. *New York Times*, March 30, 1983, p. 12.

9. *New York Times*, March 3, 1983, p. 26.

10. Cong. Peter Rodino to Attorney General Smith, February 24, 1983; author's files.

11. *New York Times*, August 18, 1983, p. A 26.

12. Reported in the *Washington Post*, August 20, 1983, p. 20.

CONCLUSION

1. Charles R. Allen to Attorney General Robert F. Kennedy, December 27, 1962; INS to Charles Allen, February 20, 1963; INS to Charles Allen, April 1, 1963. Copies in author's files.

2. *New York Times*, November 8, 1971, p. 15.

3. *New York Times*, August 29, 1975, p. 1.

4. Terrence Des Pres, "Lessons of the Holocaust," in *New York Times*, April 27, 1976.

5. *New York Times*, April 22, 1978, p. 44.

6. Theodore Sorensen, *Kennedy* (New York: Harper & Row, 1965), p. 601.

INDEX